NEW ANALYTIC GEOMETRY

REVISED EDITION

BY

PERCEY F. SMITH, Ph.D.
PROFESSOR OF MATHEMATICS IN THE SHEFFIELD SCIENTIFIC SCHOOL
OF YALE UNIVERSITY

ARTHUR SULLIVAN GALE, Ph.D.
PROFESSOR OF MATHEMATICS IN THE UNIVERSITY OF ROCHESTER

AND

JOHN HAVEN NEELLEY, Ph.D.
PROFESSOR OF MATHEMATICS IN THE CARNEGIE
INSTITUTE OF TECHNOLOGY

GINN AND COMPANY
BOSTON · NEW YORK · CHICAGO · LONDON
ATLANTA · DALLAS · COLUMBUS · SAN FRANCISCO

COPYRIGHT, 1928, BY PERCEY F. SMITH, ARTHUR SULLIVAN GALE
AND JOHN HAVEN NEELLEY
ALL RIGHTS RESERVED
PRINTED IN THE UNITED STATES OF AMERICA

653.8

PREFACE

In the revision the authors have attempted to preserve the features which have met with approval from many teachers, and, indeed, to perfect them in the light of experience. There is little change in the subject matter. A few topics have been added, which will increase the interest of the student. What changes have been made are in rearrangement. This has been done with the purpose of providing a more consistent development and of introducing at the proper time the topics which are more novel and difficult.

The authors may be pardoned for calling attention to the fact that the new material of the first edition has now become standard. Courses in analytic geometry now include, as a matter of course, chapters on transcendental curves, parametric equations, graphs, and empirical equations.

Many teachers prefer to make the course in solid analytic geometry somewhat brief. The present arrangement has been made for their accommodation. But for those teachers who desire to give a comprehensive course as preparation for the calculus the necessary material has been included.

The problems have been thoroughly revised. Some groups are preceded by the caption "For individual study or assignment." These problems are, as a rule, too difficult for general assignment and are provided for the exceptional student as an opportunity and a challenge.

CONTENTS

CHAPTER I. FORMULAS AND TABLES FOR REFERENCE

ARTICLE   PAGE
1. Formulas from Geometry, Algebra, and Trigonometry . 1
2. Natural Values. Special Angles 4
3. Rules for Signs of the Trigonometric Functions 4
4. Natural Values of Trigonometric Functions 5
5. Greek Alphabet 5

CHAPTER II. CARTESIAN COÖRDINATES

6. Analytic Geometry 6
7. Rectangular Cartesian Coördinates. Oblique Coördinates 6
8. Directed Line 9
9. Lengths 10
10. Point dividing a Line Segment in a Given Ratio 12
11. Application to Theorems in Geometry 13
12. Inclination and Slope 16
13. Test for Parallel or Perpendicular Lines 17
14. Angle Formulas 18
15. Areas 20

CHAPTER III. CURVE AND EQUATION

16. Equation of a Curve (Locus of a Point) 25
17. Locus of an Equation 28
18. Discussion of an Equation 31
19. Summary 36
20. Horizontal and Vertical Asymptotes 39
21. Points of Intersection 43

CHAPTER IV. THE STRAIGHT LINE

22. The Degree of the Equation of Any Straight Line . . 46
23. Locus of Any Equation of the First Degree 46

ARTICLE	PAGE
24. Plotting Straight Lines. Theorem. Plotting by Factoring	48
25. Point-Slope Form	51
26. Two-Point Form	51
27. Intercept Form	52
28. Condition that Three Lines shall Intersect in a Common Point	52
29. The Normal Equation of the Straight Line	55
30. Reduction to the Normal Form	56
31. The Perpendicular Distance from a Line to a Point	59
32. Systems of Straight Lines	63
33. System of Lines passing through the Point of Intersection of Two Given Lines	66

CHAPTER V. THE CIRCLE

34. Equation of the Circle	71
35. Test for a Circle	72
36. Circles determined by three Conditions	73
37. Radical Axis	78
38. Length of the Tangent	79
39. Systems of Circles	81

CHAPTER VI. PARABOLA, ELLIPSE, AND HYPERBOLA

40. The Parabola	85
41. Construction of the Parabola	87
42. Parabolic Arch	87
43. Plotting a Parabola	89
44. The Ellipse	91
45. Construction of the Ellipse	93
46. Plotting an Ellipse	95
47. Special Cases	95
48. The Hyperbola	97
49. Construction of the Hyperbola	99
50. Plotting a Hyperbola	100
51. Conjugate Hyperbolas and Asymptotes	102
52. Equilateral or Rectangular Hyperbola	105
53. Summary	105
54. Conic Sections	105
55. Systems of Conics	105

CONTENTS

CHAPTER VII. TRANSFORMATION OF COORDINATES

ARTICLE	PAGE
56. Introduction	108
57. Translation	108
58. Simplifying Equations by Translation	110
59. Theorem	114
60. Typical Equations for Conic Sections	114
61. Rotation	116
62. Simplifying Equations by Rotating the Axes	118
63. Locus of any Equation of the Second Degree	120
64. Plotting the Locus of an Equation of the Second Degree	122
65. A Special Case. Equilateral (Rectangular) Hyperbola. Construction of an Equilateral Hyperbola	127
66. Another Definition of Conic Sections (Conics)	129
67. General Transformation of Coordinates	129
68. Classification of Loci	130

CHAPTER VIII. TANGENTS

69. Equation of the Tangent	132
70. A General Theorem	135
71. Equation of the Normal	136
72. Subtangent and Subnormal	137
73. Tangent with a Given Slope	138
74. Tangent from an External Point	139
75. Formulas for Tangents when the Slope is Given	140
76. Properties of Tangents and Normals to Conics	143

CHAPTER IX. POLAR COORDINATES

77. Polar Coordinates	148
78. Plotting Polar Equations	150
79. Rapid Plotting of Polar Equations	154
80. Relations between Rectangular and Polar Coordinates	156
81. Applications. Straight Line and Circle	157
82. Polar Equation for the Conic Sections	159
83. Points of Intersection	160
84. Loci using Polar Coordinates	162

CHAPTER X. TRANSCENDENTAL CURVES

85. Natural Logarithms. Exponential and Logarithmic Curves	**166**

ARTICLE	PAGE
86. Sine Curves	171
87. Periodicity	173
88. Plotting Sine Curves	174
89. Other Trigonometric Curves	176
90. Addition of Ordinates	178
91. Boundary Curves	181

CHAPTER XI. PARAMETRIC EQUATIONS AND LOCI

92. Plotting Parametric Equations	184
93. Rectangular Equation from Parametric Equations	186
94. Various Parametric Equations for the Same Curve	187
95. Locus Problems solved by Parametric Equations	190
96. Loci defined by the Points of Intersection of Corresponding Lines	196
97. Diameters of Conics	199

CHAPTER XII. FUNCTIONS. GRAPHS, AND EMPIRICAL EQUATIONS

98. Functions. Notation of Functions	204
99. Graph of a Function. Examples of Simple Functions	205
100. Setting up and Graphing Functions	208
101. Function defined Empirically	211
102. Straight-Line Law	212
103. Method of Averages	213
104. Comments on the Preceding Example	214
105. Laws with Two Constants	217
106. Power Law	218
107. Exponential and Hyperbolic Laws	221
108. Parabolic Laws	225
109. Method of Averages applied to the General Parabolic Law	227
110. Solution of Algebraic Equations by Graphs	229
111. Graphical Solution of Transcendental Equations	232

CHAPTER XIII. CARTESIAN COÖRDINATES IN SPACE

112. Cartesian Coördinates	235
113. Important Relations	237
114. Direction Cosines of a Line	239

CONTENTS

ARTICLE	PAGE
115. Direction Numbers of a Line	239
116. Lengths	242
117. Angle between Two Directed Lines	242
118. Test for Parallel Lines or Perpendicular Lines	243
119. Point dividing a Line Segment in a Given Ratio	244
120. Loci in Space	247
121. Equation of a Surface	248
122. Equations of a Curve	248
123. Locus of an Equation. Locus of Two Simultaneous Equations	249

CHAPTER XIV. THE PLANE AND THE STRAIGHT LINE IN SPACE

124. The Normal Form of the Equation of the Plane	251
125. Locus of Any Equation of the First Degree. Reduction to the Normal Form	252
126. Special Planes	254
127. Intercepts and Traces of a Plane. To Construct a Plane	254
128. The Angle between Two Planes	257
129. Planes determined by Three Conditions	258
130. The Equation of a Plane in Terms of its Intercepts	260
131. The Perpendicular Distance from a Plane to a Point	262
132. Systems of Planes	264
133. General Equations of the Straight Line	267
134. Various Forms of the Equations of a Straight Line	271
135. The Projecting Planes of a Line. The Projections Form	272
136. Relative Positions of a Line and a Plane	276

CHAPTER XV. SPECIAL SURFACES

137. The Sphere	280
138. Cylinders	283
139. Cones	284
140. Discussion of the Equation of a Surface	287
141. Quadric Surfaces	290
142. The Ellipsoid	290
143. The Hyperboloid of One Sheet	292
144. The Hyperboloid of Two Sheets	293
145. The Elliptic Paraboloid	295
146. The Hyperbolic Paraboloid	297

CHAPTER XVI. SUPPLEMENTARY TOPICS IN THE GEOMETRY OF SPACE

ARTICLE	PAGE
147. SURFACES OF REVOLUTION	300
148. RULED SURFACES	303
149. RULED QUADRICS. RECTILINEAR GENERATORS	304
150. CYLINDERS WITH ELEMENTS OBLIQUE TO THE AXES	306
151. THE PROJECTING CYLINDERS OF A CURVE	307
152. PARAMETRIC EQUATIONS OF CURVES IN SPACE	311

CHAPTER XVII. TRANSFORMATION OF COÖRDINATES. DIFFERENT SYSTEMS OF COÖRDINATES

153. TRANSLATION OF THE AXES	314
154. ROTATION OF THE AXES	314
155. THE LOCUS OF AN EQUATION OF THE SECOND DEGREE IN x, y, AND z	317
156. SIMPLIFICATION OF THE GENERAL EQUATION OF THE SECOND DEGREE IN THREE VARIABLES	318
157. POLAR COÖRDINATES	320
158. SPHERICAL COÖRDINATES	321
159. CYLINDRICAL COÖRDINATES	321
INDEX	325

NEW ANALYTIC GEOMETRY

CHAPTER I

FORMULAS AND TABLES FOR REFERENCE

1. Occasion will arise in later chapters to make use of many of the following formulas and theorems proved in geometry, algebra, and trigonometry.

GEOMETRY

1. In the formulas, r denotes radius, a altitude, B area of base, and s slant height.

Circle. Circumference $= 2\,\pi r$. Area $= \pi r^2$.
Prism. Volume $= Ba$. *Pyramid.* Volume $= \tfrac{1}{3} Ba$.
Right circular cylinder. Volume $= \pi r^2 a$. Lateral surface $= 2\,\pi r a$. Total surface $= 2\,\pi r(r + a)$.
Right circular cone. Volume $= \tfrac{1}{3}\pi r^2 a$. Lateral surface $= \pi r s$. Total surface $= \pi r(r + s)$.
Sphere. Volume $= \tfrac{4}{3}\pi r^3$. Surface $= 4\,\pi r^2$.

ALGEBRA

2. Quadratic. $\qquad Ax^2 + Bx + C = 0.$

Solution. 1. By factoring: Factor $Ax^2 + Bx + C$, set each factor equal to zero, and solve for x.

2. By completing the square: Transpose C, divide by the coefficient of x^2, add to both members the square of half the coefficient of x, and extract the square root.

3. By the formula $\quad x = \dfrac{-B \pm \sqrt{B^2 - 4\,AC}}{2\,A}.$

Nature of the roots. The expression $B^2 - 4\,AC$ beneath the radical in the formula is called the **discriminant**. The two roots are real and unequal, real and equal, or imaginary, according as the discriminant is positive, zero, or negative.

3. Logarithms.

$$\log ab = \log a + \log b. \qquad \log a^n = n \log a. \qquad \log 1 = 0.$$
$$\log \frac{a}{b} = \log a - \log b. \qquad \log \sqrt[n]{a} = \frac{1}{n} \log a. \qquad \log_a a = 1.$$

TRIGONOMETRY

4. Right triangle. The functions of an acute angle A are defined as follows:

$$\sin A = \frac{\text{opposite side}}{\text{hypotenuse}}, \qquad \csc A = \frac{\text{hypotenuse}}{\text{opposite side}},$$
$$\cos A = \frac{\text{adjacent side}}{\text{hypotenuse}}, \qquad \sec A = \frac{\text{hypotenuse}}{\text{adjacent side}},$$
$$\tan A = \frac{\text{opposite side}}{\text{adjacent side}}, \qquad \cot A = \frac{\text{adjacent side}}{\text{opposite side}}.$$

Theorem. In a right triangle a side is equal to the product of the hypotenuse and the sine of the angle opposite to that side, or to the product of the hypotenuse and the cosine of the angle adjacent to that side.

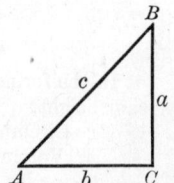

5. Angles in general. An angle XOA is considered as generated by a line rotating from OX to OA. The angle is positive when the line rotates *counterclockwise*, and negative when it rotates *clockwise*. The fixed line OX is called the *initial line*, the line OA the *terminal line*. (See figure below.)

6. Measurement of angles. There are two common methods of measuring angular magnitude; that is, there are two unit angles.

Degree measure. The unit angle is $\frac{1}{360}$ of a complete revolution, and is called a *degree*.

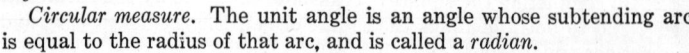

Circular measure. The unit angle is an angle whose subtending arc is equal to the radius of that arc, and is called a *radian*.

The relation between the unit angles is given by the equation

$$180 \text{ degrees} = \pi \text{ radians } (\pi = 3.14159 \cdots);$$

or also, by solving this,

1 degree $= \dfrac{\pi}{180} = .0174 \cdots$ radian; 1 radian $= \dfrac{180}{\pi} = 57.29 \cdots$ degrees.

FORMULAS AND TABLES FOR REFERENCE

From the preceding definition we have
$$\text{number of radians in an angle} = \frac{\text{subtending arc}}{\text{radius}}.$$

These equations enable us to change from one measurement to another.

7. Relations.

$$\cot x = \frac{1}{\tan x}; \quad \sec x = \frac{1}{\cos x}; \quad \csc x = \frac{1}{\sin x}.$$

$$\tan x = \frac{\sin x}{\cos x}; \quad \cot x = \frac{\cos x}{\sin x}.$$

$$\sin^2 x + \cos^2 x = 1; \quad 1 + \tan^2 x = \sec^2 x; \quad 1 + \cot^2 x = \csc^2 x.$$

8. Formulas for reducing angles.

Angle	sine	cosine	tangent	cotangent	secant	cosecant
$-x$	$-\sin x$	$\cos x$	$-\tan x$	$-\cot x$	$\sec x$	$-\csc x$
$90° - x$	$\cos x$	$\sin x$	$\cot x$	$\tan x$	$\csc x$	$\sec x$
$90° + x$	$\cos x$	$-\sin x$	$-\cot x$	$-\tan x$	$-\csc x$	$\sec x$
$180° - x$	$\sin x$	$-\cos x$	$-\tan x$	$-\cot x$	$-\sec x$	$\csc x$
$180° + x$	$-\sin x$	$-\cos x$	$\tan x$	$\cot x$	$-\sec x$	$-\csc x$
$270° - x$	$-\cos x$	$-\sin x$	$\cot x$	$\tan x$	$-\csc x$	$-\sec x$
$270° + x$	$-\cos x$	$\sin x$	$-\cot x$	$-\tan x$	$\csc x$	$-\sec x$
$360° - x$	$-\sin x$	$\cos x$	$-\tan x$	$-\cot x$	$\sec x$	$-\csc x$

9. Functions of $(x + y)$ and $(x - y)$.

$$\sin(x + y) = \sin x \cos y + \cos x \sin y.$$
$$\sin(x - y) = \sin x \cos y - \cos x \sin y.$$
$$\cos(x + y) = \cos x \cos y - \sin x \sin y.$$
$$\cos(x - y) = \cos x \cos y + \sin x \sin y.$$

$$\tan(x + y) = \frac{\tan x + \tan y}{1 - \tan x \tan y}. \quad \tan(x - y) = \frac{\tan x - \tan y}{1 + \tan x \tan y}.$$

10. Functions of $2x$ and $\frac{1}{2}x$.

$$\sin 2x = 2 \sin x \cos x; \quad \cos 2x = \cos^2 x - \sin^2 x; \quad \tan 2x = \frac{2 \tan x}{1 - \tan^2 x}.$$

$$\sin \frac{x}{2} = \pm \sqrt{\frac{1 - \cos x}{2}}; \quad \cos \frac{x}{2} = \pm \sqrt{\frac{1 + \cos x}{2}}; \quad \tan \frac{x}{2} = \pm \sqrt{\frac{1 - \cos x}{1 + \cos x}}.$$

$$\sin^2 x = \tfrac{1}{2} - \tfrac{1}{2} \cos 2x; \quad \cos^2 x = \tfrac{1}{2} + \tfrac{1}{2} \cos 2x.$$

11. Relations for any triangle. *Law of cosines.* In any triangle the square of a side equals the sum of the squares of the two other sides diminished by twice the product of those sides by the cosine of their included angle; that is, $a^2 = b^2 + c^2 - 2\,bc\cos A$.

Area of a triangle. The area of any triangle equals one half the product of two sides by the sine of the included angle; that is,

$$\text{area} = \tfrac{1}{2}\,ab\sin C = \tfrac{1}{2}\,bc\sin A = \tfrac{1}{2}\,ca\sin B.$$

2. Natural values. Special angles.

Angle in Radians	Angle in Degrees	sin	cos	tan	cot	sec	csc
0	0°	0	1	0	∞	1	∞
$\tfrac{1}{2}\pi$	90°	1	0	∞	0	∞	1
π	180°	0	-1	0	∞	-1	∞
$\tfrac{3}{2}\pi$	270°	-1	0	∞	0	∞	-1
2π	360°	0	1	0	∞	1	∞

Angle in Radians	Angle in Degrees	sin	cos	tan	cot	sec	csc
0	0°	0	1	0	∞	1	∞
$\tfrac{1}{6}\pi$	30°	$\tfrac{1}{2}$	$\tfrac{1}{2}\sqrt{3}$	$\tfrac{1}{3}\sqrt{3}$	$\sqrt{3}$	$\tfrac{2}{3}\sqrt{3}$	2
$\tfrac{1}{4}\pi$	45°	$\tfrac{1}{2}\sqrt{2}$	$\tfrac{1}{2}\sqrt{2}$	1	1	$\sqrt{2}$	$\sqrt{2}$
$\tfrac{1}{3}\pi$	60°	$\tfrac{1}{2}\sqrt{3}$	$\tfrac{1}{2}$	$\sqrt{3}$	$\tfrac{1}{3}\sqrt{3}$	2	$\tfrac{2}{3}\sqrt{3}$
$\tfrac{1}{2}\pi$	90°	1	0	∞	0	∞	1

3. Rules for signs of the trigonometric functions.

Quadrant	sin	cos	tan	cot	sec	csc
First	+	+	+	+	+	+
Second	+	−	−	−	−	+
Third	−	−	+	+	−	−
Fourth	−	+	−	−	+	−

4. Natural values of trigonometric functions.

Angle in Radians	Angle in Degrees	sin	cos	tan	cot		
.000	0°	.000	1.000	.000	∞	90°	1.571
.017	1°	.017	1.000	.017	57.29	89°	1.553
.035	2°	.035	.999	.035	28.64	88°	1.536
.052	3°	.052	.999	.052	19.08	87°	1.518
.070	4°	.070	.998	.070	14.30	86°	1.501
.087	5°	.087	.996	.088	11.43	85°	1.484
.175	10°	.174	.985	.176	5.67	80°	1.396
.262	15°	.259	.966	.268	3.73	75°	1.309
.349	20°	.342	.940	.364	2.75	70°	1.222
.436	25°	.423	.906	.466	2.14	65°	1.134
.524	30°	.500	.866	.577	1.73	60°	1.047
.611	35°	.574	.819	.700	1.43	55°	.960
.698	40°	.643	.766	.839	1.19	50°	.873
.785	45°	.707	.707	1.000	1.00	45°	.785
		cos	sin	cot	tan	Angle in Degrees	Angle in Radians

5. Greek alphabet.

Letters		Names	Letters		Names	Letters		Names
A	α	Alpha	I	ι	Iota	P	ρ	Rho
B	β	Beta	K	κ	Kappa	Σ	σ s	Sigma
Γ	γ	Gamma	Λ	λ	Lambda	T	τ	Tau
Δ	δ	Delta	M	μ	Mu	Υ	υ	Upsilon
E	ε	Epsilon	N	ν	Nu	Φ	φ	Phi
Z	ζ	Zeta	Ξ	ξ	Xi	X	χ	Chi
H	η	Eta	O	o	Omicron	Ψ	ψ	Psi
Θ	θ	Theta	Π	π	Pi	Ω	ω	Omega

CHAPTER II

CARTESIAN COÖRDINATES

6. In analytic geometry problems are solved by employing coördinates, equations, and the processes of algebra.

7. Rectangular Cartesian* coördinates. Let XX' and YY' be perpendicular lines in a plane intersecting at O. The distance of a point from YY' is called its **abscissa**; from XX', its **ordinate**. The position of a point in the plane is determined from these distances by observing the rule of signs: *The abscissa of a point P is positive when P is to the right of YY', negative when to the left. The ordinate of P is positive when P is above XX', negative when below.*

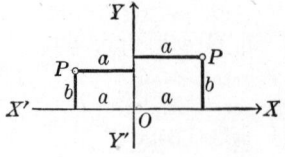

The abscissa a and ordinate b of P are its **coördinates**, and are written in a parenthesis (a, b), the abscissa preceding the ordinate. The lines XX' and YY' are the **axes of coördinates**: XX', the **x-axis** (or the **axis of abscissas**); YY', the **y-axis** (or the **axis of ordinates**). The point O is the **origin**.

The work of plotting points in a rectangular system is much simplified by the use of *coördinate* or *plotting paper*, constructed by ruling off the plane into equal squares, the sides being parallel to the axes.

In the figure several points are plotted, the unit of length

---

* So called after René Descartes (1596–1650), who first introduced the idea of coördinates into the study of geometry.

being assumed equal to one division on each axis. The method is simply this:

Count off from O along $X'X$ a number of divisions equal to the given abscissa — to the right when the abscissa is positive, to the left when negative. From the point so

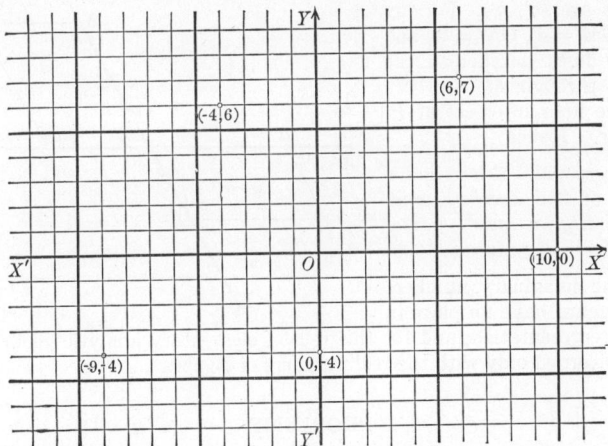

determined count off a number of divisions equal to the given ordinate, up or down according as the latter is positive or negative.

Rectangular axes divide the plane into four portions called **quadrants**; these are numbered as in the figure, in which the proper signs of the coördinates are also indicated.

As distinguished from rectangular coördinates, the term **oblique coördinates** is employed when the axes are not perpendicular (see figure on page 8). The coördinates of P are now the lines MP and NP drawn parallel to the axes. The abscissa is $NP (= OM)$, and the ordinate is MP. The rule of signs given above applies to this case also.

NEW ANALYTIC GEOMETRY

In the following problems assume rectangular coördinates unless the contrary is stated:

Any point P in the plane determines two numbers, the coördinates of P. Conversely, given two real numbers a' and b', then a point P' in the plane may always be constructed whose coördinates are (a', b'). For lay off $OM' = a'$, $ON' = b'$, and draw lines parallel to the axes through M' and N'. These lines intersect at P' (a', b') Hence

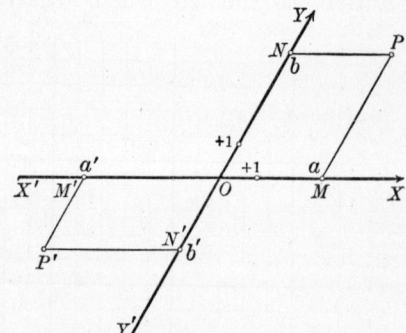

Every point determines a pair of real numbers, and, conversely, a pair of real numbers determines a point.

The imaginary numbers of algebra have no place in this representation, and for this reason elementary analytic geometry is concerned only with the real numbers of algebra.

PROBLEMS

1. Plot accurately the points $(6, 2)$, $(-2, 6)$, $(3, -3)$, $(4, 0)$, $(0, -2)$, $(-4, -3)$.

2. What is the locus of a point which moves (1) so that its abscissa is always -3? (2) so that its ordinate is always 4?

3. Draw the triangle whose vertices are as follows:

(a) $(8, 4)$, $(0, -4)$, $(2, 4)$.
(b) $(1, -1)$, $(-4, 3)$, $(-6, -2)$.
(c) $(3, 5)$, $(3, 10)$, $(0, 2.5)$.
(d) $(2, 0)$, $(-1, \sqrt{3})$, $(-1, -\sqrt{3})$.
(e) (b, d), (c, d), $(a, 0)$.

4. Find the areas of triangles (c), (d), (e) of Problem 3. *Ans.* (d) $3\sqrt{3}$

5. Draw the quadrilateral whose vertices are as follows:

(a) $(0, -4)$, $(6, 2)$, $(0, 4)$, $(-6, 2)$.
(b) $(0, 0)$, $(4, 5)$, $(8, 0)$, $(7, 3)$.
(c) (a, b), $(-a, b)$, $(a, -b)$, $(-a, -b)$.

6. What is the locus of a point (1) whose abscissa is equal to the ordinate? (2) whose abscissa is equal to the negative of the ordinate?

CARTESIAN COÖRDINATES

7. By means of geometric constructions locate accurately the points $(\sqrt{2}, 3)$, $(\sqrt{3}, 2)$, $(\sqrt{5}, \sqrt{6})$.

8. The base of an equilateral triangle whose side is 6 inches coincides with the x-axis and its mid-point is at the origin. What are the coördinates of its vertices? (Two cases.)

9. A square whose side is 6 inches has its diagonals lying along the coördinate axes. What are the coördinates of its vertices?
Ans. $(3\sqrt{2}, 0)$, $(0, 3\sqrt{2})$, $(-3\sqrt{2}, 0)$, $(0, -3\sqrt{2})$.

10. What kind of quadrilateral has its vertices at $(2, 4)$, $(0, 4)$, $(0, -4)$, $(2, -4)$? What is its area?

11. If two sides of a rectangle are of lengths a and b, and coincide with the x- and y-axes, respectively, what are the coördinates of its vertices? (Four cases.)

12. If $(0, 0)$, $(0, b)$, (a, c) are the coördinates of three vertices of a parallelogram, what are the coördinates of the fourth vertex?
Ans. $(a, b+c)$, $(a, c-b)$, $(-a, b-c)$.

13. Plot the points whose oblique coördinates are as follows, where the angle between the axes is $45°$: $(-3, 2), (4, 2), (-4, -3), (\sqrt{2}, \sqrt{3})$, $(4, 2 + \sqrt{2})$.

14. Draw the quadrilaterals of Problem 5 if the angle between the axes is $60°$.

15. If the length of a side of an equilateral triangle is b, one vertex $(0, 0)$, and one side along the y-axis, what are the coördinates of the other vertices? (Four cases.)

16. What are the coördinates of the point which is symmetric to (a, b) with respect to the x-axis? the y-axis? the origin?

17. A square of side $2a$ has one vertex at $(0, 0)$ and one diagonal along the positive x-axis. What are the coördinates of its other vertices?
Ans. $(a\sqrt{2}, a\sqrt{2})$, $(2a\sqrt{2}, 0)$, $(a\sqrt{2}, -a\sqrt{2})$.

18. One vertex of an equilateral triangle of side b is at the origin and an altitude is along the y-axis. What are the coördinates of the other vertices? (Two cases.)

8. Directed line. We mark a point M on the x-axis to the right of O when OM is determined by a positive number, and to the left when it is determined by a negative number. Accordingly we assign to $X'X$ a *positive direction* to the right. Then $X'X$ becomes a directed line; namely, a straight line upon which an origin, a unit of length, and a positive direction have been assumed. An arrowhead is usually placed upon a directed line to indicate the positive direction.

$$\overset{\longrightarrow}{\underset{B\quad A\quad O\quad A\quad B}{\bullet\quad\bullet\quad\bullet\quad\bullet\quad\bullet}}$$

If A and B are any two points of a directed line such that
$$OA = a, \quad OB = b,$$
then the length of the segment AB is always given by $b - a$.

For all positions of two points A and B on a directed line, the length AB is given by
(1) $$AB = OB - OA,$$
where O is the origin.

(I)	(II)	(III)	(IV)
0 +3 +6	-4 0 +3	-3 0 +5	-6 -2 0
O A B	B O A	A O B	B A O

The definition above is illustrated in each of the four figures.

I. $AB = OB - OA = 6 - 3 = +3.$
II. $AB = OB - OA = -4 - 3 = -7.$
III. $AB = OB - OA = +5 - (-3) = +8.$
IV. $AB = OB - OA = -6 - (-2) = -4.$

On a directed line it is obvious that
(2) $$AB = -BA.$$

(3) AB is positive if the direction from A to B agrees with the positive direction on the line, and negative if in the contrary direction.

9. Lengths. Theorem. *The length l of the line joining two points $P_1(x_1, y_1)$, $P_2(x_2, y_2)$ is given by the formula*

(I) $\quad l = \sqrt{(x_1 - x_2)^2 + (y_1 - y_2)^2}.$

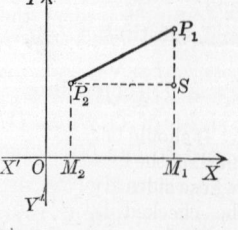

Proof. Draw lines through P_1 and P_2 parallel to the axes to form the right triangle P_1SP_2.

CARTESIAN COÖRDINATES

Then
$$P_2S = OM_1 - OM_2 = x_1 - x_2,$$
$$SP_1 = M_1P_1 - M_2P_2 = y_1 - y_2,$$
$$P_1P_2 = \sqrt{\overline{P_2S}^2 + \overline{SP_1}^2};$$
and hence
$$l = \sqrt{(x_1 - x_2)^2 + (y_1 - y_2)^2}. \qquad \text{Q.E.D.}$$

Formula (I) will give the length for *all* positions of P_1 and P_2. In the figure below, for example, assign to P_2S a positive direction to the right, and to SP_1 the upward direction. Then, in the figure and by (1) Art. 8,
$$P_2S = M_2M_1 = OM_1 - OM_2 = x_1 - x_2,$$
$$SP_1 = N_2N_1 = ON_1 - ON_2 = y_1 - y_2,$$
and the proof proceeds as before.

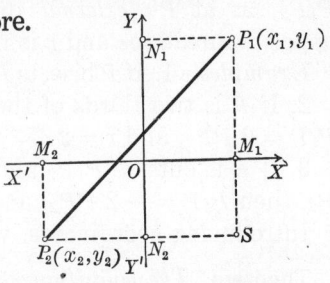

The fact that formula (I) is true for *all* positions of the points P_1 and P_2 is of fundamental importance. The application of this formula to any given problem is therefore simply a matter of direct substitution. In deriving such general formulas it is most convenient to draw the figure so that *all the quantities assumed as known shall be positive*.

EXAMPLE

Find the length of the line joining the points $(1, 3)$ and $(-5, 5)$.

Solution. Call $(1,3)$ P_1, and $(-5, 5)$ P_2.

Then $x_1 = 1, \quad y_1 = 3,$
and $x_2 = -5, \quad y_2 = 5;$
and, substituting in (I), we have
$$l = \sqrt{(1+5)^2 + (3-5)^2}$$
$$= \sqrt{40} = 6.32. \quad Ans.$$

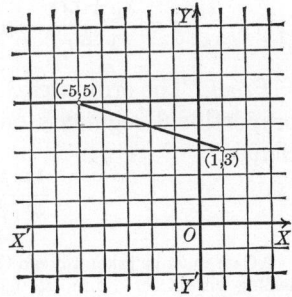

It should be noticed that we are simply finding the hypotenuse of a right triangle whose sides are 6 and 2. The result may be checked by measurement, using a strip of cross-section paper.

10. Point dividing a line segment in a given ratio. Let P_1 and P_2 be points on a directed line and P or P' a third point. Then P divides P_1P_2 in the ratio

$$\frac{P_1P}{PP_2} = r.$$

In the left-hand member note that P is written last in the numerator and first in the denominator. When P is on the segment P_1P_2 (*internal* division), P_1P and PP_2 have like directions and r is positive. When P is outside P_1P_2, as at P' (*external* division), P_1P' and $P'P_2$ have opposite directions and r is negative.

Examples. 1. If P bisects P_1P_2, then $P_1P = PP_2$ and $r = 1$.

2. If P is two thirds of the distance from P_1 to P_2, then $P_1P = 2\ PP_2$, and $r = 2$.

3. If P is outside P_1P_2 and twice as far from P_1 as from P_2, then $P_1P = -2\ PP_2$, and $r = -2$.

Introducing coördinates, we next prove the

Theorem. *The coördinates (x, y) of the point dividing the line joining $P_1(x_1, y_1)$ and $P_2(x_2, y_2)$ in the ratio*

$$\frac{P_1P}{PP_2} = r$$

are given by the formulas

(II) $\qquad x = \dfrac{x_1 + rx_2}{1+r}, \quad y = \dfrac{y_1 + ry_2}{1+r}.$

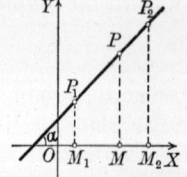

Proof. The ordinates M_1P_1, MP, and M_2P_2 will intercept proportional segments on the transversals P_1P_2 and OX; that is,*

(1) $\qquad\qquad \dfrac{M_1M}{MM_2} = \dfrac{P_1P}{PP_2} = r.$

---

* Care must be taken to read the segments on the transversals (since we are dealing with directed lines) so that they all have *positive* directions.

CARTESIAN COÖRDINATES

But $M_1M = OM - OM_1 = x - x_1,$
$MM_2 = OM_2 - OM = x_2 - x.$

Substituting in (1), $\dfrac{x - x_1}{x_2 - x} = r.$

Clearing of fractions and solving for x, we have x as in (II).

Similarly, by drawing the abscissas of P_1, P, and P_2 to the axis of y, we may prove the formula for y. Q.E.D.

Corollary. Mid-point. *The coördinates (x, y) of the mid-point of $P_1(x_1, y_1)$ and $P_2(x_2, y_2)$ are found by taking the averages of the given abscissas and ordinates; that is,*

(III) $\qquad x = \tfrac{1}{2}(x_1 + x_2), \quad y = \tfrac{1}{2}(y_1 + y_2).$

For if P is the mid-point of P_1P_2, $r = 1$ and (II) becomes (III).

EXAMPLE

The line joining $P_1(-1, -6)$ and $P_2(3, 0)$ is produced beyond P_1 to P so that P is four times as far from P_2 as from P_1. Find the coördinates of P.

Solution. By the statement,

$$\frac{P_1P}{PP_2} = -\frac{1}{4} = r.$$

Also $x_1 = -1, \ y_1 = -6, \ x_2 = 3, \ y_2 = 0.$

Hence, applying (II),

$$x = \frac{-1 - \tfrac{1}{4} \cdot 3}{1 - \tfrac{1}{4}} = \frac{-\tfrac{7}{4}}{\tfrac{3}{4}} = -2\tfrac{1}{3},$$

$$y = \frac{-6 - \tfrac{1}{4} \cdot 0}{1 - \tfrac{1}{4}} = \frac{-6}{\tfrac{3}{4}} = -8.$$

Hence P is $(-2\tfrac{1}{3}, -8)$. *Ans.*
The result is checked by plotting.

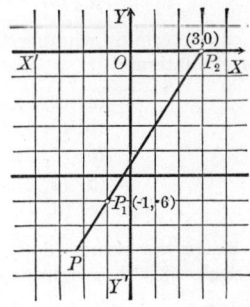

11. Application to theorems in geometry. It is often easy to prove propositions from plane geometry by introducing coördinates.

EXAMPLE

Show that the line joining the mid-points of the nonparallel sides of a trapezoid is parallel to the bases and equal to half their sum.

Proof. In this figure the x-axis is drawn along a base and the y-axis through a vertex. We read the coördinates of the vertices as follows, letting $MC = h$;

$O(0, 0)$, $A(a, 0)$, $C(c, h)$, $B(b+c, h)$.

Hence, by (III), the mid-points E, F are $E(\tfrac{1}{2}c, \tfrac{1}{2}h)$, $F[\tfrac{1}{2}(a+b+c), \tfrac{1}{2}h]$. Since the ordinates are equal, EF is parallel to OA, and its length is the difference of the abscissas, or $\tfrac{1}{2}(a+b)$.   Q.E.D.

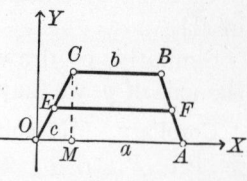

As a rule draw one axis of coördinates along a line of the figure and take O a point of the figure on this line.

PROBLEMS

1. Find the perimeters of the following triangles:

    (a) $(3, 0)$, $(5, 2)$, $(7, 6)$.   *Ans.* 14.51.
    (b) $(2, 1)$, $(7, 3)$, $(5, -4)$.
    (c) $(3, 3)$, $(-3, 4)$, $(-4, -3)$.   *Ans.* 22.38.
    (d) $(-1, 4)$, $(-4, -2)$, $(3, -4)$.
    (e) $(2, -3)$, $(-6, -3)$, $(5, 4)$.   *Ans.* 28.66.

2. Determine whether the following triangles are scalene, isosceles, or equilateral:

    (a) $(2, 6)$, $(6, 2)$, $(-3, -3)$.
    (b) $(-3, -6)$, $(-6, 5)$, $(-3, 5)$.
    (c) $(3, 0)$, $(-3, 0)$, $(0, -3\sqrt{3})$.
    (d) $(2, 2)$, $(-2, -2)$, $(2\sqrt{3}, -2\sqrt{3})$.
    (e) $(3, 0)$, $(6, 4)$, $(-1, 3)$.

3. Do the points $(3, 2)$, $(1, 2\sqrt{3})$, $(-2, 3)$, $(-2\sqrt{2}, -\sqrt{5})$ lie on a circle with the origin as center?

4. What is the value of b in $(b, 4)$ if this point is 10 units distant from $(0, -2)$?   *Ans.* $b = \pm 8$.

5. Find the mid-points of the sides of the triangles in Problem 1.

6. If one end of a line is $(-1, 2)$ and its mid-point is $(2, 1)$, what are the coördinates of the other end?   *Ans.* $(5, 0)$.

CARTESIAN COÖRDINATES

7. Find the coördinates of the point which is two thirds of the distance from the first to the second point in each of the following:

(a) $(-2, -1)$, $(3, 2)$.   *Ans.* $(1\frac{1}{3}, 1)$.
(b) $(3, -4)$, $(-1, 5)$.
(c) $(0, 0)$, $(-21, 6)$.   *Ans.* $(-14, 4)$.
(d) $(2, 6)$, $(8, 9)$.

8. Show, using coördinates, that the mid-point of the hypotenuse of a right triangle is equidistant from the three vertices.

9. Show analytically that the lines joining the mid-points of the adjacent sides of any quadrilateral form a second quadrilateral whose perimeter is equal to the sum of the diagonals of the first.

10. The lines joining $(1, 1)$ to the points $(3, 7)$ and $(5, -3)$, respectively, are extended through the latter points to three times their lengths. Find the coördinates of the points thus reached.
Ans. $(7, 19)$, $(13, -11)$.

11. What are the coördinates of the two points which divide the line joining $(5, 10)$ and $(-2, 3)$ in the ratio $3:4$?

12. Do the diagonals of the quadrilateral with vertices $(2, 1)$, $(7, 1)$, $(9, 3)$, $(4, 3)$ bisect each other?

13. Show that the points $(2, 3)$, $(4, 1)$, $(8, 2)$, and $(6, 4)$ are the vertices of a parallelogram.

14. Show analytically that

(a) the diagonals of a rectangle are equal;
(b) the diagonals of any parallelogram bisect each other;
(c) the line joining the mid-points of two sides of any triangle is equal to half the third side.

15. Find the vertices of a triangle if $(-1, 1)$, $(4, -1)$, and $(-2, -5)$ are the mid-points of its sides.   *Ans.* $(5, 5)$, $(-7, -3)$, $(3, -7)$.

16. In what ratio does the point $(-4, 3)$ divide the line segment joining $(1, -2)$ and $(-6, 5)$?

17. What algebraic equation expresses the fact that a point (x, y) is 7 units distant from $(3, -2)$?   *Ans.* $x^2 + y^2 - 6x + 4y - 36 = 0$.

18. What algebraic equation expresses the fact that

(a) the point (x, y) is equidistant from $(3, 5)$ and $(-2, -4)$?

(b) the point (x, y) is twice as far from $(3, 5)$ as from $(-2, -4)$?

19. Find the coördinates of the point of intersection of the medians of the triangle whose vertices are (x_1, y_1), (x_2, y_2), (x_3, y_3). This point is the *centroid* of the triangle. (See figure.)   *Ans.* $\frac{1}{3}(x_1 + x_2 + x_3)$, $\frac{1}{3}(y_1 + y_2 + y_3)$.

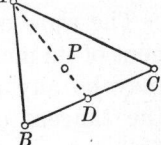

20. Show analytically that

(a) the lines joining the mid-points of the opposite sides of any quadrilateral bisect each other;

(b) the line joining the mid-points of two opposite sides of any quadrilateral and the line joining the mid-points of the diagonals of the quadrilateral bisect each other.

21. Show analytically that the sum of the squares of the distances of any point from two opposite vertices of any rectangle is equal to the sum of the squares of its distances from the other two vertices.

22. Show analytically that the line from a vertex of a parallelogram to the mid-point of one of the opposite sides intersects the opposite diagonal at a point dividing each line in the ratio 1 : 2.

12. Inclination and slope.
The angle between two intersecting directed lines is defined to be the angle made by their positive directions. In the figures this angle is marked θ (Greek "theta"). Evidently θ may have any value from 0 to 180° inclusive.

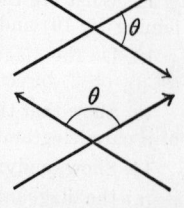

If the directed lines are parallel, the angle between them is 0 or 180°, according as the positive directions agree or do not agree.

When it is desired to assign a positive direction to a line intersecting $X'X$, we shall always assume the *upward direction as positive*.

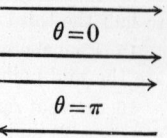

The *inclination* of a line is the angle between the axis of x and the line when the latter is given the upward direction.

This amounts to saying that the inclination is the angle *above* the x axis and to the *right* of the given line, as in the figure.

The *slope* of a line is the tangent of its inclination. The slope may be any real number, since the tangent of an angle in the first two quadrants may be any number, positive or negative.

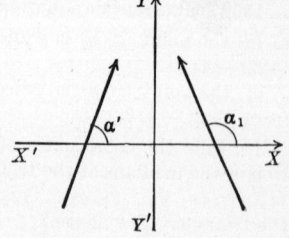

CARTESIAN COÖRDINATES

The slope of a line parallel to $X'X$ is zero, and for a line parallel to $Y'Y$ the slope is infinite.

The inclination of a line will be denoted by the Greek letter α, α_1, etc. ("alpha," etc.); its slope by m, m_1, etc., so that $m = \tan \alpha$, $m_1 = \tan \alpha_1$, etc.

Theorem. *The slope m of the line passing through two points $P_1(x_1, y_1)$, $P_2(x_2, y_2)$ is given by*

(IV) $$m = \frac{y_1 - y_2}{x_1 - x_2}.$$

Proof. In the figure P_2S is parallel to OX. Then in the right $\triangle P_2SP_1$, since $\angle P_1P_2S = \alpha$, we have

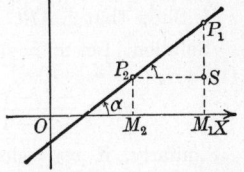

(1) $\qquad m = \tan \alpha = \dfrac{SP_1}{P_2S}.$

But
$$SP_1 = M_1P_1 - M_2P_2 = y_1 - y_2;$$
and
$$P_2S = OM_1 - OM_2 = x_1 - x_2.$$

Substituting these values in (1) gives (IV). Q.E.D.

The student should derive (IV) when α is obtuse.

To construct a line passing through a given point P_2 whose slope is a positive fraction $\dfrac{a}{b}$, we mark S a point b units to the right of P_2, and P_1 a point a units above S, and draw P_2P_1. If the slope is a negative fraction $-\dfrac{a}{b}$, then plot S a point b units to the left of P_2.

13. Test for parallel or perpendicular lines.

Theorem. *If two lines are parallel, their slopes are equal; if perpendicular, their slopes are negative reciprocals; and conversely.*

Proof. Let α_1 and α_2 be the inclinations and m_1 and m_2 the slopes of the lines.

If the lines are parallel,
$$\alpha_1 = \alpha_2. \ \therefore \ m_1 = m_2.$$

If the lines are perpendicular, as in the figure,
$$\alpha_2 = 90° + \alpha_1$$
Hence $m_2 = \tan \alpha_2 = \tan(90° + \alpha_1)$.
By trigonometry (**8**, p. 3),
$$\tan(90° + \alpha_1) = -\cot \alpha_1 = -\frac{1}{\tan \alpha_1}.$$
$$\therefore m_2 = -\frac{1}{m_1}. \qquad \text{Q.E.D.}$$

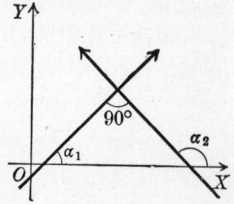

The converse is proved by retracing the steps with the assumption, in the second part, that α_2 is greater than α_1.

EXAMPLES

Draw the triangle with vertices $A(3, 4)$, $B(-2, -1)$, $C(4, 1)$.

1. Show that $\triangle ABC$ is a right triangle.

Solution. Let $m_1 =$ slope of BC. By (IV), taking B as (x_1, y_1), C as (x_2, y_2),
$$m_1 = \frac{-1-1}{-2-4} = \frac{1}{3}.$$

Similarly, if $m_2 =$ slope of CA and $m_3 =$ slope of AB, we find $m_2 = -3$ and $m_3 = 1$. Since m_1 and m_2 are negative reciprocals, $\angle C$ is $90°$.

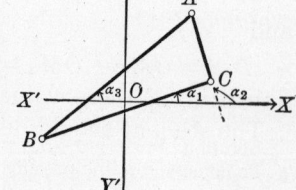

2. Find the inclinations of the sides.

Solution. From Example 1,
$$\tan \alpha_1 = \tfrac{1}{3}, \ \tan \alpha_2 = -3, \ \tan \alpha_3 = 1.$$
Hence, by tables,
$$\alpha_1 = 18° \, 26', \ \alpha_2 = 108° \, 26', \ \alpha_3 = 45°. \ \textit{Ans.}$$
In finding α_2 we have
$$\tan(180° - \alpha_2) = -\tan \alpha_2 = 3. \qquad [\text{By } \mathbf{8}, \text{p. } 3]$$
Hence
$$180° - \alpha_2 = 71° \, 34', \text{ and } \alpha_2 = 180° - 71° \, 34' = 108° \, 26'.$$

14. Angle formulas.

Theorem. *The angle θ between two directed lines is determined by*

(V) $$\tan \theta = \frac{m_1 - m_2}{1 + m_1 m_2},$$

where m_1 is the slope of the line with the greater inclination.

Proof. In the figures $\alpha_1 = \theta + \alpha_2$;
hence $\theta = \alpha_1 - \alpha_2$,
and
$$\tan \theta = \tan (\alpha_1 - \alpha_2) = \frac{\tan \alpha_1 - \tan \alpha_2}{1 + \tan \alpha_1 \tan \alpha_2}. \quad \text{[By 9, p. 3]}$$

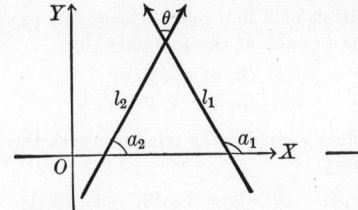

Substituting $\tan \alpha_1 = m_1$, $\tan \alpha_2 = m_2$, we have (V). Q.E.D.
If the inclinations are known, we may use the equation
(V a) $\qquad \boldsymbol{\theta = \alpha_1 - \alpha_2},$
where α_1 is the greater inclination.

EXAMPLES

1. Find $\measuredangle A$ and B of the right $\triangle ABC$ of the figure.

Solution. From Example 2, Art. 13, we have $\alpha_1 = 18° 26'$, $\alpha_2 = 108° 26'$, $\alpha_3 = 45°$. Hence, by (V a),

$\angle B = \alpha_3 - \alpha_1 = 26° 34'$;
$\angle A = \alpha_2 - \alpha_3 = 63° 26'$. *Ans.*

2. Find $\angle B$ by (V).

Solution. By Example 1, Art. 13, $m_3 = 1$, $m_1 = \frac{1}{3}$. Then
$$\tan B = \frac{m_3 - m_1}{1 + m_1 m_3} = \frac{1 - \frac{1}{3}}{1 + \frac{1}{3}} = \frac{1}{2}.$$

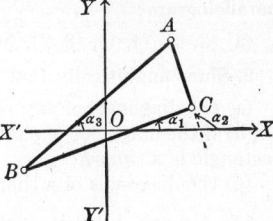

Hence $\angle B = 26° 34'$, as before. *Ans.*

PROBLEMS

1. Find the slope of the line through the points

(a) $(4, 5)$, $(7, 8)$;
(b) $(4, 7)$, $(-3, -5)$;
(c) $(2.5, 3.4)$, $(-3, 5.2)$;
(d) (a, b), $(c, -d)$;
(e) $(-3, -7)$, $(-5, 4)$;
(f) $(3, 3)$, $(5, 5)$.

2. Find the inclination of the line through the following points:

(a) $(2, -2)$, $(4, 2)$.   Ans. $m = 2$, $\alpha = 63°\ 26'$.
(b) $(1, 1)$, $(5, -5)$.   Ans. $m = -1.5$, $\alpha = 123°\ 41'$.
(c) $(5, 8)$, $(3, -4)$. (d) $(4, 8)$, $(-2, -2)$. (e) $(2, 3)$, $(-6, 7)$.

3. What are the slope and inclination of any line parallel to the x-axis? the y-axis?

4. Find the slope and inclination of a line perpendicular to the line passing through the given points in each of the following:

(a) $(1, 2)$, $(-1, 3)$.   (c) $(3, 7)$, $(-2, 7)$.
(b) $(5, -2)$, $(5, 4)$.   (d) $(5, 4)$, $(4, 7)$.

5. By means of slopes determine which of the triangles with the following vertices are right triangles:

(a) $(-2, 9)$, $(10, -7)$, $(12, -5)$.   (c) $(0, -1)$, $(3, -4)$, $(2, 1)$.
(b) $(2, 1)$, $(3, -2)$, $(-4, -1)$.   (d) $(6, 11)$, $(-4, -9)$, $(11, -4)$.

6. Which of the following sets of three points are on a line?

(a) $(6, 6)$, $(4, 7)$, $(2, 8)$.   (c) $(3, -2)$, $(5, 1)$, $(10, 0)$.
(b) $(1, 5)$, $(0, 2)$, $(2, 8)$.   (d) $(13, -2)$, $(5, 5)$, $(-7, 6)$.
(e) $(a, b + c)$, $(b, c + a)$, $(c, a + b)$.

7. Find the angles of the following triangles:

(a) $(0, 1)$, $(3, 4)$, $(2, -1)$.   (c) $(6, -6)$, $(5, 2)$, $(2, 2)$.
(b) $(7, -4)$, $(1, 1)$, $(-5, -7)$.   (d) $(0, -2)$, $(4, 2)$, $(0, 6)$.
 Ans. $39°\ 6'$, $53°\ 50'$, $87°\ 4'$.   Ans. $45°$, $45°$, $90°$.

8. Show that each of the following sets of points are vertices of a parallelogram:

(a) $(2, 3)$, $(4, 1)$, $(8, 2)$, $(6, 4)$.   (b) $(-4, -2)$, $(2, 0)$, $(8, 6)$, $(2, 4)$.

9. Show analytically that

(a) the diagonals of any square are perpendicular to each other;
(b) if the diagonals of a rectangle are perpendicular to each other, the rectangle is a square;
(c) the diagonals of a rhombus bisect each other at right angles.

15. Areas. In this section the problem of determining the area of any polygon, the coördinates of whose vertices are given, will be solved. We begin with the

Theorem. *The area of a triangle whose vertices are the origin, $P_1(x_1, y_1)$, and $P_2(x_2, y_2)$ is given by the formula*

(VI) $\qquad$ area of $\triangle OP_1P_2 = \tfrac{1}{2}(x_1y_2 - x_2y_1)$.

CARTESIAN COÖRDINATES

Proof. In the figure, the quadrilateral $OM_1P_1P_2$ is composed of $\triangle OP_1P_2$ and $\triangle OM_1P_1$, or, also, of $\triangle OM_2P_2$ and trapezoid $M_2M_1P_1P_2$. Hence, in areas,

(1) $\triangle OP_1P_2 = \triangle OM_2P_2 +$ trapezoid $M_2M_1P_1P_2 - \triangle OM_1P_1$.

But $\triangle OM_2P_2 = \frac{1}{2} OM_2 \cdot M_2P_2 = \frac{1}{2} x_2y_2$;

trapezoid $M_2M_1P_1P_2$
$= \frac{1}{2}(M_2P_2 + M_1P_1) \cdot M_2M_1$
$= \frac{1}{2}(y_2 + y_1)(x_1 - x_2)$;

$\triangle OM_1P_1 = \frac{1}{2} OM_1 \cdot M_1P_1 = \frac{1}{2} x_1y_1$.

Substituting in (1),
$\triangle OP_1P_2 = \frac{1}{2} x_2y_2 + \frac{1}{2}(y_2 + y_1)(x_1 - x_2) - \frac{1}{2} x_1y_1$
$= \frac{1}{2}(x_1y_2 - x_2y_1)$.   Q.E.D.

EXAMPLE

Find the area of the triangle whose vertices are the origin, $(-2, 4)$, and $(-5, -1)$.

Solution. Denote $(-2, 4)$ by P_1, $(-5, -1)$ by P_2. Then
$x_1 = -2, \quad y_1 = 4, \quad x_2 = -5, \quad y_2 = -1$.

Substituting in (VI),
area $= \frac{1}{2}[-2 \cdot -1 - (-5) \cdot 4] = 11$.

Then area $= 11$ *unit squares.* *Ans.*

If, however, the formula (VI) is applied by denoting $(-2, 4)$ by P_2, and $(-5, -1)$ by P_1, the result will be -11.

The two figures for this example are drawn below and illustrate the

Rule. *Passing around the perimeter in the order of the vertices* O, P_1, P_2, *if the area is on the left, as in Fig. 1, then* (VI) *gives a positive result; if*

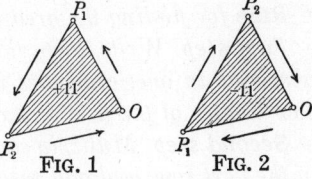

FIG. 1   FIG. 2

the area is on the right, as in Fig. 2, then (VI) *gives a negative result.*

We apply (VI) to any triangle by regarding its area as made up of triangles with the origin as a common vertex.

Theorem. *The area of a triangle whose vertices are $P_1(x_1, y_1)$, $P_2(x_2, y_2)$, $P_3(x_3, y_3)$ is given by*

(VII) $\quad$ area $\triangle P_1P_2P_3 = \frac{1}{2}(x_1y_2 - x_2y_1 + x_2y_3 - x_3y_2 + x_3y_1 - x_1y_3)$.

This formula gives a positive or negative result according as the area lies to the left or right in passing around the perimeter in the order $P_1P_2P_3$.

Proof. $\quad \triangle OP_1P_2 = \frac{1}{2}(x_1y_2 - x_2y_1),$ $\quad$ [By (VI)]

(2) $\quad\quad \triangle OP_2P_3 = \frac{1}{2}(x_2y_3 - x_3y_2),$ and

$\quad\quad\quad \triangle OP_3P_1 = \frac{1}{2}(x_3y_1 - x_1y_3).$

Fig. 1, *origin within the triangle.* By inspection,

area $\triangle P_1P_2P_3$
$= \triangle OP_1P_2 + \triangle OP_2P_3 + \triangle OP_3P_1.$

Equations (2) give these areas each with a positive sign. Adding, we have (VII).

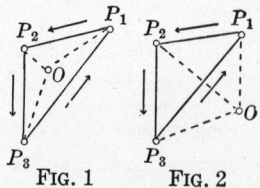

Fig. 1 $\quad\quad$ Fig. 2

Fig. 2, *origin without the triangle.* By inspection,

area $\triangle P_1P_2P_3 = \triangle OP_1P_2 + \triangle OP_2P_3 - \triangle OP_1P_3.$

The last equation in (2) gives the area of $\triangle OP_1P_3$ with a negative sign. Adding, we have (VII). $\quad$ Q.E.D.

An easy way to apply (VII) is given by the following

Rule *for finding the area of a triangle.*

First step. Write down the vertices in two columns, abscissas in one, ordinates in the other, repeating the coördinates of the first vertex.

$\quad x_1 \quad y_1$
$\quad x_2 \quad y_2$
$\quad x_3 \quad y_3$
$\quad x_1 \quad y_1$

Second step. Multiply each abscissa by the ordinate of the next row, and add results. This gives $x_1y_2 + x_2y_3 + x_3y_1$.

Third step. Multiply each ordinate by the abscissa of the next row, and add results. This gives $y_1x_2 + y_2x_3 + y_3x_1$.

CARTESIAN COÖRDINATES

Fourth step. *Subtract the result of the third step from that of the second step, and divide by 2. This gives the required area,* namely, formula (VII).

Formula (VII) may readily be memorized by remarking that the right-hand member is a determinant of simple form, namely,
$$\text{area } \triangle P_1P_2P_3 = \tfrac{1}{2}\begin{vmatrix} x_1 & y_1 & 1 \\ x_2 & y_2 & 1 \\ x_3 & y_3 & 1 \end{vmatrix}.$$

In fact, when this determinant is expanded by the usual rule, the result, when divided by 2, is precisely (VII).

It is easy to show that the above rule applies to any polygon if the following caution be observed in the first step:

Write down the coördinates of the vertices in an order agreeing with that established by passing continuously around the perimeter, and repeat the coördinates of the first vertex.

EXAMPLE

Find the area of the quadrilateral whose vertices are $(1, 6)$, $(-3, -4)$, $(2, -2)$, $(-1, 3)$.

Solution. Plotting, we have the figure from which we choose the *order* of the vertices as indicated by the arrows.
Following the rule:

First step. Write down the vertices in order.

1	6
−1	3
−3	−4
2	−2
1	6

Second step. Multiply each abscissa by the ordinate of the next row, and add. This gives
$$1 \times 3 + (-1 \times -4) + (-3 \times -2) + 2 \times 6 = 25.$$

Third step. Multiply each ordinate by the abscissa of the next row, and add. This gives
$$6 \times -1 + 3 \times -3 + (-4 \times 2) + (-2 \times 1) = -25.$$

Fourth step. Subtract the result of the third step from the result of the second step, and divide by 2.

$$\therefore \text{Area} = \frac{25 + 25}{2} = 25 \text{ unit squares. } Ans.$$

The result has the positive sign, since the area is on the *left*.

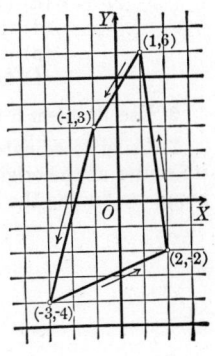

PROBLEMS

1. Find the areas of the triangles whose vertices are given below:

    (a) $(2, 3)$, $(5, 7)$, $(4, -2)$.
    (b) $(1, 3)$, $(-5, -2)$, $(7, 1)$.
    (c) $(5, 5)$, $(-6, 7)$, $(-7, -2)$.   *Ans.* 50.5.
    (d) $(3, 3)$, $(6, 2)$, $(8, -2)$.
    (e) $(-6, 7)$, $(-7, -2)$, $(2, -4)$.
    (f) $(a, 2)$, $(0, c)$, $(b, 2)$.
    (g) $(3, 0)$, $(0, 3\sqrt{3})$, $(6, 3\sqrt{3})$.   *Ans.* $9\sqrt{3}$.

2. Find the areas of the quadrilaterals whose vertices are given below:

    (a) $(2, -1)$, $(5, 6)$, $(3, 8)$, $(-4, 4)$.
    (b) $(0, 2)$, $(7, 1)$, $(12, 4)$, $(5, 5)$.
    (c) $(-2, 3)$, $(-3, -4)$, $(5, -1)$, $(2, 2)$.   *Ans.* 31.
    (d) $(0, 0)$, $(5, 0)$, $(9, 11)$, $(0, 3)$.   *Ans.* 41.
    (e) $(7, 0)$, $(10, 8)$, $(0, 5)$, $(0, 0)$.

3. Show that the quadrilateral formed by joining the mid-points of the adjacent sides of any quadrilateral of Problem 2 has an area equal to half the area of that quadrilateral.

4. Show that the lines joining the mid-points of the sides of the triangle whose vertices are $(4, 6)$, $(2, -4)$, $(-4, 2)$ divide the triangle into four triangles equal in area.

5. If the area of a triangle with given vertices is zero, the vertices lie on a straight line. By this means show that the following sets of points are in each case on a line:

    (a) $(-2, -4)$, $(10, 2)$, $(4, -1)$.
    (b) $(-3, 10)$, $(7, -10)$, $(5, -6)$.
    (c) $(\tfrac{1}{4}, 0)$, $(2\tfrac{1}{2}, 3)$, $(4, 5)$.
    (d) $(2, -3)$, $(14, 6)$, $(6, 0)$.
    (e) $(a, b+c)$, $(b, c+a)$, $(c, a+b)$.
    (f) $(a, c+a)$, $(-c, 0)$, $(-a, c-a)$.

6. Use Problem 5 to write determinants which have the value zero.

7. Using coördinates, find the area of a regular hexagon of side b with its center at the origin and one diagonal along the x-axis. Check your result by finding the areas of certain triangles.

CHAPTER III

CURVE AND EQUATION

16. Equation of a curve (locus of a point). In plane geometry a circle is defined as the locus of a point which is at a given distance from a fixed point. In analytic geometry many other curves * are defined as loci, as we shall see later.

Assume that a certain curve is defined as the locus of a point which satisfies a given condition. We wish to find the "equation" of this curve. Introduce axes of coördinates and assume the point $P(x, y)$ on the locus. Then the given condition will lead to an equation involving the variables x and y, called the *equation of the curve*. The following example illustrates this.

EXAMPLE

Find the equation of the locus of a point whose distance from $(-1, 2)$ is always equal to 4.

Solution. Assume that $P(x, y)$ is any point on the locus.

Denoting $(-1, 2)$ by C, the given condition is

(1) $PC = 4.$

By the length formula (I), p. 10,

$PC = \sqrt{(x+1)^2 + (y-2)^2}.$

Substituting in (1),

$\sqrt{(x+1)^2 + (y-2)^2} = 4.$

Squaring and reducing,

$x^2 + y^2 + 2x - 4y - 11 = 0.$

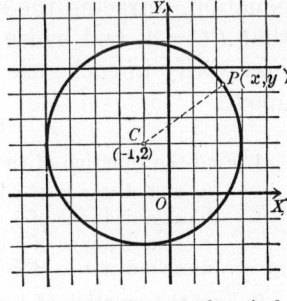

This is the required equation, namely, the equation of the circle with center $(-1, 2)$ and radius 4.

---

* The word "curve" will hereafter signify *any continuous* line, straight or curved.

DEFINITION. The equation of a curve is the equation in x and y which is satisfied by the coördinates of every point on the curve, and by those of no other point.

To find the equation of a curve we may proceed by the

Rule. *First step.* *Assume that $P(x, y)$ is any point on the curve.*

Second step. *Write down the given condition applied to P.*

Third step. *Express this condition in coördinates and simplify. The final equation, containing x, y, and the given constants of the problem, will be the required equation.*

This rule will suffice for many curves. When the condition is in a form not expressible in lengths involving P, the solution may not be so simple. In Chapter XI are many problems of a more general nature.

The point $P(x, y)$ should be plotted in a *general* position conforming to the condition, — not, for example, on one of the axes.

Referring to the example above, it is clear that the equation found is satisfied by the coördinates of every point on the circle, since for every such point $PC = 4$. Conversely, if the coördinates of a point P do satisfy the equation, retracing the steps would lead to the conclusion that $PC = 4$, and hence that P is on the circle. Thus we may verify in each case the requirements of the definition above.

PROBLEMS

1. Find the equation of the line parallel to the y-axis and
    (a) at a distance of 6 units to the left;   *Ans.* $x = -6$.
    (b) at a distance of 3 units to the right;
    (c) at a distance of 4 units to the left of the point $(3, 3)$;
    (d) at a distance of 5 units to the right of $(-2, 2)$.

2. Find the equation of a line parallel to the x-axis and
    (a) at a distance of 5 units above it;
    (b) at a distance of 3 units below it;
    (c) at a distance of 5 units below $(3, -4)$;
    (d) at a distance of 7 units above $(-6, 4)$.

3. What is the equation of the x-axis? the y-axis?

4. What is the equation of the line parallel to the line $x = 5$ and

(a) 4 units to the left of it?
(b) 7 units to the left of it?
(c) 3 units to the right of it?

5. Find the equation of the line perpendicular to the line $y = 3$ and (1) 2 units to the left of (6, 2); (2) 4 units to the right of $(-6, 1)$.

6. What is the equation of the locus of a point that moves so as to be (1) equidistant from the lines $y = -2$ and $y = 8$? (2) equidistant from the lines $x = 2$ and $x = 6$?

7. (1) If a square of side a has its center at the origin and a side perpendicular to one of the coördinate axes, what are the equations of its sides?

(2) If a square of side a has one vertex at the origin and one side along the positive y-axis, what are the equations of the sides? (Two cases.)

8. Find the equation of the line passing through

(a) (3, 4) with a slope 2; *Ans.* $2x - y - 2 = 0$.
(b) $(-3, 5)$ with a slope 3;
(c) (0, 5) with a slope $\frac{2}{3}$; *Ans.* $2x - 3y + 15 = 0$.
(d) (a, b) with a slope $-\frac{1}{4}$.

9. Find the equation of the line passing through

(a) (0, 3) with an inclination 45°;
(b) $(-4, -2)$ with an inclination 30°;
(c) $(-a, b)$ with an inclination 135°; *Ans.* $x + y + a - b = 0$.
(d) (2, 3) with an inclination 120°;
(e) $(-4, 5)$ with an inclination 150°; *Ans.* $x + \sqrt{3}y + 4 - 5\sqrt{3} = 0$.
(f) $(-1, -3)$ with an inclination 90°.

10. Find the equation of the line passing through

(a) (4, 5) and (0, 0); (c) $(-1, 6)$ and (6, 2);
(b) $(0, -3)$ and (5, 2); (d) $(-4, 8)$ and (7, 8);
(e) (2, 2) and $(-4, -4)$; *Ans.* $x = y$.
(f) $(1, -5)$ and $(-3, 1)$. *Ans.* $3x + 2y + 7 = 0$.

11. What is the equation of the locus of a point which is always

(a) at a distance of 4 units from (0, 3)? *Ans.* $x^2 + y^2 - 6y - 7 = 0$.
(b) at a distance of 6 units from the origin?
(c) at a distance of 5 units from (3, 2)?
   Ans. $x^2 + y^2 - 6x - 4y - 12 = 0$.
(d) at a distance of c units from $(a + c, a - c)$?

12. Find the equation of the following circles:

(a) With center $(6, -5)$ and radius 4.
(b) With center $(3, 4)$ and radius 5.   *Ans.* $x^2 + y^2 - 6x - 8y = 0$.
(c) With center $(-a, 2a)$ and radius $3a$.

13. Find the equation of the locus of a point equidistant from

(a) $(-3, -3)$ and $(2, 4)$;   (c) $(0, 4)$ and $(5, 0)$;
(b) $(-4, 3)$ and $(3, 2)$;   *Ans.* $10x - 8y - 9 = 0$.
    Ans. $7x - y + 6 = 0$.   (d) (a, b) and $(-a, -b)$.

14. Show analytically that the line found in each case in Problem 13 is the perpendicular bisector of the line joining the given points.

15. Find the equation of the circle for which the line joining $(5, 6)$ and $(3, -4)$ is a diameter.   *Ans.* $x^2 + y^2 - 8x - 2y - 9 = 0$.

16. Find the equation of the circle with center $(-3, 4)$ and passing through the origin.

17. Locus of an equation. When the equation of a curve has been found or is given, two problems suggest themselves, namely:

1. To draw (or plot) the curve.
2. To discuss the equation and thereby determine properties of the curve (see Art. 18).

DEFINITION. The **locus of an equation** in two variables representing coördinates is the curve (or group of curves) passing through all points whose coördinates satisfy that equation, and no other points.

From this definition follows at once

Theorem I. *If the form of an equation be changed by transposition, by multiplication by a constant, etc., the locus is entirely unaffected.*

We may now state the

Rule *for plotting the locus of a given equation.*

First step. Solve the given equation for y in terms of x (or, if easier, for x in terms of y).

Second step. By this formula compute values of the variable for which the equation has been solved by assuming successive values for the other variable.

CURVE AND EQUATION

Third step. *Plot the points corresponding to the values so determined and draw a smooth curve through them.*

Since there is no limit to the number * of points which may be computed in this way, it is evident that the locus may be drawn as *accurately as may be desired* by simply plotting a sufficiently large number of points.

NOTE. If any doubt exists as to the order in which the points should be joined, connect them in the order of increasing values of the variable for which values have been assumed.

EXAMPLES

1. Draw the locus of the equation $2x - 3y + 6 = 0$.

Solution. 1. Solving for y, $y = \frac{2}{3}x + 2$.

2. Assume values for x and compute y, arranging results in the form of the accompanying table:

Thus, if $\quad x = 1, y = \frac{2}{3} \cdot 1 + 2 = 2\frac{2}{3};$
if $\quad\quad\quad x = 2, y = \frac{2}{3} \cdot 2 + 2 = 3\frac{1}{3},$
etc.

x	y	x	y
0	2	0	2
1	$2\frac{2}{3}$	-1	$1\frac{1}{3}$
2	$3\frac{1}{3}$	-2	$\frac{2}{3}$
3	4	-3	0
4	$4\frac{2}{3}$	-4	$-\frac{2}{3}$
etc.	etc.	etc.	etc.

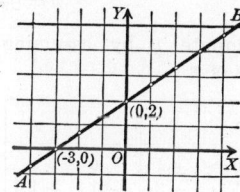

Plotting and connecting the points gives the figure, a *straight line*.

* An equation in the variables x and y is not necessarily satisfied by the coördinates of any points. For coördinates are *real* numbers, and the form of the equation may be such that it is satisfied by no *real* values of x and y. For example, the equation $\quad x^2 + y^2 + 1 = 0$

is of this sort, since, when x and y are real numbers, x^2 and y^2 are necessarily positive (or zero), and consequently $x^2 + y^2 + 1$ is always a positive number greater than or equal to 1, and therefore *not* equal to zero. Such an equation therefore has *no locus*. The expression "the locus of the equation is imaginary" is also used.

An equation may be satisfied by the coördinates of a *finite* number of points only. For example, $x^2 + y^2 = 0$ is satisfied by $x = 0, y = 0$, but by no other real values. In this case the group of points, one or more, whose coördinates satisfy the equation is called the locus of the equation.

2. Plot the locus of the equation $y = x^2 - 2x - 3$.

Solution. Computing y by assuming values of x, we find the table of values below:

x	y	x	y
0	-3	0	-3
1	-4	-1	0
2	-3	-2	5
3	0	-3	12
4	5	-4	21
5	12	etc.	etc.
6	21		
etc.	etc.		

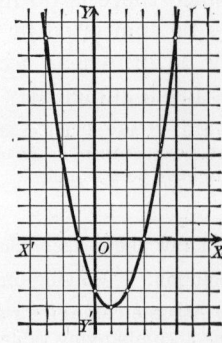

The figure shows the curve, a *parabola*. The proof that the locus is a parabola is given later.

3. Plot the locus of the equation $x^2 + y^2 + 6x - 16 = 0$.

Solution. Solving for y,
$$y = \pm \sqrt{16 - 6x - x^2}.$$

Compute y by assuming values of x.

x	y	x	y
0	± 4	0	± 4
1	± 3	-1	± 4.6
2	0	-2	± 4.9
3	imag.	-3	± 5
4	"	-4	± 4.9
5	"	-5	± 4.6
6	"	-6	± 4
7	"	-7	± 3
		-8	0
		-9	imag.

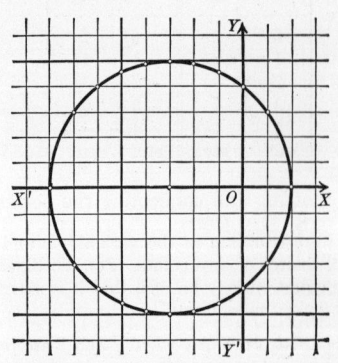

For example, if $x = -1$, $y = \pm \sqrt{16 + 6 - 1} = \sqrt{21} = \pm 4.6$;

if $x = 3$, $y = \pm \sqrt{16 - 18 - 9} = \pm \sqrt{-11}$,

an imaginary number.

The figure shows the curve, a *circle*. The proof that the locus is a circle is given later.

PROBLEMS

1. Plot the locus of each of the following equations:

(a) $2y + 5 = 0$.
(b) $x + y = 0$.
(c) $x - 3y + 5 = 0$.
(d) $y = 2x + 3$.
(e) $y = 4x^2 + 7$.
(f) $x^2 - 4y + 2x - 3 = 0$.
(g) $y^2 = x + 3$.
(h) $y = x^3$.
(i) $2x = y^3 - 3$.
(j) $x = y^3 - 3y$.
(k) $y = x^3 - 6x^2 + 11x - 6$.
(l) $y = x^4 - x^2 - 2$.
(m) $x^2 + y^2 - 9x = 0$.
(n) $x^2 + y^2 + 6y - 16 = 0$.
(o) $x^2 + y^2 = 16$.
(p) $3y^2 = x^3$.

2. Using one set of axes, construct the graphs of $2x - 3y - 4 = 0$ and $3x + 2y + 2 = 0$, and estimate the coördinates of the point of intersection. How may these coördinates be found exactly by algebra?

3. Using the same axes, construct the loci of the equations $2y = x^2$ and $2y = x^2 - 4$. How do the graphs differ?

4. Using one set of axes construct the graphs of $y = x^2$ and $y = 4x^2$. How do these graphs differ?

5. Which of the curves of Problem 1 pass through the origin? What is the necessary condition for an algebraic equation to represent a curve passing through the origin?

6. Show that the locus of $Ay^2 + By + C = 0$ is one line or two lines parallel to the x-axis according as $\Delta = B^2 - 4AC$ is zero or positive. What about the locus if $\Delta < 0$?

7. Show that the locus of $Ax^2 + 2Bxy + Cy^2 = 0$ is a pair of intersecting lines, one line, or a point according as $\Delta = B^2 - AC$ is positive, zero, or negative.

18. Discussion of an equation. The method explained of plotting a curve gives no knowledge except that the curve passes through all the points whose coördinates are determined. Joining these points gives a curve more or less like the true locus. Serious errors may be made in this way, however, since *the nature of the curve between any two successive points plotted is not known.* This objection is somewhat obviated by determining, from a discussion of the given equation *before plotting*, properties of the locus. These depend upon the form of the equation.

1. Intercepts on the axes.

The **intercepts** of a curve on the x-axis are the abscissas of the points of intersection of the curve and XX'.

The **intercepts** of a curve on the y-axis are the ordinates of the points of intersection of the curve and YY'.

Rule *to find the intercepts.*

Substitute $y = 0$ and solve for real values of x. This gives the intercepts on the x-axis.

Substitute $x = 0$ and solve for real values of y. This gives the intercepts on the y-axis.

The truth of the rule is obvious.

2. Symmetry.

DEFINITION. Two points, P and Q, are (1) symmetric with respect to an axis when the latter bisects the line PQ at right angles, and (2) symmetric with respect to a point O when O is the midpoint of PQ.

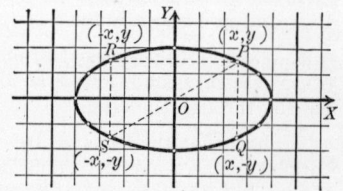

In the figure, P and Q are symmetric with respect to OX, P and R with respect to OY, P and S with respect to O.

Consider now the following

EXAMPLE

Discuss the symmetry of the locus of

(1) $$x^2 + 4y^2 = 16.$$

Solution. The equation contains no odd powers of x or y; hence it may be written in any one of the forms

(2) $(x)^2 + 4(-y)^2 = 16$, replacing (x, y) by $(x, -y)$;

(3) $(-x)^2 + 4(y)^2 = 16$, replacing (x, y) by $(-x, y)$;

(4) $(-x)^2 + 4(-y)^2 = 16$, replacing (x, y) by $(-x, -y)$.

The transformation of (1) into (2) corresponds in the figure to replacing each point $P(x, y)$ on the curve by the point $Q(x, -y)$. But the points P and Q are symmetric with respect to XX', and (1) and (2) have the same locus. Hence the locus of (1) is unchanged if each point is replaced by the symmetric point with respect to XX'. Therefore *the locus is symmetric with respect to the x-axis.* Similarly, from (3), *the locus is symmetric with respect to the y-axis,* and from (4) *the locus is symmetric with respect to the origin,* for the points $P(x, y)$ and $S(-x, -y)$ are symmetric with respect to the origin, since $OP = OS$.

In plotting the equation we take advantage of our knowledge of the symmetry of the curve by limiting the calculation to points in the first quadrant, as in the table. We plot these points, mark off the points symmetric to them with respect to the axes and the origin, and then draw the curve. The locus is called an **ellipse**.

x	y
4	0
3.5	1
2.6	1.5
0	2

The facts brought out in the example are stated in

Theorem II. Symmetry. *If an equation is unaffected by replacing y by $-y$, the locus is symmetric with respect to the x-axis.*

If an equation is unaffected by changing x to $-x$, the locus is symmetric with respect to the y-axis.

If an equation is unaffected by changing both x and y to $-x$ and $-y$, the locus is symmetric with respect to the origin.

NOTE. If two of the tests hold, the third will also.

Theorem II may be made to assume a somewhat different form if the equation is *algebraic* in x and y. In this case the locus is called an **algebraic curve**. Then from Theorem II follows

Theorem III. Symmetry of an algebraic curve. *If no odd powers of y occur in an equation, the locus is symmetric with*

respect to XX'; *if no odd powers of x occur, the locus is symmetric with respect to YY'. If every term is of even* degree, or every term of odd degree, the locus is symmetric with respect to the origin.*

3. *Extent of a curve.*

Coördinates are *real* numbers. Hence all values of x which give imaginary values of y must be excluded in the calculation. Similarly, all values of y which lead to imaginary values of x must be excluded. Determination of such values leads to knowledge of the extent of the curve.

EXAMPLES

1. What values of x or y, if any, must be excluded in plotting the locus of
$$x^2 + 4y^2 = 16?$$

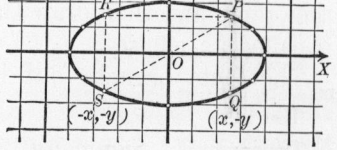

Solution. Solving for x in terms of y, and also for y in terms of x,

(5) $\qquad x = \pm 2\sqrt{4-y^2},$

(6) $\qquad y = \pm \tfrac{1}{2}\sqrt{16-x^2}.$

From the radical in (5) we see that all values of y *numerically* greater than 2 will make $4-y^2$ negative, and hence make x imaginary. Hence all values of y greater than 2 or less than -2 must be excluded.

Similarly, from the radical in (6), it is clear that values of x greater than 4 or less than -4 must be excluded.

The curve lies *entirely within* the rectangle bounded by the four lines
$$x = 4, \quad x = -4, \quad y = 2, \quad y = -2,$$
and is therefore a *closed curve.*

In determining points on the locus, we need assume for y values only between 0 and 2, as on page 33, or values of x between 0 and 4 inclusive.

2. What values, if any, of x or y are to be excluded in determining the locus of
$$y^2 - 4x + 15 = 0?$$

---

* A *constant term* is to be regarded as of zero (*even*) degree, as 16 in (1), p. 32.

Solution. Solving for x in terms of y, and also for y in terms of x,

(7) $$x = \tfrac{1}{4}(15 + y^2),$$
(8) $$y = \pm \sqrt{4x - 15}.$$

From (7) any value of y will give a real value of x. Hence no values of y are excluded.

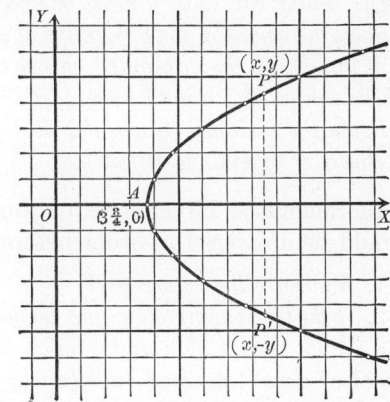

x	y
$3\tfrac{3}{4}$	0
4	± 1
$4\tfrac{3}{4}$	± 2
6	± 3
$7\tfrac{3}{4}$	± 4
10	± 5
$12\tfrac{3}{4}$	± 6
etc.	etc.

From the radical in (8) all values of x for which $4x - 15$ is negative must be excluded; that is, all values of x less than $3\tfrac{3}{4}$.

The locus therefore lies entirely to the right of the line $x = 3\tfrac{3}{4}$. Moreover, since no values of y are excluded, the locus extends to infinity, y increasing as x increases.

The locus is, by Theorem III, symmetric with respect to the x-axis, and is called a **parabola**.

3. Determine what values of x or y, if any, must be excluded in determining the locus of

$$4y = x^3.$$

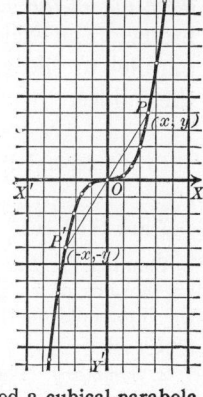

Solution. Solving for x in terms of y, and also for y in terms of x,

$$x = \sqrt[3]{4y},$$
$$y = \tfrac{1}{4} x^3.$$

From these equations it appears that no values of either coördinate need be excluded.

The locus is, by Theorem III, symmetric with respect to the origin. The coördinates increase together; the curve extends to infinity and is called **a cubical parabola**.

The method illustrated in the examples is summed up in the

Rule *to determine the extent of a curve.*

Solve the equation for x in terms of y, and determine all values of y for which the computed values of x would be imaginary. These values of y must be excluded.

Solve the equation for y in terms of x, and determine all values of x for which the computed values of y would be imaginary. These values of x must be excluded.

From the excluded values of x and y decide whether the curve is closed or extends to infinity.

19. Summary. Given an equation, the following questions should be answered in order before plotting the locus:

1. *What are the intercepts?*
2. *Is the locus symmetric with respect to the axes or the origin?*
3. *What values of x and y must be excluded? Is the curve closed or does it pass off indefinitely far?*

Answering these questions constitutes what is called a **general discussion** of the given equation. The successive results should be immediately transferred to the figure. Thus when the intercepts have been determined, *mark them off on the axes*. Indicate which axes are axes of symmetry. The excluded values of x and y will determine lines parallel to the axes which the locus *will not cross*. Draw these lines.

EXAMPLE

Give a general discussion of the equation

(1) $$x^2 - 4y^2 + 16y = 0.$$

Draw the locus.

Solution. 1. *Intercepts.* Putting $y = 0$, we find $x = 0$, the intercept on the axis of x. Putting $x = 0$, we find $y = 0$ and 4, the intercepts on the axis of y. Lay off the intercepts on the axes.

2. *Symmetry.* The equation contains no odd powers of x; hence the locus is symmetric with respect to YY'.

x	y
0	0, 4
0	0

CURVE AND EQUATION

3. *Extent.* Solving for x,

(2) $$x = \pm 2\sqrt{y^2 - 4y}.$$

The roots of $y^2 - 4y = 0$ are $y = 0$ and $y = 4$. For any value of y *between* these roots, $y^2 - 4y$ is negative. For example, $y = 2$ gives

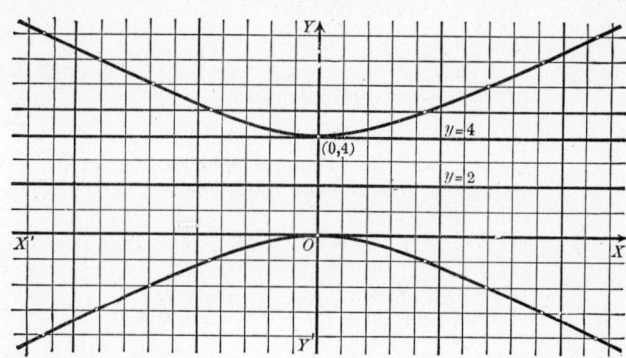

$4 - 8 = -4$. Hence all values of y between 0 and 4 must be excluded. Draw the lines $y = 0$ and $y = 4$. The locus lies below the first and above the second line.

Solving for y,

(3) $$y = 2 \pm \tfrac{1}{2}\sqrt{x^2 + 16}.$$

Hence no value of x is excluded, since $x^2 + 16$ is positive for all values of x. Obviously y increases as x increases, and the curve extends out indefinitely far from both axes.

Plotting the locus, using (2), the curve is as in the figure, a **hyperbola**.

PROBLEMS

1. Give a general discussion of each of the following equations and draw the locus. Make sure that the discussion and the figure agree.

(a) $y^2 = 4x$.
(b) $y = 8 - x^2$.
(c) $x = y^2 - 2y$.
(d) $3y = x^2 - 9$.
(e) $x^2 + y^2 = 25$.
(f) $x^2 - y^2 = 25$.
(g) $x^2 + 4y^2 = 24$.
(h) $4x^2 - y^2 = -16$.
(i) $x^2 + 9y^2 = 18$.
(j) $x^2 + y^2 - 4y = 0$.
(k) $x^2 + y^2 + 4x = 0$.
(l) $x^2 + 6y^2 + 6y = 0$.
(m) $4x^2 + 16x + y^2 = 0$.
(n) $y = 3x^3 - 6x$.
(o) $y = x^4 - 4x^2$.
(p) $3x^3 + y^2 = 0$.
(q) $9x^2 - y^2 + 18x + 6y = 0$.
(r) $x^2 + xy + y^2 - 4 = 0$.
(s) $\sqrt{x} + \sqrt{y} = 2$.

2. Discuss each of the following equations. To plot, assume some *particular* values for the arbitrary constants, but not *special* values which would give the equation an added peculiarity.*

(a) $y^2 = 2\,px$. (Parabola.)
(b) $x^2 + y^2 = r^2$. (Circle.)
(c) $\dfrac{x^2}{a^2} + \dfrac{y^2}{b^2} = 1$. (Ellipse.)
(d) $\dfrac{x^2}{a^2} - \dfrac{y^2}{b^2} = 1$. (Hyperbola.)
(e) $y = mx^3$. (Cubical parabola.)
(f) $y^2 = mx^3$. (Semi-cubical parabola.)
(g) $xy = a$. (Equilateral hyperbola.)
(h) $x^2 + my^2 = 16$.
(i) $x^2 + y^2 + 2\,rx = 0$. (Circle.)
(j) $y = ax^2 + bx + c$. (Parabola.)
(k) $x = ay^2 + by + c$. (Parabola.)
(l) $x^2 + y^2 + Dx + Ey + F = 0$. (Circle.)

The loci in Problem 2, except (e), (f), are of the class known as *conics*, or *conic sections*, — curves following straight lines and circles in the matter of their simplicity. These curves are obtained when cross sections are taken of a right circular cone. Various definitions and properties will be given later. We often use the following

DEFINITION. A **conic section** is the locus of a point whose distances from a fixed point and a fixed line are in a constant ratio.

3. Show that every conic is represented by an equation of the second degree in x and y.

Hint. Take the y-axis as the fixed line and draw the x-axis through the fixed point. If the fixed point is $(p, 0)$ and the constant ratio is e, the result is

$$(1 - e^2)x^2 + y^2 - 2\,px + p^2 = 0.$$

4. Discuss and plot the locus of the equation of Problem 3 for (1) $e = 1$; (2) $e = \tfrac{1}{2}$; (3) $e = 2$.

5. A point moves so that the sum of its distances from $(4, 0)$ and $(-4, 0)$ is always 12. What is its locus?

Ans. Ellipse $5\,x^2 + 9\,y^2 = 180$.

6. What is the equation of the locus of a point which moves so that the difference of its distances from $(0, 3)$ and $(0, -3)$ is 4?

---

* For example, in (a) $p = 0$ is a special value. In fact, in all these examples except (j), (k), (l) zero is a special value for any constant.

CURVE AND EQUATION

7. Find the equation of the locus of a point which is twice as far from $(4, 5)$ as from $(-2, 3)$. Discuss and plot this locus.

8. Find the equation of the locus of a point which moves so that its ordinate is two less than its distance from $(3, 3)$. Discuss and plot.
Ans. $x^2 - 6x - 10y + 14 = 0$.

9. A point moves so that its distances from the points $(-2, 3)$ and $(3, -2)$ are always in the ratio of 4 to 5. Find the equation of its locus, discuss and plot.

10. Find the equation of the locus of a point if its distance from $(2, -4)$ is always equal to 5 more than its ordinate. Discuss and plot.
Ans. $2y = x^2 - 4x - 5$.

11. Given the points $A(3, 1)$, $B(-1, -1)$. A point P moves so that the area of $\triangle PAB$ equals 8 square units. Find the equation of the locus of P, and plot. (Two cases.)

12. A point moves so that the slope of the line joining it to the point $(2, 2)$ is twice the slope of the line joining it to the point $(-2, 0)$. Find the equation of the locus, discuss and plot.

13. Find the equation of the locus of a point which moves so that the slope of the line joining it to the point $(2, 4)$ is 3 more than the slope of the line joining it to $(-2, 4)$. Discuss and plot.
Ans. $4y = 3x^2 + 4$.

14. Prove the statement: If an equation is unaffected when x and y are interchanged, the locus is symmetric with respect to the line $y = x$. Make use of this fact in drawing the loci of

(a) $x^2 - xy + y^2 - 4 = 0$;
(b) $\sqrt{x} + \sqrt{y} = \sqrt{a}$;
(c) $x^2 + y^2 - 4x - 4y - 1 = 0$.

15. State and prove a test for symmetry with respect to the line $x + y = 0$.

20. Horizontal and vertical asymptotes.

The following examples elucidate difficulties arising frequently in drawing the locus of an equation. We meet with lines described in the

DEFINITION. An asymptote of a curve is a straight line which the curve approaches indefinitely near as its tracing point passes off to infinity.

EXAMPLES

1. Plot the locus of the equation

(1) $$xy - 2y - 4 = 0.$$

Solution. Solving for y,

(2) $$y = \frac{4}{x-2}.$$

We observe at once, if x approaches 2, y approaches ∞. This is interpreted thus: The curve *approaches indefinitely near* the line $x = 2$ as its tracing point passes off to infinity. In fact, if we solve (1) for x and write the result in the form

(3) $$x = 2 + \frac{4}{y},$$

it is evident that x approaches 2 as y increases numerically without limit. Hence

x	y	x	y
0	-2	0	-2
1	-4	-1	$-\frac{4}{3}$
$1\frac{1}{2}$	-8	-2	-1
$1\frac{3}{4}$	-16	-4	$-\frac{2}{3}$
2	∞	-5	$-\frac{4}{7}$
$2\frac{1}{4}$	16	$\vdots$	$\vdots$
$2\frac{1}{2}$	8	-10	$-\frac{1}{3}$
3	4	etc.	etc.
4	2		
5	$\frac{4}{3}$		
6	1		
$\vdots$	$\vdots$		
12	0.4		
etc.	etc.		

the locus extends both upward and downward indefinitely far, approaching in each case the line $x = 2$. The vertical line $x = 2$ is called a *vertical asymptote*.

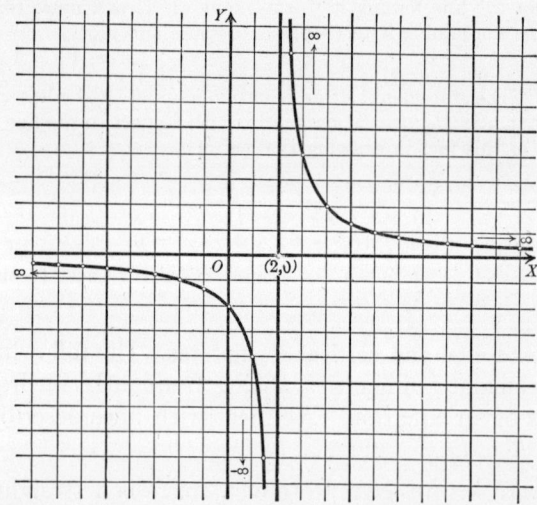

Again in (3), if y approaches 0, then x approaches ∞, and $y = 0$ is a *horizontal asymptote*.

CURVE AND EQUATION

Observe that the asymptotes $y = 0$ and $x = 2$ serve as guiding lines in drawing the curve, a **hyperbola**.

In plotting, it is necessary to assume values of x differing slightly from 2, both less and greater, as in the table.

2. Plot the locus of $\qquad y = \dfrac{2x + 3}{3x - 4}.$

Solution. This locus is shown in Fig. 1.

Asymptotes. The equation shows directly that $3x - 4 = 0$, or $x = \frac{4}{3}$, is a vertical asymptote.

Solving for x, $\qquad x = \dfrac{4y + 3}{3y - 2}.$

Hence $3y - 2 = 0$, or $y = \frac{2}{3}$, is a horizontal asymptote.

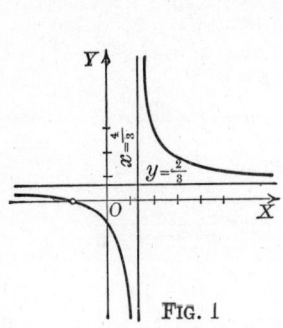

FIG. 1

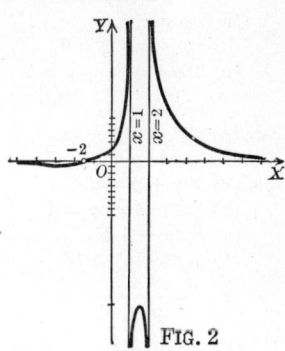

FIG. 2

3. Plot the locus of $\qquad y = \dfrac{2x + 3}{x^2 - 3x + 2}.$

Solution. This locus is shown in Fig. 2. There are two vertical asymptotes, $x = 1$ and $x = 2$, since the denominator

$$x^2 - 3x + 2 = (x - 1)(x - 2).$$

Solving for x,

$$x = \dfrac{3y + 2 \pm \sqrt{y^2 + 24y + 4}}{2y}.$$

Taking the positive sign of the radical, it appears that $y = 0$ is a horizontal asymptote.

A branch of the curve lies between the vertical asymptotes. A few points of the locus are given in the table. Note that *different* scales are used for ordinates and abscissas.

x	y
0	$\frac{3}{2}$
$-\frac{3}{2}$	0
$\frac{3}{2}$	-24
5	$\frac{13}{12}$
-5	$-\frac{1}{6}$

Rule *to find the asymptotes parallel to the axes.*

Solve the equation for y (and also for x), and set the linear factors of the denominator equal to zero.

The determination of the vertical and horizontal asymptotes of a curve should be added to the discussion outlined in Art. 19 as item 4:

4. *What are the horizontal and vertical asymptotes?*

PROBLEMS

1. Determine the horizontal and vertical asymptotes and discuss and plot each of the following:

(a) $xy = 8$.
(b) $xy - x - 2 = 0$.
(c) $2x + 2xy - y = 0$.
(d) $x^2 + 2xy - 4 = 0$.
(e) $x^2 - xy - 2x - y = 0$.
(f) $xy = x^2 + 4$.
(g) $3xy - 9y - 2x + 8 = 0$.

2. (a) $xy^2 = 4(4-x)$.
(b) $x^2y - y = 2x$.
(c) $x^2y + y = 8$.
(d) $(x^4 - 4x^2)y = 4$.
(e) $3xy + 6 = x^2y$.
(f) $y(x^2 - 4) = 12$.
(g) $x = \dfrac{y+3}{y-1}$.
(h) $x = \dfrac{y}{y^2 - 9}$.
(i) $y = \dfrac{(x-2)^2}{x+2}$.
(j) $y = \dfrac{x^2 + x - 6}{x^2 - x - 6}$.
(k) $y = \dfrac{x^2 - 4x + 4}{x^2 + 5x - 6}$.
(l) $4x = \dfrac{y^2}{y - 2}$.
(m) $y = \dfrac{x^2 - 4}{x^2 - 1}$.

3. Find the equation of the locus of a point if it moves so that its distance from the origin is always equal to the slope of the line joining it to the origin. Discuss and plot this locus. *Ans.* $y^2 - x^2y^2 - x^4 = 0$.

4. Determine the asymptotes which are parallel to OX or OY and discuss and plot each of the following:

(a) $y = \dfrac{ax+b}{x}$.
(b) $y = \dfrac{x}{ax+b}$.

PROBLEMS FOR INDIVIDUAL STUDY OR ASSIGNMENT

Discuss fully and draw carefully the following loci:

1. $y^2 - 4xy + x^3 = 0$.
2. $y^2 - 2xy - 2x^2 + x^3 = 0$.
3. $y^2 - x^2 + x^4 = 0$.
4. $(y-x)^2 - (a^2 - x^2) = 0$.

5. $(y-x)^2 - x^2(a^2-x^2) = 0$.
7. $(y-x^2)^2 - x^2(a^2-x^2) = 0$.
6. $(y-x^2)^2 - (a^2-x^2) = 0$.
8. $y^2(a-x) - x^3 = 0$. (The cissoid.)
9. $y^2(a-x) - x^2(a+x) = 0$. (The strophoid.)
10. $x^4 + 2ax^2y - ay^3 = 0$.
11. $x^4 - axy^2 + y^4 = 0$.
14. $a^3y^2 - 2abx^2y - x^5 = 0$.
12. $a^4y^2 - a^2x^4 + x^6 = 0$.
15. $y^2 - (a^2-x^2)(b^2-x^2)^2 = 0$.
13. $ay^2 - bx^4 - x^5 = 0$.
16. $x^3y^2 - a^3x^2 + ay^4 = 0$.
17. $x(y-x)^2 - b^2y = 0$.
18. $(x^2+y^2)^2 - a^2(x^2-y^2) = 0$. (The lemniscate.)
19. $(x^2-a^2)^2 = ay^2(3a+2y)$.
20. $(x^2+y^2-1)y - ax = 0$.
21. $y^2 - x^2 - x(x-4)^2 = 0$.
22. $(x^2+y^2-2ay)^2 = a^2(x^2+y^2)$. (The limaçon.)
23. $(x^4 + x^2y^2 + y^4) = x(ax^2 - 4ay^2)$.
24. $(x^2+y^2+4ay+a^2)(x^2+a^2) + 2a^2y^2 = 0$.
25. $(y^2-x^2)(x-1)(x-\tfrac{3}{2}) = 2(y^2+x^2-2x)^2$.
26. $(x^2+y^2+4ay-a^2)(x^2-a^2) + 4a^2y^2 = 0$. (The cocked hat.)
27. $(x^2-1)^2y - x^3 = 0$.

21. Points of intersection. If two curves whose equations are given intersect, the coördinates of each point of intersection must satisfy both equations. In algebra it is shown that *all* values satisfying two equations in two unknowns may be found by solving these equations as simultaneous. Hence the

Rule *to find the points of intersection of two curves whose equations are given.*

Consider the equations as simultaneous in the coördinates and solve as in algebra.

Arrange the real solutions in corresponding pairs. These will be the coördinates of all the points of intersection.

Notice that only *real* solutions correspond to common points of the two curves, since coördinates are always real numbers.

EXAMPLES

1. Find the points of intersection of

(1) $x - 7y + 25 = 0$,
(2) $x^2 + y^2 = 25$.

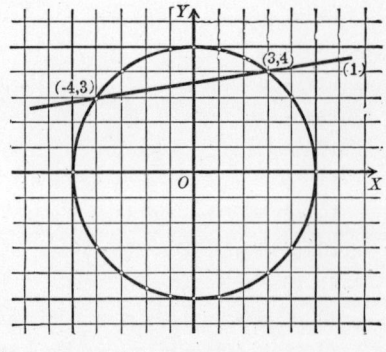

Solution. Solving (1) for x,

(3) $x = 7y - 25$.

Substituting in (2),

$(7y - 25)^2 + y^2 = 25$.

Reducing,

$y^2 - 7y + 12 = 0$.

$\therefore y = 3$ and 4.

Substituting in (3) [*not* in (2)],

$x = -4$ and $+3$.

Arranging, the points of intersection are $(-4, 3)$ and $(3, 4)$.

In the figure the straight line (1) is the locus of equation (1), and the circle the locus of (2). *Ans*.

The values of y were substituted in (1) and not in (2), because (1) is of the first degree in x and y, while (2) is of the second degree. For if we substitute $y = 3$ in (2), we obtain $x = \pm 4$. But $(4, 3)$ does not lie on the line (1).

2. Find the points of intersection of the loci of

(4) $2x^2 + 3y^2 = 35$,
(5) $3x^2 - 4y = 0$.

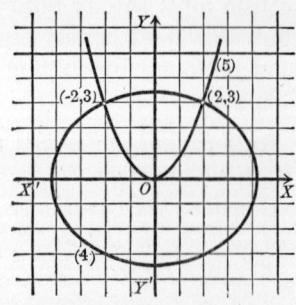

Solution. Solving (5) for x^2,

(6) $x^2 = \frac{4}{3} y$.

Substituting in (4) and reducing,

$9y^2 + 8y - 105 = 0$.

$\therefore y = 3$ and $-\frac{35}{9}$.

Substituting in (6) and solving,

$x = \pm 2$ and $\pm \frac{2}{3} \sqrt{-105}$.

Arranging the *real* values, we find the points of intersection are $(+2, 3)$, $(-2, 3)$. *Ans*.

In the figure the ellipse (4) is the locus of (4), and the parabola (5) the locus of (5).

CURVE AND EQUATION

PROBLEMS

Find the points of intersection of the following curves, and plot:

1. $3x + y - 13 = 0$,
   $x^2 + y^2 - 25 = 0$.
   Ans. $(3, 4)$, $(4.8, -1.4)$.

2. $3x + 4y = 25$,
   $x^2 + y^2 = 25$.

3. $xy = 2$,
   $x^2 + y^2 = 5$.

4. $2y = x^2$,
   $x = y$.

5. $y^2 = 2px$,
   $x^2 = 2py$.
   Ans. $(0, 0)$, $(2p, 2p)$.

6. $y = x^3$,
   $y = x^2 + 2x$.

7. $x + y = 0$,
   $x^3 - 6x - 3y = 0$.

8. $x^2 + y^2 = 5a^2$,
   $x^2 = 4ay$.
   Ans. $(2a, a)$, $(-2a, a)$.

9. $x^2 - y^2 = 16$,
   $x^2 + y^2 = 25$.

10. $x^2 + y^2 - 6x = 0$,
    $y^2 = x^3$.
    Ans. $(0, 0)$, $(2, \pm 2.83)$.

11. $x^2 - 4y^2 = 9$,
    $xy = 10$.

12. Find the length of the common chord of the circles $x^2 + y^2 = 16$, $x^2 + (y - 6)^2 = 9$.

13. Find the lengths of the sides of the triangle whose equations are $x + 2y = 5$, $2x + y = 7$, $x - y = -1$. Ans. $\sqrt{5}$, $\sqrt{2}$, $\sqrt{5}$.

14. What is the area of the triangle whose sides are $x + y = a$, $x - 2y = 4a$, $y - x + 7a = 0$? Ans. $12 a^2$.

15. Find the slope of the line joining the points of intersection of $x^2 + y^2 = 13$ and $y^2 = 3x + 3$.

16. What is the length of the chord cut off on the line $x + 2y = 4$ by the circle with center $(2, 1)$ and radius 4?

17. Find the lengths of the medians of the triangle whose sides are $x + 7y + 11 = 0$, $3x + y - 7 = 0$, $x - 3y + 1 = 0$.
Ans. $2\sqrt{5}$, $\frac{5}{2}\sqrt{2}$, $\frac{1}{2}\sqrt{170}$.

18. Find the points of intersection of $x^2 + y^2 = 9$ and $3y - 4x = 15$. What is the meaning of the result?

19. Find the coördinates of the two points which are at a distance of 6 units from each of the points $(2, 1)$ and $(-2, -3)$.

20. What are the slope and the length of the line of centers of the two circles of radius 4 that pass through $(2, 1)$ and $(-2, -2)$?

21. Find the coördinates of the points on the line $x - 2y = 4$ which are distant 4 units from $(1, -1)$.

22. Find the points which are distant 4 units from $(2, 2)$ and 3 units from $(0, -1)$. Ans. $(-1.94, 1.29)$ and $(2.87, -1.91)$.

CHAPTER IV

THE STRAIGHT LINE

22. The degree of the equation of any straight line. It will now be shown that any straight line is represented by an equation of the first degree in the variable coördinates x and y.

Theorem. *The equation of the straight line passing through $B(0, b)$ with the slope m is*

(I) $$y = mx + b.$$

Proof. Assume that $P(x, y)$ is any point on the line.

$$\text{Slope of } PB = \frac{y-b}{x}. \quad \text{[By (IV), p. 17]}$$

Then $\quad \dfrac{y-b}{x} = m, \quad \text{or} \quad y = mx + b.$ Q.E.D.

In equation (I), m and b may have any values, — positive, negative, or zero.

Equation (I) will represent any straight line which intersects the y-axis. But the equation of any line *parallel* to the y-axis has the form $x =$ a constant, since the abscissas of all points on such a line are equal. The two forms, $y = mx + b$ and $x =$ constant, will therefore represent all straight lines. Each of these equations being of the first degree in x and y, we have the following

Theorem. *The equation of any straight line is of the first degree in the coördinates x and y.*

23. Locus of any equation of the first degree. The question now arises: Given an equation of the first degree in the coördinates x and y, is the locus a straight line?

THE STRAIGHT LINE

Consider, for example, the equation
(1) $$3x - 2y + 8 = 0.$$

Let us solve this equation for y. This gives
(2) $$y = \tfrac{3}{2} x + 4.$$

Comparing (2) with the formula (I), Art. 22, we see that (2) is obtained if we set $m = \tfrac{3}{2}$, $b = 4$. Hence (2), or (1), is the equation of a straight line through $(0, 4)$ with the slope $\tfrac{3}{2}$.

The equation
(3) $$Ax + By + C = 0,$$

where A, B, and C are arbitrary constants, is called the **general equation of the first degree** in x and y because every equation of the first degree may be reduced to that form. Equation (3) represents all straight lines.

For the equation $y = mx + b$ may be written $mx - y + b = 0$, which is of the form (3) if $A = m$, $B = -1$, $C = b$; and the equation $x = $ constant may be written $x - $ constant $= 0$, which is of the form (3) if $A = 1$, $B = 0$, $C = -$ constant.

This discussion prepares the way for the general theorem.

Theorem. *The locus of $Ax + By + C = 0$ is a straight line.*

Proof. Solving (3) for y, we obtain
(4) $$y = -\frac{A}{B} x - \frac{C}{B}.$$

Comparison with (I) shows that the locus of (4) is the straight line for which
$$m = -\frac{A}{B}, \quad b = -\frac{C}{B}.$$

If, however, $B = 0$, the reasoning fails. But if $B = 0$, (3) becomes
$$Ax + C = 0, \quad \text{or} \quad x = -\frac{C}{A}.$$

The locus of this equation is a straight line parallel to the y-axis. Hence in all cases the locus of (3) is a straight line.

Q. E. D.

Corollary. *The slope of the line $Ax + By + C = 0$ is $m = -\dfrac{A}{B}$, that is, the coefficient of x with its sign changed divided by the coefficient of y.*

24. Plotting straight lines. If the line does not pass through the origin, find the intercepts, mark them off on the axes, and draw the line. If the line passes through the origin, find a second point whose coördinates satisfy the equation, and draw a line through this point and the origin.

EXAMPLE

Plot the locus of $3x - y + 6 = 0$. Find the slope.

Solution. Letting $y = 0$ and solving for x,

$x = -2 =$ intercept on x-axis.

Letting $x = 0$ and solving for y,

$y = 6 =$ intercept on y-axis.

The line therefore passes through the points $(-2, 0)$ and $(0, 6)$.

To find the slope: Comparison with the general equation (3) shows that $A = 3$, $B = -1$, $C = 6$. Hence

$$m = -\frac{A}{B} = 3.$$

Or proceed as follows: Reduce the given equation to the form $y = mx + b$ by solving it for y. This gives

$$y = 3x + 6.$$

Hence $\qquad m = 3, \quad b = 6,$
as before.

PROBLEMS

1. Find the intercepts, slope, and inclination of the lines whose equations are given below, and plot:

(a) $2x + 3y = 5$.
(b) $2x + y = 0$.
   Ans. $0, 0$; $m = -2$.
(c) $2y - 3 = 0$.
(d) $3x - 5y = 4$. *Ans.* $\frac{4}{3}, -\frac{4}{5}$; $m = \frac{3}{5}$.
(e) $5x + 2y = 3$.
(f) $2x + 5y = 2$.
(g) $4x + 7 = 0$.

THE STRAIGHT LINE

2. Find the equation and draw the line for which

(a) $m = \frac{2}{3}$, $b = 1$;
(b) $m = -\frac{4}{3}$, $b = 2$;
    Ans. $4x + 3y = 6$.
(c) $m = 1$, $b = -3$.
(d) $\alpha = 45°$, $b = \frac{5}{3}$;
    Ans. $3x - 3y + 5 = 0$.
(e) $\alpha = 60°$, $b = 0$;
(f) $\alpha = 135°$, $b = -\frac{4}{3}$.

3. Find the equation of each of the following lines:

(a) Parallel to $2x - y - 5 = 0$ passing through $(0, 0)$. *Ans.* $2x - y = 0$.
(b) Parallel to $3x + 4y - 15 = 0$ passing through $(0, 3)$.
(c) Parallel to $5y - 5x + 12 = 0$ passing through $(0, -3)$.
    Ans. $x - y - 3 = 0$.
(d) Parallel to $2x + y + 7 = 0$ passing through $(0, -4)$.

4. Find the equation of each of the following lines:

(a) Perpendicular to $3x - 4y - 5 = 0$ passing through $(0, 2)$.
(b) Perpendicular to $6x + 5y = 2$ passing through $(0, 4)$.
    Ans. $5x - 6y + 24 = 0$.
(c) Perpendicular to $x - 2y = 6$ passing through $(0, -4)$.
(d) Perpendicular to $y - 3x = 2$ passing through $(0, -7)$.

5. Find the equation of the line with

(a) $m = -2$ passing through the point of intersection of $x + y = 3$ and $2x - 3y + 9 = 0$;   *Ans.* $2x + y = 3$.
(b) $m = \frac{3}{2}$ passing through the point of intersection of $2x - y - 2 = 0$ and $5y - 5x + 11 = 0$.

6. Show that the quadrilateral whose sides are $3x - y + 2 = 0$, $x + y + 1 = 0$, $6x - 2y - 1 = 0$, and $2x + 2y = 7$ is a parallelogram. Draw the figure.

7. Show that the quadrilateral whose sides are $5x + 2y + 3 = 0$, $2x - 5y + 4 = 0$, $10x + 4y = 12$, and $6x - 15y = 8$ is a rectangle. Plot the lines.

8. Show that the quadrilateral whose sides are $5x + 3y = 30$, $3x - 4y = 16$, $10x + 6y = 4$, and $2x - y + 4 = 0$ is a trapezoid.

9. Show analytically that the locus of the point satisfying the condition given below is in each case a straight line, and plot:

(a) Its distances from the x- and y-axes are always in the ratio of 4 to 5.
(b) The difference of its distances from the axes is equal to 8 (two cases).
(c) It is equidistant from the coördinate axes.
(d) The sum of its distances from two perpendicular straight lines is constant.

NEW ANALYTIC GEOMETRY

The following example illustrates the

Theorem. *Plotting by factoring. If an equation can be put in the form of a product of variable factors equal to zero, the locus is found by setting each factor equal to zero and plotting each equation separately.*

EXAMPLE

Draw the locus of $4x^2 - 9y^2 = 0$.

Solution. Factoring,

(1) $$(2x - 3y)(2x + 3y) = 0.$$

Then, by the theorem, *the locus consists of the straight lines*

(2) $$2x - 3y = 0, \text{ and}$$
(3) $$2x + 3y = 0.$$

Proof. 1. *The coördinates of any point (x_1, y_1) which satisfy (1) will satisfy either (2) or (3).*

For if (x_1, y_1) satisfies (1),

(4) $$(2x_1 - 3y_1)(2x_1 + 3y_1) = 0.$$

This product can vanish only when one of the factors is zero. Hence either
$$2x_1 - 3y_1 = 0,$$
and therefore (x_1, y_1) satisfies (2);
or
$$2x_1 + 3y_1 = 0,$$
and therefore (x_1, y_1) satisfies (3).

2. *A point (x_1, y_1) on either of the lines defined by (2) and (3) will also lie on the locus of (1).*

For if (x_1, y_1) is on the line $2x - 3y = 0$, then

(5) $$2x_1 - 3y_1 = 0.$$

Hence the product $(2x_1 - 3y_1)(2x_1 + 3y_1)$ also vanishes, since by (5) the first factor is zero, and therefore (x_1, y_1) satisfies (1).

Therefore every point on the locus of (1) is also on the locus of (2) and (3), and conversely. This proves the theorem for this example.
Q.E.D.

PROBLEMS

1. Show that the locus of each of the following equations is a pair of straight lines, and plot:

(a) $xy = 0$.
(b) $x^2 - 5x - 6 = 0$.
(c) $9x^2 - 4y^2 = 0$.
(d) $xy - 2x = 0$.
(e) $x^2 - 3xy = 0$.
(f) $xy - 2x^2 - 3x = 0$.
(g) $x^2 - 5xy + 6x = 0$.
(h) $4y^2 - x^2 - 8y + 4x = 0$.
(i) $2x^2 - 3xy - 4x + 6y = 0$.
(j) $x^2 - 4y^2 + 5x + 10y = 0$.

THE STRAIGHT LINE

(k) $x^2 + 3xy + 2y^2 + x + y = 0$.   (m) $y^2 - 4xy - 5x^2 + 2y - 10x = 0$.
(l) $3y^2 + xy - 2x^2 + 6y - 4x = 0$.   (n) $xy - 3x + 5y - 15 = 0$.

2. Plot the complete locus of each of the following equations by using the theorem above:

(a) $x^3 + xy^2 - 4x = 0$.
(b) $x^3 - 6x^2 + 11x - 6 = 0$.
(c) $x^4 - y^4 = 0$.
(d) $(x^2 + y^2 - 8)(xy + 4) = 0$.

3. Plot the locus of a point which moves so that the difference of the squares of its distances from $(-3, 0)$ and $(2, 4)$ is always 8.

Ans. $10x + 8y = 19$ or 3.

4. A point moves so that the difference of the squares of its distances from two perpendicular lines is zero. Find and plot the locus when the perpendicular lines are taken as the coördinate axes.

5. Find the equation of the locus of a point which moves so as to be always equidistant from the lines $x - 2 = 0$ and $y + 4 = 0$. Plot the locus.   *Ans.* The perpendicular lines $x + y + 2 = 0$, $x - y - 6 = 0$.

25. Point-slope form. Theorem. *The equation of the straight line passing through $P_1(x_1, y_1)$ with the slope m is*

(II) $$y - y_1 = m(x - x_1).$$

Proof. Let $P(x, y)$ be any other point on the line. By the hypothesis,
$$\text{slope } PP_1 = m = \frac{y - y_1}{x - x_1}. \text{ [By (IV), p. 17]}$$

Clearing of fractions gives the formula.   Q.E.D.

26. Two-point form. Theorem. *The equation of the line passing through two points $P_1(x_1, y_1)$ and $P_2(x_2, y_2)$ is*

(III) $$\frac{y - y_1}{x - x_1} = \frac{y_1 - y_2}{x_1 - x_2}.$$

Proof. The slope of the line is

(1) $$\text{slope } P_1P_2 = \frac{y_1 - y_2}{x_1 - x_2}.$$

Let $P(x, y)$ be any other point on the line P_1P_2. Then
$$\text{slope } PP_1 = \frac{y - y_1}{x - x_1}.$$

Since P, P_1, and P_2 are on one line,
$$\text{slope } PP_1 = \text{slope } P_1P_2.$$

Hence we have the formula.   Q.E.D.

Equation (III) may be written in the determinant form

(2) $$\begin{vmatrix} x & y & 1 \\ x_1 & y_1 & 1 \\ x_2 & y_2 & 1 \end{vmatrix} = 0.$$

For the determinant, when expanded, is of the first degree in x and y. Hence (2) is the equation of a line. But (2) is satisfied when $x = x_1$, $y = y_1$, and also when $x = x_2$, $y = y_2$, for then two rows become identical and the determinant vanishes. Otherwise thus: Comparison of (2) with the formula at the close of Art. 15 shows that the area of the triangle PP_1P_2 is zero. Hence these three points lie on a line.

27. Intercept form. A line is determined by its intercepts on the axes. If these intercepts are a on XX' and b on YY', then the line passes through $(a, 0)$ and $(0, b)$, and the two-point form (III) gives (writing $x_1 = a$, $y_1 = 0$, $x_2 = 0$, $y_2 = b$)

$$\frac{y-0}{x-a} = \frac{0-b}{a-0} = -\frac{b}{a}.$$

Clearing of fractions, transposing, and dividing by ab, we obtain

(IV) $$\frac{x}{a} + \frac{y}{b} = 1.$$

28. Condition that three lines shall intersect in a common point. It is shown in algebra that three linear equations in two unknowns x and y, for example,

(1) $Ax + By + C = 0$, $A_1x + B_1y + C_1 = 0$, $A_2x + B_2y + C_2 = 0$,

will have a common solution when and only when the determinant formed on the coefficients vanishes; that is, when

(2) $$\begin{vmatrix} A & B & C \\ A_1 & B_1 & C_1 \\ A_2 & B_2 & C_2 \end{vmatrix} = 0.$$

Hence the three lines (1) will intersect in a common point when and only when (2) holds, *provided always that the lines are not parallel*. But this latter fact may always be determined by inspection of the equations.

THE STRAIGHT LINE

EXAMPLES

1. Find the equation of the line passing through $P_1(3, -2)$ whose slope is $-\frac{1}{4}$.

Solution. Use the point-slope equation (II), substituting $x_1 = 3$, $y_1 = -2$, $m = -\frac{1}{4}$. This gives

$$y + 2 = -\tfrac{1}{4}(x - 3).$$

Clearing and reducing,

$$x + 4y + 5 = 0. \quad Ans.$$

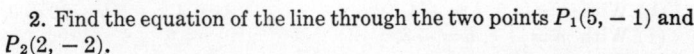

2. Find the equation of the line through the two points $P_1(5, -1)$ and $P_2(2, -2)$.

Solution. Use the two-point equation (III), substituting $x_1 = 5$, $y_1 = -1$, $x_2 = 2$, $y_2 = -2$. This gives

$$\frac{y+1}{x-5} = \frac{-1+2}{5-2} = \frac{1}{3}.$$

Clearing and reducing,

$$x - 3y - 8 = 0. \quad Ans.$$

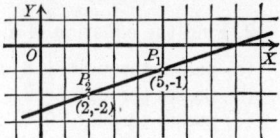

The answer should be *checked*. To do this, we must prove that the coördinates of the given points satisfy the equation. Thus for P_1, substituting $x = 5$, $y = -1$, the answer holds. Similarly for P_2. The student should supply checks for Examples 1, 3, and 4.

3. Find the equation of the line through the point $P_1(3, -2)$ parallel to the line $L_1: 2x - 3y - 4 = 0$.

Solution. The slope of the given line L_1 equals $\frac{2}{3}$. Hence the slope of the required line also equals $\frac{2}{3}$ (Theorem, Art. 13), and it passes through $P_1(3, -2)$. Using the point-slope equation (II), we have

$y + 2 = \tfrac{2}{3}(x - 3)$, or $2x - 3y - 12 = 0$. *Ans.*

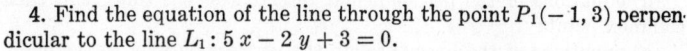

4. Find the equation of the line through the point $P_1(-1, 3)$ perpendicular to the line $L_1: 5x - 2y + 3 = 0$.

Solution. The slope of the given line L_1 equals $\frac{5}{2}$. Hence the slope of the required line equals $-\frac{2}{5}$ (Theorem, Art. 13). Since we know a point $P_1(-1, 3)$ on the line, we use the point-slope equation (II), and obtain

$y - 3 = -\tfrac{2}{5}(x + 1)$, or $2x + 5y - 13 = 0$. *Ans.*

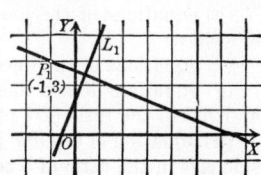

PROBLEMS

1. Find the equation of the line determined by the following conditions, and plot:

(a) Passing through $(3, 2)$ with $m = 2$.   *Ans.* $2x - y = 4$.
(b) Passing through $(-4, -3)$ with $m = \frac{3}{5}$.
(c) Passing through $(-7, 0)$ with $m = -3$.
(d) Passing through $(4, 3)$ and $(-4, 1)$.   *Ans.* $x - 4y + 8 = 0$.
(e) Passing through $(2, 5)$ and $(6, -5)$.
(f) Passing through $(-3, 4)$ with $a = -1$.
(g) Passing through $(-5, -7)$ with $b = 3$.
(h) With $a = -5$, $b = -4$.   *Ans.* $4x + 5y + 20 = 0$.
(i) With $m = -\frac{1}{3}$, $b = -3$.
(j) With $m = \frac{2}{3}$, $a = 5$.
(k) With $a = 10$, $b = -1\frac{1}{2}$.

2. Find the equation of a line and plot it if it

(a) passes through $(4, 4)$ and is parallel to $x = y$;
(b) passes through $(-2, -5)$ and is perpendicular to $x - 2y = 7$;
(c) passes through $(0, 5)$ and is perpendicular to $3x + 4y = 5$;
                             Ans. $4x - 3y + 15 = 0$.
(d) passes through $(4, -7)$ and is parallel to $3x + y + 6 = 0$;
(e) has $a = -3$ and is parallel to $4x + 7y = 1$;
                             Ans. $4x + 7y + 12 = 0$.
(f) has $b = 6$ and is parallel to $x - 7y = 4$;
(g) joins $(2, 5)$ to the mid-point of $(-2, -3)$ and $(4, -6)$.

3. The vertices of a triangle are $A(3, 3)$, $B(-1, -5)$, and $C(6, 0)$. Find the

(a) equations of the sides;
     Ans. $2x - y - 3 = 0$, $x + y - 6 = 0$, $5x - 7y - 30 = 0$.
(b) equations of the medians, and their common point;
(c) equations of the altitudes, and their common point;
     Ans. $7x + 5y = 36$, $x - y = 4$, $x + 2y = 6$; $(4\frac{2}{3}, \frac{2}{3})$.
(d) equations of the perpendicular bisectors of the sides, and their common point;
(e) equations of the lines through the vertices parallel to the opposite sides;
(f) equations of the lines joining the mid-points of the sides;
(g) equation of the line joining the points which divide both AB and AC in the ratio of 1 to 3;   *Ans.* $5x - 7y = 3$.
(h) equation of the line joining the vertex C to the point dividing the side AB in the ratio of 5 to 2.

THE STRAIGHT LINE

4. If $A(-3, 2)$, $B(3, -2)$, and $C(0, -1)$ are the vertices of a triangle, find the equations required in Problem 3.

5. Find the equations required in Problem 3 for the triangle with vertices $A(8, 0)$, $B(6, 4)$, and $C(-1, 3)$.

6. Find the equations of the diagonals of any square and show that they are perpendicular to each other.

7. Find the equations of the diagonals of any rhombus and show that they are perpendicular to each other.

8. The equations of two sides of a parallelogram are $2x + 3y - 7 = 0$ and $x - 3y + 4 = 0$. One vertex is $(5, 5)$. Find the equations of the other sides.

9. Two sides of a parallelogram are $3x - y - 2 = 0$ and $x - y - 5 = 0$. Find the equations of the other sides if one vertex is (1) $(4, 3)$; (2) $(-4, 3)$; (3) $(6, -4)$; (4) $(-3, -8)$.

Ans. (1) $3x - y - 9 = 0$, $x - y - 1 = 0$.

10. Find the perpendicular distance from the line $x - 2y = 8$ to the point $(2, 1)$. *Ans.* 3.58 units.

Hint. Find the equation of the line through $(2, 1)$ perpendicular to the given line and its point of intersection with the latter.

11. Show that the center of the circumscribed circle (circumcenter), the point of intersection of the medians (centroid), and the point of intersection of the altitudes (orthocenter) of the triangle with sides $8x + y + 34 = 0$, $x - y + 2 = 0$, $x + 2y = 7$ are on a straight line (collinear).

29. The normal equation of the straight line. Let AB be any line, and let ON be drawn from the origin perpendicular to AB at C. *Let the positive direction on ON be from O toward N.* Denote the length OC by p, and the positive angle XON, measured, as in trig-

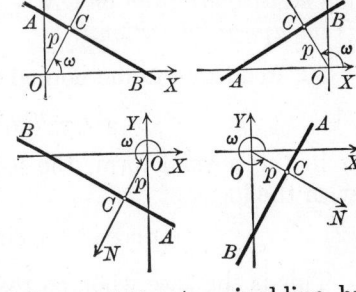

onometry, from OX as initial line to ON as terminal line, by ω (Greek letter "omega"). Then p is positive and $\omega < 360°$. Obviously, AB is determined when p and ω are given.

The problem now is this: Given for the line AB of the figure the perpendicular distance $OC (= p)$ from the origin and the angle $XON (= \omega)$, to find the equation of AB.

Solution. Let $P(x, y)$ be any point on AB. The coordinates (x_1, y_1) of C are (in all figures) $x_1 = p \cos \omega$, $y_1 = p \sin \omega$. The slope of $ON = \tan \omega$. Hence

$$\text{slope of } AB = -\cot \omega = -\frac{\cos \omega}{\sin \omega}.$$

By the point-slope form, the equation of AB is

(1) $$y - p \sin \omega = -\frac{\cos \omega}{\sin \omega}(x - p \cos \omega).$$

Reducing, and remembering that $\sin^2 \omega + \cos^2 \omega = 1$, we have

(V) $$\boldsymbol{x \cos \omega + y \sin \omega - p = 0.}$$

This equation is known as the *normal equation*.

When $p = 0$, however, AB passes through the origin, and the rule given above for the positive direction on ON becomes meaningless. *When $p = 0$ we shall assume that the positive direction on ON is the upward direction.*

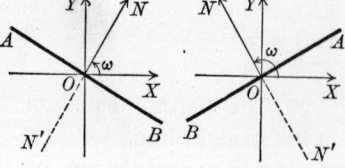

30. Reduction to the normal form.

If a given equation

(1) $$Ax + By + C = 0$$

is in the normal form, the locus of (1) must be identical with the locus of

(2) $$x \cos \omega + y \sin \omega - p = 0.$$

This is the case when corresponding coefficients are proportional. Hence

$$\frac{\cos \omega}{A} = \frac{\sin \omega}{B} = -\frac{p}{C}.$$

THE STRAIGHT LINE

Denote the common value of these ratios by r; then

(3) $$\cos \omega = rA,$$
(4) $$\sin \omega = rB, \text{ and}$$
(5) $$-p = rC.$$

To find r, square (3) and (4) and add; this gives
$$\sin^2 \omega + \cos^2 \omega = r^2(A^2 + B^2).$$
But $\sin^2 \omega + \cos^2 \omega = 1$;
and hence $r^2(A^2 + B^2) = 1$, or

(6) $$r = \frac{1}{\pm \sqrt{A^2 + B^2}}.$$

Equation (5) shows that r and C must have *opposite* signs, since p is positive.

Substituting the value of r in (3), (4), and (5),
$$\cos \omega = \frac{A}{\pm \sqrt{A^2 + B^2}},\; \sin \omega = \frac{B}{\pm \sqrt{A^2 + B^2}},\; p = -\frac{C}{\pm \sqrt{A^2 + B^2}}.$$

Hence (2) becomes

(7) $$\frac{A}{\pm \sqrt{A^2 + B^2}}\, x + \frac{B}{\pm \sqrt{A^2 + B^2}}\, y + \frac{C}{\pm \sqrt{A^2 + B^2}} = 0,$$

the normal form of (1). Hence the

Rule *to reduce $Ax + By + C = 0$ to the normal form.*

Find the numerical value of $\sqrt{A^2 + B^2}$ and give it the sign opposite to that of C. Divide the given equation by this number. The result is the required equation.

EXAMPLE

Reduce the equation

(8) $$3x - y + 10 = 0$$

to the normal form.

Solution. Divide the equation by $-\sqrt{10}$, since $A = 3$, $B = -1$, $\sqrt{A^2 + B^2} = \sqrt{10}$, and this radical must be given the negative sign, as $C (= 10)$ is positive. The normal form of (8) is accordingly

$$-\frac{3}{\sqrt{10}} x + \frac{1}{\sqrt{10}} y - \sqrt{10} = 0.\; Ans.$$

Here $\cos \omega = -\dfrac{3}{\sqrt{10}}$, $\sin \omega = \dfrac{1}{\sqrt{10}}$, $p = \sqrt{10} = 3.1 +$.

Also $\omega = 161° 34'$.

If $C = 0$, then $p = 0$, and hence $\omega < 180°$ (p. 56); then $\sin \omega$ is positive, and, from (4), r and B must have the *same* signs.

The advantages of the normal equation of a straight line are twofold. In the first place, the equation of any line may be put in the normal form. In the second place, as will be seen in the following article, from it we find the perpendicular distance from a line to a point.

PROBLEMS

1. In what quadrant will ON (see figure on page 55) lie if $\sin \omega$ and $\cos \omega$ are both positive? both negative? if $\sin \omega$ is positive and $\cos \omega$ negative? if $\sin \omega$ is negative and $\cos \omega$ positive?

2. Find the equations and plot the lines for which

(a) $\omega = 0$, $p = 5$;

(b) $\omega = \dfrac{3\pi}{2}$, $p = 3$;

(c) $\omega = \dfrac{\pi}{4}$, $p = 3$;   *Ans.* $\sqrt{2}\,x + \sqrt{2}\,y - 6 = 0$.

(d) $\omega = 45°$, $p = 4$;

(e) $\omega = 120°$, $p = 2$;

(f) $\omega = \dfrac{7\pi}{4}$, $p = 4$.   *Ans.* $x - y - 4\sqrt{2} = 0$.

3. Reduce the following equations to normal form, find p and ω, plot, and check in the figures:

(a) $4x - 3y + 1 = 0$.   *Ans.* $p = 0.2$, $\omega = 143° 8'$.
(b) $3x + y - 5 = 0$.
(c) $2x - y + 3 = 0$.
(d) $4x - y + 2 = 0$.   *Ans.* $p = \dfrac{2\sqrt{17}}{17} = 0.48$, $\omega = 165° 58'$.
(e) $x + y - 3 = 0$.
(f) $4x - y = 0$.
(g) $x + 4y = 0$.

4. By use of formula (V) find the distance from the origin to the line whose equation is

(a) $3x + 4y - 5 = 0$;   (b) $x + y - 7 = 0$;
   Ans. 1.   (c) $2x - y + 4 = 0$.

5. Find by use of (V) the inclinations of the lines of Problem 4.

THE STRAIGHT LINE

6. Find k so that the perpendicular distance of the line $kx + y + 7 = 0$ from the origin is 6 units.   *Ans.* $k = \pm \frac{1}{6}\sqrt{13}$.

7. For what values of ω will the locus of (V) be parallel to the x-axis? the y-axis?

8. Find the equations of the lines which are

(a) at a distance of 7 units from the origin, passing through $(7, 14)$;
Ans. $x = 7$, $3x - 4y + 35 = 0$.

(b) at a distance of 10 units from the origin, passing through $(5, 10)$.

9. Find the equations of the lines determined as follows:

(a) $m = -3$, $p = 10$.   (c) $m = -2$, $p = 5$.
(b) Passing through $(2, 5)$, $p = 1$.   *Ans.* $2x + y \pm 5\sqrt{5} = 0$.

10. Find the equations of the tangents to the circle with the origin as center and radius 4 which touch at the ends of the diameter whose inclination is $150°$.   *Ans.* $\sqrt{3}\,x - y \pm 8 = 0$.

31. The perpendicular distance from a line to a point.

The positive direction on the line ON drawn from the origin perpendicular to AB (Art. 29) will now be assumed to determine the positive direction on all lines perpendicular to AB. Thus in the figure the distance from AB to P_1 is positive, and from AB to P_2 is negative.

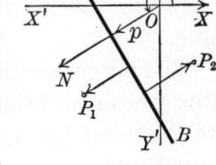

In the figure below, d is the perpendicular distance from AB to $P_1(x_1, y_1)$. The equation of AB is

(1) $\qquad x \cos \omega + y \sin \omega - p = 0.$

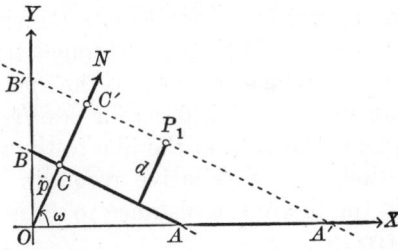

The normal equation of $A'B'$, drawn through P_1 parallel to AB, is

(2) $\qquad x \cos \omega + y \sin \omega - (p + d) = 0.$

The coördinates of P_1 satisfy (2). Substituting $x = x_1$, $y = y_1$, and solving for d, we obtain

(3) $$d = x_1 \cos \omega + y_1 \sin \omega - p.$$

In words: The perpendicular distance d is the result obtained by substituting the coördinates of P_1 for x and y in the left-hand member of the normal equation (1). Hence the

Rule *to find the perpendicular distance d from a line to a point.*

Reduce the equation of the line to normal form, set d equal to the left-hand member of this equation, and substitute the coördinates of the point for x and y.

The sign of the result will show whether the origin and the given point are on the same side (d is negative) or opposite sides (d is positive) of the line.

The perpendicular distance d from the line whose equation is $Ax + By + C = 0$ to the point (x_1, y_1) will be, by this rule, equal to

(4) $$d = \frac{Ax_1 + By_1 + C}{\pm \sqrt{A^2 + B^2}},$$

the sign of the radical being opposite to the sign of C.

When the given line AB passes through the origin, the positive direction on the normal ON is the *upward* direction. Hence the rule just stated will give a *positive* result when the perpendicular drawn from the line to the point has the upward direction, and a negative result in the contrary case. Thus in the figure the distance to P_1 is positive and to P_2 is negative.

Formula (4) may be used to find the perpendicular distance, but it is recommended that the rule be applied. The algebraic sign of the result should always be interpreted.

THE STRAIGHT LINE

EXAMPLES

1. Find the perpendicular distance from the line $4x - 3y + 15 = 0$ to the point $(2, 1)$.

Solution. The equation is reduced to the normal form by dividing by $-\sqrt{16+9} = -5$. Placing d equal to the left-hand member thus obtained,

$$d = \frac{4x - 3y + 15}{-5}.$$

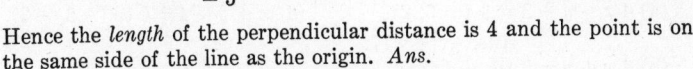

Substituting $x = 2$, $y = 1$,
$$d = \frac{8 - 3 + 15}{-5} = -4.$$

Hence the *length* of the perpendicular distance is 4 and the point is on the same side of the line as the origin. *Ans.*

2. Find the equations of the bisectors of the angles formed by the lines
$$L_1 : x + 3y - 6 = 0,$$
$$L_2 : 3x + y + 2 = 0.$$

Solution. Let $P_1(x_1, y_1)$ be any point on the bisector L_3. Then, by geometry, P_1 is equally distant from the given lines. Thus, if

$$d_1 = \text{distance from } L_1 \text{ to } P_1,$$
and $$d_2 = \text{distance from } L_2 \text{ to } P_1,$$

then d_1 and d_2 are *numerically* equal. Since, however, P_1 is on the same side of both lines as the origin, d_1 and d_2 are both negative. Hence for every point on the bisector L_3,

(5) $\qquad d_1 = d_2.$

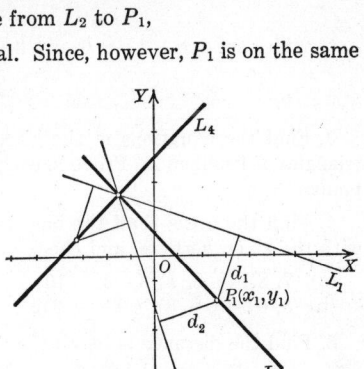

By the rule for finding d,
$$d_1 = \frac{x_1 + 3y_1 - 6}{\sqrt{10}},$$
$$d_2 = \frac{3x_1 + y_1 + 2}{-\sqrt{10}}.$$

Substituting in (5) and reducing,
$$x_1 + y_1 - 1 = 0.$$

Dropping the subscripts in order to follow the usual custom of having (x, y) denote any point on the line, we have as the equation of L_3:

$$x + y - 1 = 0. \quad Ans.$$

62 NEW ANALYTIC GEOMETRY

For any point on the bisector L_4 the distances d_1 and d_2 will be equal numerically but will differ in sign. Hence, along L_4,

$$d_1 = -d_2.$$

Proceeding as before, we find the equation of L_4 to be

$$x - y + 4 = 0. \quad Ans.$$

We note that L_3 and L_4 are perpendicular lines.

PROBLEMS

1. Find the perpendicular distance from the given line to the given point. Plot, and explain the sign of the result.

(a) $4x - y + 2 = 0$ to $(3, 2)$.
   $Ans. -\frac{12}{17}\sqrt{17}.$
(b) $4x + y = 0$ to $(-1, 3)$.
(c) $3x + 4y - 5 = 0$ to $(5, 5)$.
(d) $x + y - 4 = 0$ to $(-2, -3)$.
(e) $2x - y + 4 = 0$ to $(5, -2)$.
(f) $3x + 4y - 2 = 0$ to $(2, 7)$.
   $Ans. \ 6\frac{2}{5}.$
(g) $y - 2x + 1 = 0$ to $(-1, -3)$.

2. Find the lengths of the altitudes of the triangle whose

(a) sides are $4x - 3y + 8 = 0$, $12x - 5y + 8 = 0$, $2x - y = 0$;
(b) vertices are $(8, 7)$, $(4, -8)$, $(2, 10)$;
(c) vertices are $(1, 2)$, $(-2, 0)$, $(6, -1)$;

$$Ans. \ -\frac{19}{\sqrt{13}}, \ -\frac{19}{\sqrt{65}}, \ -\frac{19}{\sqrt{34}}.$$

(d) sides are $2x + 3y = 0$, $x + 3y + 3 = 0$, $x + y + 1 = 0$.

$$Ans. \ -\frac{3}{\sqrt{13}}, \ -\frac{6}{\sqrt{10}}, \ -\sqrt{2}.$$

3. Find the equations of the bisectors of the interior angles of the triangles of Problem 2. Prove in each case that they meet in a common point.

4. Find the areas (half the base times the altitude) of the triangles with the given vertices, and check your answer by Art. 15:

(a) $(7, 8)$, $(-8, 4)$, $(-2, -10)$.
(b) $(8, 0)$, $(0, -8)$, $(-3, -3)$.
(c) $(5, -4)$, $(-4, -5)$, $(0, 8)$.
(d) $(3, 1)$, $(2, 3)$, $(1, 2)$. $Ans. \ 1\frac{1}{2}.$

5. Find the distance between the parallel lines given below:

(a) $3x - y = 10$, $3x - y = 0$. $Ans. \ \sqrt{10}.$
(b) $12x + 5y - 1 = 0$, $12x + 5y + 7 = 0$.
(c) $3x - 4y + 1 = 0$, $6x - 8y - 9 = 0$.
(d) $2x - 7y + 8 = 0$, $4x - 14y - 3 = 0$.
(e) $x - 3y = 0$, $3x - 9y = 7$.
(f) $y = mx + 3$, $y = mx - 3$. $Ans. \ \dfrac{6}{\sqrt{1 + m^2}}.$

THE STRAIGHT LINE

6. Show that the bisectors of the interior angles of the triangles with the following sides meet in a point (are concurrent):

(a) $4x - 3y = 12$, $5x - 12y - 4 = 0$, $12x - 5y - 13 = 0$.
   Bisectors: $7x - 9y = 16$, $7x + 7y = 9$, $112x - 64y = 221$.

(b) $5x - 12y = 0$, $5x + 12y + 60 = 0$, $12x - 5y = 60$.

(c) $x + 2y - 5 = 0$, $2x - y - 5 = 0$, $2x + y + 5 = 0$.

(d) $3x + y - 1 = 0$, $x - 3y - 3 = 0$, $x + 3y + 11 = 0$.

7. Find the locus of a point which is

(a) twice as far from the line $3x + 4y - 5 = 0$ as from $4x + 3y = 6$;
   Ans. $5x + 2y = 7$.

(b) three times as far from $12x + 5y - 1 = 0$ as from the y-axis;

(c) four times as far from $5x - 12y = 0$ as from $12x - 5y = 60$;

(d) two thirds as far from $4x - 3y + 4 = 0$ as from $5x + 12y - 8 = 0$;

(e) n times as far from $4x - 3y + 1 = 0$ as from $5x - 12y = 0$.
   Ans. $(52 - 25n)x - (39 - 60n)y + 13 = 0$.

8. Find the center and the radius of the circle inscribed in the triangle whose

(a) sides are $2x + y = 12$, $2x - y = -4$, $x - 2y - 4 = 0$;
   Ans. Center $(2, 2)$, $r = \frac{6}{5}\sqrt{5}$.

(b) vertices are $(8, 1)$, $(2, 4)$, $(-2, -4)$;

(c) sides are $2x + 5y - 22 = 0$, $5x - 2y + 32 = 0$, $2x - 5y + 26 = 0$.

9. Compute the area of the polygon with vertices $(6, 1)$, $(3, -10)$, $(-3, -5)$, $(-2, 0)$.

Hint. Divide into two triangles (see Problem 4). *Ans.* 60.

10. Show that the bisector of an interior angle of the triangle with sides $x + 4y - 8 = 0$, $x - 4y + 10 = 0$, $4x - y - 15 = 0$ and the bisectors of the exterior angles at the other vertices meet in a point (are concurrent).

11. Find the equations of the lines through the center of the circle inscribed in the triangle of Problem 10 which are parallel to the sides of the triangle.

12. Find the point on each side of the triangle of Problem 10 which is equidistant from the other two sides.

32. Systems of straight lines. An equation of the first degree in x and y which contains a single arbitrary constant will represent an infinite number of lines, for the locus of the equation will be a straight line for any value of the constant, and the locus will be different for different values of the constant. These lines are said to form a *system*. The constant is called the **parameter** of the system.

Thus the equation $y = 2x + b$, where b is an arbitrary constant, represents the system of parallel lines with the slope 2. To plot lines of this system, assume values of b such as 0, ± 1, ± 2, ± 3, etc., and draw the lines $y = 2x$, $y = 2x \pm 1$, $y = 2x \pm 2$, $y = 2x \pm 3$, etc. The equation $y - 5 = m(x - 3)$, where m is an arbitrary constant, represents the system of lines passing through (3, 5).

The methods already explained suffice for solving problems involving straight lines, but shorter methods result in some cases by using systems of lines.

EXAMPLE

A line passes through $(-2, 2)$ and forms with the coördinate axes a triangle of unit area. Find its equation.

Solution. The equation of the system of lines passing through $(-2, 2)$ is

(1) $$y - 2 = k(x + 2).$$

If A and B are the points of intersection with $X'X$ and YY' respectively, then area $\triangle OAB$ must equal 1. Find the intercepts in (1) and set half their product equal to 1. This gives

$$\frac{1}{2}\left(\frac{-2k-2}{k}\right)(2k+2) = 1,$$

or $$2k^2 + 5k + 2 = 0.$$

Solving, $$k = -2, -\tfrac{1}{2}.$$

Substituting these values in (1), we obtain

$$2x + y + 2 = 0, \quad x + 2y - 2 = 0. \; Ans.$$

Both lines satisfy the above conditions.

In general, we may say this: *In finding the equation of a straight line defined by two conditions, we may begin by writing down the equation of the system of lines for which one of these conditions is satisfied, and then determine the value of the parameter so as to meet the second condition.*

THE STRAIGHT LINE

PROBLEMS

1. Write the equation of the system of lines defined by the given condition:

(a) y-intercept is -3.
(b) Slope is $-\frac{2}{3}$.
(c) Passing through $(-2, -5)$.
(d) x-intercept is 4.
(e) Distance from the origin is 5.
(f) Sum of intercepts is 7.
(g) Difference of intercepts is 2.
(h) Forming with the axes a triangle of area 10.
(i) Forming with the axes a triangle of perimeter 6.
(j) Parallel to $5x - 3y = 6$.
(k) Perpendicular to $x + 2y = 8$.
(l) Product of intercepts is 12.
(m) Perpendicular distance from the origin is 3.
(n) Passing through the point of intersection of $x - y = 6$ and $4x + 3y = 10$.
(o) Passing through the mid-point of $(2, 2)$ and $(0, -6)$.
(p) Parallel to $x \cos 45° + y \sin 45° = 6$.
(q) Perpendicular to $3x - 7y = 3$.
(r) Perpendicular to $y = mx + b$.
(s) Perpendicular to $\frac{x}{a} + \frac{y}{b} = 1$.
(t) Tangent to the circle of radius 7 about the origin.
(u) x-intercept is two thirds of the y-intercept.

2. Use the equation of a system of lines to find the equation of a line satisfying the conditions given:

(a) Passing through $(4, 5)$ and parallel to $x + 3y = 4$.
(b) Passing through $(-3, 2)$ and parallel to $3x - 2y = 7$.
(c) Passing through $(5, -6)$ and parallel to $2x - 4y = 3$.
(d) Passing through $(-1, -2)$ and perpendicular to $x - 4y = 2$.
(e) Passing through $(1, 4)$ and perpendicular to $3x - 5y + 8 = 0$.
(f) Passing through $(2, 7)$ and perpendicular to $5x - y = 4$.

3. Determine the parameter k so that

(a) $x - 2y + k = 0$ may pass through $(4, 5)$;
(b) $y = kx - 3$ may be parallel to $4x + 12y = 7$;   *Ans.* $k = -\frac{1}{3}$.
(c) $kx - y - 2k = 0$ may pass through $(5, -2)$;
(d) $4x + 7y - 2k = 0$ may be at a distance of 7 units from the origin;
(e) $3x + 4ky = 7$ has the y-intercept $\frac{1}{2}$;
(f) $kx + 3y + 8 = 0$ has the slope $\frac{2}{3}$;
(g) $7x + 2y + k = 0$ has the difference of its intercepts 3;

66 NEW ANALYTIC GEOMETRY

(h) $2x + 7y - k = 0$ forms a triangle of area 3 with the axes;
$$Ans.\ k = \pm 2\sqrt{21}.$$

(i) $4x - 3y + 6k = 0$ is distant 3 units from the origin.
$$Ans.\ k = \pm 2\tfrac{1}{2}.$$

4. (1) Given that the equations of two sides of a parallelogram are $3x - 4y + 6 = 0$ and $x + 5y - 10 = 0$ and one vertex is $(4, 9)$. Find the equations of the other sides. *Ans.* $3x - 4y + 24 = 0$, $x + 5y - 49 = 0$.

(2) The equations of two sides of a parallelogram are $3x + y - 7 = 0$ and $x - 2y + 5 = 0$ and one vertex is $(4, 5)$. Find the other sides.

5. Using the equation of the system of lines through the point $(3, 2)$, find the equations of the lines of the system each of which forms with the axes a triangle of area $13\tfrac{1}{2}$. *Ans.* $x + 3y = 9$, $4x + 3y - 18 = 0$.

6. Find the equation of the straight line which forms with the axes a triangle of area 2 and whose intercepts differ by 3.

7. Find the equation of the line perpendicular to $3x - 4y = 7$ and satisfying the condition given:

(a) Passing through $(7, -6)$.

(b) Forming with the axes a triangle of area 6.

(c) Forming with the axes a triangle of perimeter 10.

(d) Distant 4 units from the origin.

(e) At the same perpendicular distance as the given line from the origin.

(f) x-intercept is -7.

(g) Sum of the intercepts is 14.

(h) Mid-point of the part intercepted by the axes is $(3, 4)$.

33. System of lines passing through the point of intersection of two given lines. Given the two lines

(1) $$L_1:\ x + 2y - 5 = 0,$$
(2) $$L_2:\ 3x - y - 1 = 0.$$

Consider the system of lines whose equation is

(3) $$x + 2y - 5 + k(3x - y - 1) = 0,$$

where k is an arbitrary number. Each line (3) will pass through the point of intersection of the given lines L_1 and L_2. In fact, by solving (1) and (2) for x and y, we find $x = 1$, $y = 2$, and these values satisfy (3). Or, also, without

THE STRAIGHT LINE

solving, let (x_1, y_1) be the point of intersection of L_1 and L_2. When these coördinates are substituted in (3) it becomes

$$0 + k(0) = 0.$$

Note that the equation (3) is formed from the left-hand members of (1) and (2) by multiplying one of them by the parameter k and adding.

Problems requiring the equation of a line which passes through the intersection of two given lines are often much shortened by forming the equation of the system (3) and determining k to meet the given condition. The advantage of this method is that *we do not need to know the coördinates of the point of intersection of L_1 and L_2.*

EXAMPLES

1. Find the equation of the line passing through $P_1(2, 1)$ and the point of intersection of $L_1 : 3x - 5y - 10 = 0$ and $L_2 : x + y + 1 = 0$.

Solution. The system of lines passing through the intersection of the given lines is represented by

$$3x - 5y - 10 + k(x + y + 1) = 0.$$

If P_1 lies on this line, then $x = 2$, $y = 1$ must satisfy this equation.

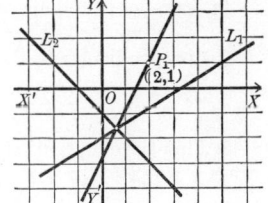

Hence $6 - 5 - 10 + k(2 + 1 + 1) = 0$;

whence $k = \frac{9}{4}$.

Substituting this value of k and simplifying, we have the required equation,

$$21x - 11y - 31 = 0. \quad Ans.$$

2. Find the equation of the line passing through the point of intersection of $L_1 : 2x + y + 1 = 0$ and $L_2 : x - 2y + 1 = 0$ and parallel to $L_3 : 4x - 3y - 7 = 0$.

Solution. The equation of the system of lines through the point of intersection of the first two lines is

$$2x + y + 1 + k(x - 2y + 1) = 0,$$

or $\qquad (2 + k)x + (1 - 2k)y + (1 + k) = 0.$

The slope of this line is $-\dfrac{2+k}{1-2k}$. This must equal the slope of L_3; that is, $\frac{4}{3}$.

$$\therefore -\frac{2+k}{1-2k} = \frac{4}{3}, \quad \text{or} \quad k = 2.$$

Substituting and simplifying, we obtain

$$4x - 3y + 3 = 0. \text{ Ans.}$$

Solve the following problems without finding the point of intersection of the two lines given.

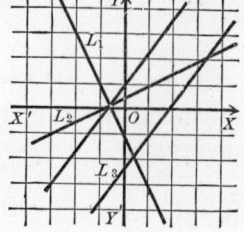

PROBLEMS

1. Find the equation of the line passing through the point of intersection of $2x - 3y + 2 = 0$ and $3x - 4y - 2 = 0$ which

(a) passes through the origin;   Ans. $5x - 7y = 0$.
(b) is parallel to $5x - 12y + 3 = 0$;
(c) is perpendicular to $3x + 2y + 4 = 0$.

2. Find the equations of the lines passing through the vertices of the triangle formed by the lines $2x - 3y + 1 = 0$, $x - y = 0$, and $3x + 4y - 2 = 0$ which are

(a) parallel to the opposite sides;

Ans. $3x + 4y = 7$, $14x - 21y + 2 = 0$, $17x - 17y + 5 = 0$.

(b) perpendicular to the opposite sides.

For individual study or assignment

3. Find the equations of the diagonals of the quadrilateral whose sides are $x + y - 2 = 0$, $x - y + 6 = 0$, $2x - y + 3 = 0$, and $x - 3y + 2 = 0$.
Ans. $19x + 3y + 26 = 0$, $13x - 23y + 58 = 0$.

Hint. The systems of lines passing through two opposite vertices are

$$x + y - 2 + k(x - y + 6) = 0$$
and
$$2x - y + 3 + k'(x - 3y + 2) = 0.$$

A line of one system will coincide with one of the other if the coefficients are proportional; that is, if

$$\frac{1+k}{2+k'} = \frac{1-k}{-1-3k'} = \frac{-2+6k}{3+2k'}.$$

Letting r be the common value of these ratios, we obtain

$$1 + k = 2r + rk',$$
$$1 - k = -r - 3rk',$$
and
$$-2 + 6k = 3r + 2rk'.$$

THE STRAIGHT LINE

From these equations we can eliminate r and k' and thus find the value of k which gives the line of the first system which belongs also to the second system.

4. Find the equation of the line passing through the point of intersection of $2x + y = 8$ and $3x + 2y = 0$ and

(a) perpendicular to the x-axis; *Ans.* $x - 16 = 0$.
(b) perpendicular to the y-axis. *Ans.* $y + 24 = 0$.

5. The equations of the sides of a parallelogram are $x + 3y + 2 = 0$, $x + 3y - 8 = 0$, $3x - 2y = 0$, and $3x - 2y - 16 = 0$. Find the equation of the line through a vertex and perpendicular to one of the opposite sides.

6. Find the equations of the lines through the point of intersection of the lines $x + 3y = 10$ and $3x - y = 0$ which are at unit distance from the origin. *Ans.* $x - 1 = 0$, $4x - 3y + 5 = 0$.

7. Find the equations of the lines through the point of intersection of $7x + 7y = 24$ and $x - y = 0$ which form with the coördinate axes
(a) a triangle of perimeter 12; *Ans.* $4x + 3y = 12$, $3x + 4y = 12$.
(b) a triangle of area $7\frac{1}{5}$.

REVIEW. TRIANGLE PROBLEMS

1. Find (1) the equations of the sides, (2) the equations of the perpendicular bisectors of the sides, (3) the equations of the medians, (4) the equations of the altitudes, (5) the equations of the lines through the vertices parallel to the opposite sides, (6) the lengths of the three medians, (7) the lengths of the three altitudes, (8) the area, (9) the three angles, (10) the equation of the circumscribed circle, for the triangle with vertices as given:

(a) $(2, 6)$, $(7, 1)$, $(-1, -3)$.   (f) $(4, 3)$, $(2, -2)$, $(-3, 4)$.
(b) $(2, 7)$, $(5, -3)$, $(-3, 2)$.   (g) $(4, 0)$, $(2, 4)$, $(-5, 3)$.
(c) $(-4, 5)$, $(-3, 8)$, $(4, 1)$.   (h) $(-3, -3)$, $(-2, 0)$, $(5, -7)$.
(d) $(3, 5)$, $(-1, -2)$, $(6, -3)$.   (i) $(5, 3)$, $(-3, 1)$, $(2, -6)$.
(e) $(4, 13)$, $(16, 5)$, $(-1, -12)$. (j) $(-1, 15)$, $(11, 7)$, $(-6, 10)$.

2. Find (1) the equations of the sides, (2) the equations of the perpendicular bisectors of the sides, (3) the equations of the bisectors of the interior angles, (4) the equation of the circumscribed circle, (5) the equation of the inscribed circle, for the triangle with vertices as given:

(a) $(2, 4)$, $(8, 4)$, $(6, 0)$.   (d) $(3, -2)$, $(3, -6)$, $(0, -3)$.
(b) $(0, -4)$, $(6, -2)$, $(5, -6)$.   (e) $(8, 1)$, $(2, 4)$, $(-2, -4)$.
(c) $(0, 3)$, $(6, 0)$, $(4, 4)$.   (f) $(-6, -30)$, $(-36, 10)$, $(24, 10)$.
           (g) $(5, 5)$, $(-5, 8)$, $(-7, -2)$.

3. Find (1) the angles, (2) the equations of the bisectors of the interior angles, (3) the equations of the bisectors of the exterior angles, (4) the equation of the inscribed circle, for the triangle with sides as given:

(a) $x + 4y - 8 = 0$, $x - 4y + 10 = 0$, $4x - y - 15 = 0$.
(b) $4x - 3y - 4 = 0$, $3x + 4y - 8 = 0$, $5x - 12y - 60 = 0$.
(c) $3x + 4y - 10 = 0$, $8x - 6y + 3 = 0$, $12x + 5y + 15 = 0$.
(d) $5x + 12y - 24 = 0$, $12x + 5y + 7 = 0$, $5x - 12y - 48 = 0$.
(e) $5x - 12y - 42 = 0$, $12x + 5y - 2 = 0$, $5x + 12y - 66 = 0$.
(f) $7x + y - 7 = 0$, $5x - 5y + 19 = 0$, $x + 7y + 15 = 0$.
(g) $4x - 3y + 25 = 0$, $5x - 12y + 1 = 0$, $3x + 4y - 5 = 0$.
(h) $12x + 5y + 50 = 0$, $5x + 12y - 16 = 0$, $5x - 12y - 16 = 0$.
(i) $x + 2y - 5 = 0$, $2x + y - 7 = 0$, $x - 2y - 9 = 0$.
(j) $3x + y - 7 = 0$, $x + 3y - 5 = 0$, $x - 3y + 1 = 0$.

CHAPTER V

THE CIRCLE

34. Equation of the circle. Theorem. *The equation of the circle whose center is (h, k) and whose radius equals r is*

(I) $$(x-h)^2 + (y-k)^2 = r^2.$$

Proof. Assume that $P(x, y)$ is any point on the circle.

Then $\quad r = \sqrt{(x-h)^2 + (y-k)^2}.\quad$ [By (I), p. 10]

Squaring, we have (I). Q.E.D.

Corollary. *The equation of the circle whose center is the origin $(0, 0)$ and whose radius is r is*

$$x^2 + y^2 = r^2.$$

If (I) is expanded and transposed, we obtain

(1) $\quad x^2 + y^2 - 2hx - 2ky + h^2 + k^2 - r^2 = 0.$

The form of this equation is

$$x^2 + y^2 + \textit{terms of lower degree} = 0.$$

In words: Any circle is defined by an equation of the *second degree* in the variables x and y, in which *the terms of the second degree are the sum of the squares of x and y.*

Equation (1) is of the form

(2) $\quad\quad\quad x^2 + y^2 + Dx + Ey + F = 0.$

We shall take up in Art. 35 the question of the locus of any equation of this form.

EXAMPLES

1. Find the locus of the equation
$x^2 + y^2 - 4x + 8y - 5 = 0$.

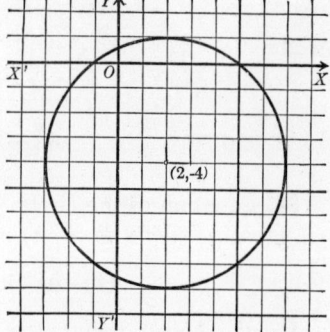

Solution. Collecting terms,

$(x^2 - 4x) + (y^2 + 8y) = 5$.

Completing the squares,

$(x^2 - 4x + 4) + (y^2 + 8y + 16) = 25$.

Or, also, $(x-2)^2 + (y+4)^2 = 25$.

Comparing with (I), the locus is a circle, and

$h = 2, \quad k = -4, \quad r = 5$. *Ans.*

2. Show that the locus of $5x^2 + 5y^2 - 14x + 7y - 24 = 0$ is a circle.

Solution. Divide through by 5 and complete the squares. The result is

$$(x - \tfrac{7}{5})^2 + (y + \tfrac{7}{10})^2 = \tfrac{29}{4}.$$

Comparing with (I), we see that the locus is a circle. The center is $(\tfrac{7}{5}, -\tfrac{7}{10})$, and $r = \tfrac{1}{2}\sqrt{29}$. *Ans.*

35. Test for a circle. Can we infer, conversely, that the locus of every equation of the form (2) in the preceding article is a circle? To decide this question transform (2) into the form of (I) by completing the squares of the terms in x and the terms in y. Then (2) may be written

(3) $\quad (x + \tfrac{1}{2}D)^2 + (y + \tfrac{1}{2}E)^2 = \tfrac{1}{4}(D^2 + E^2 - 4F)$.

If $D^2 + E^2 - 4F$ is positive, (3) is in the form (I), and the locus is <u>a circle with</u> center $(-\tfrac{1}{2}D, -\tfrac{1}{2}E)$ and radius $r = \tfrac{1}{2}\sqrt{D^2 + E^2 - 4F}$.

If $D^2 + E^2 - 4F = 0$, the only real values satisfying (3) are $x = -\tfrac{1}{2}D$, $y = -\tfrac{1}{2}E$. The locus, therefore, is the single point $(-\tfrac{1}{2}D, -\tfrac{1}{2}E)$, and is called a **point circle**, or a **circle whose radius is zero**.

If $D^2 + E^2 - 4F$ is negative, no real values satisfy (3), and (2) has no locus.

THE CIRCLE

The equation

(4) $$Ax^2 + Bxy + Cy^2 + Dx + Ey + F = 0$$

is called the **general equation of the second degree** in x and y because it contains all possible terms in x and y of the second and lower degrees. This equation can be reduced to the form (2) (by dividing by A) when and only when $A = C$ and $B = 0$.

Hence *the locus of an equation of the second degree in which the coefficients of x^2 and y^2 are equal and the xy-term is lacking is a circle or a point circle or there is no locus.*

36. Circles determined by three conditions. The equation of any circle may be written in one of the forms

$$(x - h)^2 + (y - k)^2 = r^2$$
or $$x^2 + y^2 + Dx + Ey + F = 0.$$

Each equation has three arbitrary constants. To determine these constants three equations are necessary. Each equation means that the circle satisfies some geometrical condition. Hence a circle may be determined from three conditions.

Rule *to derive the equation of a circle satisfying three conditions.*

First step. *Let the required equation be*

(1) $\qquad (x - h)^2 + (y - k)^2 = r^2$, *or*

(2) $\qquad x^2 + y^2 + Dx + Ey + F = 0$,

as may be more convenient.

Second step. *Find three equations between the constants h, k, and r [or D, E, and F] which express that the circle (1) [or (2)] satisfies the three given conditions.*

Third step. *Solve these equations for h, k, and r [or D, E, and F], and substitute the results in (1) [or (2)].*

In some problems, however, a more direct method results by constructing the center of the required circle from the given conditions and then finding the equations and points of intersection of the lines of the figure (see Example 3 below).

EXAMPLES

1. Find the equation of the circle passing through the three points $P_1(0, 1)$, $P_2(0, 6)$, and $P_3(3, 0)$.

Solution. *First step.* Let the required equation be

(3) $\quad x^2 + y^2 + Dx + Ey + F = 0.$

Second step. Since P_1, P_2, and P_3 lie on (3), their coördinates must satisfy (3).

Substituting $x = 0$, $y = 1$, the coördinates of P_1, and then those of P_2 and P_3 in turn, we get

(4) $\quad\quad 1 + E + F = 0,$

(5) $\quad\quad 36 + 6E + F = 0,$

(6) $\quad\quad 9 + 3D + F = 0.$

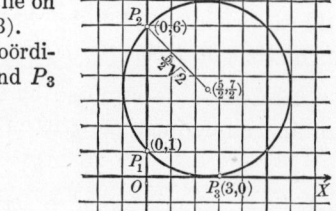

Third step. Solving (4), (5), and (6), we obtain $E = -7$, $F = 6$, $D = -5$.

Substituting in (3), the required equation is

$$x^2 + y^2 - 5x - 7y + 6 = 0. \text{ Ans.}$$

The center is $(\frac{5}{2}, \frac{7}{2})$, and the radius is $\frac{5}{2}\sqrt{2} = 3.5$.

2. Find the equation of the circle passing through the points $P_1(0, -3)$ and $P_2(4, 0)$ which has its center on the line $x + 2y = 0$.

Solution. *First step.* Let the required equation be

(7) $\quad\quad (x - h)^2 + (y - k)^2 = r^2.$

Second step. Since P_1 and P_2 lie on the locus of (7), we have

(8) $\quad\quad h^2 + (-3 - k)^2 = r^2,$ and

(9) $\quad\quad (4 - h)^2 + k^2 = r^2.$

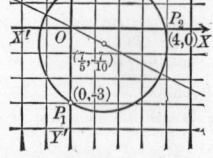

The center (h, k) lies on the given line. Hence

(10) $\quad\quad h + 2k = 0.$

Third step. Solving (8), (9), and (10), we get $h = \frac{7}{5}$, $k = -\frac{7}{10}$, $r = \frac{1}{2}\sqrt{29}$.

Substituting in (7) and reducing, we obtain the required equation,

$$x^2 + y^2 - \tfrac{14}{5}x + \tfrac{7}{5}y - \tfrac{24}{5} = 0,$$

or $\quad\quad 5x^2 + 5y^2 - 14x + 7y - 24 = 0. \text{ Ans.}$

THE CIRCLE

3. Find the equation of the circle inscribed in the triangle whose sides are

(11)
$$AB : 3x - 4y - 19 = 0,$$
$$BC : 4x + 3y - 17 = 0,$$
$$CA : x + 7 = 0.$$

Solution. The center is the point of intersection of the bisectors of the angles of the triangle. We therefore find the equations of the bisectors of the angles A and C.

Reducing equations (11) to the normal form,

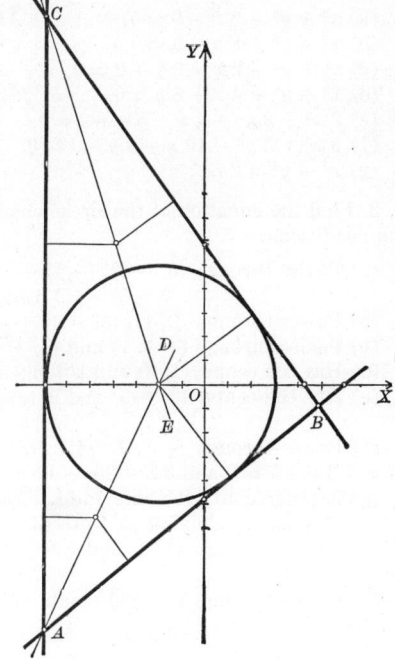

(12) $AB : \dfrac{3x - 4y - 19}{5} = 0;$

$BC : \dfrac{4x + 3y - 17}{5} = 0;$

$CA : \dfrac{x + 7}{-1} = 0.$

Then (see Example 2, Art. 31) the bisectors are

(13) $AD : \dfrac{3x - 4y - 19}{5} = \dfrac{x + 7}{-1},$

or $\quad 2x - y + 4 = 0,$

$CE : \dfrac{4x + 3y - 17}{5} = \dfrac{x + 7}{-1},$

or $\quad 3x + y + 6 = 0.$

The point of intersection of AD and CE is $(-2, 0)$. This is therefore the center of the inscribed circle. The radius is the perpendicular distance from any of the lines (11) to $(-2, 0)$. Taking the side AB, then, from (12),

$$r = \dfrac{3(-2) - 4(0) - 19}{5} = -5.$$

Hence, by (I), the equation of the required circle is

$$(x + 2)^2 + (y - 0)^2 = 25, \quad \text{or} \quad x^2 + y^2 + 4x - 21 = 0. \quad Ans.$$

NEW ANALYTIC GEOMETRY

PROBLEMS

1. Find the equation of the circle

(a) with center $(0, 1)$ and radius 3; $\quad$ *Ans.* $x^2 + y^2 - 2y - 8 = 0$.

(b) with center $(7, 2)$ and radius 5;

(c) with center $(-6, 4)$ and radius 7;

(d) with center $(-4, -8)$ and radius 8.

2. Determine the locus of each of the following equations, and plot:

(a) $x^2 + y^2 - 8x - 9 = 0$. $\quad$ *Ans.* Circle, center $(4, 0)$, $r = 5$.

(b) $x^2 + y^2 + 8y - 9 = 0$.

(c) $x^2 + y^2 - 2x + 2y + 2 = 0$. $\quad$ *Ans.* Point circle $(1, -1)$.

(d) $x^2 + y^2 - 4x + 6y = 0$.

(e) $2x^2 + 2y^2 + 4x - 5y + 2 = 0$.

(f) $5x^2 + 5y^2 - 10x + 4y - 1 = 0$.

(g) $x^2 + y^2 = 2rx$.

3. Find the equation of the circle which is determined by the following conditions:

(a) Passes through $(6, -6)$, $(-1, -5)$, $(7, -5)$.
$\quad$ *Ans.* $x^2 + y^2 - 6x + 4y - 12 = 0$.

(b) Passes through $(2, 1)$, $(3, -2)$, $(-4, 0)$.

(c) Passes through $(-1, 1)$ and $(1, 3)$ with center on the x-axis.

(d) Has the center $(1, 3)$ and is tangent to $2x + y + 5 = 0$.

(e) Has the center $(3, -5)$ and is tangent to $x - 7y + 2 = 0$.
$\quad$ *Ans.* $x^2 + y^2 - 6x + 10y + 2 = 0$.

(f) Passes through $(-1, 1)$ with center at the point of intersection of $x + 3y + 7 = 0$ and $3x - 2y - 12 = 0$.

(g) Is tangent to both axes and has radius 4. (Four solutions.)

(h) Has the line joining $(4, 7)$ to $(2, -3)$ as diameter.

(i) Passes through $(4, 2)$ and $(-6, -2)$ with center on the y-axis.
$\quad$ *Ans.* $x^2 + y^2 + 5y - 30 = 0$.

(j) Passes through the mid-points of the sides of the triangle with vertices $(a, 0)$, $(b, 0)$, and $(0, c)$. $\quad$ *Ans.* $x^2 + y^2 - \dfrac{a+b}{2}x + \dfrac{ab - c^2}{2c}y = 0$.

4. Find the equation of the circle determined by the given conditions:

(a) Circumscribes the triangle $(4, 3)$, $(3, -3)$, $(-1, 2)$.

(b) Circumscribes the triangle formed by the axes and $x + 2y = 4$.

(c) Circumscribes the triangle formed by the lines $x = y$, $2x - y = 2$, $2x + 3y - 3 = 0$.

(d) Passes through $(5, -3)$ and $(0, 6)$ with its center on $2x - 3y = 6$.
$\quad$ *Ans.* $3x^2 + 3y^2 - 114x - 64y + 276 = 0$.

(e) Is tangent to the x-axis with radius 5 and center on the line $x = 6$.

THE CIRCLE

(f) Passes through $(5, 1)$ and $(3, -2)$ with its center on $x + 2y = 3$.

(g) Is tangent to $4x + 7y = 4$, with center at the origin.

Ans. $65x^2 + 65y^2 = 16$.

5. Show that the following loci are circles. Find the center and the radius in each case.

(a) A point moves so that the sum of the squares of its distances from $(3, 0)$ and $(-3, 0)$ is always 68. *Ans.* $x^2 + y^2 = 25$.

(b) A point moves so that its distances from $(4, 5)$ and $(-4, 3)$ are always in the ratio of 3 to 2.

(c) A moving point is always one half as far from $(2, -1)$ as from $(0, 4)$. *Ans.* $3x^2 + 3y^2 - 16x + 16y + 4 = 0$.

(d) A point moves so that its distance from the y-axis is four times the square of its distance from $(1, -3)$.

(e) A point moves so that its distance from $3x + 4y - 1 = 0$ is always equal to the square of its distance from $(2, 3)$.

Ans. $5x^2 + 5y^2 - 23x - 34y + 66 = 0$.

(f) A point moves so that the square of its distance from $x + y = 6$ is always equal to the area of the rectangle formed by the axes and perpendiculars from the point to the axes.

Ans. $x^2 + y^2 - 12x - 12y + 36 = 0$.

(g) The locus of the vertex of a right triangle which has $(0, -4)$ and $(6, 3)$ as the ends of its hypotenuse.

(h) The sum of the squares of the distances of a point from the two lines $x - 2y = 7$ and $2x + y = 3$ is 7.

Ans. $5x^2 + 5y^2 - 26x + 22y + 23 = 0$.

6. Find the equation of the inscribed circle of the triangle whose sides are given below:

(a) $x + 2y = 5$, $2x - y = 5$, $2x + y + 5 = 0$.
(b) $3x + y = 1$, $x - 3y = 3$, $x + 3y + 11 = 0$.
(c) $3x + 4y = 22$, $4x - 3y + 29 = 0$, $y - 5 = 0$.
(d) $x = 0$, $y = 0$, $x + y = 7$.

For individual study or assignment

7. Find the equation of the circle which is

(a) tangent to $4x + 3y - 70 = 0$ at $(10, 10)$ with radius 10;

Ans. $x^2 + y^2 - 4x - 8y - 80 = 0$, $x^2 + y^2 - 36x - 32y + 480 = 0$.

(b) tangent to $3x - 4y = 19$ and $4x + 3y = 17$ and passes through $(3, 2)$;

(c) tangent to $x + 3y = 26$ at the point $(8, 6)$ and passes through $(-2, -4)$.

8. Prove analytically that an angle inscribed in a semicircle is a right angle.

9. Show analytically that a straight line can cut a circle in no more than two points.

10. Show analytically that the circle through the mid-points of the sides of a triangle passes through the feet of the altitudes of the triangle and bisects the lines joining the vertices to the point of intersection of the altitudes. (The nine-point circle.)

11. If a point moves so that the sum of the squares of its distances from two fixed points is constant, show that its locus is a circle.

12. A point moves so that the sum of the squares of its distances from two fixed perpendicular lines is constant. Show that its locus is a circle.

13. What is the locus of a point which moves so that the ratio of its distances from two fixed points is constant?

14. What is the locus of a point which moves so that the square of its distance from a fixed point is proportional to its distance from a fixed line?

15. What is the locus of the mid-point of a line of given length $2\,a$ which moves so that its ends rest on two perpendicular lines?

16. What is the locus of the vertex of a triangle with the base fixed if one of the medians from one end of the base remains constant in length?

17. Show analytically that the perpendicular let fall from a point of a circle to a diameter is the mean proportional between the segments formed on the diameter.

18. Show analytically that a radius perpendicular to a chord of a circle bisects the chord.

19. If $(3, -5)$ is the mid-point of a chord of the circle $x^2 + y^2 = 277$, what are the equation of the chord and its length?

37. Radical axis. When x^2 and y^2 are eliminated between the equations of two circles

(1) $\qquad C_1 : x^2 + y^2 + D_1 x + E_1 y + F_1 = 0,$

(2) $\qquad C_2 : x^2 + y^2 + D_2 x + E_2 y + F_2 = 0,$

we obtain (by subtraction)

(3) $\qquad (D_1 - D_2)x + (E_1 - E_2)y + F_1 - F_2 = 0.$

The straight line (3) is called the *radical axis* of C_1 and C_2.

THE CIRCLE

Theorem 1. *The radical axis is perpendicular to the line of centers of C_1 and C_2.*

The proof is immediate, since the centers of C_1 and C_2 are $(-\tfrac{1}{2} D_1, -\tfrac{1}{2} E_1)$ and $(-\tfrac{1}{2} D_2, -\tfrac{1}{2} E_2)$ respectively.

Theorem 2. *If C_1 and C_2 intersect (or touch each other), the radical axis is their common chord (or their common tangent).*

Proof. To solve (1) and (2) for x and y, we subtract, obtaining (3), and take (3) and (1), or (2), as simultaneous. Hence a point of intersection (or tangency) of C_1 and C_2 is also a point on the radical axis. Q.E.D.

EXAMPLE

The radical axis of the circles

(4) $x^2 + y^2 + 3x - 3y - 52 = 0$,

(5) $x^2 + y^2 - 2x + 2y - 32 = 0$,

is (by subtraction)

(6) $\qquad x - y - 4 = 0$.

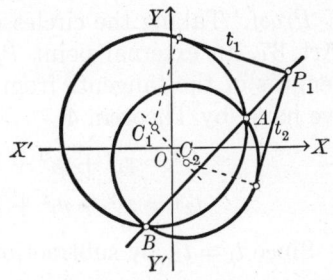

Solving (6) and (4), we obtain $(6, 2)$ and $(-2, -6)$ as the points of intersection of the circles. The line (6) is their common chord.

38. Length of the tangent. To obtain a geometrical property of the radical axis true for all relative positions of C_1 and C_2, we need

Theorem 3. *The length t of the tangent from $P_1(x_1, y_1)$ to a circle with center $C(h, k)$ and radius r is given by*

(II) $\quad t^2 = (x_1 - h)^2 + (y_1 - k)^2 - r^2$.

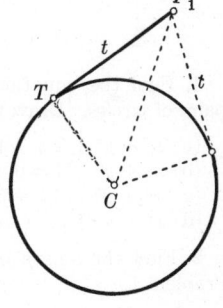

Proof. In the right $\triangle P_1CT$, $t^2 = \overline{P_1C}^2 - r^2$.

Using the length formula for P_1C, we obtain (II). Q.E.D.

NEW ANALYTIC GEOMETRY

From (II) follows at once

Theorem 4. *The square of the length of the tangent from $P_1(x_1, y_1)$ to the circle*

$$x^2 + y^2 + Dx + Ey + F = 0$$

is the value of the left-hand member when x_1 and y_1 are substituted for x and y.

This theorem should be compared with the rule for perpendicular distance in Art. 31.

We may now prove

Theorem 5. *The locus of a point from which the lengths of the tangents to two circles are equal is their radical axis.*

Proof. Taking the circles C_1 and C_2 as in (1) and (2) of Art. 37, an external point $P_1(x_1, y_1)$, and t_1 and t_2 as the lengths of the tangents from P_1 to C_1 and C_2 respectively, we have, by Theorem 4,

$$t_1{}^2 = x_1{}^2 + y_1{}^2 + D_1 x_1 + E_1 y_1 + F_1,$$
$$t_2{}^2 = x_1{}^2 + y_1{}^2 + D_2 x_1 + E_2 y_1 + F_2.$$

Since $t_1 = t_2$, by subtraction we get

$$(D_1 - D_2)x_1 + (E_1 - E_2)y_1 + F_1 - F_2 = 0.$$

That is, P_1 lies on the radical axis (3), Art. 37. Q.E.D.
See the figure for the example on page 79.

PROBLEMS

1. Find the equation of the radical axis of each of the following pairs of circles. Draw the circles and the radical axis.

(a) $x^2 + y^2 + 2y - 4 = 0$ and $x^2 + y^2 - 2y - 4 = 0$.
(b) $x^2 + y^2 - 4 = 0$ and $x^2 + y^2 + 2x - 3 = 0$.
(c) $x^2 + y^2 - 3x - 5y - 8 = 0$ and $x^2 + y^2 + 8x = 0$.
(d) $x^2 + y^2 + ax + by + c = 0$ and $x^2 + y^2 + mx + ny + p = 0$.

2. Find the length of the common chord of each pair of circles of Problem 1.

THE CIRCLE

3. Find the radical axes of the following sets of circles taken in pairs, and show that they meet in a point:

(a) $x^2 + y^2 + 4x + 7 = 0, \ 2x^2 + 2y^2 + 3x + 5y + 9 = 0, \ x^2 + y^2 + y = 0$.
(b) $x^2 + y^2 - 4x = 0, \ x^2 + y^2 + 6x - 8y = 0, \ x^2 + y^2 + 6x - 8 = 0$.
(c) $x^2 + y^2 - 9 = 0, \ 3x^2 + 3y^2 - 6x + 8y - 1 = 0, \ x^2 + y^2 + 8y = 0$.
(d) $x^2 + y^2 + 4x - 3y + 5 = 0, \ 2x^2 + 2y^2 + 5x - 6y + 1 = 0,$
$x^2 + y^2 + 5x - 4y + 5 = 0$.

4. Prove that the line of centers of each pair of circles of Problem 1 is perpendicular to the radical axis.

5. Show in Problem 1 that the lengths of the tangents to each pair of circles drawn from a definite point on their radical axis are equal.

6. Find the lengths of the following tangents:

(a) From $(7, 2)$ to the circle $x^2 + y^2 - 4 = 0$. *Ans.* 7.
(b) From $(-3, 2)$ to the circle $x^2 + y^2 - 6x - 2y = 0$.
(c) From $(1, 1)$ to the circle $2x^2 + 2y^2 + 2x + 4y - 1 = 0$.
(d) From $(-4, 0)$ to the circle $x^2 + y^2 - 6x + 2y - 3 = 0$. *Ans.* $\sqrt{37}$.

For individual study or assignment

7. Show analytically that the radical axes of any three circles taken by pairs meet in a point.

8. Find the longest and shortest distances from the given points to the given circles in Problem 6.

9. Find the locus of a point such that the lengths of the tangents drawn from it to two concentric circles are in the same ratio as the radii of the circles.

10. Find the locus of a point which moves so that the length of the tangent from it to a given circle is in a constant ratio to its distance from a given point.

11. By considering the length of the common chord of the circles $(x-a)^2 + (y-b)^2 = c^2$ and $(x-b)^2 + (y-a)^2 = c^2$, find the condition for tangency of these circles. *Ans.* $(a-b)^2 = 2c^2$.

39. Systems of circles. If one or more of the constants D, E, F, in the equation

(1) $$x^2 + y^2 + Dx + Ey + F = 0$$

is arbitrary, the locus is a *system of circles* obtained by assigning sets of values to the arbitrary constants and plotting the circles. Thus $x^2 + y^2 - r^2 = 0$
defines a system of concentric circles with different radii.

82 NEW ANALYTIC GEOMETRY

A simple and interesting case arises by proceeding from the equations of two circles in a manner analogous to Art. 33. Namely, given two circles

(2) $\quad C_1 : x^2 + y^2 + D_1 x + E_1 y + F_1 = 0,$

(3) $\quad C_2 : x^2 + y^2 + D_2 x + E_2 y + F_2 = 0,$

consider the locus of

(4) $x^2 + y^2 + D_1 x + E_1 y + F_1 + k(x^2 + y^2 + D_2 x + E_2 y + F_2) = 0,$

where k is an arbitrary constant. The coefficients of x^2 and y^2 are equal ($= 1 + k$). When $k = -1$, (4) becomes the equation of the radical axis (3), Art. 37. In other cases, the locus is a circle (Art. 35), and (4) defines a system of circles.

EXAMPLE

Plot the system of circles represented by

$$x^2 + y^2 + 8x - 9 + k(x^2 + y^2 - 4x - 9) = 0.$$

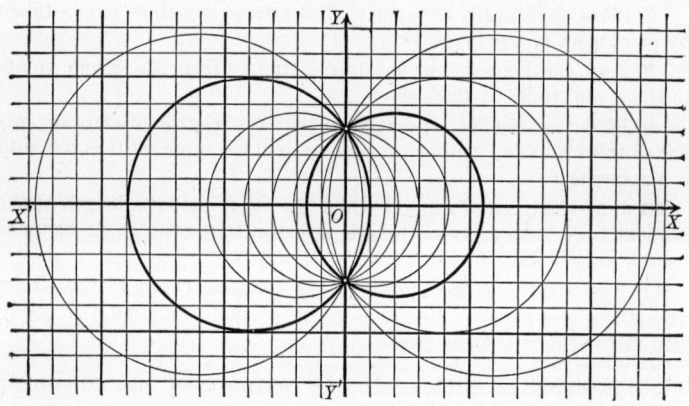

Solution. The figure shows the circles

$$x^2 + y^2 + 8x - 9 = 0 \quad \text{and} \quad x^2 + y^2 - 4x - 9 = 0,$$

plotted in heavy lines, and the circles corresponding to

$$k = 2,\ 5,\ 1,\ \tfrac{1}{2},\ -4,\ -\tfrac{5}{2},\ \text{and}\ -\tfrac{1}{4};$$

these circles all pass through the points of intersection of the first two.

The radical axis of the two circles plotted in heavy lines, which corresponds to $k = -1$, is the y-axis.

THE CIRCLE

The following facts concerning the system (4) are easily established:

1. *The circles have a common line of centers.* (See Problem 6 below.)

2. *If C_1 and C_2 intersect in two points A, B (or touch each other at A), then all the circles (4) will pass through A and B (or touch one another at A).*

For, obviously, if x_1 and y_1 satisfy (2) and (3), they will satisfy (4).

3. *The radical axis of any pair of circles of (4) is identical with that of C_1 and C_2.*

For writing down (4) with $k = k_1$ and then with $k = k_2$, and eliminating x^2 and y^2 between these equations, we obtain (3), Art. 37. In the above example the y-axis is the radical axis for any pair of circles.

PROBLEMS

1. Draw the given pair of circles C_1 and C_2. From their equations write down the equation of the system corresponding to (4) above (p. 82), and draw the circles of this system for the given values of k.

Find the equations of the line of centers and the radical axis, and plot them.

(a) $C_1: x^2 + y^2 + 4y = 0$; $C_2: x^2 + y^2 - 4 = 0$; $k = 3, 1, -\frac{1}{2}$.
(b) $C_1: x^2 + y^2 - 2x + 4y = 0$; $C_2: x^2 + y^2 + 2x - 4y = 0$; $k = 1, -2, 3, -3$.
(c) $C_1: x^2 + y^2 - 8x + 4y - 5 = 0$; $C_2: x^2 + y^2 + 8x - 4y - 5 = 0$; $k = 1, -2, 3, -3$.

2. Find the equation of the circle which

(a) passes through the points of intersection of the circles $x^2 + y^2 = 1$ and $x^2 + y^2 + 2x = 0$ and also through $(3, 2)$;
Ans. $7x^2 + 7y^2 - 24x - 19 = 0$.

(b) passes through the points of intersection of the circles $x^2 + y^2 = 4$, and $x^2 + y^2 - 6x = 0$ and through $(2, -2)$;

(c) belongs to the system $x^2 + y^2 - 4x - 3 + k(x^2 + y^2 - 4y - 3) = 0$ and passes through $(0, 1)$.

3. Find the equation of the circle of the system

(a) $x^2 + y^2 + 6x - 5 + k(x^2 + y^2 + 6y - 7) = 0$ whose center is on the line $x - y = 4$;

(b) $x^2 + y^2 - 4x + 2y + k(x^2 + y^2 - 2y - 4) = 0$ whose center is on the line $2x + 4y = 1$. *Ans.* $x^2 + y^2 - 3x + y - 1 = 0$.

4. Describe the system of circles represented by each of the following:

(a) $x^2 + y^2 + kx + 4y = 0$.
(b) $x^2 + y^2 + kx + ky = 0$.
  Ans. Centers on $x = y$ and passing through the origin.
(c) $x^2 + y^2 + 4x - 2y = k^2$.
(d) $x^2 + y^2 - 2kx - 2ky + k^2 = 0$.
(e) $x^2 + y^2 + 2kx = 0$.

5. Show that the centers of the circles of the system in Problem 3(a) and in 3(b) lie on a line.

6. Show that if P_1 and P_2 are, respectively, the centers of the circles (2) and (3) of Art. 39, then the center P of a circle (4) is the point which divides P_1P_2 in a ratio equal to k.

CHAPTER VI

PARABOLA, ELLIPSE, AND HYPERBOLA

40. The parabola. Consider the following locus problem. A point moves so that its distances from a fixed line and a fixed point are equal. Determine the nature of the locus.

Solution. Let DD' be the fixed line and F the fixed point. Draw the x-axis through F perpendicular to DD'. Take the origin midway between F and DD'.

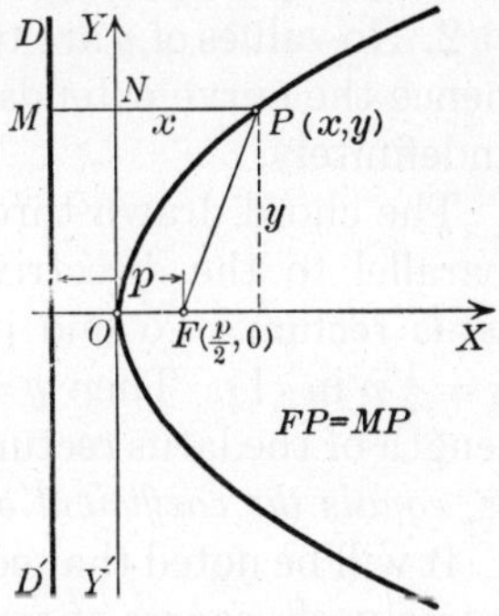

Let

(1) distance from $D'D$ to $F = p$.

Then, if $P(x, y)$ is any point on the locus,

(2) $\qquad FP = MP$.

But $FP = \sqrt{(x - \frac{1}{2} p)^2 + y^2}$, $MP = MN + NP = \frac{1}{2} p + x$.
Substituting in (2),

$$\sqrt{(x - \tfrac{1}{2} p)^2 + y^2} = \tfrac{1}{2} p + x.$$

Squaring and reducing,

(3) $\qquad\qquad y^2 = 2\, px.$

The locus is called a *parabola*. The fixed line DD' is called the **directrix**, the fixed point F, the **focus**. From (3) it is clear that the x-axis is an axis of symmetry. For this reason the x-axis is called the **axis** of the parabola. Furthermore, the origin is on the curve. This point midway between focus and directrix is called the **vertex**.

85

NEW ANALYTIC GEOMETRY

Theorem. *If the origin is the vertex and the x-axis the axis of a parabola, then its equation is*

(I) $$y^2 = 2\,px.$$

The focus is the point $(\tfrac{1}{2}p, 0)$, *and the equation of the directrix is* $x = -\tfrac{1}{2}p$.

A discussion of (I) gives us the following properties of the parabola in addition to those already obtained.

1. Values of x having the sign opposite to that of p are to be excluded. Hence the curve lies to the *right* of YY' when p is *positive* and to the *left* when p is *negative*.

2. No values of y are to be excluded; hence the curve extends up and down indefinitely.

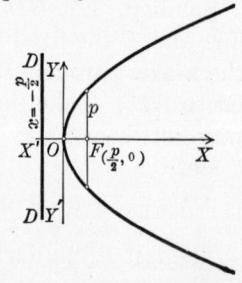

The chord drawn through the focus parallel to the directrix is called the **latus rectum**. To find its length, put $x = \tfrac{1}{2}p$ in (I). Then $y = \pm p$, and the length of the latus rectum $= 2\,p$; that is, *equals the coefficient of x in* (I).

It will be noted that equation (I) contains two terms only; namely, *the square of one coördinate and the first power of the other*. Obviously, the locus of

$$x^2 = 2\,py$$

is also a parabola (figure, p. 87), and thus we have the

Theorem. *If the origin is the vertex and the y-axis the axis of a parabola, then its equation is*

(II) $$x^2 = 2\,py.$$

The focus is the point $(0, \tfrac{1}{2}p)$, *and the equation of the directrix is* $y = -\tfrac{1}{2}p$.

Equations (I) and (II) are called the *typical forms* of the equation of the parabola.

Equations of the forms
$$Ax^2 + Ey = 0 \quad \text{and} \quad Cy^2 + Dx = 0,$$
where A, E, C, and D are different from zero, may, by transposition and division, be written in one of the forms (I) or (II).

Equations (I) and (II) are extraordinarily simple types of equations of the second degree. The problem

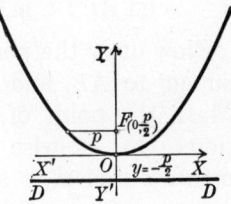

To derive a test for determining whether the locus of a given equation of the second degree is a parabola

will be solved in Art. 63.

41. Construction of the parabola. A parabola whose focus and directrix are given is readily constructed by rule and compasses as follows:

Draw the axis MX. Construct the vertex V, the midpoint of MF. Through any point A to the right of V draw a line AB parallel to the directrix. From F as a center with a radius equal to MA strike arcs to intersect AB at P and Q. Then P and Q are points on

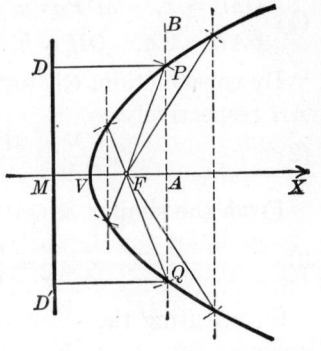

the parabola. For $FP = MA$, by construction, and hence P is equidistant from focus and directrix.

By changing the position of A we may construct as many points on the curve as desired.

42. Parabolic arch. When the span AB and height OH of a parabolic arch are given, points on the arch may be constructed as follows:

Draw the rectangle $ABCD$ (first figure, p. 88).

Divide AH and AC into the same number of equal parts.

Starting from A, let the successive points of division be

on AH: a, b, c;
on AC: l, m, n.

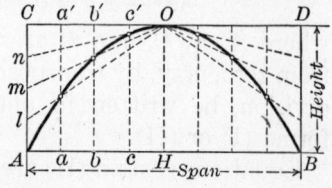

Now draw the perpendicular aa' to AB, and draw Ol. Mark the point of intersection. Do likewise for the points b and m, c and n. The points of intersection are points on the parabola required.

Proof. Take axes OX and OY, as in the figure. Let

(1) $\quad OM' = x, \quad M'P = y,$
$\quad AB = 2a, \quad OH = h.$

By construction, CN and MH are equal parts of CA and AH respectively.

(2) $\quad \therefore \dfrac{CN}{CA} = \dfrac{MH}{AH}, \quad \text{or} \quad \dfrac{CN}{h} = \dfrac{-x}{a}.$

From the similar $\triangle$ $OM'P$ and OCN,

(3) $\quad \dfrac{y}{x} = \dfrac{CN}{OC} = \dfrac{CN}{-a}.$

Substituting the value of CN from (2) into (3), and reducing,

(4) $\quad x^2 = \dfrac{a^2}{h} y.$

This is the typical form (II), and the locus passes through O, $A(-a, h)$, and $B(a, h)$, as required.

Solving (4) for y, we get

(5) $\quad y = \dfrac{h}{a^2} x^2.$

x	$\tfrac{1}{4}a$	$\tfrac{1}{2}a$	$\tfrac{3}{4}a$	a
y	$\tfrac{1}{16}h$	$\tfrac{1}{4}h$	$\tfrac{9}{16}h$	h

Hence y varies as the square of x. By (5), we may compute values of y, as in the table.

PARABOLA, ELLIPSE, AND HYPERBOLA

43. Plotting a parabola. To plot a parabola quickly from its typical equation, determine its axis and its position (above or below XX', to the right or left of YY') by *discussion* of the equation. Compute a few values of x and y and plot. Find $2p$ by comparison with (I) or (II), and plot the focus and directrix.

EXAMPLES

1. Plot the locus of $x^2 + 4y = 0$ and plot the focus and directrix.

Solution. The given equation may be written

$$x^2 = -4y.$$

The y-axis is an axis of symmetry; positive values of y must be excluded. Hence the parabola lies below the x-axis. The table gives a few points on the curve.

x	y
0	0
± 2	-1
± 4	-4

Comparing with (II), $p = -2$. The focus is therefore the point $(0, -1)$ and the directrix the line $y = 1$. The length of the latus rectum is 4. Every point on the locus is equidistant from $(0, -1)$ and the line $y = 1$.

2. Find the equation of the parabola whose focus is $(4, -2)$ and whose directrix is the line $x = 1$.

Solution. In the figure, by definition,

(1) $FP = MP.$

But $FP = \sqrt{(x-4)^2 + (y+2)^2},$
and $MP = x - 1.$

Substituting in (1) and reducing,

(2) $y^2 - 6x + 4y + 19 = 0.$ *Ans.*

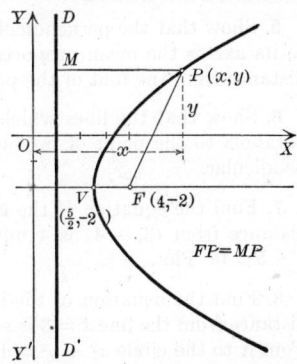

PROBLEMS

1. Plot the locus of each of the following equations and construct the focus and directrix. Also find the length of the latus rectum and draw it.

(a) $y^2 = 12\,x$.
(b) $x^2 = 10\,y$.
(c) $2\,y^2 = 9\,x$.
(d) $3\,y = 5\,x^2$.
(e) $7\,x + 4\,y^2 = 0$.
(f) $x^2 + 10\,y = 0$.

2. Using ruler and compasses, construct a parabola if its focus is

(a) 6 units from its directrix;
(b) 10 units from its directrix;
(c) 15 units from its directrix.

3. Find the equation of the parabola with

(a) vertex $(3, 4)$ and directrix the y-axis;

Ans. $y^2 - 8\,y - 12\,x + 52 = 0$.

(b) vertex $(4, 2)$ and focus $(2, 2)$;
(c) vertex $(0, 0)$, axis the y-axis, and passing through $(-4, 5)$;

Ans. $5\,x^2 = 16\,y$.

(d) directrix $y + 3 = 0$ and focus $(1, -7)$;
(e) directrix $x + 2\,y = 1$ and focus at the origin;

Ans. $4\,x^2 + y^2 - 4\,xy + 2\,x + 4\,y = 1$.

(f) axis $x - y = 0$, vertex $(0, 0)$, and latus rectum $= 4$ (two cases);
(g) vertex at the origin, axis the x-axis, and passing through the point (h, k).

4. Derive the equation of, and construct, a parabolic arch with

(a) span 20 ft. and height 10 ft.; (b) span 15 ft. and height 8 ft.

5. Show that the perpendicular let fall from any point of a parabola to its axis is the mean proportional between the latus rectum and the distance from the foot of the perpendicular to the vertex.

6. Show that the lines which join the ends of the latus rectum of a parabola to the point of intersection of its axis and directrix are perpendicular.

7. Find the equation of the locus of a point which moves so that its distance from $(3, -4)$ is 4 units less than its distance from the line $x + 5 = 0$. Plot. *Ans.* $y^2 + 8\,y - 8\,x + 24 = 0$.

8. Find the equation of the locus of a point which moves so that its distance from the line $x = 3$ is equal to the length of the tangent drawn from it to the circle $x^2 + y^2 = 16$.

PARABOLA, ELLIPSE, AND HYPERBOLA

44. The ellipse. Let us solve the following locus problem:

Given two fixed points F and F'. A point P moves so that the sum of its distances from F and F' remains constant. Determine the nature of the locus.

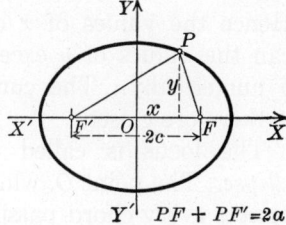
$PF + PF' = 2a$

Solution. Draw the x-axis through F and F', and take for origin the middle point of $F'F$. By definition,

(1) $\quad PF + PF' =$ a constant.

Let us denote this constant by $2a$. Then (1) becomes

(2) $\qquad PF + PF' = 2a$.

Let $F'F = 2c$. Then

$$PF = \sqrt{(x-c)^2 + y^2}, \quad PF' = \sqrt{(x+c)^2 + y^2},$$

since the coördinates of F are $(c, 0)$, and of F', $(-c, 0)$.

Hence (2) becomes

(3) $\qquad \sqrt{(x-c)^2 + y^2} + \sqrt{(x+c)^2 + y^2} = 2a$.

Transposing one of the radicals, squaring and reducing, the result is

(4) $\qquad (a^2 - c^2)x^2 + a^2y^2 = a^2(a^2 - c^2)$.

For added simplicity, set *

(5) $\qquad a^2 - c^2 = b^2$.

Then (4) becomes the simple equation

(6) $\qquad b^2x^2 + a^2y^2 = a^2b^2$.

Discussion. The intercepts are, on XX', $\pm a$; on YY', $\pm b$. The axes XX' and YY' are axes of symmetry and O is a center of symmetry.

---

* This is permissible. For $PF + PF' > F'F$, or $2a > 2c$; that is, $a > c$, and $a^2 - c^2$ is a *positive* number.

Solving (6) for x and for y,
$$x = \pm \frac{a}{b}\sqrt{b^2 - y^2}, \quad y = \pm \frac{b}{a}\sqrt{a^2 - x^2}.$$

Hence the values of x cannot exceed a numerically, nor can the values of y exceed b numerically. The curve is therefore closed.

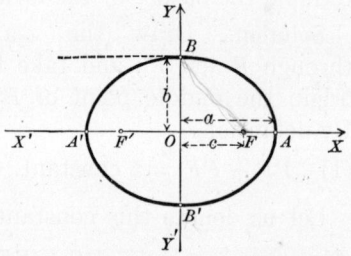

The locus is called an *ellipse*. The point O, which bisects every chord passing through it, is called the **center**. The given fixed points F and F' are called the **foci**. The longest chord AA' through O is called the **major axis**; the shortest chord BB', the **minor axis**. Obviously,

(7) $\qquad major\ axis = 2\,a, \quad minor\ axis = 2\,b.$

Dividing (6) through by a^2b^2, and summarizing, gives the

Theorem. *The equation of an ellipse whose center is the origin and whose foci are on the x-axis is*

(III) $\qquad \dfrac{x^2}{a^2} + \dfrac{y^2}{b^2} = 1,$

where $2\,a$ is the major axis and $2\,b$ the minor axis. If $c^2 = a^2 - b^2$, then the foci are $(\pm c, 0)$ (figure above).

If the foci are on the y-axis, and if we keep the above notation, the equation of the ellipse is

(8) $\qquad a^2x^2 + b^2y^2 = a^2b^2, \quad \text{or} \quad \dfrac{x^2}{b^2} + \dfrac{y^2}{a^2} = 1.$

Equations (6), (8), and (III) are *typical* equations of the ellipse, and are of the form

(9) $\qquad\qquad\qquad Ax^2 + By^2 = C,$

where A, B, and C **agree in sign**.

PARABOLA, ELLIPSE, AND HYPERBOLA

In the figure $\overline{BF}^2 = b^2 + c^2$. Substituting the value of c^2 from (5), then $\overline{BF}^2 = a^2$. Hence the property: *The distance from either focus to the end of the minor axis equals the semimajor axis.*

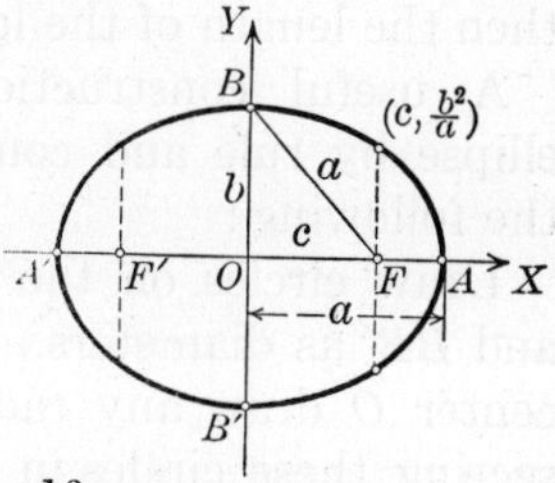

The chord drawn through either focus perpendicular to the major axis is called the **latus rectum**. Its length is determined by setting $x = c$ in (III), and solving for y. This gives

$$y = \frac{b}{a}\sqrt{a^2 - c^2} = \frac{b^2}{a}.$$ Hence

(10) $$\text{length of latus rectum} = \frac{2b^2}{a}.$$

Eccentricity. When the foci are very near together the ellipse differs but little from a circle. The value of the ratio $OF : OA$ may, in fact, be said to determine the divergence of the ellipse from a circle. The value of this ratio is called the *eccentricity* of the ellipse, and is denoted by e. Hence

(11) $$e = \frac{OF}{OA} = \frac{c}{a}.$$

The value of e varies from 0 to 1. If the major axis AA' remains of fixed length, then the "flatness" of the ellipse increases as e increases from 0 to 1, the limiting forms being a circle of diameter AA' and the line segment AA'.

From (11) and (5),

(12) $$b^2 = a^2 - c^2 = a^2(1 - e^2).$$

45. Construction of the ellipse. The definition (2) of the preceding article affords a simple method of drawing an ellipse.

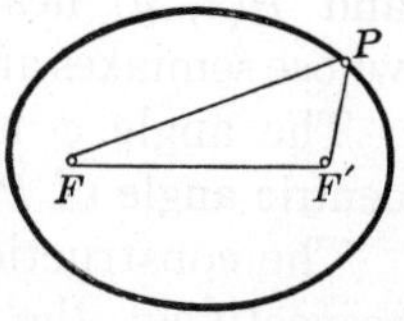

Place two tacks in the drawing board at the foci F and F' and wind a string about them as indicated. If a pencil is placed in the loop FPF' and is moved so as to keep the string taut, then $PF + PF'$ is constant and P describes an ellipse. If the major axis is to be $2\,a$, then the length of the loop FPF' must be $2\,a + 2\,c$.

A useful construction of an ellipse by rule and compasses is the following:

Draw circles on the axes AA' and BB' as diameters. From the center O draw any radius intersecting these circles in M and N respectively. From M draw a line MR parallel to the minor axis,

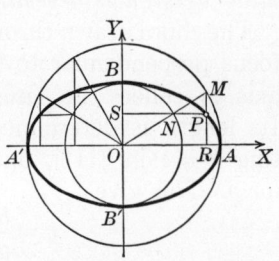

and from N a line NS parallel to the major axis. These lines will intersect in a point P on the ellipse.

Proof. Take the coördinate axes as in the figure below. Let $OA = x$, $AP = y = OD$, $\angle BOX = \phi$.

Clearly,

OB = semimajor axis = a, OC = semiminor axis = b.

Then in the right $\triangle OAB$,

(1) $$\cos \phi = \frac{OA}{OB} = \frac{x}{a}.$$

Similarly, in the right $\triangle ODC$, $\angle OCD = \angle COA = \phi$, and

(2) $$\sin \phi = \frac{OD}{OC} = \frac{y}{b}.$$

But $\cos^2 \phi + \sin^2 \phi = 1$. Hence, from (1) and (2),

$$\frac{x^2}{a^2} + \frac{y^2}{b^2} = 1,$$

and $P(x, y)$ lies on the ellipse whose semiaxes are a and b. Q.E.D.

The angle ϕ is called the **eccentric angle** of P.

The construction circles used in this problem are called, respectively, the major and minor **auxiliary circles**.

PARABOLA, ELLIPSE, AND HYPERBOLA

46. Plotting an ellipse. To draw an ellipse quickly when its equation is in the typical form, proceed thus:

1. Find the intercepts, mark them off on the coördinate axes, and set the larger one equal to a, the smaller equal to b. Letter the major axis AA' and the minor axis BB'.

2. Find c from $c^2 = a^2 - b^2$. Mark the foci F and F' on the major axis.

3. Calculate directly one or more sets of values of the coördinates, and sketch in the curve.

EXAMPLE

Draw the ellipse $4x^2 + y^2 = 16$.

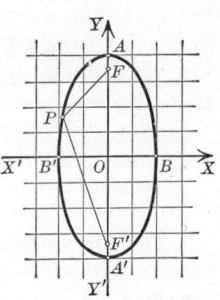

Solution. The intercepts are, on XX', ± 2; on YY', ± 4. Hence the major axis falls on YY', and $a = 4, b = 2, c = \sqrt{12} = 2\sqrt{3} = 3.5$. The foci are on the y-axis. The length of the latus rectum equals $\dfrac{2 b^2}{a} = 2$. The eccentricity $e = \dfrac{c}{a} = \tfrac{1}{2}\sqrt{3}$. The points found in the table are the ends of the latus rectum. If P is any point on the ellipse, then $PF + PF' = 2a = 8$.

x	y
± 1	± 3.5

47. Special cases. Equations (6) and (8) of Art. 44 are simple equations of the second degree. We may ask the question,

What is the test that determines whether the locus of a given equation of the second degree is an ellipse?

We reserve for a later article the answer to this question. (See Art. 63.)

At this point two special cases of the equation

$$Ax^2 + By^2 = C,$$

in which A and B have like signs, should be noted.

1. $C = 0$. Then the locus is a **point ellipse** (both axes zero).

2. *C not zero and differing in sign from A and B.* The equation now has no locus. This is sometimes expressed by the words "imaginary ellipse."

NEW ANALYTIC GEOMETRY

PROBLEMS

1. Plot, locate the foci, and find the eccentricity and the length of the latus rectum:

(a) $x^2 + 4y^2 = 16$.
(b) $4x^2 + 9y^2 = 36$.
(c) $x^2 + 2y^2 = 8$.
(d) $2x^2 = 1 - y^2$.
(e) $25y^2 + x^2 = 25$.
(f) $3x^2 + 5y^2 = 30$.
(g) $8x^2 + 3y^2 = 63$.
(h) $9x^2 + 49y^2 = 250$.

2. Write the equation of the ellipse with its center at the origin, using the data given:

(a) $a = 8$, $b = 4$, foci on the y-axis.
(b) $a = 10$, $c = 6$, foci on the x-axis.
(c) $a = 6$, latus rectum = 3, foci on the x-axis.
(d) $b = 5$, latus rectum = 7, foci on the y-axis.
(e) $a = 5b$ and passing through $(7, 2)$.

3. Write the equation of the ellipse with its center at the origin and axes along the coördinate axes and

(a) passing through $(-3, 0)$ and $(0, -2)$;
(b) passing through $(2, 3)$ and $(-1, 4)$;   *Ans.* $7x^2 + 3y^2 = 55$.
(c) passing through $(5, 1)$ and $(-4, -2)$;
(d) with the major axis 3 times the minor and passing through $(6, 2)$.

4. Find the equation of the locus of a point which bisects the abscissas of the points of the circle $x^2 + y^2 = 16$.

5. Find the equation of the locus of a point which divides the ordinates of points of the circle $x^2 + y^2 = 25$ in the ratio $2 : 3$.

6. Find the locus of a point which moves so that

(a) its distance from the line $x = 8$ is twice its distance from the point $(2, 0)$;   *Ans.* $3x^2 + 4y^2 = 48$.
(b) its distance from the line $y = 6$ is twice its distance from the point $(0, 3)$;
(c) its distance from the line $x = -18$ is 3 times its distance from $(-2, 0)$;   *Ans.* $8x^2 + 9y^2 = 288$.
(d) its distance from the line $2y = -15$ is $1\frac{1}{2}$ times its distance from $(0, -3\frac{1}{3})$.

7. Find the locus of the vertex of a triangle with $(0, 6)$ and $(0, -6)$ as the ends of one side if the product of the slopes of the other two sides is $-\frac{4}{9}$.

8. Show that the latus rectum of an ellipse is the third proportional to the two axes.

9. A line of fixed length moves so that its ends remain on two perpendicular lines. Find the locus of any point of the line.

PARABOLA, ELLIPSE, AND HYPERBOLA 97

48. The hyperbola. Turn now to a third locus problem.

Given two fixed points F and F'. A point P moves so that the **difference** between its distances from F and F' remains constant. Determine the nature of the locus.

Solution. Draw the x-axis through the fixed points, and take for origin the mid-point of $F'F$. By definition,

(1) $\quad PF' - PF = $ a constant.

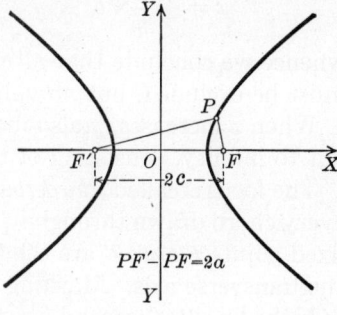

Let us denote this constant by $2\,a$. Then (1) becomes

(2) $\quad PF' - PF = 2\,a$.

Let $F'F = 2\,c$. Then
$$PF = \sqrt{(x-c)^2 + y^2},$$
$$PF' = \sqrt{(x+c)^2 + y^2},$$

since the coördinates of F are $(c, 0)$, and of F' are $(-c, 0)$.

Substituting in (2),

(3) $\quad \sqrt{(x+c)^2 + y^2} - \sqrt{(x-c)^2 + y^2} = 2\,a$.

Transposing either radical, squaring and reducing, we obtain the result

(4) $\quad (a^2 - c^2)x^2 + a^2y^2 = a^2(a^2 - c^2)$.

For added simplicity,* set

(5) $\quad a^2 - c^2 = -b^2$,

or $\quad c^2 - a^2 = b^2$.

Then (4) becomes the simple equation

(6) $\quad b^2x^2 - a^2y^2 = a^2b^2$.

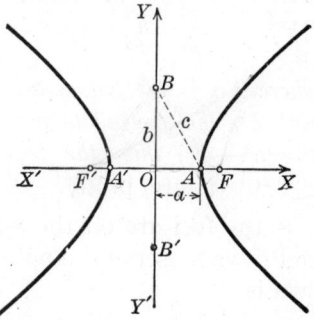

Discussion. The intercepts are, on XX', $\pm a$; on YY', $\pm b\sqrt{-1}$; that is, the locus

---

* This is permissible. For in the figure, $PF' - PF < F'F$, or $2\,a < 2\,c$; that is, $a < c$, and $a^2 - c^2$ is a *negative* number.

does not cross the y-axis. The coefficient of the $\sqrt{-1}$ in the imaginary intercept on the y-axis is, however, b. The axes XX' and YY' are axes of symmetry and O is a center of symmetry.

Solving (6) for x and for y,
$$x = \pm \frac{a}{b}\sqrt{b^2 + y^2}, \quad y = \pm \frac{b}{a}\sqrt{x^2 - a^2},$$

whence we conclude that all values of x between $-a$ and a must be excluded, but no values of y.

When x increases, y also increases, and the curve extends out to infinity, consisting of two distinct **branches**.*

The locus is called a *hyperbola*. The point O, which bisects every chord drawn through it, is called the **center**. The given fixed points F and F' are the **foci**. The chord AA' is named the **transverse axis**. Marking off on YY' from O the lengths $\pm b$, the line BB' (second figure, p. 97) is called the **conjugate axis**. Thus the

(7) $\quad$ *transverse axis* $= 2\,a, \quad$ *conjugate axis* $= 2\,b.$

Dividing (6) through by a^2b^2, and summarizing, gives the

Theorem. *The equation of a hyperbola whose center is the origin and whose foci are on the x-axis is*

(IV) $\quad \dfrac{x^2}{a^2} - \dfrac{y^2}{b^2} = 1,$

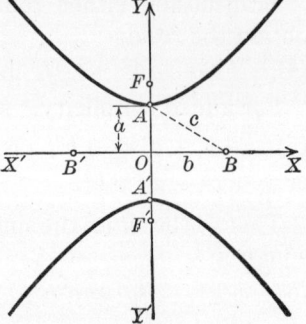

where $2\,a$ is the transverse axis and $2\,b$ the conjugate axis. If $c^2 = a^2 + b^2$, then the foci are $(\pm c, 0)$ (figure, p. 97).

If the foci are on the y-axis, and if we preserve the notation, the equation of the hyperbola is

(8) $\quad a^2x^2 - b^2y^2 = -a^2b^2, \quad$ or $\quad \dfrac{x^2}{b^2} - \dfrac{y^2}{a^2} = -1.$

---

* On the left-hand branch, (2) is replaced by $PF - PF' = 2\,a$.

PARABOLA, ELLIPSE, AND HYPERBOLA

Equations (6) and (8) are typical equations of the hyperbola. They are of the form

(9) $$Ax^2 + By^2 = C,$$

where *A and B differ in sign*.

In the preceding figures $\overline{AB}^2 = a^2 + b^2$. Substituting the value of b^2 from (5), $\overline{AB}^2 = c^2$. Hence the property: *The distance between the extremities of the axes equals half the distance between the foci.*

The chord drawn through a focus and perpendicular to the transverse axis is called the **latus rectum**. We may determine its length by setting $x = c$ in (IV) and solving for y. Thus, by (5) we obtain

$$y = \pm \frac{b}{a} \sqrt{c^2 - a^2} = \pm \frac{b^2}{a}.$$

Hence

(10) $$\text{length of latus rectum} = \frac{2\,b^2}{a}.$$

Eccentricity. The value of the ratio $OF : OA$ in the hyperbola is called the *eccentricity* of the curve, as in the case of the ellipse. Denoting the eccentricity by e, then

(11) $$e = \frac{OF}{OA} = \frac{c}{a}.$$

For a hyperbola, $e > 1$. The relation of the value of e to the shape of the curve will be made clear later. From (5) and (11),

(12) $$b^2 = c^2 - a^2 = a^2(e^2 - 1).$$

49. Construction of the hyperbola. A mechanical construction, depending upon the definition (1) of Art. 48, is the following:

Fasten thumb tacks at the foci. Pass *over F′* and *around F* a string whose ends are held together (figure, p. 100).

If a pencil is tied to the string at P, and both strings are pulled in or let out the same length, then $PF' - PF$ will be constant and P will describe a hyperbola. If the transverse axis is to be $2\,a$, the strings must be adjusted at the start so that the difference between PF' and PF equals $2\,a$.

50. Plotting a hyperbola. To draw a hyperbola quickly when its equation is in the typical form (9), proceed thus:

1. Find the intercepts and mark them off on the proper axis. Set a equal to the real intercept and b equal to the coefficient of $\sqrt{-1}$ in the imaginary intercept. Lay off the conjugate axis; letter it BB' and the transverse axis AA'.

2. Find c from $c^2 = a^2 + b^2$. Mark the foci F and F' on the transverse axis.

3. Calculate directly one or more sets of values of the coördinates, and sketch the curve.

EXAMPLE

Draw the hyperbola

$$4\,x^2 - 5\,y^2 + 20 = 0.$$

Solution. The intercepts are, on XX', $\pm\sqrt{-5} = \pm\sqrt{5}\sqrt{-1}$; on YY', ± 2. Hence $b = \sqrt{5}$, $a = 2$, $c = \sqrt{a^2 + b^2} = 3$, and the transverse axis and the foci are on YY'. The eccentricity is $\frac{3}{2}$. The length of the latus rectum is $\dfrac{2\,b^2}{a} = 5$. If P is any point

x	y
0	± 2
$\pm \frac{5}{2}$	± 3

on the hyperbola, then, by the definition of Art. 48, $PF' - PF = 4$.

PARABOLA, ELLIPSE, AND HYPERBOLA

PROBLEMS

1. Plot the following equations and locate the foci. Find the eccentricity and the length of the latus rectum and draw the latus rectum.

(a) $16\,x^2 - 9\,y^2 = 144$.
(b) $5\,x^2 - 4\,y^2 = 20$.
(c) $9\,x^2 - 16\,y^2 = 144$.
(d) $x^2 - 8\,y^2 + 8 = 0$.
(e) $x^2 - y^2 = 4$.
(f) $9\,x^2 - y^2 + 9 = 0$.
(g) $9\,x^2 - 16\,y^2 + 144 = 0$.
(h) $3\,x^2 - y^2 = 12$.
(i) $x^2 - 3\,y^2 + 3 = 0$.
(j) $4\,x^2 - 9\,y^2 = 36$.
(k) $9\,x^2 - 7\,y^2 = 36$.
(l) $7\,x^2 - 2\,y^2 + 8 = 0$.

2. Find the equations of the following hyperbolas with centers at $(0,0)$:

(a) $a = 4$, $b = 5$, foci on the y-axis.
(b) $b = 5$, $c = 8$, foci on the x-axis.
(c) $a = 6$, $e = 2$, transverse axis along the x-axis.
(d) $a = \sqrt{6}$, $c = 6$, conjugate axis along the x-axis.
(e) $a = 7$, latus rectum $= 14$, conjugate axis along the y-axis.
(f) $c = \sqrt{15}$, latus rectum $= 4$, foci on the y-axis.

3. Find the equations of the following hyperbolas with centers at the origin and axes along the coördinate axes:

(a) Transverse axis along the y-axis and passes through $(2, -4)$ and $(6, -7)$.

(b) Transverse axis along the y-axis and passes through $(0, 4)$ and $(6, 5)$.

(c) Transverse axis along the x-axis and passes through $(6, 7)$ and $(-3, 3)$.

(d) Foci on the x-axis and passes through $(2, 0)$ and $(\sqrt{11}, -3)$.
Ans. $9\,x^2 - 7\,y^2 = 36$.

4. Find the equation of the locus of a point which moves so that

(a) its distance from the point $(3, 0)$ is twice its distance from the line $4\,x - 3 = 0$; *Ans.* $12\,x^2 - 4\,y^2 = 27$.

(b) its distance from the point $(0, 4)$ is $\tfrac{3}{2}$ of its distance from the line $9\,y - 16 = 0$;

(c) its distance from the point $(0, -2)$ is 3 times its distance from the line $9\,y + 2 = 0$;

(d) its distance from the point $(-5, 0)$ is 4 times its distance from the line $16\,x + 5 = 0$.

5. If two vertices of a triangle are fixed at $(0, 5)$ and $(0, -5)$, find the locus of the third vertex if the product of the slopes of the variable sides is 7. *Ans.* $7\,x^2 - y^2 + 25 = 0$.

6. Find the equation of the hyperbola with center at the origin and foci on the y-axis if the transverse axis is 10 and the conjugate axis is one half of the distance between the foci.

51. Conjugate hyperbolas and asymptotes.

Two hyperbolas are called **conjugate hyperbolas** if the transverse and conjugate axes of one are, respectively, the conjugate and transverse axes of the other.

If the equation of a hyperbola is given in typical form, then *the equation of the conjugate hyperbola is found by changing the signs of the coefficients of x^2 and y^2 in the given equation.*

Thus the loci of the equations

(1) $\quad 16\,x^2 - y^2 = 16 \quad$ and $\quad -16\,x^2 + y^2 = 16$

are conjugate hyperbolas. They may be written

$$\frac{x^2}{1} - \frac{y^2}{16} = 1 \quad \text{and} \quad -\frac{x^2}{1} + \frac{y^2}{16} = 1.$$

The foci of the first are on the x-axis, those of the second on the y-axis. The transverse axis of the first and the conjugate axis of the second are both equal to 2, while the conjugate axis of the first and the transverse axis of the second are both equal to 8.

The foci of two conjugate hyperbolas are equally distant from the origin. For c^2 equals the sum of the squares of the semitransverse and semiconjugate axes, and that sum is the same for two conjugate hyperbolas.

Thus in the first of the hyperbolas above, $c^2 = 1 + 16$, while in the second $c^2 = 16 + 1$.

If in one of the typical forms of the equation of a hyperbola we replace the constant term by zero, then the locus of the new equation is a pair of lines (Theorem, Art. 24), which are called the **asymptotes** of the hyperbola.

Thus the asymptotes of the hyperbola

(2) $\qquad\qquad b^2x^2 - a^2y^2 = a^2b^2$

are the lines

(3) $\qquad\qquad b^2x^2 - a^2y^2 = 0$, or

(4) $\qquad bx + ay = 0 \quad$ and $\quad bx - ay = 0.$

PARABOLA, ELLIPSE, AND HYPERBOLA

These may be written

(5) $$y = -\frac{b}{a}x \quad \text{and} \quad y = \frac{b}{a}x.$$

They pass through the origin and their slopes are, respectively, $-\frac{b}{a}$ and $\frac{b}{a}$.

The property of these lines which they have in common with the vertical or horizontal asymptotes of Art. 20 is expressed in the

Theorem. *The branches of the hyperbola approach indefinitely near its asymptotes as the tracing point recedes to infinity.*

Proof. Let $P_1(x_1, y_1)$ be a point on either branch of (2) near the asymptote $bx - ay = 0.$

The perpendicular distance from this line to P_1 is

(6) $$d = \frac{bx_1 - ay_1}{-\sqrt{b^2 + a^2}}.$$

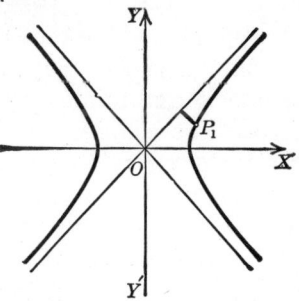

We may find a value for the numerator as follows:

Since P_1 lies on (2),

$$b^2 x_1^2 - a^2 y_1^2 = a^2 b^2.$$

Factoring and dividing,

$$bx_1 - ay_1 = \frac{a^2 b^2}{bx_1 + ay_1}.$$

Substituting in (6),

$$d = \frac{a^2 b^2}{-\sqrt{b^2 + a^2}(bx_1 + ay_1)}.$$

As P_1 recedes to infinity in the first quadrant, x_1 and y_1 become infinite and d approaches zero.

Hence the curve approaches closer and closer to its asymptotes. Q.E.D.

Two conjugate hyperbolas have the same asymptotes.

Thus the asymptotes of the conjugate hyperbolas (1) are, respectively, the loci of $16x^2 - y^2 = 0$ and $-16x^2 + y^2 = 0$, which are the same.

A hyperbola may be drawn with fair accuracy by the following construction:

Lay off $OA = OA' = a$ on the axis on which the foci lie, and $OB = OB' = b$ on the other axis. Draw lines through A, A', B, B', parallel to the axes, forming a rectangle. Draw the diagonals of the rectangle. The diagonals produced are the asymptotes. For the equations of the diagonals are readily seen to be $bx - ay = 0$ and

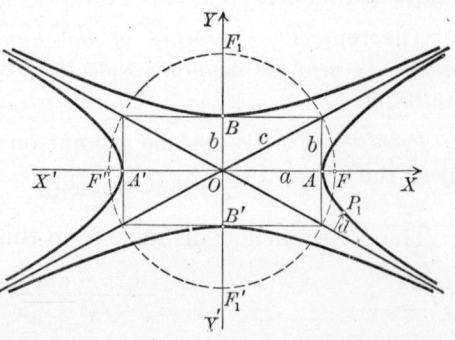

$bx + ay = 0$, and these are the same as (4). Draw the branches of the hyperbola tangent to the sides of the rectangle at A and A' and approaching nearer and nearer to the diagonals. The conjugate hyperbola is tangent to the sides of the rectangle at B and B' and approaches the diagonals. The length of each diagonal is $2c$ (since $a^2 + b^2 = c^2$). The foci of both hyperbolas are on the circle which circumscribes the rectangle.

From this construction the influence of the value of the eccentricity upon the shape of the hyperbola can easily be discussed. In the figure, let AA' be fixed. Now, from (12), Art. 48,
$$b^2 = a^2(e^2 - 1).$$

When e diminishes toward unity, b decreases, the altitude BB' of the rectangle diminishes, the asymptotes turn toward the x-axis, and the hyperbola flattens.

PARABOLA, ELLIPSE, AND HYPERBOLA

When e increases, the asymptotes turn from the x-axis, and the hyperbola broadens.

52. Equilateral or rectangular hyperbola. When the axes of a hyperbola are equal ($a = b$), the hyperbola is said to be *equilateral*. If we set $a = b$ in equation (IV), we obtain

(1) $\qquad x^2 - y^2 = a^2,$

which is accordingly the equation of an equilateral hyperbola whose transverse axis lies on XX'.

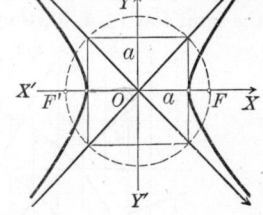

Its asymptotes are the lines

$$x - y = 0 \quad \text{and} \quad x + y = 0.$$

These lines are perpendicular, whence the designation "rectangular" hyperbola. (See also Art. 65.)

53. Summary. Reserving for a later section (Art. 63) the problem of finding a test for a hyperbola, we may at this point summarize results as follows:

The locus of the equation $Ax^2 + By^2 = C$ is

(1) an *ellipse* when A, B, and C have like signs;

(2) a *point ellipse* when A and B have like signs and $C = 0$;

(3) a *hyperbola* when A and B have unlike signs and C is not zero;

(4) a *pair of intersecting lines* when A and B have unlike signs and $C = 0$.

There is *no locus* when C is not zero and differs in sign from both A and B.

54. Conic sections. Historically, the parabola, ellipse, and hyperbola were discovered as plane sections of a right circular cone. Hence the generic term used for them, — *conic sections*, or **conics**. We discuss this subject in Art. 155.

55. Systems of conics. When the equation of a conic contains one or more arbitrary constants, the locus is a *system of conics*.

EXAMPLE

Discuss the system represented by $\dfrac{x^2}{25-k} + \dfrac{y^2}{9-k} = 1$.

Solution. When $k < 9$ the locus is an ellipse whose foci are $(\pm c, 0)$, where $c^2 = (25 - k) - (9 - k) = 16$. When $9 < k < 25$ the locus is a hyperbola whose foci are $(\pm c, 0)$, where $c^2 = (25 - k) - (9 - k) = 16$. When $k > 25$ there is no locus. Since the ellipses and hyperbolas have the same foci $(\pm 4, 0)$, they are called **confocal**.

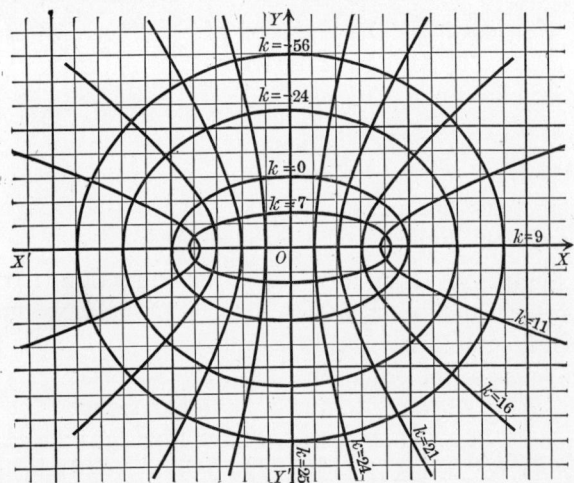

In the figure the locus is plotted for $k = -56, -24, 0, 7, 9, 11, 16, 21, 24, 25$. As k increases and approaches 9, the ellipses flatten out and finally degenerate into the x-axis, and as k decreases and approaches 9, the hyperbolas flatten out and degenerate into the x-axis. As k increases and approaches 25, the two branches of the hyperbolas lie closer to the y-axis, and in the limit they coincide with the y-axis.

PROBLEMS

1. Find the equations of the conjugate hyperbola and the asymptotes, and plot:

(a) $4x^2 - y^2 = 16$.
(b) $9x^2 - 4y^2 = 36$.
(c) $9x^2 - 16y^2 = 144$.
(d) $16y^2 - x^2 + 64 = 0$.
(e) $25x^2 - 16y^2 + 400 = 0$.
(f) $x^2 - y^2 = 10$.
(g) $x^2 - 16y^2 + 16 = 0$.
(h) $x^2 - 9y^2 + 9 = 0$.

PARABOLA, ELLIPSE, AND HYPERBOLA

2. Show that the perpendicular distance from an asymptote of a hyperbola to either focus is numerically equal to the semiconjugate axis.

3. Show that the product of the perpendicular distances from the asymptotes to any point of a hyperbola is constant.

4. Show that the point of intersection of the lines $bx + ay = k$ and $bx - ay = \dfrac{l}{k}$ is on a hyperbola for all values of k.

5. Show that the product of the distances from a point of an equilateral hyperbola to its foci is equal to the square of the distance of the point from the center of the hyperbola.

6. Find the equation of the hyperbola with transverse axis on the y-axis which has $3y - 2x = 0$ for one asymptote and one focus at $(0, -4)$. *Ans.* $117 y^2 - 52 x^2 = 576$.

7. Show that the eccentricity of an equilateral hyperbola is $\sqrt{2}$.

8. Show that the segments on any line intercepted between a hyperbola and its asymptotes are equal.

9. Plot the conics of the following systems for the given values of k:

(a) $9x^2 + y^2 = k$; $k = 0, 4, 9, 25$.
(b) $9x^2 - 4y^2 = k$; $k = 0, \pm 4, \pm 9, \pm 36$.
(c) $x^2 = 4y - k$; $k = 0, \pm 4, \pm 8$.
(d) $ky^2 - 16 kx^2 = 64$; $k = \pm 1, \pm 2, \pm 4$.
(e) $y^2 = 2 kx$; $k = \pm 1, \pm 4$.

10. Plot the following systems of conics and show that those of each system are confocal:

(a) $\dfrac{x^2}{4-k} + \dfrac{y^2}{9-k} = 1$; $k = \pm 1, \pm 2, \pm 10, \pm 20$.
(b) $y^2 = 2 kx + k^2$; $k = \pm 1, \pm 4, \pm 6$.
(c) $\dfrac{x^2}{16-k} + \dfrac{y^2}{64-k} = 1$; $k = 0, \pm 9, \pm 20, \pm 50$.

11. Derive an equation for all ellipses with foci $(0, \pm 3)$.

12. What change will be necessary to make the result of Problem 11 represent all hyperbolas with the same foci?

13. Find the relation connecting the eccentricities e_1 and e_2 of two conjugate hyperbolas. *Ans.* $e_1^2 + e_2^2 = e_1^2 e_2^2$.

CHAPTER VII

TRANSFORMATION OF COÖRDINATES

56. When we are at liberty to choose the axes as we please we generally take them so that our results shall have the simplest possible form. When the axes are given, it is useful to find the equation of a given curve referred to other axes. The operation of changing from one pair of axes to a second pair is known as a **transformation of coördinates**. We regard the axes as moved from their given position to a new position and we seek formulas which express the old coördinates in terms of the new coördinates.

57. Translation. If the axes are moved from a first position OX and OY to a second position $O'X'$ and $O'Y'$ such that $O'X'$ and $O'Y'$ are respectively parallel to OX and OY, then they are said to be **translated** from the first to the second position.

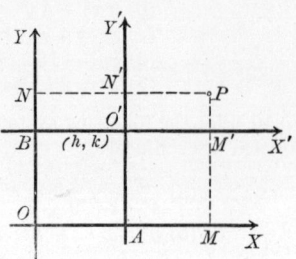

Theorem. *If the axes are translated to a new origin (h, k), and if (x, y) and (x', y') are, respectively, the coördinates of any point P before and after the translation, then*

(I)
$$\begin{cases} x = x' + h, \\ y = y' + k. \end{cases}$$

Proof. In the figure,

$$OM = x. \quad OA = h. \quad O'M' = x'.$$
$$MP = y, \quad AO' = k, \quad M'P = y'.$$

TRANSFORMATION OF COÖRDINATES

But $\quad OM = OA + AM = OA + O'M';$

$\quad\quad MP = MM' + M'P = AO' + M'P.$

Substituting, we have (I). Q.E.D

Equations (I) are called the **equations for translating the axes**. To find the equation of a curve referred to the new axes when its equation referred to the old axes is given, substitute in the given equation the values of x and y given by (I) and reduce.

EXAMPLE

Transform the equation

$$x^2 + y^2 - 6x + 4y - 12 = 0$$

when the axes are translated to the new origin $(3, -2)$.

Solution. Here $h = 3$ and $k = -2$; so equations (I) become

$\quad x = x' + 3, \quad y = y' - 2.$

Substituting in the given equation, we obtain

$\quad (x'+3)^2 + (y'-2)^2 - 6(x'+3)$
$\quad\quad + 4(y'-2) - 12 = 0,$

or, reducing,

$\quad x'^2 + y'^2 = 25. \ Ans.$

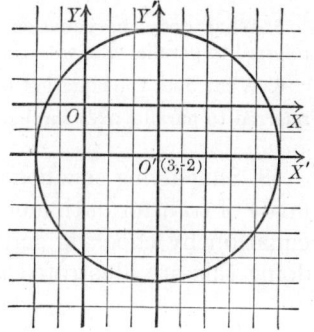

This result could easily be foreseen. For the locus of the given equation is a circle whose center is $(3, -2)$ and whose radius is 5. When the origin is translated to the center the equation of the circle must necessarily have the form obtained.

PROBLEMS

1. Find the new coördinates of the points $(3, -5)$, $(-4, 3)$, and $(-2, -5)$ if the axes are translated to the new origin

(a) $(3, 6)$; (b) $(-5, 3)$; (c) $(-6, -7)$; (d) $(4, -3)$.

2. Find the new coördinates of the points $(3, 0)$, $(0, 0)$, $(0, 3)$ if the axes are translated to the new origin

(a) $(2, -1)$; (b) (a, b); (c) $(-a, b)$; (d) $(a, -b)$.

3. Find the equations of each of the following curves if the axes are translated to the new origin indicated. Plot the curves and draw the old and the new axes.

(a) $3x - 4y = 6$; $(2, 0)$.   *Ans.* $3x' - 4y' = 0$.
(b) $5x - y + 2 = 0$; $(3, -2)$.
(c) $x^2 + y^2 - 4x - 2y = 0$; $(2, 1)$.   *Ans.* $x'^2 + y'^2 = 5$.
(d) $x^2 + y^2 - 6x + 4y + 12 = 0$; $(3, 5)$.
(e) $y^2 - 4x + 8 = 0$; $(2, 0)$.   *Ans.* $y'^2 = 4x'$.
(f) $x^2 + y^2 - 4x - 6y = 18$; $(-2, 3)$.
(g) $y^2 - 2x^2 - 2y + 6x = 3$; $(\frac{3}{2}, 1)$.
(h) $x^2 - 2hx - 4y + 4k + h^2 = 0$; (h, k).
(i) $y = 4 + (x-3)^3$; $(3, 4)$.
(j) $y^2 - 6x + 9 = 0$; $(\frac{3}{2}, 0)$.   *Ans.* $y'^2 = 6x'$.
(k) $x^2 - 4y^2 + 8x + 24y = 20$; $(-4, 3)$.
(l) $y^2 = x^3$; $(-2, -3)$.

4. Prove equations (I) if the new origin is in (1) the second quadrant; (2) the third quadrant; (3) the fourth quadrant.

5. What does the equation $(x - h)^2 + (y - k)^2 = r^2$ become when referred to parallel axes with the origin at (1) $(h - r, k)$? (2) $(h, k - r)$?

6. What does the equation $(m - n)(x^2 + y^2) - 2mny = 0$ become if referred to parallel axes through the point $\left(0, \dfrac{mn}{m-n}\right)$?

58. Simplifying equations by translation.
The principal use made of transformation of coördinates is to simplify a given equation by choosing suitable new axes. The methods of doing this are illustrated in the following examples.

EXAMPLES

1. Simplify the equation $y^2 - 8x + 6y + 17 = 0$ by translating the axes.

Solution. Rewrite the given equation, collecting the terms in y in the left-hand member.

(1) $$(y^2 + 6y) = 8x - 17.$$

Complete the square in the left-hand member, adding 9 to both members.
$$(y^2 + 6y + 9) = 8x - 17 + 9 = 8x - 8.$$

If we write this equation in the form

(2) $$(y + 3)^2 = 8(x - 1),$$

it is obvious by inspection that if we substitute in this equation

$$x - 1 = x', \quad y + 3 = y', \text{ or}$$
(3) $\quad x = x' + 1, \quad y = y' - 3,$

the transformed equation is

$$y'^2 = 8x'. \quad Ans.$$

Equations (3) translate the axes to the new origin $(1, -3)$ since, comparing (3) and (I), we have $h = 1$, $k = -3$.

Plotting $y'^2 = 8x'$ on the new axes $O'X'$, $O'Y'$, we see that the locus is a parabola with focus $x' = 2$, $y' = 0$, and directrix $x' = -2$. Hence, by (3), the locus of (2) is a parabola with focus $x = 3$, $y = -3$, and directrix $x = -1$.

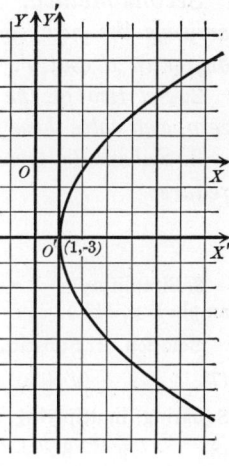

2. Simplify $x^2 + 4y^2 - 2x - 16y + 1 = 0$ by translating the axes.

Solution. Collect the terms in x and y in the left-hand member. Complete the squares within the parentheses, adding the corresponding numbers to the right-hand member.

(4) $\quad (x^2 - 2x + 1) + 4(y^2 - 4y + 4) = -1 + 1 + 16 = 16.$

If we write this in the form

(5) $\quad (x-1)^2 + 4(y-2)^2 = 16,$

it is obvious by inspection that by substituting

$$x - 1 = x', \quad y - 2 = y', \text{ or}$$
(6) $\quad x = x' + 1, \quad y = y' + 2,$

we obtain the simple equation

$$x'^2 + 4y'^2 = 16. \quad Ans.$$

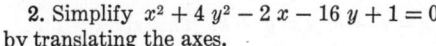

Equations (6) translate the axes to the new origin $(1, 2)$.

Plotting $x'^2 + 4y'^2 = 16$ on the new axes, we see that the locus is an ellipse with center $x' = y' = 0$, $a = 4$, $b = 2$, and foci on the x'-axis. Hence (5) is an ellipse with center $x = 1$, $y = 2$ and with axes of symmetry $x = 1$, $y = 2$; etc.

The method used may be summed up as the

First method. *Complete the squares of the terms in* x *and in* y, *factor, and choose the transformation indicated by the result.*

A more general method may be described as the

Second method. 1. *Substitute $x = x' + h$, $y = y' + k$, and arrange the new equation according to terms of descending degree in x' and y'.*

2. *Set two of the coefficients containing h or k equal to zero, and solve these for h and k.*

3. *Substitute these values in the equation in x', y', and reduce.*

EXAMPLES

3. Simplify $y^2 - 8x + 6y + 17 = 0$ by translation. (Compare Example 1, p. 111.)

Solution. 1. Substitute $x = x' + h$, $y = y' + k$. This gives

(7) $\quad (y' + k)^2 - 8(x' + h) + 6(y' + k) + 17 = 0.$

Squaring, multiplying, and arranging according to x' and y', we get

(8) $\quad y'^2 - 8x' + (2k + 6)y' + k^2 - 8h + 6k + 17 = 0.$

2. Set $\quad 2k + 6 = 0, \quad k^2 - 8h + 6k + 17 = 0.$

Solving these, $k = -3$, $h = 1$.

3. Substituting these values in (8), we obtain

$$y'^2 - 8x' = 0. \ Ans.$$

Hence the given equation reduces to $y'^2 - 8x' = 0$ by the translation $x = x' + 1$, $y = y' - 3$, the same result as was obtained by the other method.

4. Simplify $3xy - 2x - 4y - 3 = 0$ by translation.

Solution. 1. Following the directions, we obtain

(9) $\quad 3(x' + h)(y' + k) - 2(x' + h) - 4(y' + k) - 3 = 0.$

(10) $\quad 3x'y' + (3k - 2)x' + (3h - 4)y' + 3hk - 2h - 4k - 3 = 0.$

2. Set the coefficients of x' and y' equal to zero. This gives

$$3k - 2 = 0, \quad 3h - 4 = 0;$$

whence $h = \frac{4}{3}$, $k = \frac{2}{3}$.

3. Substitute these values in (10), and the result is

(11) $\quad\quad\quad 3x'y' - \frac{17}{3} = 0. \ Ans.$

The given equation reduces to (11) by the translation $x = x' + \frac{4}{3}$, $y = y' + \frac{2}{3}$.

TRANSFORMATION OF COÖRDINATES

In (11), $x' = 0$ and $y' = 0$ are asymptotes. Hence for the given curve, $x = \frac{4}{3}$ and $y = \frac{2}{3}$ are asymptotes. This example is significant, since it cannot be done by completing squares.

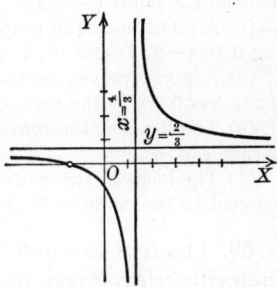

What coefficients in the new equation shall be made to disappear? In Example 3, if the coefficient of y' in (8) is set equal to zero, no odd power of y' remains, and $y' = 0$ becomes an axis of symmetry. Setting the constant term equal to zero places the new origin on the curve. In Example 4, when the terms of the first degree in x' and y' are made to disappear from (10), the new origin becomes a center of symmetry. Simplification is secured in these examples by taking advantage of *symmetry with respect to the new axes or the new origin.*

PROBLEMS

1. Simplify each of the following equations by translating the **axes**; plot the curve and both sets of axes:

(a) $x^2 + 6x + 4y + 8 = 0$. *Ans.* $x'^2 + 4y' = 0$.
(b) $4x^2 - 32x - 4y - 13 = 0$.
(c) $y^2 - 6x - 10y + 19 = 0$. *Ans.* $y'^2 - 6x' = 0$.
(d) $2x^2 - 6x + 7y + 15 = 0$.
(e) $x^2 - y^2 + 32x + 4y + 40 = 0$.
(f) $3x^2 + 4y^2 - 12x - 6y + 7 = 0$.
(g) $x^2 + 4y^2 + 10x - 12y + 14 = 0$.
(h) $x^2 - y^2 + 8x - 14y - 35 = 0$.

2. Translate the axes so that the new equation shall contain no term of the first degree:

(a) $x^2 - 4xy + 6y = 0$.
  Ans. $4x'^2 - 16x'y' + 9 = 0$.
(b) $x^2 + xy + y^2 + 6x = 0$.
(c) $2xy - 8x + 6y = 0$.
(d) $3xy - 4x + 2 = 0$.

3. Find the equations of the following loci and simplify them by translation. Plot, showing both sets of axes.

(a) A point moves so as to be four times as far from $(3, -2)$ as from the line $x + 1 = 0$. *Ans.* $225 x'^2 - 15 y'^2 = 256$.

(b) A point moves so as to be always half as far from the line $y - 7 = 0$ as from the point $(-3, 4)$.

(c) A point moves so that the product of the slopes of the lines joining it to $(-2, 4)$ and $(6, 4)$ is always 3.

(d) A point moves so that its distances from $(3, 3)$ and the line $2x + 5 = 0$ are in the ratio of 1 to 3.

(e) The locus of the center of a circle tangent to $y = 2$ and passing through $(3, 6)$.

(f) The locus of the center of a circle tangent to the y-axis and also tangent to the circle $x^2 + y^2 - 12x + 4y + 31 = 0$.

59. The first method (Art. 58), of completing squares and factoring, developed in the above examples can easily be applied to prove the

Theorem. *By translating the axes we are able to transform*

(1) $\qquad Ay^2 + Bx + Cy + F = 0 \text{ into}^* Ay'^2 + Bx' = 0;$

(2) $\qquad Ax^2 + Cx + By + F = 0 \text{ into } Ax'^2 + By' = 0;$

(3) $\; Ax^2 + By^2 + Dx + Ey + F = 0 \text{ into } Ax'^2 + By'^2 + F' = 0.$

Hence the locus of (1) *is a parabola with its axis parallel to the x-axis, of* (2) *a parabola with its axis parallel to the y-axis, and of* (3) *an ellipse* (*A and B like signs*), *or hyperbola* (*A and B unlike signs*), *with its axes parallel to the axes of coördinates.* (See Art. 53.)

Equations (1) and (2) are often written

(4) $\qquad x = ay^2 + by + c, \quad y = ax^2 + bx + c,$

respectively.

60. Typical equations for conic sections. For the typical forms (I)–(IV) of Chapter VI we may now write the following more general equations:

Parabola. $(y - k)^2 = 2\,p(x - h).$

Vertex (h, k); axis of symmetry, $y = k$.

$(x - h)^2 = 2\,p(y - k).$

Vertex (h, k); axis of symmetry, $x = h$.

---

* We assume that A and B are different from 0.

TRANSFORMATION OF COÖRDINATES

Ellipse. Center (h, k); axes of symmetry, $x = h$, $y = k$.

$$\frac{(x-h)^2}{a^2} + \frac{(y-k)^2}{b^2} = 1, \quad \frac{(x-h)^2}{b^2} + \frac{(y-k)^2}{a^2} = 1.$$

Hyberbola. Center (h, k); axes of symmetry, $x = h$, $y = k$.

$$\frac{(x-h)^2}{a^2} - \frac{(y-k)^2}{b^2} = 1, \quad \frac{(x-h)^2}{b^2} - \frac{(y-k)^2}{a^2} = -1.$$

To verify these, translate the axes by substituting $x = x' + h$, $y = y' + k$. Then they reduce to the corresponding typical forms in Chapter VI.

EXAMPLES

1. Find the equation of the parabola with focus $(3, -3)$ and directrix the line $x = -1$.

Solution. The vertex is $(1, -3)$, and $p = 4$. The axis of the parabola is parallel to the x-axis. Hence, by the first formula of this article,

$$(y + 3)^2 = 8(x - 1). \quad Ans.$$

By translation to the vertex $(1, -3)$ as new origin, this becomes

$$y'^2 = 8 x'.$$

The figure shows both sets of axes.

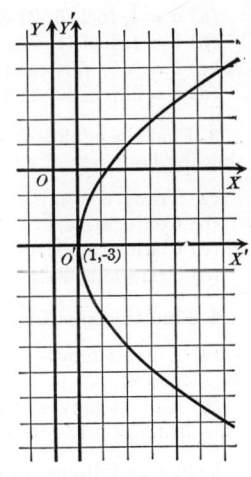

2. Find the equation of an ellipse if the extremities of the major axis are $(-3, 2)$ and $(5, 2)$ and the minor axis equals 4.

Solution. The center is $(1, 2)$. Also $a = 4$, $b = 2$. Hence the equation is

$$\frac{(x-1)^2}{16} + \frac{(y-2)^2}{4} = 1. \quad Ans.$$

Translating to the center as new origin, and reducing, we obtain

$$x'^2 + 4\, y'^2 = 16.$$

The figure shows both sets of axes.

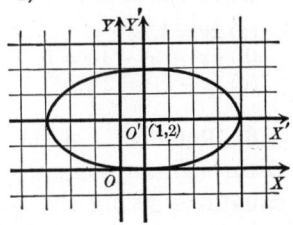

PROBLEMS

1. Find the equations of the following parabolas and transform each to one of the typical forms of Art. 40 by translation; plot and draw both sets of axes:

(a) Vertex (3, 4), directrix the y-axis.
(b) Focus (−2, 3), vertex (3, 3).
(c) Focus (0, −3), vertex (2, −3).   *Ans.* $y'^2 + 8\,x' = 0$.
(d) Axis the y-axis, vertex (0, −4), passes through (6, 0).
   Ans. $x'^2 - 9\,y' = 0$.
(e) Focus (0, 0), directrix $y = 4$.
(f) Axis the x-axis, vertex (6, 0), passes through (0, 4).
   Ans. $3\,y'^2 + 8\,x' = 0$.

2. Find the equations of the following ellipses and simplify them by translation; plot, showing both sets of axes:

(a) $a = 4$, foci (5, 2) and (−1, 2).   *Ans.* $7\,x'^2 + 16\,y'^2 = 112$.
(b) $b = 4$, foci (1, 0) and (−4, 0).
(c) $b = \sqrt{7}$, vertices (−2, 0) and (8, 0).   *Ans.* $7\,x'^2 + 25\,y'^2 = 175$.
(d) $b = 2$, foci (0, 2) and (0, −4).

3. Find the equations of the following hyperbolas; simplify and plot, showing both sets of axes:

(a) Transverse axis 6, foci (−2, 0) and (6, 0).   *Ans.* $7\,x'^2 - 9\,y'^2 = 63$.
(b) Conjugate axis 4, foci (0, 2) and (0, −10).
(c) Conjugate axis 6, vertices (1, 2) and (−5, 2).
(d) Transverse axis $2\sqrt{3}$, foci (0, 0) and (−4, 0).

4. Find the equations of the following loci, simplify, and plot:

(a) A point moves so that the sum of its distances from (3, 4) and (3, −2) is 8.
(b) A point moves so that the difference between its distances from (3, −3) and (−1, −3) is 3.

5. Plot and discuss each of the following systems:

(a) $xy = k$.
(b) $kx^2 + y^2 - 4\,x = 0$.
(c) $(x - k)^2 = 2\,y$.
(d) $(x - k)^2 + 9\,y^2 = 36$.
(e) $4(y - k)^2 - 9\,x^2 = 144$.
(f) $4(x - k)^2 - 9(y - k)^2 = 36$.

61. Rotation. Let the axes OX and OY be rotated about O through an angle θ to the positions OX' and OY'. The equations giving the coördinates of any point referred to

TRANSFORMATION OF COÖRDINATES

OX and OY in terms of its coördinates referred to OX' and OY' are called the **equations for rotating the axes.**

Theorem. *The equations for rotating the axes through an angle θ are*

(II) $\begin{cases} x = x' \cos \theta - y' \sin \theta, \\ y = x' \sin \theta + y' \cos \theta. \end{cases}$

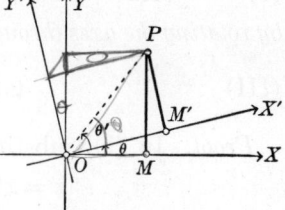

Proof. Let P be any point whose old and new coördinates are, respectively, (x,y) and (x',y'). Draw OP.

Now $x = OM = OP \cos \angle MOP = OP \cos (\theta' + \theta)$.

Expanding $\cos (\theta' + \theta)$ by trigonometry (**9**, p. 3), we get

(1) $\qquad x = OP \cos \theta' \cos \theta - OP \sin \theta' \sin \theta$.

But $\quad x' = OM' = OP \cos \theta', \quad y' = M'P = OP \sin \theta'$.

Substituting in (1), we obtain the formula for x as in (II). Similarly for y. Q.E.D.

EXAMPLE

Transform the equation $x^2 - y^2 = 16$ by rotating the axes through **45°**.

Solution. Since

$$\sin 45° = \tfrac{1}{2}\sqrt{2} = \frac{1}{\sqrt{2}}$$

and $\quad \cos 45° = \dfrac{1}{\sqrt{2}},$

equations (II) become

$$x = \frac{x' - y'}{\sqrt{2}}, \quad y = \frac{x' + y'}{\sqrt{2}}.$$

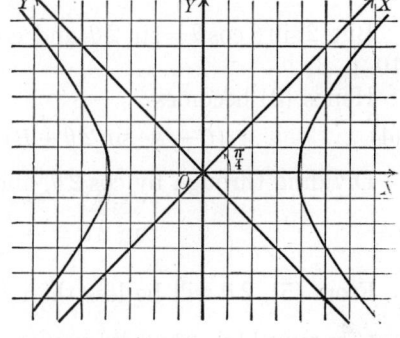

Substituting in the given equation, we obtain

$$\left(\frac{x' - y'}{\sqrt{2}}\right)^2 - \left(\frac{x' + y'}{\sqrt{2}}\right)^2 = 16,$$

or, simplifying, $\qquad x'y' + 8 = 0.$ *Ans.*

62. Simplifying equations by rotating the axes.

Theorem. *The term in xy may always be removed from an equation of the second degree,*

(1) $$Ax^2 + Bxy + Cy^2 + Dx + Ey + F = 0,$$

by rotating the axes through an angle θ such that

(III) $$\tan 2\theta = \frac{B}{A - C}.$$

Proof. In (1), substitute formulas (II), Art. 61,

$$x = x' \cos \theta - y' \sin \theta,$$
and $$y = x' \sin \theta + y' \cos \theta.$$

This gives, after squaring, multiplying, and arranging* the terms according to x', y', the transformed equation

(2) $\begin{vmatrix} A\cos^2\theta \\ +B\sin\theta\cos\theta \\ +C\sin^2\theta \end{vmatrix} x'^2 \begin{vmatrix} -2A\sin\theta\cos\theta \\ +B(\cos^2\theta-\sin^2\theta) \\ +2C\sin\theta\cos\theta \end{vmatrix} x'y' \begin{vmatrix} +A\sin^2\theta \\ -B\sin\theta\cos\theta \\ +C\cos^2\theta \end{vmatrix} y'^2$
$\qquad\qquad\qquad\qquad\qquad + \begin{vmatrix} +D\cos\theta \\ +E\sin\theta \end{vmatrix} x' \begin{vmatrix} -D\sin\theta \\ +E\cos\theta \end{vmatrix} y' + F = 0.$

The term $x'y'$ will disappear from (2) if its coefficient is equal to zero, that is, if

(3) $\quad -2A\sin\theta\cos\theta + B(\cos^2\theta - \sin^2\theta) + 2C\sin\theta\cos\theta = 0.$

But $2\sin\theta\cos\theta = \sin 2\theta$ and $\cos^2\theta - \sin^2\theta = \cos 2\theta$ (by **10**, p. 3).

Hence (3) becomes

(4) $$(C - A)\sin 2\theta + B\cos 2\theta = 0.$$

Dividing through by $\cos 2\theta$, and transposing,

(5) $$\tan 2\theta = \frac{B}{A - C}. \qquad \text{Q.E.D.}$$

From (5), 2θ will be less than $180°$, and θ less than $90°$.

---

* The vertical bars take the place of parentheses. For example, the coefficient of x'^2 is $A\cos^2\theta + B\sin\theta\cos\theta + C\sin^2\theta$.

TRANSFORMATION OF COÖRDINATES

EXAMPLE

Simplify $x^2 + 4xy + y^2 = 4$ by rotating the axes.

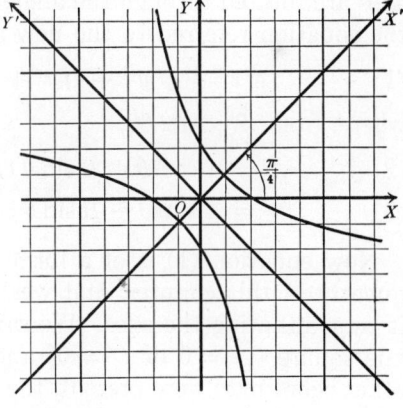

Solution. Here $A = 1$, $B = 4$, $C = 1$.

Hence, by (III),

$\tan 2\theta = \infty$, and $\theta = 45°$.

Then (II) becomes (cf. example, Art. 61)

$$x = \frac{x' - y'}{\sqrt{2}}, \quad y = \frac{x' + y'}{\sqrt{2}}.$$

Substituting and reducing, we obtain the hyperbola

$3x'^2 - y'^2 = 4$. *Ans.*

PROBLEMS

1. Transform the following equations by rotating the axes through the indicated angle; plot the curve, showing both sets of axes:

(a) $x + y = 0$; $45°$.   *Ans.* $x' = 0$.
(b) $x^2 + y^2 = 9$; $60°$.
(c) $y^2 - x^2 = 8$; $90°$.
(d) $x^2 + 4xy + y^2 = 16$; $45°$.   *Ans.* $3x'^2 - y'^2 = 16$.
(e) $4xy - 3x^2 = 10$; $\tan \theta = 2$.   *Ans.* $x'^2 - 4y'^2 = 10$.
(f) $3x^2 - 3xy - y^2 = 5$; $\tan \theta = 3$.
(g) $x^2 + 4xy + 4y^2 + 12x - 6y = 0$; $\tan \theta = 2$.

2. Show that the equation $x^2 + y^2 = r^2$ is invariant under any rotation whatever.

3. Remove the xy-term from the following equations by rotation of the axes and plot the curve, showing both pairs of axes:

(a) $x^2 - 2xy + y^2 = 12$.   *Ans.* $y'^2 = 6$.
(b) $x^2 + 2\sqrt{3}xy - y^2 = 4$.   *Ans.* $x'^2 - y'^2 = 2$.
(c) $17x^2 - 16xy + 17y^2 = 225$.
(d) $3x^2 - 4\sqrt{3}xy - y^2 = 9$.
(e) $x^2 + 4xy + y^2 = 16$.
(f) $x^2 - 2xy + y^2 - 2x - 2y + 1 = 0$.
(g) $3x^2 - 2\sqrt{3}xy + y^2 + 4x + 4\sqrt{3}y = 0$.
(h) $xy = 12$.   *Ans.* $x'^2 - y'^2 = 24$.
(i) $25x^2 + 14xy + 25y^2 = 288$.   *Ans.* $16x'^2 + 9y'^2 = 144$.
(j) $3x^2 - 10xy + 3y^2 = 0$.

63. Locus of any equation of the second degree.
When the axes are rotated through the angle θ given by (III), p. 118, the equation referred to the new axes is

(1) $$A'x'^2 + C'y'^2 + D'x' + E'y' + F = 0,$$

where, from (2), Art. 62,

(2) $$A' = A\cos^2\theta + B\sin\theta\cos\theta + C\sin^2\theta,$$

(3) $$C' = A\sin^2\theta - B\sin\theta\cos\theta + C\cos^2\theta.$$

Now equation (1) is of a form which we have met frequently in this chapter, and we have learned to simplify it by translating the axes. We saw in Art. 59 that if only one square ($A' = 0$ or $C' = 0$) and the first power of the other coördinate were present, the equation could be transformed into one of the typical forms of the parabola.

Suppose, however, that the first power of the other coördinate does not appear. For example, suppose that in (1) $A' = 0$ and $D' = 0$. Then the equation is

(4) $$C'y'^2 + E'y' + F = 0.$$

This is a quadratic in y. If the roots are real, the locus will be two lines parallel to the x'-axis. These lines will coincide if the roots are equal. There will be no locus if the roots are imaginary.

If neither A' nor C' is zero, we may, by translation to the new origin $\left(-\dfrac{D'}{2A'}, -\dfrac{E'}{2C'}\right)$, transform the equation into

(5) $$A'x''^2 + C'y''^2 + F' = 0.$$

Consider the locus of (5).

A' and C' like signs, assumed positive. Then we have an *ellipse*, a *point ellipse* ($x'' = y'' = 0$), or *no locus*, according as F' is negative, zero, or positive.

A' and C' unlike signs. Then the locus is a hyperbola or a pair of intersecting lines, according as F' is not zero or zero.

TRANSFORMATION OF COÖRDINATES

We seek now a test to apply to an equation containing an xy-term in order to decide in advance the nature of the locus. To do this we eliminate the angle θ from equations (2) and (3), making use of (4), Art. 62. The result is the simple equation,

(IV) $$-4\,A'C' = B^2 - 4\,AC.$$

The steps in the elimination process are as follows:
Adding and subtracting (2) and (3),

(6) $\quad A' + C' = A + C,\qquad$ [since $\sin^2\theta + \cos^2\theta = 1$]

(7) $\quad A' - C' = (A - C)\cos 2\theta + B\sin 2\theta.\qquad$ [**10**, p. 3]

Squaring (7),

(8) $(A' - C')^2 = (A - C)^2\cos^2 2\theta + 2\,B(A - C)\sin 2\theta\cos 2\theta$
$\qquad\qquad\qquad\qquad + B^2\sin^2 2\theta.$

Squaring (4), Art. 62,

(9) $0 = (A - C)^2\sin^2 2\theta + 2\,B(C - A)\sin 2\theta\cos 2\theta$
$\qquad\qquad\qquad\qquad + B^2\cos^2 2\theta.$

Adding (8) and (9),

(10) $\qquad\qquad (A' - C')^2 = (A - C)^2 + B^2.$

Squaring (6),

(11) $\qquad\qquad (A' + C')^2 = (A + C)^2.$

Subtracting (11) from (10), we obtain (IV).

If the locus of (1) is a parabola, $A' = 0$ or $C' = 0$. Hence, from (IV), $B^2 - 4\,AC = 0$.

If the locus of (1) is an ellipse, A' and C' agree in sign. Hence $A'C'$ is positive, and, from (IV), $B^2 - 4\,AC$ is negative.

If the locus of (1) is a hyperbola, A' and C' differ in sign. Hence $A'C'$ is negative, and, from (IV), $B^2 - 4\,AC$ is a positive number.

Collecting all the results in tabular form, we have the
Theorem. *Given any equation of the second degree,*
$$Ax^2 + Bxy + Cy^2 + Dx + Ey + F = 0,$$
the possible loci may be classified thus:

Test	General Case	Exceptional Cases *
$B^2 - 4AC$ † zero	parabola	two parallel lines one line
$B^2 - 4AC$ negative	ellipse	point-ellipse
$B^2 - 4AC$ positive	hyperbola	two intersecting lines

The exceptional cases are recognizable by the condition that the equation is then *factorable into two factors of the first degree in x and y.* A number of problems of this kind were given on page 50.

A point-ellipse is often called a "degenerate ellipse," two intersecting lines a "degenerate hyperbola," and two parallel lines a "degenerate parabola."

In algebra, $B^2 - 4AC$ is called the *discriminant* of the terms of the second degree in the equation.

64. Plotting the locus of an equation of the second degree.
FIRST METHOD. *After transformation.* We have seen that if the xy-term is lacking, the equation may be simplified by translating the axes. The transformed equation is then readily plotted on the new axes.

When the xy-term is present, rotate ‡ the axes through the angle θ given by (III),
$$(1) \qquad \tan 2\theta = \frac{B}{A - C}.$$

The term in xy will then disappear and further simplification is accomplished by translation.

---
* For tests to distinguish the exceptional cases, see Smith and Gale's "Elements of Analytic Geometry," p. 277.

† This case is recognizable by inspection, for the terms of the second degree, $Ax^2 + Bxy + Cy^2$, now will form a *perfect square*.

‡ See below, following Example 2, and also Art. 65.

TRANSFORMATION OF COÖRDINATES

To rotate, we substitute

(2) $x = x' \cos \theta - y' \sin \theta, \quad y = x' \sin \theta + y' \cos \theta.$

We find $\sin \theta$ and $\cos \theta$ as follows. First compute $\cos 2\theta$ from

(3) $$\cos 2\theta = \pm \frac{1}{\sqrt{1 + \tan^2 2\theta}}, \qquad [7, \text{p. } 3]$$

and remember that $\cos 2\theta$ and $\tan 2\theta$ must have like signs.

From **10**, p. 3, we have

(4) $\sin \theta = +\sqrt{\dfrac{1 - \cos 2\theta}{2}}, \quad \cos \theta = +\sqrt{\dfrac{1 + \cos 2\theta}{2}}.$

EXAMPLES

1. Construct and discuss the locus of

(5) $x^2 + 4xy + 4y^2 + 12x - 6y = 0.$

Solution. Here $A = 1, \quad B = 4, \quad C = 4.$
$$\therefore B^2 - 4AC = 0,$$

and the locus is a parabola.

Write the equation (5) in the form

(6) $(x + 2y)^2 + 12x - 6y = 0.$

We rotate the axes through an angle θ such that

$$\tan 2\theta = \frac{4}{1 - 4} = -\frac{4}{3}.$$

Then, by (3), $\cos 2\theta = -\frac{3}{5},$
and, by (4),

(7) $\sin \theta = \dfrac{2}{\sqrt{5}} \quad \text{and} \quad \cos \theta = \dfrac{1}{\sqrt{5}}.$

The equations for rotating the axes are therefore

$$x = \frac{x' - 2y'}{\sqrt{5}}, \quad y = \frac{2x' + y'}{\sqrt{5}}.$$

Substituting in the equation (6), we obtain

$$x'^2 - \frac{6}{\sqrt{5}} y' = 0,$$

The figure shows both sets of axes; also the parabola, its focus $x' = 0$, $y' = \frac{3}{10}\sqrt{5}$, and directrix $y' = -\frac{3}{10}\sqrt{5}$. The axis OX' has the slope $\tan\theta = \frac{\sin\theta}{\cos\theta} = 2$, from (7). Hence OX' is the line through the origin whose slope equals 2.

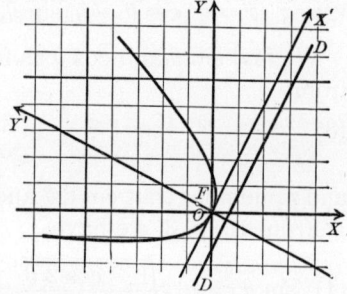

A good check in the figure is secured by finding the intercepts on OX and OY from the given equation (5). These are $x = 0$ and -12, and $y = 0$ and $\frac{3}{2}$.

2. Construct the locus of
$$5x^2 + 6xy + 5y^2 + 22x - 6y + 21 = 0.$$

Solution. Here $A = 5$, $B = 6$, $C = 5$.

$\therefore B^2 - 4AC = 36 - 100 = -64 = $ a negative number.

Hence the locus is an ellipse.

By (III), $\tan 2\theta = \frac{6}{5-5} = \infty$, and $\theta = 45°$.

Hence the equations of the rotation are
$$x = \frac{x' - y'}{\sqrt{2}}, \quad y = \frac{x' + y'}{\sqrt{2}}.$$

Substituting in the given equation and reducing, we obtain
$$4x'^2 + y'^2 + 4\sqrt{2}\,x' - 7\sqrt{2}\,y' + \tfrac{21}{2} = 0.$$

Translating to the new origin $(-\tfrac{1}{2}\sqrt{2},\ \tfrac{7}{2}\sqrt{2})$, the final equation is
$$4x''^2 + y''^2 = 16.$$

Hence the major axis is 8, minor axis 4, and the foci are on the y''-axis.

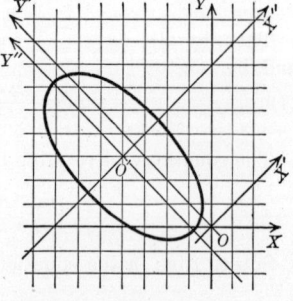

The figure shows the three sets of axes and the ellipse. The coördinates of the new origin $O'(-\tfrac{1}{2}\sqrt{2},\ \tfrac{7}{2}\sqrt{2})$ refer to the axes OX' and OY', and this must be remembered in plotting.

Remark. When the conic has a center, we may translate the axes to this point as new origin, and then rotate to eliminate $x'y'$. We substitute $x = x' + h$,

TRANSFORMATION OF COÖRDINATES

$y = y' + k$, set the coefficients of x' and y' equal to zero, and solve for h and k. The center is this point (h, k).

To illustrate, take Example 2 on page 124. The equations to solve for h and k are $10h + 6k + 22 = 0$, $6h + 10k - 6 = 0$. Solving, $h = -4$, $k = 3$. These are the coördinates of O' in the figure referred to OX and OY. The new equation is $5x'^2 + 6x'y' + 5y'^2 - 32 = 0$. Rotating through $45°$ gives $4x''^2 + y''^2 = 16$, as before.

SECOND METHOD. *By direct plotting.* Test by the theorem at the end of the preceding section, and then discuss and plot the equation directly.

EXAMPLES

1. Plot the locus of
(8) $$x^2 - 2xy + 4y^2 - 4x = 0.$$

Solution. Here $A = 1$, $B = -2$, $C = 4$.

$$\therefore B^2 - 4AC = 4 - 16 = -12 = \text{a negative number.}$$

Hence the locus is an ellipse.

Discussion. 1. *Intercepts.* On the x-axis, 0 and 4. On the y-axis, 0.
2. *Symmetry.* Not symmetric to x-axis, y-axis, or origin.
3. *Extent.* Solve the equation for x as follows:

(9) $$x^2 - (2y + 4)x + \left(\frac{2y+4}{2}\right)^2 = -4y^2 + \left(\frac{2y+4}{2}\right)^2.$$

[Collecting terms in x and completing the square.]

(10) $$\therefore x = y + 2 \pm \sqrt{(2-y)(2+3y)}.$$

Solving for y,
(11) $\quad y = \tfrac{1}{4}x \pm \tfrac{1}{4}\sqrt{x(16 - 3x)}.$

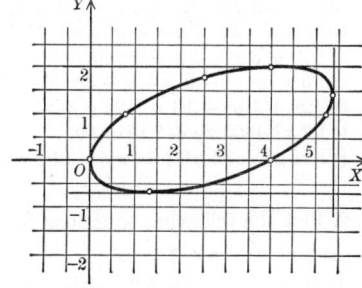

x	y
$\tfrac{4}{3}$	$-\tfrac{2}{3}$
0, 4	0
$3 \pm \sqrt{5}$	1
4	2
$5\tfrac{1}{3}$	$\tfrac{4}{3}$

From the radicals in (10) and (11) we see that

y may have values from $-\tfrac{2}{3}$ to 2 inclusive;

x may have values from 0 to $\tfrac{16}{3}$ inclusive.

Hence the ellipse lies within the rectangle
$$y = -\tfrac{2}{3}, \quad y = 2, \quad x = 0, \quad x = 1\tfrac{6}{3}.$$

Points on the locus may be found from (10) as in the table.

2. Determine the locus of
$$5x^2 + 4xy - y^2 + 24x - 6y - 5 = 0.$$

Solution. $A = 5$, $B = 4$, $C = -1$.
$$\therefore B^2 - 4AC = 16 + 20 = 36.$$

Hence, from the table of Art. 63, we may expect a hyperbola or a pair of intersecting lines.

Solve the equation for y as follows:
$$y^2 - (4x - 6)y + (2x - 3)^2 = 5x^2 + 24x - 5 + (2x - 3)^2$$
$$= 9x^2 + 12x + 4 = (3x + 2)^2.$$

[Collecting terms in y and completing the square.]
$$\therefore y - (2x - 3) = \pm (3x + 2).$$

Hence the locus is the pair of intersecting lines
$$y = 5x - 1 \quad \text{and} \quad y = -x - 5. \; Ans.$$

PROBLEMS

1. Simplify each of the following equations. Plot, and draw all sets of axes:

(a) $x^2 + 3xy + 5y^2 = 11$.
(b) $x^2 - 2xy + y^2 - 5y = 0$.   *Ans.* $4y'^2 - 5\sqrt{2}\, x' = 0$.
(c) $x^2 + 3xy + y^2 + 4y = 0$.
(d) $x^2 + 2xy + y^2 + 4x - 4y = 0$.   *Ans.* $x'^2 - 2\sqrt{2}\, y' = 0$.
(e) $3xy + 4x + 8y + 4 = 0$.
(f) $x^2 + 6x - 3y + 6 = 0$.   *Ans.* $x'^2 - 3y' = 0$.
(g) $3x^2 + y^2 - 9x + y + 4 = 0$.
(h) $x^2 + 4y^2 - 16x + 24y + 84 = 0$.   *Ans.* $x'^2 + 4y'^2 = 16$.
(i) $7x^2 + 50xy + 7y^2 = 50$.
(j) $13x^2 + 13y^2 + 10xy - 42x + 6y - 27 = 0$.
     Ans. $9x'^2 + 4y'^2 = 36$.

2. Plot the following equations by the second method given above:

(a) $3x^2 - 4xy - 1 = 0$.   (c) $x^2 - 4y^2 - 4x - 32y - 60 = 0$.
(b) $4xy + 4y^2 - 2x + 3 = 0$.   (d) $x^2 + y^2 - 4x - 6y - 18 = 0$.
(e) $4xy - 3x^2 = 9$.
(f) $2x^2 + 3y^2 - 16x + 18y + 53 = 0$.
(g) $x^2 + 4xy + 4y^2 + 12x - 6y = 0$.
(h) $3x^2 + 4xy + y^2 - 2x - 1 = 0$.

TRANSFORMATION OF COÖRDINATES 127

3. Test and plot each of the following equations, using transformations or direct plotting, as seems better:

(a) $3x^2 - 2xy + y^2 - 4x - 6 = 0$.
(b) $x^2 - xy + y^2 - 2x - 6y = 0$.
(c) $x^2 + \sqrt{3}xy + y^2 - 4x - 6y + 5 = 0$.
(d) $2x^2 + 4xy + 5y^2 - 4x - 22y + 7 = 0$.
(e) $xy - x^2 + 4 = 0$.
(f) $xy - 2x - y + 3 = 0$.
(g) $x^2 - 2xy + y^2 - 2x - 2y + 1 = 0$.
(h) $2x^2 - 5xy - 3y^2 - 2x + 13y - 12 = 0$.
(i) $x^2 - 3xy + y^2 + 10x - 10y + 21 = 0$.
(j) $y^2 + 4xy + 4x^2 - 4 = 0$.

For individual study or assignment

4. Show that the general equation
$$Ax^2 + Bxy + Cy^2 + Dx + Ey + F = 0$$
may be simplified by translation so that the new equation contains no terms of the first degree if the coördinates of the new origin (h, k) satisfy the equations $2Ah + Bk + D = 0$, $Bh + 2Ck + E = 0$. Hence show that the new origin is the center of the locus unless $B^2 - 4AC = 0$. In that case the transformation fails.

5. Show by clearing the equation of radicals that the locus of $x^{\frac{1}{2}} + y^{\frac{1}{2}} = a^{\frac{1}{2}}$ is a conic, and determine the type. Plot for particular values of a.

6. Describe the system of curves represented by each of the following:

(a) $(x - y)^2 + (y - k)^2 = 0$.
(b) $xy + h^2 - h(x + y) = 0$.
(c) $x^3 - y^3 - (x - h)(x^2 - y^2) = 0$.

65. A special case. Equilateral (rectangular) hyperbola.

Theorem. *The equation of an equilateral hyperbola referred to its asymptotes is*

(V) $\qquad 2xy + a^2 = 0.$

Proof. Start with the equation of Art. 52 and rotate the axes through 45°. The result is (V) (see Example, p. 117), and the new axes are the asymptotes. Q.E.D.

To simplify

(1) $\qquad Bxy + Dx + Ey + F = 0,$

translate the axes, set the coefficients of x' and y' in the new equation equal to zero, and thus transform (1) into

(2) $$Bx'y' + F' = 0,$$

which is in the form (V). It now appears that (1) is the equation of a rectangular hyperbola with asymptotes parallel to OX and OY respectively (see Example 4, p. 112).

Two special forms of (1) are used below. These are

(3) $$y = \frac{ax+b}{x} \quad \text{and} \quad y = \frac{x}{ax+b}.$$

Construction of an equilateral hyperbola. A construction often used for an equilateral hyperbola when the asymptotes and one point A on the curve are given is as follows (Fig. 1):

Let OX and OY be the asymptotes and A the given point. Draw any line through A to meet OX at M and OY at N.

Lay off $MP = AN$. Then P is a point on the required hyperbola.

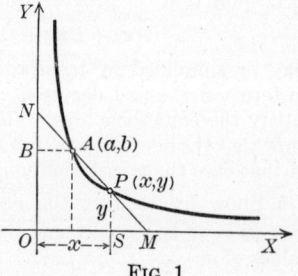

Fig. 1

Proof. Choose the asymptotes as axes. Let the coördinates of A be (a, b) and of P, (x, y). Then

$$OS = x, \quad SP = y,$$
$$OB = b, \quad BA = a.$$

By construction, $AN = MP$.

$\therefore \triangle PSM = \triangle NBA$,

and $\qquad BN = SP = y, \quad SM = BA = a.$

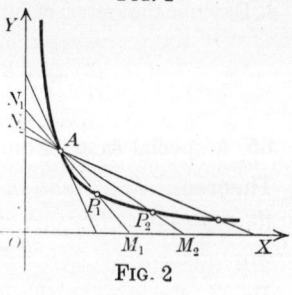

Fig. 2

Since $\triangle OMN$ and BAN are similar,

$$\frac{BN}{BA} = \frac{ON}{OM} = \frac{OB + BN}{OS + SM}.$$

Substituting, $\dfrac{y}{a} = \dfrac{b+y}{a+x}$, or $xy = ab$.

Comparing with (V), we see that $P(x, y)$ lies upon an equilateral hyperbola which has OX and OY for its asymptotes and which passes through (a, b). Q.E.D.

By drawing different lines through A, and laying off $M_1P_1 = AN_1$, $M_2P_2 = AN_2$, etc., we determine as many points P_1, P_2, etc., as we wish on the hyperbola (Fig. 2).

66. Another definition of conic sections (conics). *When a point P moves so that its distances from a given fixed point and a given fixed line are in a constant ratio, the locus is a conic.*

The given fixed line is called the **directrix**, the fixed point the **focus**, and the ratio of the distances of P from the focus and directrix is called the **eccentricity**.

In Problem 3, p. 38, we found the equation for any conic to be

(1) $\qquad (1 - e^2)x^2 + y^2 - 2\,px + p^2 = 0,$

if e is the eccentricity, YY' the directrix, and $(p, 0)$ the focus. Now (1) has no xy-term. Hence we see at once by comparison with our previous results that a conic is

a parabola when $e = 1$,
an ellipse when $e < 1$,
a hyperbola when $e > 1$.

Clearly, when $e = 1$ the definition of the conic agrees with that already given for the parabola.

The ellipse and hyperbola, each having a center, are called **central conics**.

Focus and eccentricity, as used in this section, agree with these terms as already introduced. This fact is left to the student to prove in the following problems.

67. General transformation of coördinates. If the axes are moved in any manner, they may be brought from the old position to the new position by translating them to the new origin and then rotating them through the proper angle.

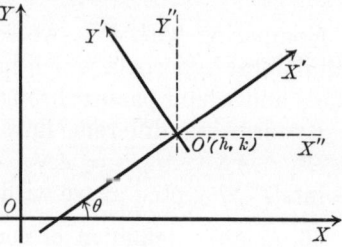

Theorem. *If the axes are translated to a new origin (h, k) and then rotated through an angle θ, the equations of the transformation are*

(VI) $\quad\begin{cases} x = x' \cos \theta - y' \sin \theta + h, \\ y = x' \sin \theta + y' \cos \theta + k. \end{cases}$

Proof. To translate the axes to $O'X''$ and $O'Y''$ we have, by (I),
$$x = x'' + h, \qquad y = y'' + k,$$
where (x'', y'') are the coördinates of any point P referred to $O'X''$ and $O'Y''$.

To rotate the axes we set, by (II),
$$x'' = x' \cos \theta - y' \sin \theta,$$
$$y'' = x' \sin \theta + y' \cos \theta.$$

Substituting these values of x'' and y'', we obtain (VI).
Q.E.D.

68. Classification of loci. The loci of algebraic equations are classified according to the *degree* of the equations. This classification is justified by the following

Theorem. *The degree of the equation of a curve is unchanged by a transformation of coördinates.*

Proof. Since equations (VI) are of the first degree in x' and y', the degree of an equation cannot be *raised* when the values of x and y given by (VI) are substituted. Neither can the degree be *lowered*; for then the degree must be raised if we transform back to the old axes.

As the degree can be neither raised nor lowered by a transformation of coördinates, it must remain unchanged. Q.E.D.

PROBLEMS

1. By the proper translation of the coördinate axes, refer the following rectangular hyperbolas to their asymptotes as axes, and plot:

(a) $xy - 2x - y + 8 = 0$. *Ans.* $x'y' + 6 = 0$.
(b) $3xy - 6x - 12y + 30 = 0$.
(c) $2xy - 6x + 4y - 16 = 0$.
(d) $4xy + 12x - 4y - 6 = 0$.
(e) $5xy + 5x + 20y + 24 = 0$.
(f) $3xy + x + 4y + 1 = 0$.

2. What is the conic $A(x-h)(y-k) + C = 0$?

3. Simplify $(1-e^2)x^2 + y^2 - 2px + p^2 = 0$ by translation of the axes.

For individual study or assignment

4. Show analytically that in a central conic the focus coincides with the focus already adopted.

5. Prove that e in Problem 3 agrees with e as defined in Art. 44 and Art. 48.

6. Prove that the distances from a point (x, y) on the ellipse $\dfrac{x^2}{a^2} + \dfrac{y^2}{b^2} = 1$ to the foci (focal radii) are $a \pm ex$.

7. Show analytically that if three points are taken on any ellipse whose abscissas are in arithmetic progression, the corresponding focal radii are also in arithmetic progression.

8. Show that the focal radii of a point of the hyperbola $\dfrac{x^2}{a^2} - \dfrac{y^2}{b^2} = 1$ are $ex \pm a$.

LOCUS PROBLEMS

1. Find the equations of the following loci and discuss and construct them.

The base of a triangle is fixed in length and position. Find the locus of the opposite vertex if

(a) the sum of the two variable sides is constant;
(b) the difference between the two variable sides is constant;
(c) the sum of the slopes of the variable sides is constant;
(d) the slope of one variable side is proportional to the reciprocal of the slope of the other variable side;
(e) one base angle is double the other;
(f) the sum of the base angles is constant;
(g) the difference between the base angles is constant.

CHAPTER VIII

TANGENTS

69. Equation of the tangent. A tangent to a curve at a point P_1 is obtained as follows. Take a second point P_2 on the curve near P_1. Draw the secant through P_1 and P_2. Now let P_2 move along the curve toward P_1. The secant will turn around P_1. The limiting position of the secant when P_2 reaches P_1 is called the *tangent* at P_1.

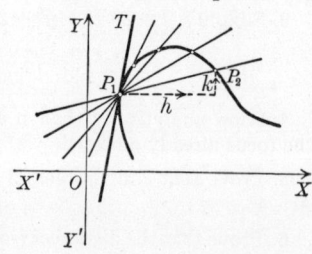

Let the coördinates of P_1 be (x_1, y_1) and of P_2 $(x_1 + h, y_1 + k)$. Then

$$\text{slope of secant } P_1P_2 = \frac{k}{h}.$$

To find the slope of the tangent, we begin by finding a value for $\frac{k}{h}$, as in the following example, in which is proved the

Theorem. *The equation of the tangent to the circle*

$$x^2 + y^2 = r^2$$

at the point of contact $P_1(x_1, y_1)$ *is*

(I) $$x_1 x + y_1 y = r^2.$$

EXAMPLE

Find the equation of the tangent to the circle

$$x^2 + y^2 = r^2$$

at the point of contact (x_1, y_1).

TANGENTS

Solution. Let $P_1(x_1, y_1)$ and $P_2(x_1 + h, y_1 + k)$ be two points on the circle C.

Since these coördinates satisfy the equation of the circle, we have

(1) $x_1^2 + y_1^2 = r^2$,

and $(x_1 + h)^2 + (y_1 + k)^2 = r^2$; or

(2) $x_1^2 + 2 x_1 h + h^2 + y_1^2 + 2 y_1 k + k^2 = r^2$.

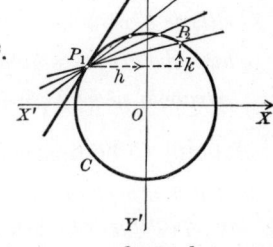

Subtracting (1) from (2), we have

$2 x_1 h + h^2 + 2 y_1 k + k^2 = 0$.

Transposing and factoring, we obtain

$k(2 y_1 + k) = - h(2 x_1 + h)$,

whence, by division,

(3) $\dfrac{k}{h}$ = slope of the secant through P_1 and $P_2 = -\dfrac{2 x_1 + h}{2 y_1 + k}$.

The secant becomes the tangent at P_1 when h and k equal zero. Hence m, the slope of the tangent at P_1, is the value of the right-hand member of (3) when $h = k = 0$; that is,

$$m = -\frac{x_1}{y_1}.$$

The equation of the tangent at P_1 is then

$$y - y_1 = -\frac{x_1}{y_1}(x - x_1),$$

or, by (1), $x_1 x + y_1 y = x_1^2 + y_1^2 = r^2$. *Ans.*

The method employed in this example is general and may be formulated in the following

Rule *to determine the slope of the tangent to a curve C at a point P_1 on C.*

First step. *Let $P_1(x_1, y_1)$ and $P_2(x_1 + h, y_1 + k)$ be two points on C. Substitute these coördinates in the equation of C and subtract. Factor this result and find a value for $\dfrac{k}{h}$. This is the slope of the secant through P_1 and P_2.*

Second step. *Find the value of the slope of the secant when h and k equal zero. This is the slope of the tangent.*

Having the slope of the tangent, we find its equation by the point-slope formula. The point P_1 is called the **point of contact**.

By this rule we may prove the following

Theorem. *The equation of the tangent at the point of contact $P_1(x_1, y_1)$ to the*

ellipse $b^2x^2 + a^2y^2 = a^2b^2$ *is* $b^2x_1x + a^2y_1y = a^2b^2$;
hyperbola $b^2x^2 - a^2y^2 = a^2b^2$ *is* $b^2x_1x - a^2y_1y = a^2b^2$;
parabola $y^2 = 2\,px$ *is* $y_1y = p(x + x_1).$

A point to be observed in the proofs is this:

Always simplify the equation of the tangent by making use of the equation obtained when x_1 and y_1 are substituted for x and y in the equation of the given curve.

PROBLEMS

1. Find the equation of the tangent to each of the following curves at the point of contact (x_1, y_1):

(a) $3\,y^2 = 4\,x.$ *Ans.* $2\,x - 3\,y_1y + 2\,x_1 = 0.$
(b) $x = Ay^2 + By + C.$
(c) $x^2 + y^2 + 2\,hx + 2\,ky + r^2 = 0.$
(d) $x^2 + 6\,y^2 = 16.$ *Ans.* $x_1x + 6\,y_1y = 16.$
(e) $4\,x^2 - 2\,y^2 = 7.$
(f) $xy = k.$ *Ans.* $x_1y + y_1x = 2\,k.$
(g) $Ax^2 + By^2 + Dx + Ey + F = 0.$
(h) $y = x^3.$ *Ans.* $3\,x_1^2x - y - 2\,y_1 = 0.$
(i) $3\,x^2 = 4\,y^3.$
(j) $xy^2 = xy - y - x.$

2. Find the equation of the tangent to each of the following curves at the point indicated:

(a) $x^2 + 9\,y^2 = 40,\ (-2,\,2).$
(b) $x^2 + 4\,y^2 + 2\,x + 8\,y - 20 = 0,\ (2,\,-3).$ *Ans.* $3\,x - 8\,y = 30.$
(c) $2\,x^2 + 3\,y^2 = 50,\ (-1,\,-4).$
(d) $y = x^3 + 2\,x,\ (1,\,3).$ *Ans.* $5\,x - y = 2.$
(e) $2\,y^2 = x^3,\ (2,\,2).$
(f) $y = 2\,x^3 + 3,\ (-2,\,-13).$
(g) $2\,x^2 - 3\,y^2 = 12,\ (3,\,\sqrt{2}).$ *Ans.* $\sqrt{2}\,x - y = 2\,\sqrt{2}.$
(h) $y = 2\,x - x^2,\ (0,\,0).$ *Ans.* $y = 2\,x.$
(i) $xy = x + 3,\ (3,\,2).$
(j) $xy - 2\,x + y = 0,\ (x_1 = 3).$

TANGENTS

70. A general theorem. Taking next any equation of the second degree, we may prove the

Theorem. *The equation of the tangent to the locus of*
$$Ax^2 + Bxy + Cy^2 + Dx + Ey + F = 0$$
at the point of contact $P_1(x_1, y_1)$ is

$$Ax_1x + B\frac{y_1x + x_1y}{2} + Cy_1y + D\frac{x + x_1}{2} + E\frac{y + y_1}{2} + F = 0.$$

Proof. Let $P_1(x_1, y_1)$ and $P_2(x_1 + h, y_1 + k)$ be two points on the conic. Then

(1) $\quad Ax_1^2 + Bx_1y_1 + Cy_1^2 + Dx_1 + Ey_1 + F = 0$, and

(2) $\ A(x_1 + h)^2 + B(x_1 + h)(y_1 + k) + C(y_1 + k)^2 + D(x_1 + h)$
$\hfill + E(y_1 + k) + F = 0.$

Clearing (2) of parentheses, and subtracting (1) from (2), we obtain

(3) $\quad 2Ax_1h + Ah^2 + Bx_1k + By_1h + Bhk + 2Cy_1k + Ck^2 + Dh + Ek = 0.$

Transposing all the terms containing h, factoring and dividing, we get

$$\frac{k}{h} = -\frac{2Ax_1 + By_1 + D + Ah + Bk}{Bx_1 + 2Cy_1 + E + Ck}.$$

This is the slope of the secant P_1P_2.

If we let P_2 approach P_1, h and k will approach zero, and the slope m of the tangent is
$$m = -\frac{2Ax_1 + By_1 + D}{Bx_1 + 2Cy_1 + E}.$$

The equation of the tangent line is then

$$y - y_1 = -\frac{2Ax_1 + By_1 + D}{Bx_1 + 2Cy_1 + E}(x - x_1).$$

To reduce this equation to the required form we first clear of fractions and transpose. This gives

$(2Ax_1 + By_1 + D)x + (Bx_1 + 2Cy_1 + E)y$
$\hfill - (2Ax_1^2 + 2Bx_1y_1 + 2Cy_1^2 + Dx_1 + Ey_1) = 0.$

But from (1) the last parenthesis in this equation equals
$$-(Dx_1 + Ey_1 + 2F).$$

Substituting, the equation of the tangent line is

$$(2Ax_1 + By_1 + D)x + (Bx_1 + 2Cy_1 + E)y + (Dx_1 + Ey_1 + 2F) = 0.$$

Removing the parentheses, collecting the coefficients of $A, B, C, D, E,$ and F, and dividing by 2, we obtain the equation of the theorem. Q.E.D.

The result above enables us to write down the equation of the tangent to the locus of any equation of the second degree. For, by comparing the equation of the curve and the equation of the tangent, we obtain the following

Rule *to write the equation of the tangent at the point of contact* $P_1(x_1, y_1)$ *to the locus of an equation of the second degree.*

Substitute x_1x *and* y_1y *for* x^2 *and* y^2, $\dfrac{y_1x + x_1y}{2}$ *for* xy, *and* $\dfrac{x + x_1}{2}$ *and* $\dfrac{y + y_1}{2}$ *for* x *and* y *in the given equation.*

For example, the equation of the tangent at the point of contact (x_1, y_1) to the conic $x^2 + 3xy - 4y + 5 = 0$ is

$$x_1x + \tfrac{3}{2}(x_1y + y_1x) - \tfrac{4}{2}(y + y_1) + 5 = 0;$$

or, also, $\quad (2x_1 + 3y_1)x + (3x_1 - 4)y - 4y_1 + 10 = 0.$

71. Equation of the normal. The normal to a curve at a point P_1 is the line drawn through P_1 perpendicular to the tangent at P_1. When the equation of the tangent has been found, we may find at once the equation of the normal in the manner of Chapter IV. Thus, using the equations of the tangents given on page 134, we find the

Theorem. *The equation of the normal at* $P_1(x_1, y_1)$ *to the ellipse* $b^2x^2 + a^2y^2 = a^2b^2$ *is* $a^2y_1x - b^2x_1y = (a^2 - b^2)x_1y_1$; *hyperbola* $b^2x^2 - a^2y^2 = a^2b^2$ *is* $a^2y_1x + b^2x_1y = (a^2 + b^2)x_1y_1$; *parabola* $y^2 = 2px$ *is* $y_1x + py = x_1y_1 + py_1.$

For example, for the ellipse the slope of the tangent

$$b^2x_1x + a^2y_1y = a^2b^2$$

is $\quad\quad m = -\dfrac{A}{B} = -\dfrac{b^2x_1}{a^2y_1}.$

Hence the equation of the normal is

$$y - y_1 = \frac{a^2y_1}{b^2x_1}(x - x_1),$$

and this reduces to the equation in the theorem.

TANGENTS

In numerical examples the student should use the rule given to write down the equation of the tangent and then find the normal as a perpendicular line, and should not use the special formulas.

72. Subtangent and subnormal. If the tangent and normal at P_1 intersect the x-axis in T and N respectively, then we define

(1) $\quad P_1T =$ length of tangent at P_1,
$\quad\quad P_1N =$ length of normal at P_1.

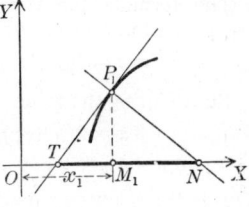

The projections on XX' of P_1T and P_1N are called, respectively, the *subtangent* and *subnormal* at P_1; that is, in the figure,

(2) $\quad\quad M_1T =$ *subtangent* at P_1,
$\quad\quad\quad M_1N =$ *subnormal* at P_1.

Theorem. *If m is the slope of the tangent at (x_1, y_1), then*

(3) $\quad -\dfrac{y_1}{m} = subtangent, \quad my_1 = subnormal.$

Proof. In the figure, since $\angle P_1TM_1 = \angle M_1P_1N$ (sides mutually perpendicular), and m is the tangent of $\angle P_1TM_1$, then

$$\text{in } \triangle P_1TM_1, \ m = \frac{M_1P_1}{TM_1} = \frac{y_1}{TM_1};$$

$$\text{in } \triangle M_1P_1N, \ m = \frac{M_1N}{M_1P_1} = \frac{subnormal}{y_1}.$$

From these, noting that $TM_1 = -M_1T$, we have equations (3). Q.E.D.

Since the subtangent and subnormal are measured in opposite directions from the foot of the ordinate M_1P_1, they will have opposite signs.

The lengths of the tangent P_1T and normal P_1N are now easily found by geometry.

EXAMPLE

Find the equations of tangent and normal, and the lengths of subtangent and subnormal, at the point on the parabola $x^2 = 4y$ whose abscissa equals 3.

Solution. The point of contact (x_1, y_1) is
$$x_1 = 3, \quad y_1 = \tfrac{9}{4}.$$

The formula for the tangent at (x_1, y_1) is, by the rule, Art. 70
$$x_1 x = 2(y + y_1).$$

Substituting the values of x_1 and y_1,
$$3x = 2(y + \tfrac{9}{4}),$$
or $\quad 6x - 4y - 9 = 0.$ *Ans.*

This is the required equation of the tangent.

The slope of this line is $\tfrac{3}{2}$. Hence the equation of the normal at $(3, \tfrac{9}{4})$ is
$$y - \tfrac{9}{4} = -\tfrac{2}{3}(x - 3), \quad \text{or} \quad 8x + 12y - 51 = 0. \ \textit{Ans.}$$

Using (3), we have $m = \tfrac{3}{2}$, $y_1 = \tfrac{9}{4}$. Hence the subtangent $= -\tfrac{3}{2}$, and the subnormal $= \tfrac{27}{8}$. *Ans.*

The lengths of the tangent and normal may be found by geometry, for the lengths of the legs of the triangles $P_1 T M_1$ and $M_1 P_1 N$ are now known.

73. Tangent with a given slope. The method of finding the equation of the tangent in this case is illustrated in the following

EXAMPLE

Find the equation of a tangent to the ellipse
(1) $\qquad 5x^2 + y^2 = 5$
with a slope equal to 2.

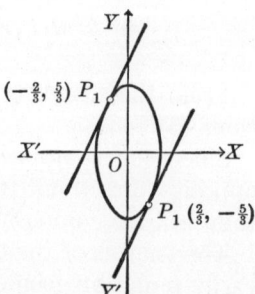

Solution. Let $P_1(x_1, y_1)$ be the point of contact. The equation of the required tangent is (Art. 70)
(2) $\qquad 5x_1 x + y_1 y = 5.$

The slope of (2) must equal 2. Hence

(3) $\quad -\dfrac{5x_1}{y_1} = 2, \quad \text{or} \quad y_1 = -\dfrac{5}{2} x_1.$

TANGENTS

Since P_1 is on the ellipse (1), we have

(4) $$5 x_1^2 + y_1^2 = 5.$$

Solving (3) and (4), we obtain the points of contact of two parallel tangents, namely, $(\frac{2}{3}, -\frac{5}{3})$ and $(-\frac{2}{3}, \frac{5}{3})$. Substituting in (2), we get

$$2x - y - 3 = 0, \quad 2x - y + 3 = 0. \quad Ans.$$

74. Tangent from an external point.
We may readily find the equation of a tangent drawn from an external point, as in the following

EXAMPLE

Find the equation of a tangent to the ellipse

(1) $$5 x^2 + y^2 = 5$$

from the point $A(-2, -1)$.

Solution. Let $P_1(x_1, y_1)$ be the point of contact. The equation of the required tangent is (Art. 70)

(2) $$5 x_1 x + y_1 y = 5.$$

But the point $A(-2, -1)$ lies on this tangent. Hence

(3) $$-10 x_1 - y_1 = 5.$$

Also x_1 and y_1 satisfy (1); that is,

(4) $$5 x_1^2 + y_1^2 = 5.$$

Solving (3) and (4), we obtain the points of contact of two tangents from A, namely, $(-\frac{2}{3}, \frac{5}{3})$ and $(-\frac{2}{7}, -1\frac{5}{7})$. Substituting in (2), we get

$$2x - y + 3 = 0, \quad 2x + 3y + 7 = 0. \quad Ans.$$

PROBLEMS

1. Find the equation of the normal to each of the following curves at the point indicated:

(a) $2 x^2 + 3 y^2 = 35$, $(2, 3)$. *Ans.* $9x - 4y = 6$.
(b) $y^2 = 4x + 4$, $(3, 4)$.
(c) $x^2 + xy = 4$, $(-2, 0)$. *Ans.* $x - 2y + 2 = 0$.
(d) $xy^2 = 9$, $(1, -3)$.
(e) $3 y^2 = x^3$, $(3, 3)$.
(f) $x^2 + 4 y^2 + 5 x = 0$, $(-4, 1)$. *Ans.* $8x + 3y + 29 = 0$.

2. Find the lengths of the subtangent and subnormal in each part of Problem 1. *Ans.* (a) $6\frac{3}{4}$, $-1\frac{1}{3}$.

3. Show that the subtangent for the parabola $y^2 = 2\,px$ is twice the abscissa of the point of contact, and that the subnormal is constant and equal to p.

4. Find the equations of tangent and normal, and the lengths of subtangent and subnormal, to the given curve at the point of contact given:

(a) $y^2 - 6\,y - 8\,x - 31 = 0$, $(-3, -1)$.
Ans. $x + y + 4 = 0$, $x - y + 2 = 0$; $-1, 1$.
(b) $2\,x^2 - y^2 = 14$, $(3, -2)$.
(c) $x^2 - 3\,y^2 + 6\,x + 12\,y = 9$, $(0, 3)$.
(d) $5\,x^2 + 9\,y^2 + 20\,x + 36\,y + 11 = 0$, $(1, -2)$.
(e) $4\,x^2 + 9\,y^2 + 24\,x + 36\,y = 0$, $(0, 0)$.
Ans. $2\,x + 3\,y = 0$, $3\,x - 2\,y = 0$; $0, 0$.

5. Derive the equations of the tangents drawn from the point given to the given curve:

(a) $x^2 + y^2 = 5$, $(3, -1)$. *Ans.* $x - 2\,y - 5 = 0$, $2\,x + y - 5 = 0$.
(b) $x^2 + 4\,y^2 = 4$, $(2, 2)$.
(c) $12\,x^2 - 10\,y^2 = 120$, $(0, 2)$.
(d) $3\,x^2 + y^2 = 16$, $(2, 2)$.
(e) $y^2 = 6\,x$, $(8, 13)$. *Ans.* $x - 8\,y + 96 = 0$, $3\,x - 2\,y + 2 = 0$.

6. Find the equations of the tangents to the conics below with the slope or inclination indicated:

(a) $2\,x^2 + 3\,y^2 = 6$, $m = -1$. *Ans.* $x + y = \pm\sqrt{5}$.
(b) $y^2 = 4\,x$, $\alpha = 30°$.
(c) $x^2 + y^2 = 25$, $m = -\frac{3}{4}$.
(d) $2\,y^2 - 16\,x^2 = 1$, $m = 2$.
(e) $y^2 - 12\,y - 8\,x + 20 = 0$, $\alpha = 90°$. *Ans.* $x + 2 = 0$.
(f) $15\,x^2 - 8\,y^2 + 30\,x + 32\,y - 137 = 0$, $m = \sqrt{2}$.
Ans. $\sqrt{2}\,x - y + 3 + \sqrt{2} = 0$, $\sqrt{2}\,x - y + 1 + \sqrt{2} = 0$.
(g) $8\,x^2 + 9\,y^2 = 72$, $m = 1$.

7. Find the equations of the normals to the following conics with slope as indicated:

(a) $xy = 4$, $m = \frac{1}{4}$. *Ans.* $x - 4\,y \pm 15 = 0$.
(b) $4\,x^2 + 6\,y^2 = 25$, $m = -6$.
(c) $x^2 - 4\,y^2 = 9$, $m = \frac{1}{2}$.
(d) $2\,y^2 - 16\,x^2 = 1$, $m = \pm 1$.

75. Formulas for tangents when the slope is given. For later reference we collect in this section formulas giving the equations of tangents to the conics with the slope m. The

TANGENTS

student should derive these formulas, following the method of Art. 73.

Theorem. *The equation of a tangent with the slope m to the circle $x^2 + y^2 = r^2$ is $y = mx \pm r\sqrt{1+m^2}$;
ellipse $b^2x^2 + a^2y^2 = a^2b^2$ is $y = mx \pm \sqrt{a^2m^2 + b^2}$;
hyperbola $b^2x^2 - a^2y^2 = a^2b^2$ is $y = mx \pm \sqrt{a^2m^2 - b^2}$;
parabola $y^2 = 2\,px$ is $y = mx + \dfrac{p}{2m}$.*

A second method is set forth in the following

EXAMPLE

Find the equations of the tangents to the ellipse

(1) $$5x^2 + y^2 = 5$$

whose slope equals 2.

Solution. The equation of the system of lines whose slope equals 2 is

(2) $$y = 2x + k,$$

where k is an arbitrary parameter.

For what value of k is the line (2) a tangent? To answer this, we *start to solve for the points of intersection with the ellipse* (1). Substituting from (2) into (1),

(3) $5x^2 + (2x + k)^2 = 5.$

Squaring and collecting terms,

(4) $9x^2 + 4kx + k^2 - 5 = 0.$

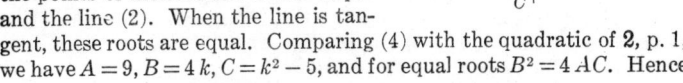

The roots of (4) are the abscissas of the points of intersection of the ellipse and the line (2). When the line is tangent, these roots are equal. Comparing (4) with the quadratic of **2**, p. 1, we have $A = 9, B = 4k, C = k^2 - 5$, and for equal roots $B^2 = 4AC$. Hence

(5) $16k^2 - 36(k^2 - 5) = 0,$ or $k = \pm 3.$

The equations of the required tangents are therefore

$AB: y = 2x + 3$ and $CD: y = 2x - 3$. *Ans.*

Check. Writing $k = 3$ in (4), we obtain

$9x^2 + 12x + 4 = 0,$ or $(3x + 2)^2 = 0.$

The equal roots have the common value $x = -\frac{2}{3}$. This is the abscissa of the point of contact P. From $y = 2x + 3$ the ordinate is found to be $y = \frac{5}{3}$. Hence P is $(-\frac{2}{3}, \frac{5}{3})$.

Similarly, putting $k = -3$ in (4), we find Q to be $(\frac{2}{3}, -\frac{5}{3})$.

The method followed may be described as follows:

To find the equation of the tangent to a conic when the slope of the tangent is given,

1. Write down the equation of the system of lines with the given slope $(y = mx + k)$. This equation contains a parameter (k) whose value must be found.

2. Eliminate x or y from the equations of the line and conic and arrange the result in the form of a quadratic,

(6) $\qquad Ay^2 + By + C = 0 \quad \text{or} \quad Ax^2 + Bx + C = 0.$

3. The roots of this quadratic must be equal. Hence set

(7) $\qquad\qquad\qquad B^2 - 4AC = 0,$

solve this for the parameter k, and substitute the values in the equation of the system of lines.

4. *Check.* When each value of the parameter satisfying (7) is substituted in (6), the quadratic becomes a perfect square.

PROBLEMS

1. Find the equations of the tangents to the following conics which satisfy the condition indicated. Find the points of contact and verify by plotting:

(a) $x^2 + y^2 = 16$, $m = -\frac{4}{3}$.

$\qquad$ *Ans.* $4x + 3y \pm 20 = 0$; $(3\frac{1}{5}, 2\frac{2}{5})$, $(-3\frac{1}{5}, -2\frac{2}{5})$.

(b) $y^2 = 4x$, $m = 1$. $\qquad$ *Ans.* $x - y + 1 = 0$; $(1, 2)$

(c) $x^2 + y^2 - 2x + 3y - 8 = 0$, $m = 2$.

(d) $x^2 + y^2 - 2y = 0$, $\alpha = 90°$.

(e) $xy - 12 = 0$, $m = -\frac{3}{2}$.

(f) $x^2 - 4y^2 = 4$, perpendicular to $x - 2y - 5 = 0$.

(g) $x^2 + 9y^2 = 4$, perpendicular to $9x - y = 0$.

(h) $x^2 - y^2 - 4x + 6y + 7 = 0$, parallel to $x + 2y = 7$.

(i) $9x^2 - 16y^2 = 32$, parallel to $18x - 8\sqrt{7}y = 15$.

$\qquad$ *Ans.* $9x - 4\sqrt{7}y = \pm 8$; $(4, \sqrt{7})$, $(-4, -\sqrt{7})$.

TANGENTS

(j) $4x^2 + 7y^2 = 79$, $m = \frac{8}{21}$.
 Ans. $8x - 21y = \pm 79$; $(-2, 3)$, $(2, -3)$.
(k) $2x^2 + 5y^2 = 10$, $\alpha = 60°$.
(l) $x^2 + 2y^2 = 22$, parallel to $2x - 6y + 11 = 0$.
 Ans. $x - 3y \pm 11 = 0$; $(-2, 3)$, $(2, -3)$.
(m) $4x^2 - 9y^2 + 36 = 0$, perpendicular to $5x + 2y = 7$.
(n) $x^2 - 2y^2 = 1$, $m = \frac{3}{4}$.
(o) $xy + y^2 - 4x + 8y = 0$, $m = \frac{1}{2}$.
(p) $x^2 + 2xy + y^2 + 8x - 6y = 0$, $m = \frac{4}{3}$.
 Ans. $4x - 3y = 0$; $(0, 0)$.
(q) $x^2 + 2xy - 4x + 2y = 0$, $m = 2$.
 Ans. $y = 2x$, $2x - y + 10 = 0$; $(0, 0)$, $(-2, 6)$.

2. Find the points of contact for each of the tangents given in the theorem on page 141.

Ans. Points of contact of tangent with slope m to the ellipse are

$$\left(-\frac{a^2 m}{\sqrt{a^2 m^2 + b^2}},\ \frac{b^2}{\sqrt{a^2 m^2 + b^2}}\right);\ \text{etc.}$$

76. Properties of tangents and normals to conics. If we draw the tangent AB and the normal CD at any point P_1 on the ellipse, and if we draw also the **focal radii** P_1F and P_1F', we may prove the following

Theorem. *The tangent and normal to an ellipse bisect, respectively, the external and internal angles formed by the focal radii of the point of contact.*

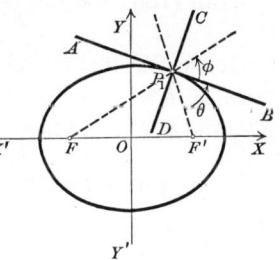

Proof. In the figure we wish to prove $\theta = \phi$. To do this we find $\tan \phi$ and $\tan \theta$ by (V), Art. 14.

The slopes of the lines joining $P_1(x_1, y_1)$ on the ellipse

$$b^2 x^2 + a^2 y^2 = a^2 b^2$$

to the foci $F'(c, 0)$ and $F(-c, 0)$ are

$$\text{slope of } F'P_1 = \frac{y_1}{x_1 - c}; \quad \text{slope of } FP_1 = \frac{y_1}{x_1 + c}.$$

The slope of the tangent AB is $-\dfrac{b^2 x_1}{a^2 y_1}$.

Now $\tan \theta = \dfrac{m_1 - m_2}{1 + m_1 m_2}$, where $m_1 =$ slope of AB, $m_2 =$ slope of $P_1 F'$.

Substituting the above values of the slopes.

$$\tan \theta = \frac{-\dfrac{b^2 x_1}{a^2 y_1} - \dfrac{y_1}{x_1 - c}}{1 - \dfrac{b^2 x_1 y_1}{a^2 y_1 (x_1 - c)}} = \frac{-b^2 x_1^2 + b^2 c x_1 - a^2 y_1^2}{a^2 x_1 y_1 - a^2 c y_1 - b^2 x_1 y_1}$$

$$= \frac{(a^2 y_1^2 + b^2 x_1^2) - b^2 c x_1}{a^2 c y_1 - (a^2 - b^2) x_1 y_1}.$$

But since P_1 lies on the ellipse, $a^2 y_1^2 + b^2 x_1^2 = a^2 b^2$ and also $a^2 - b^2 = c^2$.

Hence
$$\tan \theta = \frac{a^2 b^2 - b^2 c x_1}{a^2 c y_1 - c^2 x_1 y_1} = \frac{b^2(a^2 - c x_1)}{c y_1 (a^2 - c x_1)} = \frac{b^2}{c y_1}.$$

In like manner,
$$\tan (180° - \phi) = \frac{-b^2 x_1^2 - b^2 c x_1 - a^2 y_1^2}{a^2 x_1 y_1 + a^2 c y_1 - b^2 x_1 y_1} = -\frac{b^2}{c y_1}.$$

Hence $\tan \theta = \tan \phi$; and since θ and ϕ are both less than π, $\theta = \phi$. That is, AB bisects the external angle of FP_1 and $F'P_1$, and hence, also, CD bisects the internal angle.

Q.E.D.

An obvious application of this theorem is to the problem

To draw a tangent and normal at a given point P_1 on an ellipse.

This is done by connecting P_1 with the foci and bisecting the internal and external angles formed by these lines.

The phenomenon observed in "whispering galleries" depends upon this property. Let the elliptic arc $A'PA$ be a vertical section of such a gallery. The waves of sound from a voice at the focus F will, after meeting the ceiling of the gallery at P, be reflected in the direction PF'. For if PN is the normal at P, $\angle NPF = \angle NPF'$, and the

TANGENTS

law of reflection of sound waves is precisely that the angles of incidence ($=\angle NPF$) and reflection ($=\angle NPF'$) are equal. Hence sound waves emanating from F in all directions will converge at F'. A whisper at F, which would not carry over the distance FF', might consequently, through reflection, be audible at F'.

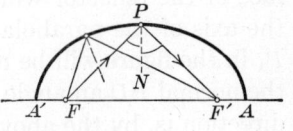

In like manner we prove the following theorems:

The tangent and normal to a hyperbola bisect respectively the internal and external angles formed by the focal radii of the point of contact.

The tangent and normal to a parabola bisect respectively the internal and external angles formed by the focal radius of the point of contact and the line through that point parallel to the axis.

These theorems give rules for constructing the tangent and normal to these conics by means of ruler and compasses.

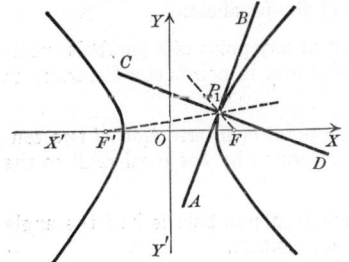 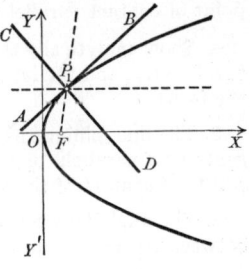

To construct the tangent and normal to a hyperbola at any point, join that point to the foci and bisect the angles formed by these lines. To construct the tangent and normal to a parabola at any point, draw lines through it to the focus and parallel to the axis, and bisect the angles formed by these lines.

The principle of parabolic reflectors depends upon the property of tangent and normal just enunciated. Namely, the reflecting surface of such a reflector is obtained by revolving a parabolic arc about its axis. If, now, a light be placed at the focus, the rays of light which meet the surface of the reflector will all be reflected in the direction of the axis of the parabola; for a ray meeting the surface at P_1 in the figure will be reflected in a direction making with the normal PD an angle equal to the angle FP_1D. But this direction is, by the above property, parallel to the axis OX of the parabola.

PROBLEMS

1. Show analytically that the point of contact of a tangent to a hyperbola bisects the segment of the tangent between the asymptotes.

2. Show analytically (1) that the perpendicular to a focal chord of a parabola erected at the focus meets both tangents at the ends of the focal chord on the directrix; (2) that these tangents are perpendicular to each other.

3. Show analytically that the perpendicular from the focus of a parabola to a tangent meets the directrix on the line drawn from the point of contact parallel to the axis of the parabola.

4. Show analytically that a tangent at any point of a parabola meets the directrix and the latus rectum produced in points equidistant from the focus.

5. The line joining the focus to the point of intersection of two tangents to a parabola bisects the angle formed by the focal radii to the points of contact of the tangents.

6. The angle between two tangents to a parabola is half the angle between the focal radii to the points of contact.

For individual study or assignment

7. Show analytically that the product of the perpendicular distances to the foci from a tangent to an ellipse (or hyperbola) is constant.

8. An ellipse and a hyperbola which are confocal intersect at right angles.

9. Find the equations of the parabola $y^2 = 2\,px$ when referred to the tangents (perpendicular) at the extremities of its latus rectum as axes.

Ans. $x^{\frac{1}{2}} + y^{\frac{1}{2}} = \sqrt{p\sqrt{2}}$.

TANGENTS

10. Show that a point P on a central conic divides the segment AB intercepted by the axes on the normal at P in a constant ratio (a^2 to b^2).

11. A tangent at one vertex of a hyperbola meets the conjugate hyperbola in two points. Show that tangents at these points pass through the other vertex.

12. Show that the foci of a hyperbola and the points where a tangent meets the tangents at the vertices are on a circle.

13. Find the points of an ellipse such that the subtangent and subnormal are equal.
$$Ans. \left(\pm \frac{a^2}{\sqrt{a^2 + b^2}},\ \pm \frac{b^2}{\sqrt{a^2 + b^2}} \right).$$

14. Show that the two equilateral hyperbolas so placed that the asymptotes of one are the axes of the other intersect at right angles.

15. Show analytically that the triangle formed by a tangent to a hyperbola and the asymptotes has a constant area.

CHAPTER IX

POLAR COÖRDINATES

77. Polar coördinates. In this chapter we shall consider a second method of determining points in the plane by coördinates. We suppose given a fixed point O, called the **pole**, and a fixed line OA, passing through O, called the **polar axis**. Then the position of a point P is determined by the length $OP = \rho$ (Greek letter "rho") and the angle $AOP = \theta$. The numbers ρ and θ are called the **polar coördinates** of P; ρ is called the **radius vector** and θ the **vectorial angle**. The vectorial angle θ is *positive* or *negative* as in trigonometry (see **5**, p. 2). The radius vector is *positive* if P lies on the terminal line of θ, and *negative* if P lies on that line produced through the pole O.

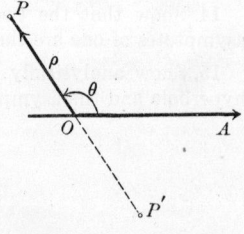

Thus, in the figure the radius vector of P is positive, and that of P' is negative.

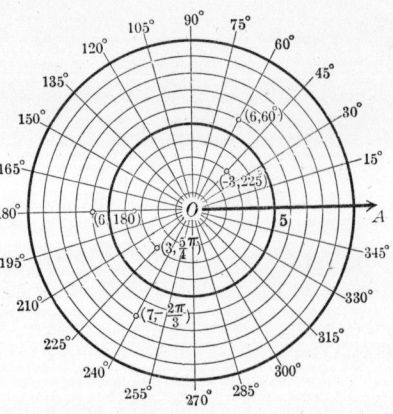

It is evident that *every pair of real numbers (ρ, θ) determines a single point*, which may be plotted by the

Rule *to plot a point whose polar coördinates (ρ, θ) are given.*

POLAR COÖRDINATES

Construct the terminal line of the vectorial angle θ, as in trigonometry. If the radius vector is positive, lay off a length $OP = \rho$ on the terminal line of θ; if negative, produce the terminal line through the pole and lay off OP equal to the numerical value of ρ. Then P is the required point.

In the figure on page 148 are plotted the points whose polar coördinates are (6, 60°), (3, $\frac{5}{4}\pi$), (−3, 225°), (6, 180°), and (7, −$\frac{2}{3}\pi$).

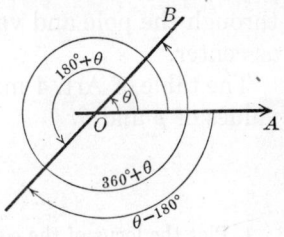

Every point has an infinite number of polar coördinates.

Thus, if $OB = \rho$, the coördinates of B may be written in any one of the forms (ρ, θ), $(-\rho, 180° + \theta)$, $(\rho, 360° + \theta)$, $(-\rho, \theta - 180°)$, etc.

Unless the contrary is stated, *we shall always suppose that θ is positive or zero, and less than 360°*; that is, $0 \leqq \theta < 360°$.

PROBLEMS

1. Plot the points (3, 30°), (6, 120°), (− 5, − 145°), (− 10, − 20°), (− 4, 60°).

2. Plot the points (10, 0°), (− 2, 90°), (5, 180°), (5, 18°), (5, 100°), ($4\frac{1}{2}$, 135°).

3. Show that the points (ρ, θ) and $(\rho, -\theta)$ are symmetric with respect to the polar axis.

4. Show that the points (ρ, θ) and $(-\rho, \theta)$ are symmetric with respect to the pole.

5. Show that the points (ρ, θ) and $(\rho, 180° - \theta)$ are symmetric with respect to the line $\theta = 90°$.

6. Give another pair of coördinates for each of the points of Problems 1 and 2.

7. What is the distance (1) between the points (3, 210°) and (4, 30°)? (2) between the points (4, 45°) and (− 6, 15°)?

8. What is the angle made with the polar axis by the line joining (4, 60°) and (3, 30°)?

9. Find the distance between (1, 30°) and (− 2, 240°). (Use the law of cosines, 11, p. 4.) *Ans.* 1.24.

150 NEW ANALYTIC GEOMETRY

78. Plotting polar equations. Solve the equation for ρ in terms of θ. Substitute convenient values for θ and calculate the corresponding values of ρ until the coördinates of enough points are obtained to determine the form of the curve. Connect the points by a curve.

The plotting is facilitated by the use of polar coördinate paper, which enables us to plot values of θ by lines drawn through the pole and values of ρ by circles having the pole as center.

The table of Art. 4 may be used in constructing tables of values of ρ and θ.

EXAMPLES

1. Plot the locus of the equation

(1) $$\rho = 10 \cos \theta.$$

Solution. Assume values for θ as in the table below, and calculate ρ, making use of 8, p. 3. For example, if

$$\theta = 105°, \rho = 10 \cos 105° = 10 \cos(180° - 75°) = -10 \cos 75° = -2.6.$$

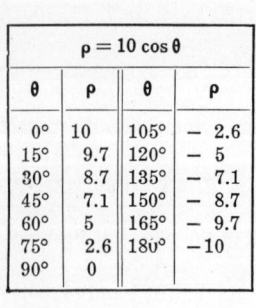

$\rho = 10 \cos \theta$			
θ	ρ	θ	ρ
0°	10	105°	− 2.6
15°	9.7	120°	− 5
30°	8.7	135°	− 7.1
45°	7.1	150°	− 8.7
60°	5	165°	− 9.7
75°	2.6	180°	−10
90°	0		

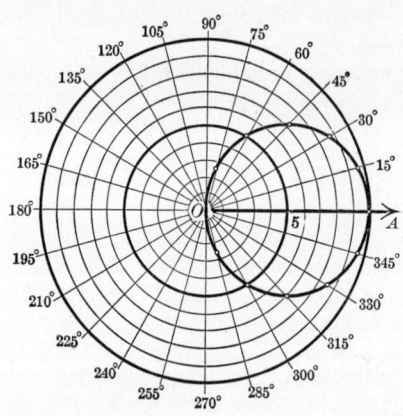

The complete locus is found in this example without going beyond 180° for θ.

POLAR COÖRDINATES

Discussion. 1. *Symmetry.* Since $\cos(-\theta) = \cos\theta$ (8, p. 3), equation (1) may be written $\rho = 10\cos(-\theta)$; that is, for every point (ρ, θ) on the locus there is also a second point $(\rho, -\theta)$ on the locus. Since these points are symmetric with respect to the polar axis, we have this result: *The locus of* (1) *is symmetric with respect to the polar axis.*

2. *Extent.* θ may have any value, but ρ ranges from 0 to 10. Hence the curve is closed. In Art. 81 we learn that it is a circle.

2. Draw the locus of
(2) $$\rho^2 = a^2 \cos 2\theta.$$

Solution. Before plotting, discuss the equation.

Discussion. 1. *Symmetry.* We may change θ to $-\theta$ in (2) without affecting the equation. Also we may replace ρ by $-\rho$. Hence the locus is symmetric with respect to the polar axis, and with respect to the pole.

2. *Extent.* Since the maximum value of $\cos 2\theta$ is 1, the maximum value of ρ is a, and the curve must be *closed*.

When $\cos 2\theta$ is negative, ρ will be imaginary. Now $\cos 2\theta$ is negative when 2θ is an angle in the second or third quadrant; that is, when
$$90° < 2\theta < 270°, \text{ or } 45° < \theta < 135°,$$

ρ is imaginary. There is no part of the curve between the 45° and 135° lines.

In the table θ is given values from 0° to 45°.

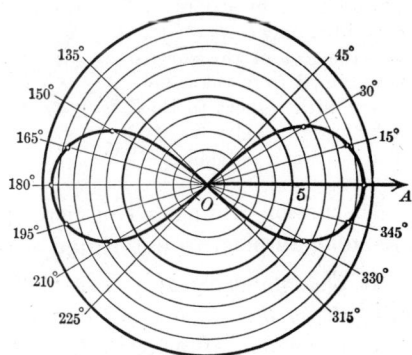

$\rho^2 = a^2 \cos 2\theta$			
θ	2θ	$\cos 2\theta$	ρ
0°	0°	1	$\pm a$
15°	30°	.866	$\pm .93\,a$
30°	60°	.500	$\pm .7\,a$
45°	90°	0	0

The complete curve results by plotting these points and the points symmetric to them with respect to the polar axis. It is called a lemniscate. In the figure a is taken equal to 9.5.

3. Discuss and plot the locus of the equation

$$(3) \qquad \rho = \frac{2a}{1+\cos\theta}.$$

$\rho = 2 \div (1+\cos\theta)$							
θ	$\cos\theta$	$1+\cos\theta$	ρ	θ	$\cos\theta$	$1+\cos\theta$	ρ
0°	1	2	1	105°	−.259	.741	2.7
15°	.966	1.966	1.02	120°	−.500	.500	4
30°	.866	1.866	1.07	135°	−.707	.293	6.8
45°	.707	1.707	1.2	150°	−.866	.134	15
60°	.500	1.500	1.3	165°	−.966	.034	59
75°	.259	1.259	1.6	180°	−1	0	∞
90°	0	1	2				

Solution. *Discussion.* 1. *Symmetry.* The curve is symmetric with respect to the polar axis, since θ may be replaced by $-\theta$.

2. *Extent.* ρ becomes infinite when $1+\cos\theta = 0$, or $\cos\theta = -1$, and hence $\theta = 180°$. The curve recedes to infinity in the direction $\theta = 180°$. No values of θ are excluded.

The table of values is computed only to $\theta = 180°$, and the rest of the curve is obtained from the symmetry with respect to the polar axis. Take $a = 1$. The locus is a parabola.

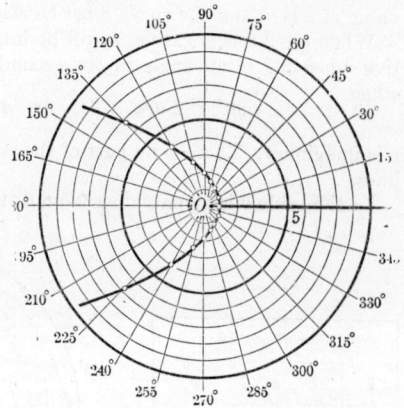

Discussion of a polar equation. It is usually easy (see the above examples) to determine

1. *The symmetry of a curve with respect to the polar axis, the pole, or the line $\theta = 90°$* (see Problem 5, Art. 77).

2. *The extent of the curve (closed or not closed).*

Before plotting polar equations, the student should establish such simple facts as result from a discussion, as illustrated above.

POLAR COÖRDINATES

PROBLEMS

Discuss and plot the loci of the following equations:

1. $\rho = 8$.
2. $\theta = 135°$.
3. $\rho = 10 \sin \theta$.
4. $\rho = 2 \sin \theta + 3 \cos \theta$.
5. $\rho \sin \theta = 5$.
6. $\rho = \dfrac{4}{1 + \cos \theta}$.
7. $\rho = \dfrac{8}{2 + \cos \theta}$.
8. $\rho = \dfrac{8}{1 + 2 \cos \theta}$.
9. $\rho = a \sin 2\theta$.
10. $\rho = 2(1 + \tan \theta)$.
11. $\rho^2 \sin 2\theta = 9$.
12. $\rho^2 \cos 2\theta = a^2$.
13. $\rho = a \sin \theta \tan \theta$.

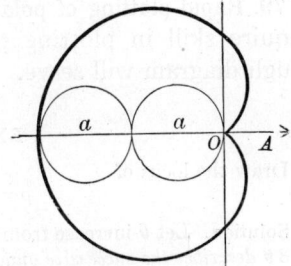

15. $\rho = a(1 - \cos \theta)$.
CARDIOID

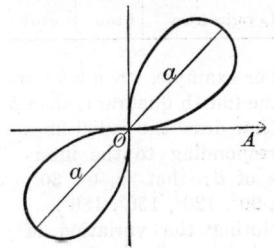

16. $\rho^2 = a^2 \sin 2\theta$.
TWO-LEAVED ROSE LEMNISCATE

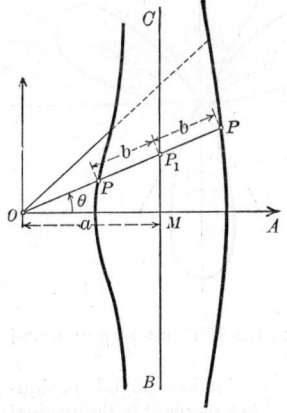

14. $\rho = a \sec \theta \pm b;\ b < a$.
CONCHOID OF NICOMEDES

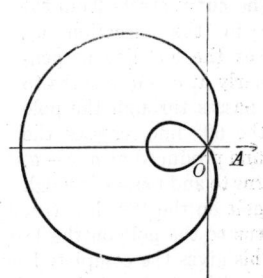

17. $\rho = b - a \cos \theta;\ b < a$.
LIMAÇON

18. Plot the conchoid (Problem 14) for $b = a$; $b > a$.

19. Plot the limaçon (Problem 17) for $b > a$.

79. Rapid plotting of polar equations. The student should acquire skill in plotting polar equations rapidly when a rough diagram will serve.

EXAMPLE

Draw the locus of
(1) $$\rho = a \sin 3\theta,$$

Solution. Let θ increase from $0°$. Follow the variation of ρ from (1) *as 3θ describes the successive quadrants.*

When 3θ varies from	0° to 90°	90° to 180°	180° to 270°	270° to 360°	360° to 450°	450° to 540°
then θ varies from	0° to 30°	30° to 60°	60° to 90°	90° to 120°	120° to 150°	150° to 180°
and ρ varies from	0 to a	a to 0	0 to $-a$	$-a$ to 0	0 to a	a to 0

For example, when 3θ varies from $270°$ to $360°$, that is, is an angle in the fourth quadrant, then ρ is negative and increases from $-a$ to 0.

Now draw the radial lines corresponding to the intervals of θ; that is, $0°$, $30°$, $60°$, $90°$, $120°$, $150°$, $180°$.

Noting the variation of ρ and the corresponding variation of θ, we sketch the curve as follows:

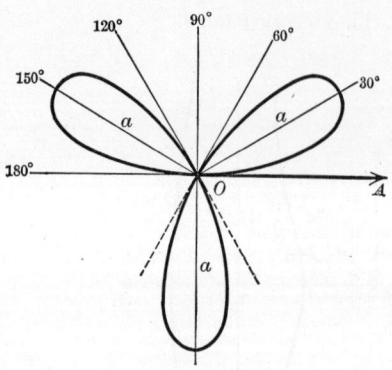

The curve starts from the pole in the direction $0°$, crosses the $30°$ line perpendicularly at $\rho = a$, returns to and passes through the pole on the $60°$ line, crosses the $90°$ line produced at $\rho = -a$, returns to and passes through the pole on the $120°$ line (produced), crosses the $150°$ line at $\rho = a$, and returns to the pole on the $180°$ line.

This gives the complete locus. The pencil point has moved continuously without *abrupt change in direction, and has returned to the original position and direction.*

The curve is called the **three-leaved rose.**

POLAR COÖRDINATES

PROBLEMS

Sketch the locus of each of the following equations:

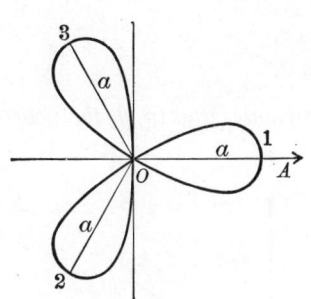

1. $\rho = a \cos 3\theta$.

THREE-LEAVED ROSE

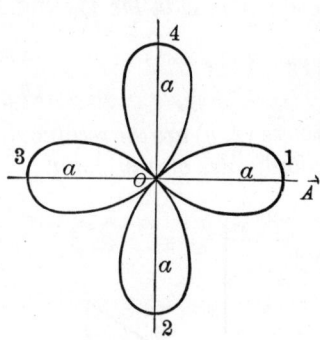

3. $\rho = a \cos 2\theta$.

FOUR-LEAVED ROSE

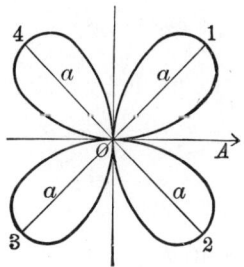

2. $\rho = a \sin 2\theta$.

FOUR-LEAVED ROSE

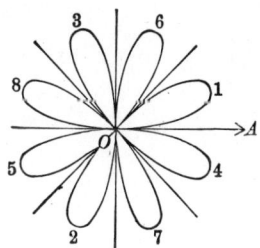

4. $\rho = a \sin 4\theta$.

EIGHT-LEAVED ROSE

5. $\rho = a \cos \frac{1}{2}\theta$.

6. $\rho = a \sin \frac{2}{3}\theta$.

7. $\rho = a \cos 4\theta$.

8. $\rho = a(1 + 2\sin\theta)$.

9. $\rho = a(2 + \cos\theta)$.

10. $\rho = a \sin(\theta + 45°)$.

11. $\rho = a \cos\left(\theta + \dfrac{\pi}{6}\right)$.

12. $\rho = a \sin \frac{1}{3}\theta$.

13. $\rho = a \cos \frac{2}{3}\theta$.

14. $\rho = a \cos \frac{1}{3}\theta$.

15. $\rho = a \sin^2 \frac{1}{2}\theta$.

16. $\rho = a \cos^2 \frac{1}{2}\theta$.

17. $\rho = a \sin^3 \frac{1}{3}\theta$.

18. $\rho = a \cos^3 \frac{1}{3}\theta$.

80. Relations between rectangular and polar coördinates.

Theorem. *If the pole coincides with the origin and the polar axis with the positive x-axis, then*

(I) $$\begin{cases} x = \rho \cos \theta, \\ y = \rho \sin \theta, \end{cases}$$

where (x, y) are the rectangular coördinates and (ρ, θ) the polar coördinates of any point.

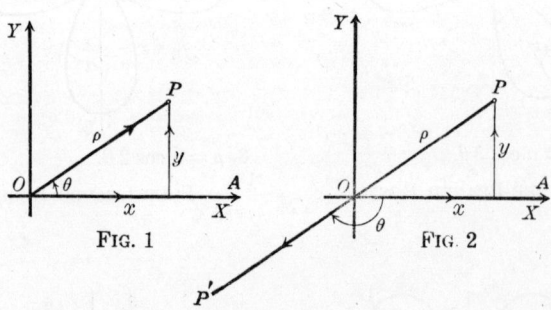

Proof. When ρ is *positive* (Fig. 1) we have, by definition,

$$\cos \theta = \frac{x}{\rho}, \quad \sin \theta = \frac{y}{\rho},$$

whatever quadrant P is in. Solving, we get

(1) $\qquad x = \rho \cos \theta, \quad y = \rho \sin \theta.$

When ρ is *negative* (Fig. 2) we plot the point P', whose rectangular and polar coördinates are respectively $(-x, -y)$ and $(-\rho, \theta)$. Hence for P', by (1), since $-\rho$ is positive,

$$-x = -\rho \cos \theta, \quad -y = -\rho \sin \theta;$$
or $\qquad x = \rho \cos \theta, \qquad y = \rho \sin \theta,$
as before. Q.E.D.

Equations (I) enable us to find the equation of a curve in polar coördinates when its equation in rectangular co-

POLAR COÖRDINATES

ordinates is known. From the figures we also have the useful relations

(2) $$\begin{cases} \rho^2 = x^2 + y^2, & \theta = \tan^{-1}\dfrac{y}{x}, \\ \sin\theta = \dfrac{y}{\pm\sqrt{x^2+y^2}}, & \cos\theta = \dfrac{x}{\pm\sqrt{x^2+y^2}}. \end{cases}$$

These equations express the polar coördinates of any point in terms of the rectangular coördinates.

EXAMPLES

1. Find the equation of the circle $x^2 + y^2 = 25$ in polar coördinates.

Solution. From the first equation of (2), we have at once $\rho^2 = 25$; hence $\rho = \pm 5$, which is the required equation. It expresses the fact that the distance of the point (ρ, θ) from the origin is five units.

2. Find the equation of the lemniscate (Example 2, p. 151) $\rho^2 = a^2 \cos 2\theta$ in rectangular coördinates.

Solution. By 10, p. 3, since $\cos 2\theta = \cos^2\theta - \sin^2\theta$,
$$\rho^2 = a^2(\cos^2\theta - \sin^2\theta).$$
Substituting from (2),
$$x^2 + y^2 = a^2\left(\frac{x^2}{x^2+y^2} - \frac{y^2}{x^2+y^2}\right).$$
$$\therefore (x^2 + y^2)^2 = a^2(x^2 - y^2). \quad Ans.$$

81. Applications. Straight line and circle.

Theorem. *The general equation of a straight line in polar coördinates is*

(II) $$\rho(A\cos\theta + B\sin\theta) + C = 0,$$

where A, B, and C are arbitrary constants.

Proof. The general equation of the line in rectangular coördinates is
$$Ax + By + C = 0.$$
By substitution from (I) we obtain (II). Q.E.D.

Special cases of (II) are $\rho\cos\theta = a$, $\rho\sin\theta = b$, which result, respectively, when $B = 0$ or $A = 0$, that is, when the line is parallel to OY or OX.

In like manner we obtain from (2), Art. 34, the

Theorem. *The general equation of a circle in polar coördinates is*

(III) $\qquad \rho^2 + \rho(D \cos \theta + E \sin \theta) + F = 0,$

where D, E, and F are arbitrary constants.

If the pole is on the circumference and the polar axis is a diameter, the equation is

$$\rho = 2\, r \cos \theta,$$

where r is the radius of the circle.

Similarly, if the circle touches the polar axis at the pole, the equation is $\rho = 2\, r \sin \theta$. These results may easily be derived directly from the accompanying figures.

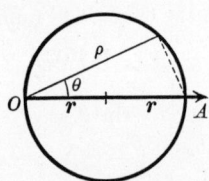 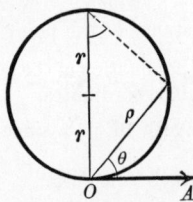

Theorem. *The length l of the line joining two points $P_1(\rho_1, \theta_1)$ and $P_2(\rho_2, \theta_2)$ is given by*

(IV) $\qquad l^2 = \rho_1^2 + \rho_2^2 - 2\,\rho_1\rho_2 \cos(\theta_1 - \theta_2).$

Proof. Let the rectangular coördinates of P_1 and P_2 be respectively (x_1, y_1) and (x_2, y_2). Then, by (I), Art. 80,

$$x_1 = \rho_1 \cos \theta_1, \quad x_2 = \rho_2 \cos \theta_2,$$
$$y_1 = \rho_1 \sin \theta_1, \quad y_2 = \rho_2 \sin \theta_2.$$

But $\qquad l^2 = (x_1 - x_2)^2 + (y_1 - y_2)^2,$

and hence

$$l^2 = (\rho_1 \cos \theta_1 - \rho_2 \cos \theta_2)^2 + (\rho_1 \sin \theta_1 - \rho_2 \sin \theta_2)^2.$$

Removing parentheses and using formulas from 7 and 9, p. 3, we obtain (IV). Q.E.D.

Formula (IV) may also be derived directly from a figure by using the law of cosines (11, p. 4).

POLAR COÖRDINATES

82. Polar equation for the conic sections.

Theorem. *The polar equation of a conic section is*

(V) $$\rho = \frac{ep}{1 - e \cos \theta}$$

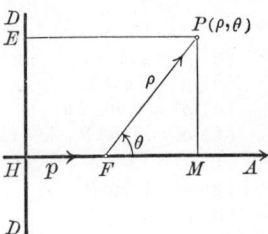

if the pole is at the focus and the polar axis is perpendicular to the directrix, if we assume that e is the eccentricity and p the distance from the focus to the directrix.

Proof. For let P be any point on the conic. Then, by definition (see Art. 66),

$$\frac{FP}{EP} = e.$$

From the figure, $FP = \rho$,

and $EP = HM = p + \rho \cos \theta.$

Substituting these values of FP and EP, we have

$$\frac{\rho}{p + \rho \cos \theta} = e.$$

Solving for ρ, we obtain (V).   Q.E.D.

PROBLEMS

1. Find the polar coördinates of the points $(5, 12)$, $(13, 12)$, $(-4, -3)$, $(\sqrt{3}, 1)$, $(-2\sqrt{3}, 2)$, $(1, -1)$, $(5, 5)$.

2. Transform the following equations into polar equations and plot the loci:

(a) $2x - 5y = 0.$ *Ans.* $\tan \theta = \frac{2}{5}.$

(b) $4x - 3y + 6 = 0.$

(c) $x^2 + y^2 = 25.$ *Ans.* $\rho = \pm 5.$

(d) $x^2 + y^2 + 2x = 0.$

(e) $x^2 + y^2 - 2x + 4y = 5.$ *Ans.* $\rho^2 - \rho(2 \cos \theta - 4 \sin \theta) = 5.$

(f) $xy = a.$

(g) $x^2 - y^2 = a^2.$ *Ans.* $\rho^2 \cos 2\theta = a^2.$

(h) $(x^2 + y^2)^2 = a^2(x^2 - y^2).$

(i) $(x^2 + y^2 + bx)^2 - a^2(x^2 + y^2) = 0.$

(j) $(1 - e^2)x^2 + y^2 - 2px + p^2 = 0.$

(k) $y^2 = 3x^3.$

3. Transform the following polar equations into rectangular equations:

(a) $\rho = 7$.
(b) $\theta = 15°$.
(c) $\rho = 4 \sin \theta$.
(d) $\rho = 6 \cos \theta$.
(e) $\rho^2 = 9 \cos 2\theta$.
(f) $\rho^2 = 4 \cot \theta$.
  Ans. $x^2 y + y^3 = 4x$.
(g) $\rho = \frac{1}{3} \tan \theta$.
(h) $\rho = 4 \sec \theta$.

(i) $\rho(2 \cos \theta + 3 \sin \theta) + 5 = 0$.
  Ans. $2x + 3y + 5 = 0$.
(j) $\rho(7 \cos \theta - 5 \sin \theta) = 7$.
(k) $\rho = 5 \csc \theta$.
(l) $\rho^2 \cos 2\theta = 16$.
(m) $\rho + 6 \cot \theta \csc \theta = 0$.
  Ans. $y^2 + 6x = 0$.
(n) $\rho = \dfrac{6}{1 + 2 \cos \theta}$.

4. If we rotate the polar axis through an angle α about the pole, what are the relations between the old coördinates (ρ, θ) and the new (ρ', θ') of any point?

5. If the polar axis is rotated 90° about the pole, that is, so that it is parallel to the directrix of the conic as discussed in Art. 82, what form does the equation (V) assume?   *Ans.* $\rho = \dfrac{ep}{1 + e \sin \theta}$.

6. Compare the equations of each of the following conics with (V), Art. 82, or Problem 5, and find e and p. Plot and draw the directrix.

(a) $\rho = \dfrac{7}{2 - 2 \cos \theta}$. *Ans.* $e = 1$, $p = \frac{7}{2}$.   (c) $\rho = \dfrac{12}{1 + 3 \cos \theta}$.

(b) $\rho = \dfrac{16}{2 + \sin \theta}$. *Ans.* $e = \frac{1}{2}$, $p = 16$.   (d) $\rho = \dfrac{10}{2 - \sin \theta}$.

83. Points of intersection. By a method analogous to that used in rectangular coördinates we find the coördinates of the points of intersection of two polar curves by solving their equations simultaneously. This is best done by eliminating ρ, which will give rise in general to a transcendental equation in θ.

The following example will illustrate the method:

EXAMPLE

Find the points of intersection of

(1) $$\rho = 1 + \cos \theta,$$

(2) $$\rho = \frac{1}{2(1 - \cos \theta)}$$

POLAR COÖRDINATES

Solution. Eliminating ρ,

$$1 + \cos \theta = \frac{1}{2(1 - \cos \theta)},$$

or $\quad 1 - \cos^2 \theta = \tfrac{1}{2},$

$$\cos \theta = \pm \frac{\sqrt{2}}{2}.$$

$$\therefore \theta = \pm 45°, \pm 135°.$$

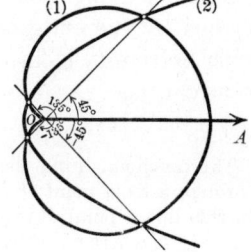

Substituting these values in either equation, we obtain the following four points,

$$\left(1 + \frac{\sqrt{2}}{2}, \pm 45°\right), \left(1 - \frac{\sqrt{2}}{2}, \pm 135°\right). \; Ans.$$

The result checks in the figure. The locus of (1) is a cardioid; of (2), a parabola.

PROBLEMS

Find the points of intersection of the following pairs of curves and check by drawing the figure:

1. $\begin{cases} \rho = 4 \sin \theta, \\ \rho = 2. \end{cases}$
   Ans. $(2, 30°), (2, 150°)$.

2. $\begin{cases} \rho = 1 + \cos \theta, \\ \rho = \tfrac{1}{2}. \end{cases}$

3. $\begin{cases} \rho = 2a \sin \theta, \\ \rho = 2a. \end{cases}$

4. $\begin{cases} \rho \cos \theta = 4a, \\ \rho = 4a \cos \theta. \end{cases}$
   Ans. $(4a, 0°), (-4a, 180°)$.

5. $\begin{cases} \rho = \sin \theta, \\ \rho = \cos 2\theta. \end{cases}$
   Ans. $(\tfrac{1}{2}, 30°), (\tfrac{1}{2}, 150°)$.

6. $\begin{cases} \rho = \cos 2\theta, \\ \rho = \tfrac{1}{2}. \end{cases}$

7. $\begin{cases} \rho = 4 + 4 \cos \theta, \\ \rho(1 - \cos \theta) = 3. \end{cases}$
   Ans. $(6, \pm 60°), (2, \pm 120°)$.

8. $\begin{cases} \rho^2 = \sin 2\theta, \\ \rho = \sqrt{2} \sin \theta. \end{cases}$

9. $\begin{cases} \rho = 5 - 2 \sin \theta, \\ \rho = \dfrac{6}{1 + \sin \theta}. \end{cases}$

10. $\begin{cases} \rho^2 \cos 2\theta = a^2, \\ \rho = \sqrt{2}\, a. \end{cases}$

11. $\begin{cases} \rho \cos (\theta - 60°) = a, \\ \rho \cos (\theta - 30°) = a. \end{cases}$

12. $\begin{cases} \rho = \dfrac{3}{2 - \cos \theta}, \\ \rho = 2. \end{cases}$

13. $\begin{cases} \rho = 6 \sin \theta, \\ \rho = 2(1 + \cos \theta). \end{cases}$

14. $\begin{cases} \rho = a \sin \theta, \\ \rho = a \sin 2\theta. \end{cases}$

15. $\begin{cases} \rho = 2 + \cos \theta, \\ 4\rho (1 - \cos \theta) = 9. \end{cases}$ *Ans.* $(\tfrac{3}{2}, 120°), (\tfrac{3}{2}, 240°)$.

84. Loci using polar coördinates.

When a curve is described by the end-point of a line of variable length whose other extremity is fixed, polar coördinates may be employed to advantage.

EXAMPLE

The conchoid. Find the locus of a point P constructed as follows: Through a fixed point O a line is drawn cutting a fixed line BC at P_1. On this line a point P is taken so that $P_1P = \pm b$, where b is a constant.

Solution. The required locus is the locus of the end-point P of the line OP, and O is fixed. Hence we use polar coördinates, taking O for the pole and the perpendicular OM to BC for the polar axis. Then

(1) $\quad OP = \rho, \quad \angle MOP = \theta.$

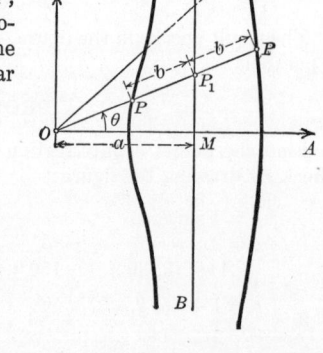

By construction,

(2) $\quad \rho = OP = OP_1 \pm b.$

But in the right $\triangle\, OMP_1$,

(3) $\quad OP_1 = OM \sec \angle MOP_1 = a \sec \theta.$

Substituting from (3) in (2),

(4) $\quad \rho = a \sec \theta \pm b.$

The locus of this equation is called the *conchoid of Nicomedes*. It has three distinct forms according as a is greater, equal to, or less than b.

PROBLEMS

1. Find the equation of the locus of the mid-points of chords of the circle $\rho = 2\, r \cos \theta$ drawn from the pole.

2. The chord OB of a fixed circle $\rho = a \cos \theta$ drawn from O is produced to P so that BP is determined as below. Find the locus of P and plot.

(a) BP equals the perpendicular distance of B from the polar axis.

Ans. $\rho = a \cos \theta (1 + \sin \theta).$

(b) BP = diameter = a. (See Fig. 1.)

Ans. The **cardioid** $\rho = a(1 + \cos \theta).$

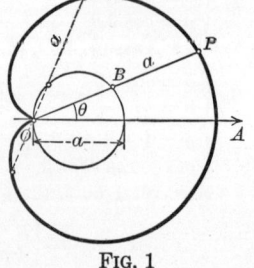

Fig. 1

POLAR COÖRDINATES

(c) $BP = $ radius $= \frac{1}{2} a$. (See Example 17, p. 153.)

Ans. The limaçon $\rho = a(\frac{1}{2} + \cos \theta)$.

(d) $BP = MB$. (See Fig. 2.)   Ans. The circle $\rho = a(\sin \theta + \cos \theta)$.

(e) $BP = 2\, MB$.

(f) $BP = \frac{3}{2} a$.

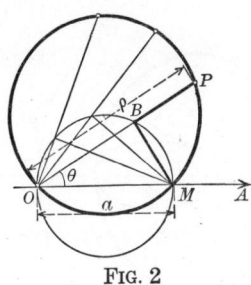

Fig. 2

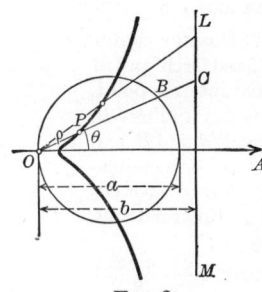

Fig. 3

3. Lines are drawn from the fixed point O on a fixed circle to meet a fixed line LM which is perpendicular to the diameter through O. On any such line OC lay off $OP = BC$. What is the locus of P? (Fig. 3.)

Ans. $\rho = b \sec \theta - a \cos \theta$.

Plot the locus when (1) $b = 4, a = 3$; (2) $b = 3, a = 4$; (3) $a = b = 4$. When $a = b$ the curve is the **cissoid** (Problem 8, Art. 95).

4. A line is drawn from the pole O to meet the line $\rho \cos \theta = 4$ at M. Find the equation of the locus of a point P on OM under the condition given, and plot.

    (a) $MP = 4$.   (b) $MP = OM + 4$.   (c) $OM \cdot OP = 12$.

PROBLEMS FOR INDIVIDUAL STUDY OR ASSIGNMENT

Plot carefully the following loci:

1. $\rho = a \sin \theta + b \sec \theta$.
2. $\left(\rho - \dfrac{a}{2}\right)^2 = a^2 \cos 2\theta$.
3. $\rho = a(\cos 2\theta + \sin 2\theta)$.
4. $\rho = a \cos 2\theta + \frac{1}{2} a \sec \theta$.
5. $\rho = a \sin 2\theta + \frac{1}{2} a \sec \theta$.
6. $\rho = a \cos 2\theta + b \cos \theta$.
7. $\rho = a \sin 2\theta + b \cos \theta$.
8. $\rho = a \cos 2\theta + b(\sin \theta + 1)$.
9. $\rho = a \cos 3\theta - b \cos \theta$.
10. $\rho = \cos 3\theta + \cos \theta + 1$.
11. $\rho = \cos 3\theta + \cos 2\theta$.
12. $\rho = \cos 3\theta - \sin 2\theta$.
13. $\rho^2 \cos \theta = a^2 \sin 3\theta$.
14. $\rho^2 = \dfrac{2 \cos \theta}{\cos 2\theta} + 1$.
15. $\rho^2 = \dfrac{2 \cos 2\theta}{\cos \theta + 2} + 1$.

16. On a radius vector (focal radius) FQ of the ellipse $\rho = \dfrac{6}{2 - \cos \theta}$ lay off from Q toward F a segment $QP = 4$. Find the locus of P. (The segment QP = semi-major axis.)

17. O is the center of a fixed circle and M a fixed interior point. Draw any radius OB, connect M and B, and draw MP perpendicular to MB to meet OB at P. Required the locus of P.

Ans. $\rho = e \dfrac{e - a \cos \theta}{e \cos \theta - a}$

if $OB = a$, $OM = e$.

Draw the locus when $a = 4, e = 2$, and show that it is the same as in Problem 16.

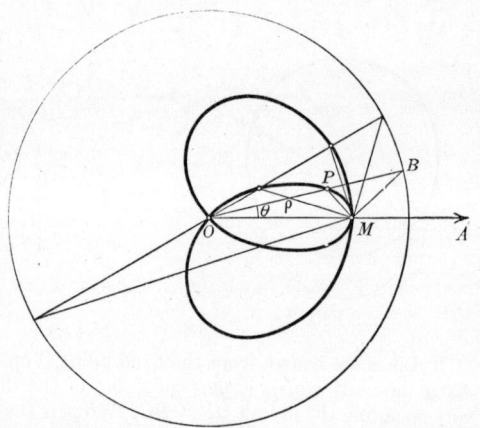

18. Let the x-axis cut the circle $x^2 + y^2 = a^2$ at C. An arc CB is laid off on the circle equal to the abscissa x_0 of a point (x_0, y_0) on the parabola $y^2 = 4cx$, and the radius OB is produced to P, making $BP = y_0$. Show that the locus of P is the **parabolic spiral** $(\rho - a)^2 = 4 ac\theta$ (see figure).

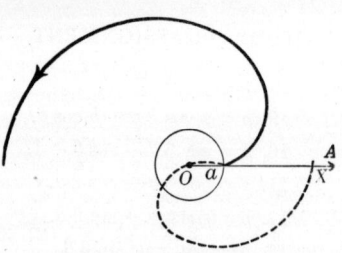

PARABOLIC SPIRAL

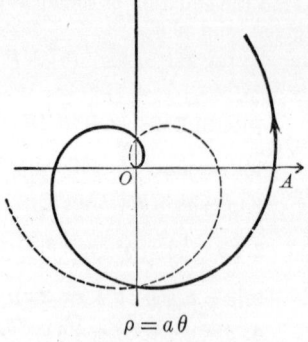

$\rho = a\theta$

SPIRAL OF ARCHIMEDES

19. Find the locus of a point such that

(a) its radius vector is proportional to its vectorial angle;

Ans. The spiral of Archimedes, $\rho = a\theta$.

(b) its radius vector is inversely proportional to its vectorial angle;

Ans. The **hyperbolic** or **reciprocal spiral**, $\rho\theta = a$.

(c) the square of its radius vector is inversely proportional to its vectorial angle;

Ans. The lituus, $\rho^2\theta = a^2$.

(d) the logarithm of its radius vector is proportional to its vectorial angle.

Ans. The logarithmic spiral, $\log \rho = a\theta$.

20. *Theorem on the logarithmic spiral.* When two points, P_1 and P_2, have been plotted on a logarithmic spiral, points between them on the locus may be constructed geometrically by the following theorem:

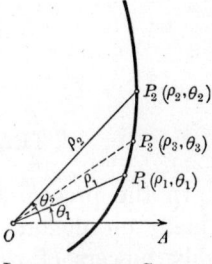

LOGARITHMIC SPIRAL

If the angle P_2OP_1 is bisected, and if on this bisector OP_3 is laid off equal to the mean proportional between OP_1 and OP_2, then P_3 is on the locus.

Prove this theorem (see figure).

CHAPTER X

TRANSCENDENTAL CURVES

In the preceding chapters the emphasis has been laid chiefly on algebraic equations, that is, equations involving only powers of the coördinates x, y. We now turn our attention to equations such as

$$y = \log x, \quad y = 2^x, \quad x = \sin y,$$

which are called *transcendental equations*, and their loci, *transcendental curves*.

85. Natural logarithms. The *common* logarithm of a given number N is the exponent x of the base 10 in the equation

(1) $\qquad 10^x = N; \text{ that is, } x = \log_{10} N.$

In a second system of logarithms, known as *natural* or *Naperian* logarithms, the base is denoted by e, called the *natural base*. Numerically, to three decimal places,

(2) $\qquad\qquad\qquad e = 2.718.$

The *natural* logarithm of a given number N is the exponent y in the equation

(3) $\qquad\qquad e^y = N; \text{ that is, } y = \log_e N.$

To find the equation connecting the *common* and *natural* logarithms of a given number, we may take the logarithms of both members of (3) to the base 10, which gives

(4) $\qquad \log_{10} e^y = \log_{10} N, \text{ or } y \log_{10} e = \log_{10} N.$ [3, p. 2]

Substituting the value of y from (3), we obtain

(5) $\qquad\qquad \log_{10} N = \log_{10} e \cdot \log_e N.$

TRANSCENDENTAL CURVES

Hence the common logarithm of any number equals the product of its natural logarithm by the constant $\log_{10} e$. This constant is called the **modulus** ($= M$) of the **common** system; that is, using a table of logarithms,

(6) $\qquad M = \log_{10} e = 0.434;$ also $\dfrac{1}{M} = 2.303.$

We may summarize in the equations

(A)   **Common log = natural log times 0.434,**
         Natural log = common log times 2.303.

These equations show us how to find the natural logarithm from the common logarithm, or vice versa.

Exponential and logarithmic curves. The locus of the equation

(7) $\qquad\qquad y = e^x$

is called an *exponential curve*. From the preceding we may write (7) also in the form

(8) $\quad x = \log_e y = 2.303 \log_{10} y.$

The locus of (7) is therefore the curve whose abscissas are the natural logarithms of the ordinates. Let us now discuss and plot (7) (see figure).

Discussion. 1. *Intercepts.* From (8), if $y = 0$, $x = \log_e 0 = -\infty$. From (7), if $x = 0$, $y = e^0 = 1$. Results are put down in the table.

2. There is no symmetry.

3. Since negative numbers have no logarithms, negative values of y are excluded,

x	y
$-\infty$	0
0	1

but no values of x. Moreover, x increases as y increases.

4. The x-axis is an asymptote, for y approaches 0 as the negative values of x increase numerically.

The coördinates of a few points on the locus are set down in the table. A table of values of e^x and e^{-x} is given below.

If the curve is carefully drawn, natural logarithms may be measured off. Thus, in the figure, if $y = 4$, by measurement $x = 1.39 = \log_e 4$.

x	y	x	y
0	1	0	1
1	$e = 2.7$	-1	$\dfrac{1}{e} = .37$
2	$e^2 = 7.4$	-2	$\dfrac{1}{e^2} = .14$
etc.	etc.	etc.	etc.

The locus of

(9) $\qquad y = be^{ax}$,

where a and b are constants, is also an *exponential curve*. The discussion is left to the student.

Table of values of the exponential function e^x.

x	.0		.1		.2		.3		.4	
	e^x	e^{-x}	e^x	e^{-x}	e^x	e^{-x}	e^x	e^{-x}	e^x	e^{-x}
0	1.00	1.00	1.11	0.90	1.22	0.82	1.35	0.74	1.49	0.67
1	2.72	0.37	3.00	0.33	3.32	0.30	3.67	0.27	4.06	0.25
2	7.39	0.14	8.17	0.12	9.03	0.11	9.97	0.10	11.0	0.09
3	20.1	0.05	22.2	0.05	24.5	0.04	27.1	0.04	30.0	0.03
4	54.6	0.02	60.3	0.02	66.7	0.02	73.7	0.01	81.5	0.01
5	148	0.01	164	0.01	181	0.01	200	0.00	221	0.00

x	.5		.6		.7		.8		.9	
	e^x	e^{-x}	e^x	e^{-x}	e^x	e^{-x}	e^x	e^{-x}	e^x	e^{-x}
0	1.65	0.61	1.82	0.55	2.01	0.50	2.23	0.45	2.46	0.41
1	4.48	0.22	4.95	0.20	5.47	0.18	6.05	0.17	6.69	0.15
2	12.2	0.08	13.5	0.07	14.9	0.07	16.4	0.06	18.2	0.06
3	33.1	0.03	36.6	0.03	40.4	0.02	44.7	0.02	49.4	0.02
4	90.0	0.01	99.5	0.01	110	0.01	122	0.01	134	0.01
5	245	0.00	270	0.00	299	0.00	330	0.00	365	0.00

For example, to find the value of $e^{2.3}$, we look in the column under x for the value 2 and then pass to the right under .3. The value sought is found in the column under e^x to be 9.97. The next value to the right of this under e^{-x} is $e^{-2.3} = 0.10$.

TRANSCENDENTAL CURVES

The locus of the equation

(10) $$y = \log_{10} x,$$

called a *logarithmic curve*, differs from the locus of (9) only in its relation to the axes. In fact, both curves are exponential or logarithmic curves, depending upon the point of view.

Solving (10) for x,

(11) $$x = 10^y = e^{2.303\,y}.$$

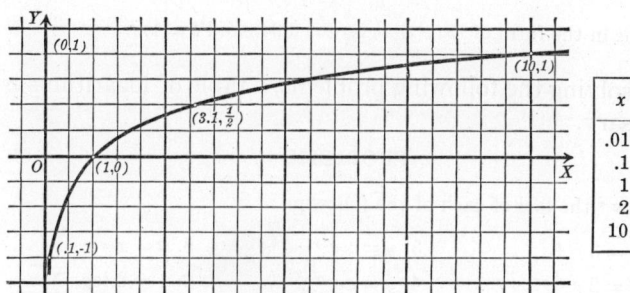

x	y
.01	-2
.1	-1
1	0
2	.301
10	1

Discussion. 1. The intercepts are 1 on OX, $-\infty$ on OY.

2. There is no symmetry.

3. Negative values of x are excluded, but no values of y, which increases with x.

4. The y-axis is a vertical asymptote.

The locus of (10) is given in the figure. Some coördinates are given in the table. The scales chosen are

unit length on OX equals 2 divisions,
unit length on OY equals 4 divisions.

Compound-interest curve. The problem of compound interest introduces exponential curves. For if $r =$ rate per cent of interest, and $n =$ number of years, then the amount ($= A$) of one dollar in n years, if the interest is compounded annually, is given by the formula

$$A = (1 + r)^n.$$

For example, if the rate is 5 per cent, the formula is

(12) $$A = (1.05)^n.$$

170 NEW ANALYTIC GEOMETRY

If we plot years as abscissas and the amounts as ordinates, the corresponding curve will be an exponential curve. For $\log_{10} 1.05 = 0.021$. Hence, from (A),

$$\log_e 1.05 = 2.303 \text{ times } 0.021$$
$$= 0.048 \text{ (to three decimal places)}.$$

Hence, by (3), $\qquad e^{.048} = 1.05,$

and equation (12) becomes

(13) $\qquad A = e^{.048 n},$

which is in the form of (9); that is, $a = 0.048$ and $b = 1$.

In solving the following problems, a table of logarithms is necessary.

PROBLEMS

Draw * the loci of each of the following:

1. $y = 3\, e^{-x}$.
2. $y = 2\, e^{-\frac{1}{2}x}$.
3. $y = \frac{1}{2}\, e^{2x}$.
4. $y = xe^{-2x}$.
5. $y = x^2 e^{-x}$.
6. $y = 2 \log_{10} \sqrt{x}$.
7. $y = \log_{10} (2 + x)$.
8. $y = \log_e (9 - x^2)$.
9. $y = \log_{10} \sqrt{x + 3}$.
10. $y = \log_e (4\, x - x^2)$.

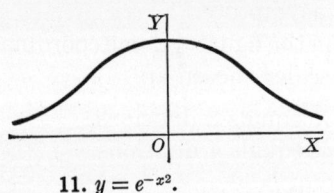

11. $y = e^{-x^2}$.
PROBABILITY CURVE

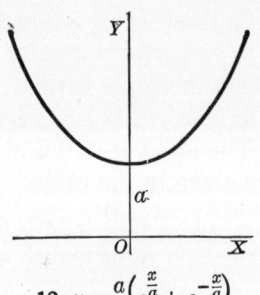

12. $y = \dfrac{a}{2}\Big(e^{\frac{x}{a}} + e^{-\frac{x}{a}}\Big)$.

The locus in Problem 12 is called the **catenary** (see figure). The shape of the curve is that assumed by a heavy flexible cord freely suspended from its extremities.

* If the *shape* only of the curves 1–5 is desired, we may replace e by the approximate value 3.

TRANSCENDENTAL CURVES

86. Sine curves. As already explained (**6**, p. 2), the two common methods of angular measurement, namely, *circular measure* and *degree measure*, employ as units of measurement the *radian* and the *degree* respectively. The relation between these units is

(1) $\qquad\qquad \pi \text{ radians} = 180°.$

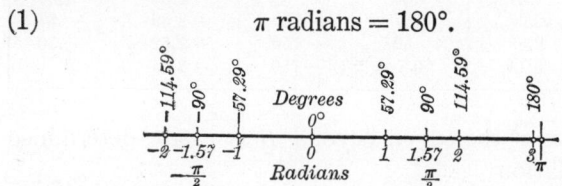

Thus $\frac{1}{2}\pi$ radians $= 90°$, $\frac{1}{4}\pi$ radians $= 45°$, etc. The two scales laid off on the same line give the figure above.

In advanced mathematics, circular measure is commonly used. The numerical value of $\sin 2x$ for $x = 1$ radian, for example, is found as follows:

(2) $\qquad \sin 2x = \sin 2 \text{ radians} = \sin 114° 35' = 0.909.$

Let us now draw the locus of the equation

(3) $\qquad\qquad y = \sin x.$

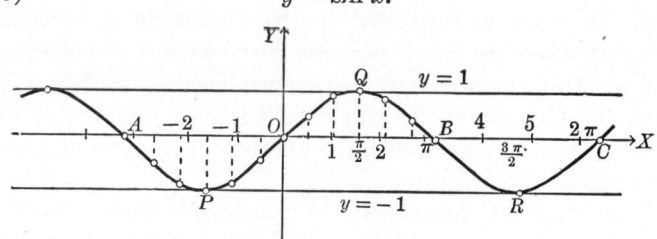

Solution. In making the calculation (see page 172) for plotting, it is convenient to choose values of x at intervals of, say, 30°, then find the values of x in radians, and y from the table of Art. 4 (see also **8**, p. 3).

To plot, choose a convenient unit of length on XX' to represent 1 radian, and use the same unit for ordinates. Plotting, the curve $APOQB$ is the result.

x degrees	x radians	y	x degrees	x radians	y
0	0	0	0	0	0
30	.52	.50	− 30	− .52	− .50
60	1.05	.87	− 60	− 1.05	− .87
90	1.57	1.00	− 90	− 1.57	− 1.00
120	2.09	.87	− 120	− 2.09	− .87
150	2.62	.50	− 150	− 2.62	− .50
180	3.14	0	− 180	− 3.14	0

The course of the curve beyond B is easily determined from the relation

$$\sin(2\pi + x) = \sin x.$$

Hence $\qquad y = \sin x = \sin(2\pi + x);$

that is, the values of y will be repeated if each value of x is increased by 2π. This means that any point on the curve will be also on the curve when moved a distance 2π to the right parallel to OX. Hence the arc APO may be moved parallel to XX' until A falls on B, that is, into the position BRC, and *it will also be a part of the curve in its new position.* This property is expressed by the following statement: The curve $y = \sin x$ is a periodic curve with a **period** equal to 2π. Also, the arc OQB may be displaced parallel to XX' until O falls upon C. In this way it is seen that the entire locus consists of an indefinite number of congruent arcs, alternately above and below XX'.

Discussion. 1. *Intercepts.* If $x = 0$, $y = \sin 0 = 0 =$ intercept on the y-axis. If $y = 0$, then $\sin x = 0$, and $x = n\pi$, n being any integer. Hence the curve cuts the axis of x an indefinite number of times on both the right and left of O, these points being at a distance of π from one another.

2. *Symmetry.* The origin is a center of symmetry, for $\sin(-x) = -\sin x$ (**8**, p. 3). Hence, replacing (x, y) in (3) by $(-x, -y)$, we have $-y = \sin(-x) = -\sin x$, or, changing signs, equation (3) as before.

TRANSCENDENTAL CURVES

3. *Extent.* The curve extends indefinitely along XX' in both directions, but lies between the lines $y = +1$ and $y = -1$.

If the axes are translated to $(\tfrac{1}{2}\pi, 0)$, then (3) becomes

(4) $\quad y' = \sin(x' + \tfrac{1}{2}\pi) = \sin(90° + x') = \cos x'.$

The locus of $y = \cos x$ is therefore a sine curve, as in the figure. This curve differs from the locus of $y = \sin x$ only in the position of the y-axis.

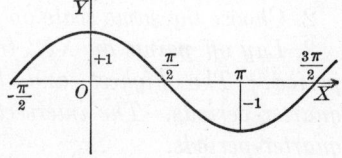

In the figure, p. 171, the curve $APOQB$ may be regarded as a "pattern curve." When this is displaced parallel to $X'X$, either to the right or to the left, a distance equal to any multiple of the period, it will belong to the locus in its new position.

87. Periodicity. The equations

(1) $\quad \sin x = \sin(x + 2\pi), \quad \tan x = \tan(x + \pi)$

indicate that $\sin x$ and $\tan x$ are **periodic functions**. The formal definition is

A function of x is a periodic function if its value is repeated when x is replaced by $x + P$, P being a constant and x any value.

The constant P is called the **period** if it is the *least* number for which the function has the specified property. From (1), $\sin x$ and $\tan x$ are periodic functions, the former with the period 2π, the latter, π. Of course, $\tan(x + 2\pi) = \tan x$, also, but the period is π.

The period of $\sin kx$ is $\dfrac{2\pi}{k}$. In fact, replace x by $x + \dfrac{2\pi}{k}$. Then kx becomes $kx + 2\pi$, and $\sin kx$ becomes $\sin(kx + 2\pi)$. But these are equal.

In the same way it may be shown that *the period of $\tan ax$ is $\dfrac{\pi}{a}$.*

88. Plotting sine curves. Assume the equation

(1) $$y = a \sin kx.$$

The period is $\frac{2\pi}{k}$. The values of y range from $-a$ to $+a$ inclusive. The maximum value a is called the **amplitude**.

As it is important to sketch sine curves quickly, the following directions are useful:

1. *Find the amplitude a and the period P.*
2. *Choose the same scale on both axes.*
3. *Lay off points on XX' from O at intervals of a quarter-period. The highest and lowest points are at the odd quarter-periods. The intersections with XX' are at the even quarter-periods.*

Thus, in the figure, p. 171, where $\frac{1}{4}P = \frac{1}{2}\pi$, at Q, $x = \frac{1}{2}\pi$; at R, $x = \frac{3}{2}\pi$; at B, $x = \pi$; etc.

EXAMPLES

1. Sketch the sine curve

(2) $$y = 2 \sin \frac{\pi x}{3}.$$

Solution. Amplitude $a = 2$. Period $P = 6$. Hence $\frac{1}{4}P = 1\frac{1}{2}$. Mark the points $x = 0$, $\pm 1\frac{1}{2}$, ± 3, etc. on the x-axis. The corresponding values of y are given in the table. The curve from $x = -3$ to $x = 3$ is shown in the figure.

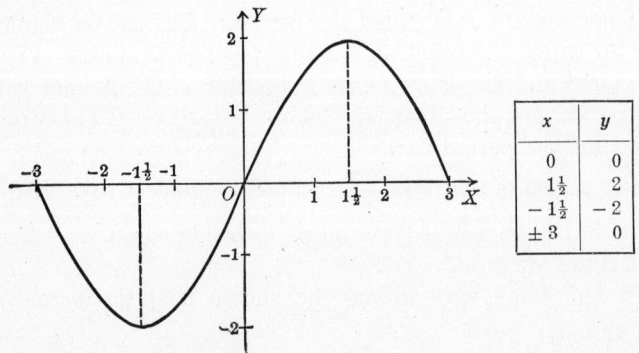

x	y
0	0
$1\frac{1}{2}$	2
$-1\frac{1}{2}$	-2
± 3	0

TRANSCENDENTAL CURVES

2. Sketch the curve

(3) $$y = 2 \sin \left(\tfrac{1}{3} \pi x + \tfrac{1}{6} \pi\right).$$

Solution. Taking the coefficient of x (that is, $\tfrac{1}{3}\pi$) outside the parenthesis, (3) becomes

(4) $$y = 2 \sin \tfrac{1}{3} \pi (x + \tfrac{1}{2}).$$

Set $x + \tfrac{1}{2} = x'$, that is, $x = x' - \tfrac{1}{2}$, and $y = y'$. Then (4) becomes

(5) $$y' = 2 \sin \tfrac{1}{3} \pi x',$$

the same as (2). The figure for (5) is that on page 174, with $x' = 0$ at O. But the transformation $x = x' - \tfrac{1}{2}$, $y = y'$ translates the axes to the new origin $(-\tfrac{1}{2}, 0)$. The point O in the figure is therefore $(-\tfrac{1}{2}, 0)$ referred to the axes of (3). Hence the figure for (3) is obtained by drawing the y-axis at a distance of half a unit to the right of OY.

General sine curves. The locus of

(6) $$y = a \sin (kx + c) \quad \text{or} \quad y = a \cos (kx + c)$$

is a sine curve with amplitude a and period $\dfrac{2\pi}{k}$; for the translation

$$x = x' - \frac{c}{k}, \ y = y'$$

transforms (6) into

$$y' = a \sin kx' \quad \text{and} \quad y' = a \cos kx'$$

respectively.

PROBLEMS

1. Make out a table of values of $\cos x$ (see Art. 86) and plot and discuss fully $y = \cos x$.

Sketch each of the following for a full period. Compute y for the value of x given, plot, and check in the figures.

2. $y = \sin 3x$, $x = \tfrac{1}{2}$.

3. $y = 2 \sin \tfrac{1}{2} x$, $x = \tfrac{1}{2} \pi$.

4. $y = 2 \cos \pi x$, $x = \tfrac{2}{3}$.

5. $y = \tfrac{1}{2} \cos 2x$, $x = 1$.

6. $y = \cos \tfrac{1}{2} \pi x$, $x = 3$.

7. $y = 2 \sin \tfrac{1}{3} \pi x$, $x = 2$.

8. $y = 3 \cos \tfrac{1}{4} \pi x$, $x = -3$.

9. $y = 3 \sin (x + 2)$, $x = 1$.

10. $y = 2 \cos (1 - 3x)$, $x = -\tfrac{1}{3}$.

11. $y = 2 \cos (2\pi x + \tfrac{2}{3} \pi)$, $x = \tfrac{2}{3}$.

12. $y = \tfrac{1}{2} \sin (\tfrac{1}{3} x + \tfrac{1}{2})$, $x = 2$.

13. $y = \sin (\tfrac{1}{3} \pi x - \tfrac{1}{5} \pi)$, $x = 2$.

14. $y = a \sin (kx + \pi)$.

15. $s = a \cos \left(\dfrac{2\pi t}{P} + \beta\right).$

176 NEW ANALYTIC GEOMETRY

89. Other trigonometric curves. *The tangent curve.* The figure shows the tangent curve, locus of

(1) $$y = \tan x.$$

x	y	x	y
0	0	0	0
$\frac{1}{4}\pi$	1	$-\frac{1}{4}\pi$	-1
$\frac{1}{2}\pi$	∞	$-\frac{1}{2}\pi$	∞
$\frac{3}{4}\pi$	-1	$-\frac{3}{4}\pi$	1
π	0	π	0

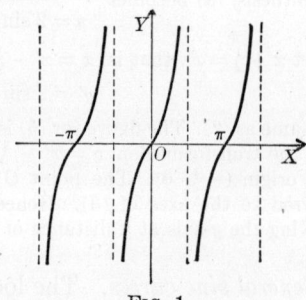

FIG. 1

The period $P = \pi$, and values of y for multiples of a quarter period are shown in the table.

Discussion. 1. *Intercepts.* On the y-axis, 0; on the x-axis, $\pm n\pi$, n any integer.

2. *Symmetry.* The curve is symmetric with respect to O.

3. *Extent.* No values of x or y excluded.

4. *Asymptotes.* $x = \frac{1}{2}\pi \pm n\pi$, n any integer.

Note that the distance between consecutive asymptotes equals the period π.

The secant curve. The locus of

(2) $$y = \sec x$$

is shown in the figure.

x	y	x	y
0	1	$\frac{1}{3}\pi$	2
$\frac{1}{2}\pi$	∞	$-\frac{1}{3}\pi$	2
π	-1		

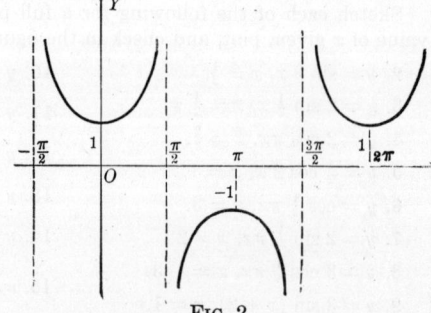

FIG. 2

TRANSCENDENTAL CURVES

The period is $P = 2\pi$. Lay off points on the x-axis at intervals of a quarter-period $\frac{1}{2}\pi$, write (2) in the form

$$(3) \qquad y = \frac{1}{\cos x},$$

and recall the values of $\cos x$ for these values of x. The table gives also values of y for other values of x.

The pattern for a tangent curve may be taken as the branch between the asymptotes $x = -\frac{1}{2}P$, $x = \frac{1}{2}P$; for a secant curve, the two branches between the asymptotes $x = -\frac{1}{4}P$, $x = \frac{3}{4}P$.

The cotangent curve. The figure for the locus of $y = \cot x$ is shown in Art. 111. The following discussion shows that this curve can be obtained from the tangent curve by a simple geometric transformation.

In Fig. 1 translate the axes to $(\frac{1}{2}\pi, 0)$. Then (1) becomes

$$(4) \qquad y' = \tan(\tfrac{1}{2}\pi + x') = -\cot x'. \quad [\text{By } \mathbf{8}, \text{p. 3}]$$

The figure for (4) is Fig. 1 except that the y'-axis lies along the asymptote $x = \frac{1}{2}\pi$. In (4), replace y' by $-y'$. Then we obtain

$$(5) \qquad -y' = -\cot x', \text{ or } y' = \cot x'.$$

The figure for (5) is obtained from Fig. 1 by drawing $O'Y'$ along the asymptote $x = \frac{1}{2}\pi$, and replacing* each point (x, y) by the point $(x, -y)$.

The cosecant curve. In Fig. 2 translate the axes to $(-\frac{1}{2}\pi, 0)$. Then (2) becomes

$$(6) \qquad y' = \sec(x' - \tfrac{1}{2}\pi) = \csc x'. \quad [\text{By } \mathbf{8}, \text{p. 3}]$$

In Fig. 2, therefore, if $O'Y'$ is drawn along the first asymptote to the left, we obtain the figure for (6). The cosecant curve is, accordingly, a secant curve.

---

* Called a reflection in the x-axis.

178   NEW ANALYTIC GEOMETRY

PROBLEMS

1. Plot directly and discuss (1) $y = \cot x$; (2) $y = \csc x$.

2. Sketch each of the following for one period, compute y for the values of x given, plot, and check in the figure:

(a) $y = 3 \tan x$; $x = \frac{1}{4}\pi$.
(b) $y = 3 \tan(\frac{1}{2}\pi x - \frac{2}{3}\pi)$; $x = \frac{3}{2}$.
(c) $y = \cot \frac{2}{3}\pi x$; $x = 2$.
(d) $y = 4 \cot(\frac{1}{4}\pi x + \frac{3}{4}\pi)$; $x = -1.2$.
(e) $2y = 3 \cot 3x$; $x = \frac{1}{2}$.
(f) $3y = \sec[-(x+1)]$; $x = 0.8$.
(g) $2y = \sec \frac{1}{2} x$; $x = 5$.
(h) $4y = \csc \frac{1}{4}\pi x$; $x = 3$.
(i) $y = \csc(\frac{1}{3}x + \frac{2}{3})$; $x = 5$.
(j) $2y = 3 \csc 3x$; $x = 1.2$.

Plot the following loci and discuss:

3. $x = \sin y$. Also written $y = \arcsin x$ or $\sin^{-1} x$, and read "the angle whose sine is x."

4. $x = 2\cos y$, or $y = \arccos \frac{1}{2} x$.

5. $x = \tan y$, or $y = \arctan x$ (see figure).

6. $x = 2 \sin \frac{2}{3} \pi y$.

7. $x = \frac{1}{2} \cos \frac{1}{3} \pi y$.

8. $y = \arctan 2x$.

9. $y = \frac{1}{2}\pi \arccos \frac{1}{2} x$.

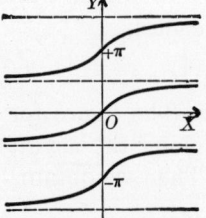

90. Addition of ordinates. When the equation of a curve has the form

$y = $ *the algebraic sum of two expressions,*

as, for example, $y = \sin x + \cos x$, $y = \frac{1}{2}x + \sin^2 x$, etc., the principle known as addition of ordinates may be employed with advantage. For example, to construct the locus of

(1) $\qquad y = 2 \sin \frac{1}{4}\pi x + \frac{1}{2} x,$

we employ the auxiliary curves

(2) $\qquad y_1 = 2 \sin \frac{1}{4}\pi x,$
(3) $\qquad y_2 = \frac{1}{2} x.$

Plot these curves one below the other, keeping the y-axes in a straight line. The *same scales* must be used in both figures. The locus of (2) is the sine curve of Fig. 1. The locus of (3) is the straight line in Fig. 2.

The ordinates of Fig. 1 are now added to the corresponding ones in Fig. 2, attention being given to the algebraic

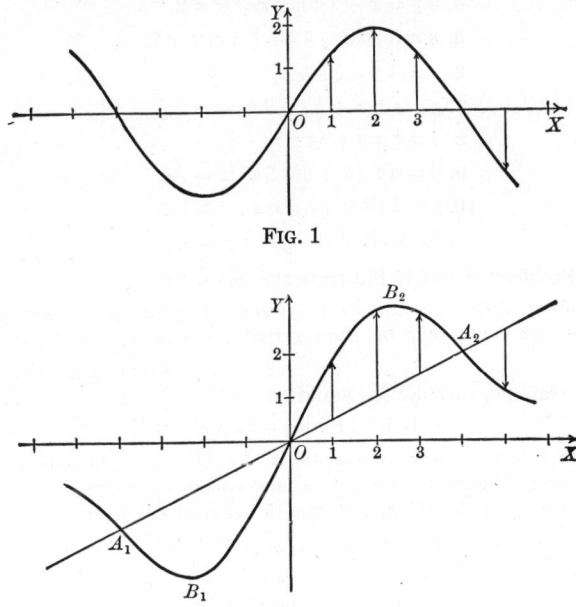

FIG. 1

FIG. 2

signs. The derived compound curve $A_1B_1OB_2A_2$ has the equation

(4) $\qquad y = y_1 + y_2 = 2 \sin \tfrac{1}{4} \pi x + \tfrac{1}{2} x$

as required. The locus winds back and forth across the line $y = \tfrac{1}{2} x$, crossing the line at $x = 0, \pm 4, \pm 8, \pm 12$, etc., that is, directly under the points where the sine curve in Fig. 1 crosses the x-axis.

PROBLEMS

Draw the following curves, calculate y accurately for the given value of x, and check in the figure:

1. $y = 2 \sin x + \frac{1}{3} x$; $x = 1$.
2. $y = 2 \cos x + \frac{1}{10} x^2$; $x = \frac{1}{2}$.
3. $y = \sin x - \cos 2x$; $x = -\frac{1}{2}$.
4. $3y = x - 3 \sin \frac{1}{3} \pi x$; $x = 2$.
5. $y = \log_{10} x - 4 \cos \frac{1}{4} \pi x$; $x = 2$.
6. $y = e^{\frac{1}{4}x} - \cos \pi x$; $x = \frac{1}{2}$.
7. $y = \sin x + \frac{1}{2} \sin 2x$; $x = 1.8$.
8. $y = \frac{1}{2} x + e^{-x}$; $x = -\frac{1}{2}$.
9. $y = \sin 2x + \cos 2x$; $x = \frac{9}{10}$.
10. $y = 2 \sin x + 3 \cos x$; $x = 1.5$.
11. $y = 2 \sin 2x - e^{-\frac{1}{4}x}$; $x = 1$.

12. Problems 9 and 10 illustrate the following

Theorem. *The compound curve obtained by adding corresponding ordinates of sine curves with the same period is also a sine curve with equal period.*

For example, consider the equation

(5) $$y = a \sin(kx + \alpha) + b \sin(kx + \beta),$$

in which $a, b, \alpha, \beta,$ and k are constants. Expand the right-hand member by the rule (9, p. 3) for $\sin(x + y)$ and collect the terms in $\sin kx$ and $\cos kx$. Then equation (5) assumes the form

(6) $$y = A \sin kx + B \cos kx,$$

where A and B are constants, independent of x. Let us now introduce the angle γ of the right triangle whose legs are A and B. Let the hypotenuse $\sqrt{A^2 + B^2} = C$. Then $B = C \sin \gamma$, $A = C \cos \gamma$. Substituting these values in (6) gives

(7) $$y = C(\sin kx \cos \gamma + \cos kx \sin \gamma) = C \sin(kx + \gamma).$$

This is a sine curve with period $\frac{2\pi}{k}$ (the same as for both terms in (5)), and amplitude $C = \sqrt{A^2 + B^2}$.   Q.E.D.

The compound curve resulting from the addition of ordinates of sine curves with *unequal* periods is, however, *not* a simple sine curve.

13. What is the amplitude of the compound sine curve of Problem 10? Show that the equation may be written $y = \sqrt{13} \sin(x + \alpha)$, where $\alpha = \arctan 1.5 = 0.98$. Plot, and compare with the compound curve.

TRANSCENDENTAL CURVES

91. Boundary curves. In plotting the locus of an equation of the form

(1) $\qquad y = \text{product of two factors}$

one of which is a sine or cosine, much aid is obtained by the following considerations.

For example, consider the locus of

(2) $\qquad y = e^{-\frac{1}{4}x} \sin \frac{1}{2}\pi x.$

We make the following observations:

1. Since the numerical value of the sine never exceeds unity, the values of y in (2) will not exceed in numerical value the value of the first factor, $e^{-\frac{1}{4}x}$. Moreover, the extreme values of $\sin \frac{1}{2}\pi x$ are $+1$ and -1 respectively. *Hence y has the extreme values $e^{-\frac{1}{4}x}$ and $-e^{-\frac{1}{4}x}$.*

Consequently, if the curves

(3) $\qquad y = e^{-\frac{1}{4}x} \quad \text{and} \quad y = -e^{-\frac{1}{4}x}$

are drawn, the locus of (2) will lie entirely *between* these curves. They are accordingly called *boundary curves*.

Draw these curves (see figure on page 182). The second is obviously symmetric to the first with respect to the x-axis. To plot, find three points on the first curve, as in the accompanying table. (Use the table of Art. 85.)

x	y
0	1
2	$e^{-\frac{1}{2}} = .61$
4	$e^{-1} = .37$

2. When $\sin \frac{1}{2}\pi x = 0$, then in (2) $y = 0$, since the first factor is always *finite*. Hence *the locus of* (2) *meets the x-axis in the same points as the auxiliary sine curve*

(4) $\qquad y = \sin \frac{1}{2}\pi x.$

3. The required curve *touches** the boundary curves when the second factor, $\sin \frac{1}{2}\pi x$, is $+1$ or -1, that is, when the ordinates of the auxiliary curve (4) have a maximum or minimum value.

---
* The discussion shows merely that the curve (2) *reaches* the boundary curves. *Tangency* is shown by calculus.

Hence draw the sine curve (4). The period is 4 and the amplitude is 1. This curve is the dotted line of the figure.

The discussion shows these facts:

The locus of (2) *crosses* XX' *at* $x = 0, \pm 2, \pm 4, \pm 6$, *etc., and touches the boundary curves* (3) *at* $x = \pm 1, \pm 3, \pm 5$, *etc.*

We may then readily sketch the curve, as in the figure; that is, the winding curve between the boundary curves (3).

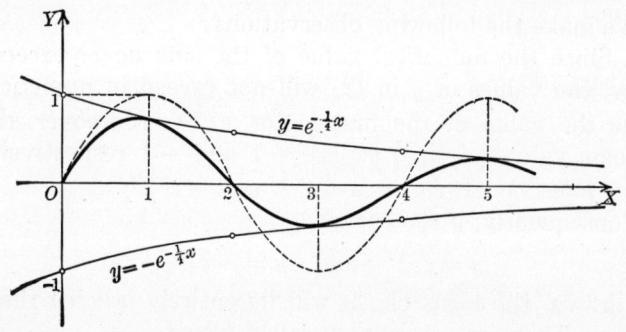

4. For a check remember that the ordinate of (2) is the *product* of the ordinates of the boundary curve $y = e^{-\frac{1}{4}x}$ and the sine curve (4). In the figure, for example, the required curve lies above XX' between $x = 0$ and $x = 2$, for the ordinates of $y = e^{-\frac{1}{4}x}$ and of the sine curve are now all positive. But between $x = 2$ and $x = 4$ the required curve lies below XX', for the ordinates of $y = e^{-\frac{1}{4}x}$ and the sine curve now have unlike signs.

PROBLEMS

Draw the following loci, calculate y accurately for the given values of x, plot, and check in the figure:

1. $y = x \sin x$; $x = 3, \frac{1}{3}\pi$.
2. $xy = \sin x$; $x = \frac{1}{2}$.
3. $xy = \cos x$; $x = 1$.
4. $3y = x \cos \pi x$; $x = 3$.
5. $10y = x^2 \sin \frac{1}{2} \pi x$; $x = \frac{1}{2}, 3$.
6. $y = 3 e^{-\frac{1}{2}x} \sin 2x$; $x = 1, 2$.
7. $y e^x = \cos 2x$; $x = 1.5, 2$.
8. $y = e^{-\frac{1}{4}x^2} \sin \frac{1}{3} \pi x$; $x = 1, 3$.

TRANSCENDENTAL CURVES

9. $y = (x+1)\sin 2x$; $x = \tfrac{1}{3}\pi$.

10. $x^2 y = \cos \tfrac{1}{2} x$; $x = 2, \tfrac{1}{2}\pi$.

11. $y e^{\tfrac{1}{4}x} = \cos \tfrac{1}{4}\pi x$; $x = 1.6$.

12. $y = 2 e^{-\tfrac{1}{3}x} \sin \pi(x+1)$; $x = -\tfrac{1}{2}, \tfrac{2}{3}$.

13. $y = 3 e^{-x} \sin \tfrac{1}{3}\pi(x + \tfrac{1}{2})$; $x = -\tfrac{1}{2}$.

14. $y = 2 e^{-\tfrac{1}{2}x} \cos (\pi x - \tfrac{1}{3}\pi)$; $x = 0$.

For individual study or assignment

15. Draw the two loci obtained (1) by adding and (2) by multiplying the ordinates of the following pairs of curves:

(a) $y = \sin 2x$,
$y = e^{-x}$.

(b) $y = e^{\tfrac{1}{2}x}$,
$y = \cos \tfrac{1}{2} x$.

(c) $y = 2 + \tfrac{1}{16} x^2$,
$y = \cos \tfrac{1}{2}\pi x$.

(d) $y = \tfrac{1}{8}(16 - x^2)$,
$y = \cos \tfrac{1}{3}\pi x$.

(e) $y = e^x$,
$y = \log_e x$.

(f) $y = x$,
$y = \tfrac{1}{3} \cos (\tfrac{1}{3}\pi x + \tfrac{2}{3})$.

16. Plot the compound sine curves

(a) $y = 2 \sin (\pi x + \tfrac{1}{4}\pi) + 3 \sin (\pi x - \tfrac{1}{3}\pi)$.

(b) $y = 3 \cos (2x + \tfrac{3}{4}\pi) - \cos (2x - \tfrac{1}{4}\pi)$.

(c) $y = \sin (x + \tfrac{1}{12}\pi) - 2 \cos (x - \tfrac{1}{12}\pi)$.

17. Express each equation in Problem 16 in the form $y = A \sin (\pi x + \alpha)$ and find A and α, plot, and compare with the compound curve.

CHAPTER XI

PARAMETRIC EQUATIONS AND LOCI

92. Plotting parametric equations. If x and y are rectangular coördinates, and if each is expressed in terms of a variable or parameter t, as, for example,

(1) $$x = \tfrac{1}{2} t^2, \quad y = \tfrac{1}{4} t^3,$$

then these equations are called the *parametric equations* of the curve, — the locus of (x, y).

To plot the curve, give values to t *increasing algebraically* and compute values of x and y, arranging the results in a table. Plot the points (x, y) and draw a smooth curve through them in the order of the table.

EXAMPLES

1. Plot the curve whose parametric equations are

(2) $$x = \tfrac{1}{2} t^2, \quad y = \tfrac{1}{4} t^3.$$

t	x	y
-3	4.5	-6.75
-2	2	-2
-1	0.5	-0.25
0	0	0
1	0.5	0.25
2	2	2
3	4.5	6.75
etc.	etc.	etc.

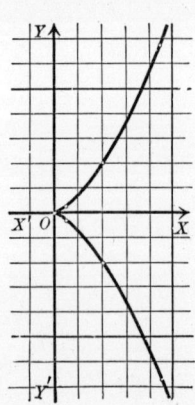

184

PARAMETRIC EQUATIONS AND LOCI 185

Solution. The table is easily made. For example, if $t = 2$, then $x = 2$, $y = 2$, etc.

The curve is called a **semicubical parabola**.

2. Draw the curve whose parametric equations are

(3) $\quad x = 2r\cos\theta + r\cos 2\theta,$
$\quad\quad\quad y = 2r\sin\theta - r\sin 2\theta,$

where θ is the parameter.

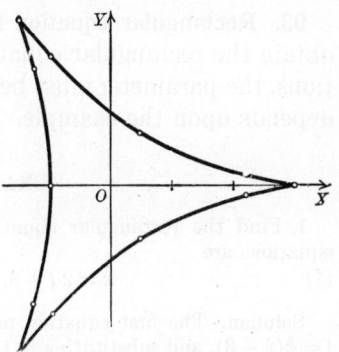

Solution. Take $r = 5$. Arrange the computation as below:

$x = 10\cos\theta + 5\cos 2\theta, \quad y = 10\sin\theta - 5\sin 2\theta$							
θ	cos θ	2θ	cos 2θ	x	sin θ	sin 2θ	y
0°	1	0°	1	15	0	0	0
30°	.866	60°	.5	11.2	.5	.866	0.7
60°	.5	120°	− .5	2.5	.866	.866	4.3
90°	0	180°	− 1	− 5	1	0	10
120°	− .5	240°	− .5	− 7.5	.866	− .866	13.0
150°	− .866	300°	.5	− 6.2	.5	− .866	9.3
180°	− 1	360°	1	− 5	0	0	0
210°	− .866	420°	.5	− 6.2	− .5	.866	− 9.3
240°	− .5	480°	− .5	− 7.5	− .866	.866	− 13.0
270°	0	540°	− 1	− 5	− 1	0	− 10
300°	.5	600°	− .5	2.5	− .866	− .866	− 4.3
330°	.866	660°	.5	11.2	− .5	− .866	− 0.7
360°	1	720°	1	15	0	0	0

The three-pointed curve thus obtained is called a **hypocycloid of three cusps**.

93. Rectangular equation from parametric equations.

To obtain the rectangular equation from the parametric equations, the parameter must be eliminated. The method used depends upon the example.

EXAMPLES

1. Find the rectangular equation of the curve whose parametric equations are

(1) $$x = 2t + 3, \quad y = \tfrac{1}{2} t^2 - 4.$$

Solution. The first equation may readily be solved for t. We find $t = \tfrac{1}{2}(x - 3)$, and substituting in the second equation gives

$$y = \tfrac{1}{8}(x - 3)^2 - 4,$$

or, expanding and simplifying

$$x^2 - 6x - 8y - 23 = 0, \text{ a parabola. } Ans.$$

2. Find the rectangular equation of the curve whose parametric equations are

(2) $$x = 3 + 4 \cos \theta, \quad y = 3 \sin \theta.$$

Solution. Remembering that $\sin^2 \theta + \cos^2 \theta = 1$, we solve the first equation for $\cos \theta$, the second for $\sin \theta$. This gives

(3) $$\cos \theta = \tfrac{1}{4}(x - 3), \quad \sin \theta = \tfrac{1}{3} y.$$

Hence the rectangular equation is

(4) $$\frac{(x - 3)^2}{16} + \frac{y^2}{9} = 1, \text{ an ellipse. } Ans.$$

PROBLEMS

Plot the following parametric equations, t and θ being the parameters. Find the rectangular equation in each case.

1. $x = t, y = 2 - t.$
2. $x = 2 + t, y = 2 - 3t.$
3. $x = t^2, y = \tfrac{1}{2} t.$
4. $x = \tfrac{1}{2} t, y = t^2 - 8.$
5. $x = t^2 - 2t, y = t^2 + 2.$
6. $x = t^2 + t, y = \tfrac{1}{2} t^2 - 3t.$
7. $x = \dfrac{2}{t}, y = 4t.$
8. $x = t + 2, y = \dfrac{t}{t - 2}.$
9. $x = \tfrac{1}{2} t^2 + 1, y = \tfrac{1}{3} t^3 - 2$
10. $x = 2 \cos \theta, y = 2 \sin \theta.$
11. $x = 3 \sin \theta, y = 4 \cos \theta.$
12. $x = 5 + \cos \theta, y = \sin \theta - 5.$
13. $x = 3 \sec \theta, y = 3 \tan \theta.$
14. $x = \csc \theta, y = 5 \cot \theta.$

PARAMETRIC EQUATIONS AND LOCI

15. $x = 2 \cos \theta$, $y = \cos 2\theta$.

16. $x = 3 \tan \theta$, $y = \cot \theta$.

17. $x = 5 t \cos 30°$, $y = 5 t \sin 30° - 16 t^2$.

18. $x = 3 + 4 \cos \theta$, $y = 3 \sin \theta - 2$.

19. $x = 6 + 4 \sec \theta$, $y = 3 \tan \theta - 2$.

20. Plot the following parametric equations:
  (a) $x = t^2 - 4 t$, $y = t^3 - 3 t^2 - 3 t$.
  (b) $x = t + \sin t$, $y = 1 + \cos t$.
  (c) $x = 2 r \cos \theta - r \cos 2\theta$, $y = 2 r \sin \theta - r \sin 2\theta$.
  (d) $x = 3 r \cos \theta - \frac{1}{2} r \cos 3\theta$, $y = 3 r \sin \theta - \frac{1}{2} r \sin 3\theta$.
  (e) $x = r \cos \theta + r\theta \sin \theta$, $y = r \sin \theta - r\theta \cos \theta$.

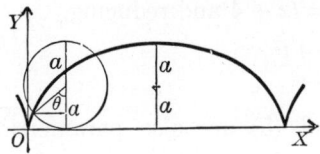

21. (a) $\begin{cases} x = a(\theta - \sin \theta), \\ y = a(1 - \cos \theta). \end{cases}$
(b) $\begin{cases} x = a(\theta + \sin \theta), \\ y = a(1 - \cos \theta). \end{cases}$

CYCLOID, CUSP AT ORIGIN   CYCLOID, VERTEX AT ORIGIN

22. $x = a\theta - \frac{1}{2} a \sin \theta$, $y = a - \frac{1}{2} a \cos \theta$.

23. $x = a\theta - 2 a \sin \theta$, $y = a - 2 a \cos \theta$.

24. $x = b \cos^2 \theta$, $y = a \tan \theta$.

94. Various parametric equations for the same curve. When the rectangular equation of a curve is given, any number of parametric equations may be obtained for the curve.

For example, given the ellipse

(1) $\qquad 4 x^2 + y^2 = 16.$

Let $x = 2 \cos \theta$, where θ is a parameter. Substituting in (1),

$$16 \cos^2 \theta + y^2 = 16, \quad \text{or} \quad y^2 = 16(1 - \cos^2 \theta) = 16 \sin^2 \theta.$$

Hence the equations

(2) $$x = 2\cos\theta, \quad y = 4\sin\theta,$$

are parametric equations of the ellipse (1).

Again, substitute in (1),
$$y = tx + 4,$$
where t is a parameter.

This gives

(3) $\quad 4x^2 + t^2x^2 + 8tx + 16 = 16$, or $(4 + t^2)x^2 + 8tx = 0.$

(4) $$\therefore x = -\frac{8t}{4 + t^2}.$$

Substituting this value in $y = tx + 4$ and reducing,

(5) $$y = \frac{16 - 4t^2}{4 + t^2}.$$

Hence the equations (4) and (5) are also parametric equations of the ellipse.

The point is: *We obtain parametric equations by setting one of the coördinates equal to a function of a parameter, substituting for this coördinate in the given rectangular equation, and solving for the other coördinate in terms of the parameter.*

To obtain *simple* parametric equations we must, of course, assume the *right function* for one coördinate. No general rule can be given for this purpose, but the study of the problems below will aid the student.

In some cases the parametric equations represent only a portion of the curve; for example, the equations

$$x = \sin\theta, \quad y = \cos 2\theta$$

represent the arc of the parabola $2x^2 + y - 1 = 0$ on which the numerical values of x and y do not exceed 1.

Many rectangular equations difficult to plot directly are treated by deriving parametric equations and plotting the latter.

EXAMPLE

Draw the locus of the equation

(6) $$x^3 + y^3 - 3\,axy = 0.$$

Solution. Set $y = tx$, where t is the parameter. Then, from (6),

(7) $$x^3 + t^3x^3 - 3\,atx^2 = 0.$$

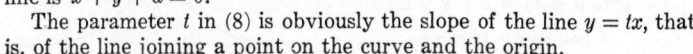

Dividing out x^2, solving for x, and remembering that $y = tx$, we obtain the desired parametric equations

(8) $$x = \frac{3\,at}{1 + t^3}, \quad y = \frac{3\,at^2}{1 + t^3}.$$

The locus is the curve of the figure, called the **folium of Descartes**.

The line drawn in the figure is an oblique asymptote. The equation of this line is $x + y + a = 0$.

The parameter t in (8) is obviously the slope of the line $y = tx$, that is, of the line joining a point on the curve and the origin.

The *reason* for assuming the relation $y = tx$ in the preceding example is that x^2 divides out in (7), leaving an equation of the first degree to solve for x. Problems 1 (a) and (b) below are worked on the same principle. In many cases trigonometric functions are employed with advantage, as in (c).

PROBLEMS

1. Find parametric equations for the following curves by making the substitution indicated in the given equation and solving. The parameter is t or θ. Plot the locus in each case.

(a) $y^2 = 4\,x^2 - 5\,x^3$; $y = tx$.   Ans. $x = \frac{1}{5}(4 - t^2)$; $y = \frac{1}{5}t(4 - t^2)$.
(b) $y^3 = 5\,x^2 - 8\,x^3$; $y = tx$.
(c) $4\,x^2 + y^2 - 16\,x + 12 = 0$; $y = 2\cos\theta$. Ans. $x = 2 \pm \sin\theta$.
(d) $x^2 - 4\,xy + 13\,y^2 = 9$; $y = \sin\theta$.   Ans. $x = 2\sin\theta \pm 3\cos\theta$.
(e) $x^2y^2 = b^2x^2 - a^2y^2$; $y = b\sin\theta$.   Ans. $x = a\tan\theta$.
(f) $x^2y^2 = a^2y^2 + b^2x^2$; $y = b\csc\theta$.
(g) $x^2 + 2\,xy + y^2 + 2\,x - 2\,y = 0$; $x = t - t^2$.
(h) $17\,x^2 - 16\,xy + 4\,y^2 - 34\,x + 16\,y + 13 = 0$; $x = 1 + 2\cos\theta$.

NEW ANALYTIC GEOMETRY

For individual study or assignment

2. Plot the following curves by deriving parametric equations:

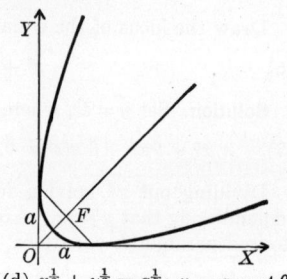
(d) $x^{\frac{1}{2}} + y^{\frac{1}{2}} = a^{\frac{1}{2}}$; $x = a\cos^4\theta$.

PARABOLA

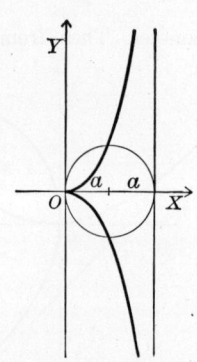

(a) $y^2(2a - x) = x^3$; $y = tx$.

CISSOID OF DIOCLES

(b) $y^2 = x^2 \dfrac{2+x}{2-x}$; $y = tx$.

Ans. $x = \dfrac{2t^2 - 2}{1 + t^2}$; $y = \dfrac{2t^3 - 2t}{1 + t^2}$.

(c) $x^2 + xy + 2y^2 + 2x + 1 = 0$; $x = ty - 1$.

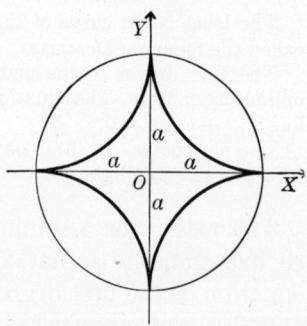

(e) $x^{\frac{2}{3}} + y^{\frac{2}{3}} = a^{\frac{2}{3}}$; $x = a\sin^3\theta$.

HYPOCYCLOID OF FOUR CUSPS

(f) $x^4 + 2ax^2y - ay^3 = 0$; $y = tx$.
(g) $(x^2 + y^2 + 4ay - a^2)(x^2 - a^2) + 4a^2y^2 = 0$; $x^2 = a^2 - t^2y^2$.
(h) $x^2 = y(y - 2)^2$; $y - 2 = tx$.
(i) $(x^2 - \frac{1}{2}b^2)^2 + y^2(x^2 - b^2) = 0$; $x^2 = \frac{1}{2}b^2 + ty$.
(j) $(a - x)y^2 = (a + x)x^2$; $x = a\cos\theta$.

95. Locus problems solved by parametric equations. Parametric equations are important because it is sometimes easy in locus problems to express the coördinates of a point on the locus in terms of a parameter, when it would be difficult to obtain directly the rectangular equation. The following examples illustrate this statement.

EXAMPLES

1. ABP is a rigid line. The points A and B move along two perpendicular intersecting lines. What is the locus of the point P on AB?

In the figure, A moves on XX', B moves on YY'; required the locus of the point $P(x, y)$.

Solution. Take the coördinate axes as indicated, and consider the line in any one of its positions. Choose for parameter $\angle XAB = \theta$.

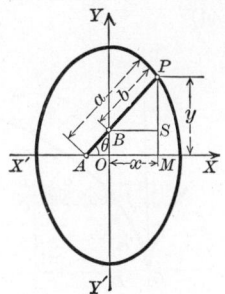

Let $AP = a$, $BP = b$.

Now $OM = x$, $MP = y$.

In the right $\triangle MPA$,

(1) $\qquad \sin \theta = \dfrac{MP}{AP} = \dfrac{y}{a}.$

In the right $\triangle BSP$, $\angle PBS = \theta$.

(2) $\quad \therefore \cos \angle PBS = \cos \theta = \dfrac{BS}{BP} = \dfrac{x}{b}.$

From (1) and (2),

(3) $\qquad x = b \cos \theta, \quad y = a \sin \theta.$

These are the parametric equations of the locus.

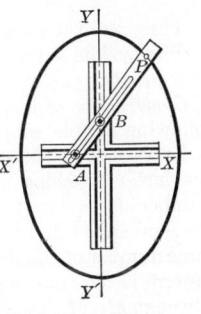

Squaring (1) and (2) and adding,

$$\frac{x^2}{b^2} + \frac{y^2}{a^2} = 1.$$

Hence the point P moves on an ellipse whose axes, $2a$ and $2b$, lie along the given perpendicular lines.

A method commonly employed for drawing ellipses depends upon this result. The instrument consists of two grooved perpendicular bars $X'X$ and YY' and a crossbar ABP. At A and B are screw nuts fitting the grooves and adjustable along ABP. If the crossbar is moved, a pencil at P will describe an ellipse whose semiaxes are PA and PB.

2. The cycloid. Find the parametric equations of the locus of a point P on a circle which rolls along the axis of x.

Solution. Take for origin a point O at which the moving point P touched the axis of x (see figure on page 192). Let the circle drawn be any position of the rolling circle. Let a be the radius of the circle, and take for the parameter θ the variable angle CBP.

From the figure, if (x, y) are the coördinates of P,

$$x = OD = OA - PC, \quad y = DP = AB - CB.$$

But $PC = a \sin \theta$, $CB = a \cos \theta$, and, by definition,
$$OA = \text{arc } AP = a\theta.$$

(For an arc of a circle equals its radius times the subtended angle, from the definition of a radian.) Hence

(4)
$$\begin{cases} x = a(\theta - \sin \theta), \\ y = a(1 - \cos \theta). \end{cases}$$

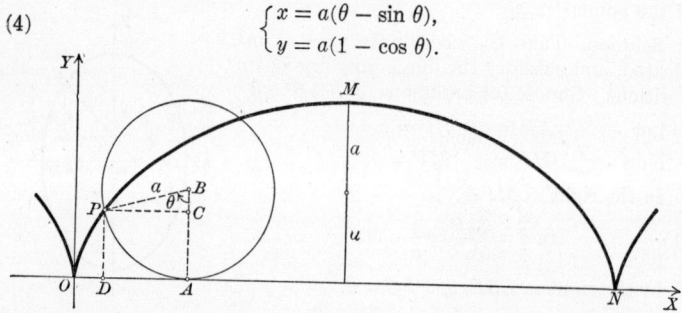

These are the parametric equations of the *cycloid*.

The cycloid extends indefinitely to the right and left and consists of arcs equal to OMN.

Construction of a cycloid. The definition of the cycloid suggests the following simple construction:

Lay off $ON = 2\pi a = $ circumference of the generating circle. Draw the latter touching at C, the mid-point of ON. Divide OC into any number of equal parts, and the semicircle CM into the same number of equal arcs. Letter as in the figure. Through M_1, M_2, etc. draw lines parallel to ON. Lay off $M_1D_1 = CC_1$, $M_2D_2 = CC_2$, $M_3D_3 = CC_3$, etc.

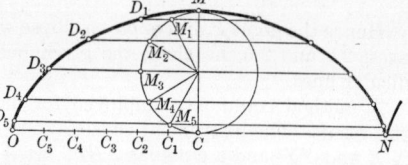

Then D_1, D_2, D_3, etc. are points on the cycloid.

For, let the generating circle roll to the left, the point M tracing the curve. When the circle touches ON at C_1, M will lie on a level with M_1, and at a distance to the left of M_1 equal to CC_1. Similarly for D_2, D_3, etc.

The arc MN of the cycloid may be constructed by using CM as an axis of symmetry.

3. The hypocycloid. Find the parametric equations of the locus of a point P on a circle which rolls on the inside of a fixed circle.

Solution. Take the center of the fixed circle for the origin and let the x-axis pass through a point A where the tracing point $P(x, y)$

PARAMETRIC EQUATIONS AND LOCI

touched the large circle. Let $OA = R$, $BC = r$. Then $OC = R - r$.
Now

(5) $\qquad x = OF = OE + DP, \quad y = FP = EC - DC.$

In the right $\triangle OEC$,

(6) $\qquad OE = (R - r) \cos \theta,$
$\qquad\qquad EC = (R - r) \sin \theta.$

In the right $\triangle DPC$,

(7) $\qquad DP = r \sin \angle PCD,$
$\qquad\qquad DC = r \cos \angle PCD.$

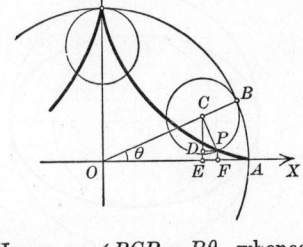

But
$\angle BCP + \angle PCD = 90° + \theta$, whence

(8) $\quad \angle PCD = 90° - \angle BCP + \theta.$

By definition, arc BP = arc AB. Hence $r \cdot \angle BCP = R\theta$, whence $\angle BCP = \dfrac{R\theta}{r}$; and, substituting in (8), we obtain

(9) $\qquad\qquad \angle PCD = 90° - \dfrac{R-r}{r} \theta.$

Then, from (7) and (9),

(10) $\qquad DP = r \cos \left(\dfrac{R-r}{r}\right)\theta, \quad DC = r \sin \left(\dfrac{R-r}{r}\right)\theta.$

Substituting from (6) and (10) in (5) gives the result

(11) $\begin{cases} x = (R - r) \cos \theta + r \cos \left(\dfrac{R-r}{r}\right)\theta, \\ y = (R - r) \sin \theta - r \sin \left(\dfrac{R-r}{r}\right)\theta. \end{cases}$ Ans.

The curve is closed when r and R are commensurable. In the figure, $R = 4r$, and we have the hypocycloid of four cusps, p. 190, called the astroid, a special case. See also Example 2, p. 185, where $R = 3r$ in (11).

PROBLEMS

In the following problems express x and y in terms of the parameter and the lengths of the given lines of the figure. Sketch the locus.

1. Find parametric equations for the ellipse, using as parameter the *eccentric angle* ϕ, that is, the angle between the major axis and the radius of the point B on the circle $x^2 + y^2 = a^2$ which has the same abscissa as the point $P(x, y)$ on the ellipse (see figure on page 194 and Art. 45.)

$\qquad\qquad$ Ans. $x = a \cos \phi, \; y = b \sin \phi$

2. In the right-hand figure below, ABP is a rigid equilateral triangle. A moves on YY', B moves on XX'. Find the locus of the vertex P.

Ans. $x = a \cos\theta + a \cos(120° - \theta)$, $y = a \sin(120° - \theta)$;
ellipse $x^2 - \sqrt{3}\,xy + y^2 = \tfrac{1}{4} a^2$.

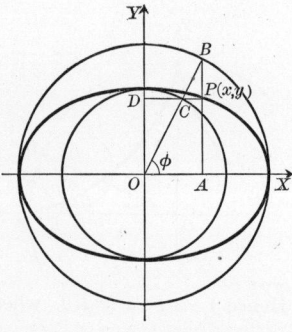
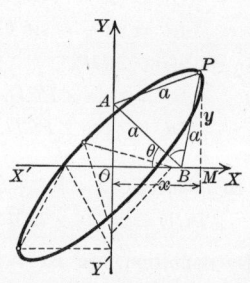

3. The epicycloid. A circle of radius r rolls on the outside of a circle of radius R. Find the equations of the locus of a point on the rolling circle.

Ans. $x = (R + r)\cos\theta - r\cos\dfrac{R + r}{r}\theta$;

$y = (R + r)\sin\theta - r\sin\dfrac{R + r}{r}\theta$.

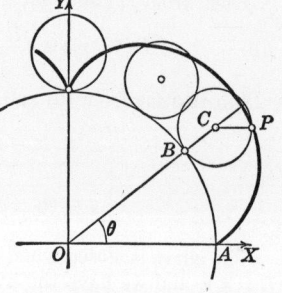

Replacing r by $-r$ in equations (11) on page 193 for the hypocycloid gives this result.

The curve is closed when r and R are commensurable. In the figure $R = 4\,r$.

4. Describe constructions for the epicycloid and hypocycloid analogous to that given on page 192 for the cycloid.

5. The witch of Agnesi. Find the locus of a point P constructed as follows: Let OA be a diameter of a circle, and let any line OB be drawn through

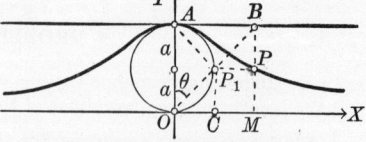

O to meet the circle at P_1 and the tangent at A at B. Draw $P_1 P \perp$ to OA and $BP \parallel$ to OA.

Ans. $x = 2 a \tan\theta$, $y = 2 a \cos^2\theta$;
rectangular equation, $y(x^2 + 4 a^2) = 8 a^3$.

6. Find the locus of a point Q on the radius BP (figure, Example 2, p. 192) if $BQ = b$.

Ans. $x = a\theta - b\sin\theta,\; y = a - b\cos\theta$. The locus is called a prolate or curtate cycloid according as a is greater or less than b.

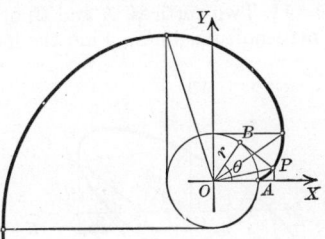

7. The involute of a circle. Given a string wrapped around a circle; find the locus of the end of the string as it is unwound.

Ans. $x = r\cos\theta + r\theta\sin\theta,\; y = r\sin\theta - r\theta\cos\theta$.

Hint. Take the center of the circle for origin and let the x-axis pass through the point A at which the end of the string rests. If the string is unwound to a point B, let $\angle AOB = \theta$ (see figure).

8. The cissoid of Diocles. A chord OP_1 of the circle $x^2 + y^2 - 2ax = 0$ meets the line $x = 2a$ at a point A. Find the locus of a point P on the line OP_1 such that $OP = P_1A$.   Ans. $y^2(2a - x) = x^3$ (see figure).

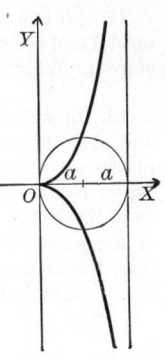

For individual study or assignment

9. AB is a fixed line and O a fixed point. Through O draw OX parallel to AB and ON perpendicular to AB. Draw a line from O through any point Q on AB. Mark on this line a point P such that $MP = NQ$, MP being perpendicular to OX. What is the locus of P?

Ans. Parabola $y^2 = ax$.

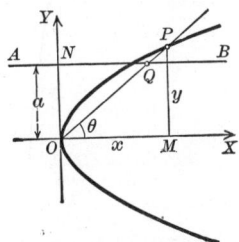 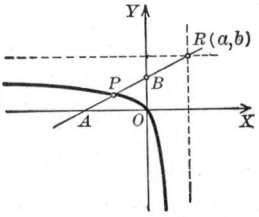

10. Through the fixed point $R(a, b)$ lines are drawn meeting the coördinate axes in A and B. What is the locus of the mid-point of AB?

Ans. Equilateral hyperbola $(2x - a)(2y - b) = ab$.

11. Two vertices, A and B, of a rigid isosceles right $\triangle ABP$ move on perpendicular lines. Find the locus of the vertex P.

Ans. Ellipse $x^2 - 2xy + 2y^2 = a^2$.

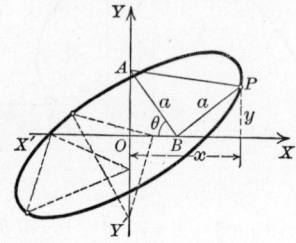
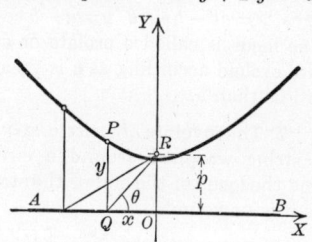

12. AB is a fixed line and R a fixed point. Draw RQ to any point Q on AB and erect the perpendicular QP, making $QP \div QR$ equal to a constant e. What is the locus of P?

Ans. Hyperbola $\dfrac{x^2}{p^2} - \dfrac{y^2}{p^2 e^2} = -1$.

13. OB is the crank of an engine and AB the connecting rod. B moves on the crank circle whose center is O, and A moves on the fixed line OX. What is the locus of any point P on AB?

Ans. Ellipse when $r = a + b$; otherwise an egg-shaped curve.

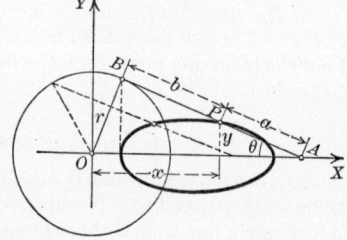

14. OB is an engine crank revolving about O, and AB is the connecting rod, the point A moving on OX. Draw $AP \perp$ to OX to meet OB produced at P.* What is the locus of P?

Ans. $(x^2 + r^2 - c^2)\sqrt{x^2 + y^2} = 2rx^2$.

When $c = r$, the locus is the circle
$$x^2 + y^2 = 4r^2.$$

96. Loci defined by the points of intersection of corresponding lines.
If the equations of two systems of lines involve the same parameter, the

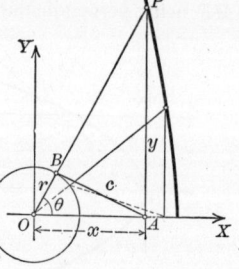

lines belonging to the same value of the parameter are called **corresponding lines**. In some cases a curve may be defined as the locus of the point of intersection of corresponding lines.

* P is the "instantaneous center" of the motion of the connecting rod.

EXAMPLE

1. In the figure, LM is any half-chord of the circle parallel to the diameter AB. Find the locus of P, the intersection of BL and OM.

Solution. The equation of OM is $y = x \tan t$, if $\angle XOM = t$. The coördinates of M are $(a \cos t, a \sin t)$; of L, $(0, a \sin t)$. Hence the equation of BL is $y = \sin t(a - x)$. Then the two systems of lines are

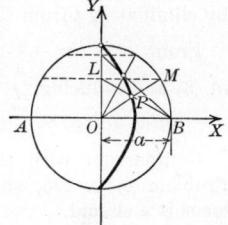

(1) $\qquad y = x \tan t, \quad y = \sin t(a - x).$

Solving for x and y, we obtain

(2) $\qquad x = \dfrac{a \cos t}{1 + \cos t}, \quad y = \dfrac{a \sin t}{1 + \cos t},$

the parametric equations of the locus. The rectangular equation is found by eliminating t from (2) or from (1), and is

$$y^2 = a^2 - 2\,ax. \quad \textit{Ans.}$$

The locus is the parabolic arc within the circle.

The method of solving Example 1 may be summed up in the

Rule *to find the equation of the locus of the point of intersection of corresponding lines of two systems.*

First step. *Find the equations of the two systems of lines defining the locus in terms of the same parameter.*

Second step. *Solve these equations for x and y in terms of the parameter. This gives the parametric equations of the locus. Or eliminate the parameter from the equations of the lines. This gives the rectangular equation.*

EXAMPLE

Find the locus of the foot of the perpendicular drawn from the vertex of a parabola to the tangent.

Solution. If we take the typical equation $y^2 = 2\,px$, the equation of a tangent AB in terms of the slope t is (Art. 75)

(3) $\qquad\qquad\qquad y = tx + \dfrac{p}{2\,t}.$

The equation of the perpendicular OP is

(4) $$y = -\frac{1}{t}x.$$

The rectangular equation is found by eliminating t from (3) and (4).

From (4), $t = -\dfrac{x}{y}$. Substituting in (3) and reducing,

$$y^2(x + \tfrac{1}{2}p) = -x^3. \text{ Ans.}$$

Comparison with the answer to Problem 8, p. 195, shows that the locus is a cissoid.

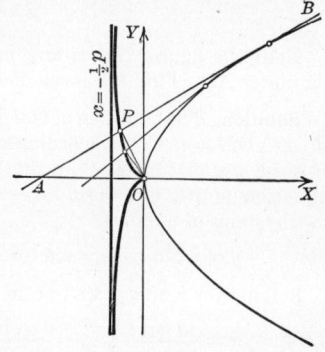

PROBLEMS

1. Find the locus of the point of intersection of a tangent to an equilateral hyperbola (Art. 52), and the line drawn through the center perpendicular to that tangent.

Ans. The lemniscate $(x^2 + y^2)^2 = a^2(x^2 - y^2)$ (Example 2, p. 157).

2. Find the locus of the point of intersection of the altitudes of a triangle if its base is fixed and the altitude on this base has a fixed length. *Ans.* A parabola.

3. Find the locus of the point of intersection of two perpendicular tangents to the ellipse

$$b^2x^2 + a^2y^2 = a^2b^2.$$

Ans. The *director circle*

$$x^2 + y^2 = a^2 + b^2.$$

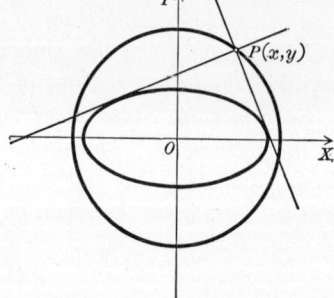

Hint. By Art. 75, the equations of tangents with slopes t and $-\dfrac{1}{t}$, respectively, may be written

$$y - tx = \sqrt{a^2t^2 + b^2}, \quad ty + x = \sqrt{a^2 + b^2t^2}.$$

Eliminate t by squaring and adding.

4. A tangent to the ellipse $b^2x^2 + a^2y^2 = a^2b^2$ meets the axes of x and y in A and B respectively. From A draw a line ∥ to OY, and from B a line ∥ to OX. What is the locus of their point of intersection?

Ans. $x^2y^2 = a^2y^2 + b^2x^2$ (Problem 1 (f), p. 189).

5. Work out Problem 4 when the ellipse is replaced by a hyperbola.

PARAMETRIC EQUATIONS AND LOCI

6. Find the locus of the point of intersection of perpendicular tangents to (1) the parabola, (2) the hyperbola (IV), Art. 48 (see Problem 3).
  Ans. (1) The directrix; (2) $x^2 + y^2 = a^2 - b^2$.

7. Find the locus of the point of intersection of a tangent to (1) an ellipse, (2) a parabola, (3) a hyperbola, with the line drawn through a focus perpendicular to the tangent.
  Ans. (1) $x^2 + y^2 = a^2$; (2) $x = 0$; (3) $x^2 + y^2 = a^2$ (see Problem 3).

8. Find the locus of the point of intersection of a tangent to the circle $x^2 + y^2 + 2ax + a^2 - b^2 = 0$ and the line drawn through the origin perpendicular to it.
  Ans. The limaçon $(x^2 + y^2 + ax)^2 = b^2(x^2 + y^2)$ (Problem 17, p. 153).

9. A tangent is drawn at any point M on the ellipse $b^2x^2 + a^2y^2 = a^2b^2$. The perpendicular drawn from the center upon this tangent meets the ordinate at M (produced if necessary) at P. Find the locus of P (see Problem 2, p. 143).   Ans. The ellipse $a^2x^2 + b^2y^2 = a^4$.

10. A tangent is drawn at any point M on a parabola. The perpendicular drawn from the vertex upon this tangent meets the focal radius of M (produced if necessary) at P. What is the locus of P?
  Ans. A circle.

For individual study or assignment

11. Find the locus of the foot of the perpendicular drawn from the origin to a tangent to the parabola $y^2 + 4ax + 4a^2 = 0$.
  Ans. The strophoid, $y^2 = x^2 \dfrac{a+x}{a-x}$ (see figure).

12. Find the locus of the point of intersection of the normals drawn at points on the ellipse $\dfrac{x^2}{a^2} + \dfrac{y^2}{b^2} = 1$ and major auxiliary circle $x^2 + y^2 = a^2$ which have the same abscissas.
  Ans. Circle $x^2 + y^2 = (a+b)^2$.

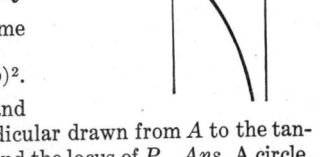

13. AB is a fixed diameter of a circle and M any point on the circle. The perpendicular drawn from A to the tangent at M meets BM produced at P. Find the locus of P. Ans. A circle.

14. A and B are fixed points and LM a fixed line. Lines PA and PB are drawn so that they intercept a given length on LM. What is the locus of P?

97. Diameters of conics. A somewhat different class of locus problems is illustrated in the following example.

EXAMPLE

What is the locus of the mid-points of a system of parallel chords of an ellipse?

Solution. Let the equation of the system of parallel chords be

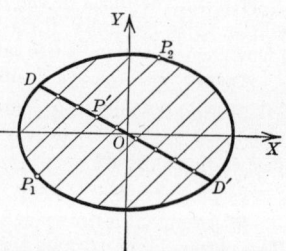

(1) $\qquad y = mx + k.$

Let the value of k for the chord P_1P_2 be k_1; that is,

(2) $\qquad y = mx + k_1$

is the equation of P_1P_2. Assume that the coördinates of P_1 are (x_1, y_1), and of P_2, (x_2, y_2).

If $P'(x', y')$ is the middle point of P_1P_2, then

(3) $\qquad x' = \tfrac{1}{2}(x_1 + x_2), \quad y' = \tfrac{1}{2}(y_1 + y_2).$

Since (x_1, y_1) and (x_2, y_2) are the points of intersection of the chord (2) and the ellipse, we shall find their values by solving

(4) $\qquad y = mx + k_1 \quad \text{and} \quad b^2x^2 + a^2y^2 = a^2b^2.$

Eliminating y, we obtain the equation

(5) $\qquad (a^2m^2 + b^2)x^2 + 2\,a^2k_1mx + a^2k_1^2 - a^2b^2 = 0.$

The roots of this equation are x_1 and x_2, and, from (3), x' equals one half the sum of these roots. Hence *we need to know in* (5) *only the sum of the roots*. But, by algebra,*

(6) $\qquad x_1 + x_2 = -\dfrac{2\,a^2k_1m}{a^2m^2 + b^2}.$

Hence, from (3),

(7) $\qquad x' = -\dfrac{a^2m}{a^2m^2 + b^2}\,k_1.$

Since (x', y') satisfy (2),

(8) $\qquad y' = mx' + k_1 = \dfrac{-a^2m^2k_1}{a^2m^2 + b^2} + k_1 = \dfrac{b^2}{a^2m^2 + b^2}\,k_1.$

Eliminating k_1 from (7) and (8) and dropping the accents gives the equation of the locus,

(9) $\qquad b^2x + a^2my = 0.$

The locus is the straight line DD' in the figure.

In a circle a diameter may be defined as the locus of the mid-points of a system of parallel chords. The correspond-

---

* In the quadratic $Ax^2 + Bx + C = 0$, *sum of roots* $= -\dfrac{B}{A}$; *product of roots* $= \dfrac{C}{A}$.

ing locus for a conic section is called a **diameter** of the conic. Hence we have the

Theorem. *The diameter of the ellipse*
$$b^2x^2 + a^2y^2 = a^2b^2$$
which bisects all chords with the slope m is
$$b^2x + a^2my = 0.$$

In like manner we may prove the

Theorem. *The diameter of the hyperbola*
$$b^2x^2 - a^2y^2 = a^2b^2$$
which bisects all chords with the slope m is
$$b^2x - a^2my = 0;$$
the diameter of the parabola
$$y^2 = 2\,px$$
which bisects all chords with the slope m is
$$my = p.$$

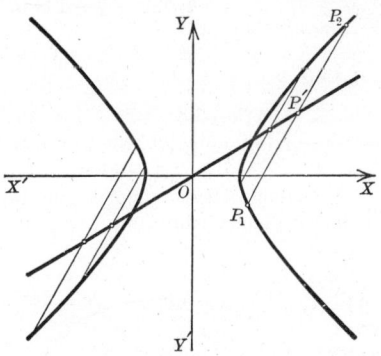
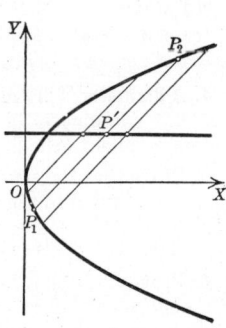

Every line through the center of an ellipse or hyperbola is a diameter, while in a parabola every line parallel to its axis is a diameter.

The method of the above example should be analyzed so that the student can apply it to the equation of any conic.

PROBLEMS

1. Find the equation of the diameter of each of the following conics which bisects the chords described. Draw a figure in every case.

(a) $4x^2 + 9y^2 = 36$, slope of chords $= \frac{1}{2}$.
(b) $x^2 = 8y$, chords $x + y = k$. *Ans.* $x + 4 = 0$.
(c) $4x^2 - y^2 = 16$, chords $3x - y + k = 0$.
(d) $xy = 12$, slope of chords $= -2$. *Ans.* $2x - y = 0$.
(e) $x^2 - 4y^2 + 4x - 16 = 0$, chords $x + y = k$. *Ans.* $x + 4y + 2 = 0$.
(f) $xy - y^2 + 2x - 4 = 0$, chords $3y = 2x + k$.

2. Find the equation of the diameter of the given conic which is determined by the given condition, and the slope of the system of chords bisected by the diameter.

(a) $y^2 = 6x$, passing through $(3, -1)$.
    Ans. $y + 1 = 0$; slope of chords $= -3$.
(b) $9x^2 + 36y^2 = 324$, passing through $(4, 2)$.
(c) $4x^2 - 16y^2 = 25$, passing through $(1, -2)$.
    Ans. $2x + y = 0$; slope of chords $= -\frac{1}{8}$.
(d) $x^2 + 2y^2 - 4x - 2y - 6 = 0$, passing through $(8, 0)$.
(e) $y^2 + xy - 8 = 0$, passing through $(3, -3)$.

3. Find the equation of the chord

(a) of $y^2 = 6x$ which is bisected by the point $(4, 3)$;
    Ans. $x - y - 1 = 0$.
(b) of $9x^2 + 36y^2 = 324$ which is bisected by $(4, 2)$;
(c) of $4x^2 - y^2 = 9$ which is bisected by $(4, 2)$; *Ans.* $8x - y - 30 = 0$.
(d) of $xy - 4 = 0$ which is bisected by $(2, -1)$.

4. A diameter is drawn to the point $(2, 3)$ on the ellipse $4x^2 + y^2 = 25$. Find the coördinates of the extremities of the diameter which bisects chords parallel to the first diameter. *Ans.* $(\frac{3}{2}, -4)$ and $(-\frac{3}{2}, 4)$.

5. Prove that the tangent drawn at the point where a diameter meets a conic is parallel to the chords which that diameter bisects.

For individual study or assignment

6. Prove the following theorem: If the slopes m and m' of two diameters of the ellipse $b^2x^2 + a^2y^2 = a^2b^2$ satisfy the relation $mm' = -\dfrac{b^2}{a^2}$, then each diameter bisects chords parallel to the other. They are called **conjugate diameters**. AB and CD in the figure are conjugate diameters.

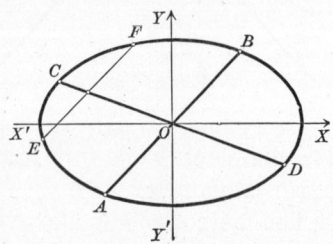

7. The point $A\ (x_0,\ y_0)$ on the ellipse $b^2x^2 + a^2y^2 = a^2b^2$ is one extremity of a diameter. Prove the following theorems:

(a) The extremities of the conjugate diameter CD are

$$\left(\pm \frac{ay_0}{b},\ \pm \frac{bx_0}{a}\right).$$

(b) The area of the parallelogram formed by the tangents drawn at the extremities of two conjugate diameters AB and CD equals eight times the area of $\triangle\ OAC$, and is equal to $4\ ab$.

(c) If OB and OC are the lengths of any two semiconjugate diameters, then $\overline{OB}^{\,2} + \overline{OC}^{\,2} = a^2 + b^2$.

8. A line drawn through a focus perpendicular to a diameter of an ellipse intersects the conjugate diameter, produced, at P. Find the locus of P.

9. State and prove the theorems corresponding to those in Problems 6 and 7 for the hyperbola $b^2x^2 - a^2y^2 = a^2b^2$ (see the figure, in which AB and CD are conjugate diameters).

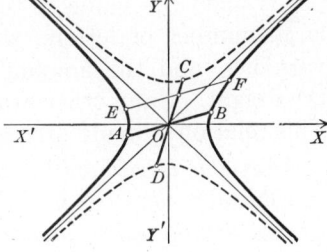

CHAPTER XII

FUNCTIONS, GRAPHS, AND EMPIRICAL EQUATIONS

98. Functions. In many practical problems two variables are involved in such a manner that the value of one depends upon the value of the other. For example, given a large number of letters, the postage and the weight are variables, and the amount of the postage depends upon the weight. Many other examples will occur to the student. This relation is made precise by the following definition:

A variable is said to be a function of a second variable when its value depends upon the value of the latter and is determined when a definite value is assumed for the second variable.

Thus the *postage* is *determined* when a *definite* weight is assumed.

Notation of functions. The symbol $f(x)$ is used to denote a function of x, and is read "*f of x*." In order to distinguish between different functions, the prefixed letter is changed, as $F(x)$, $\phi(x)$ (read "*phi of x*"), $f'(x)$, etc.

During any investigation the same functional symbol always indicates the same law of dependence of the function upon the variable. In the simpler cases this law takes the form of a series of analytical operations upon that variable. Hence, in such a case, the same functional symbol will indicate the same operations or series of operations, even though applied to different quantities. Thus, if

$$f(x) = x^2 - 9x + 14,$$
then
$$f(y) = y^2 - 9y + 14;$$
also
$$f(0) = 0^2 - 9 \cdot 0 + 14 = 14,$$
$$f(-1) = (-1)^2 - 9(-1) + 14 = 24, \text{ etc.}$$

FUNCTIONS, GRAPHS, EMPIRICAL EQUATIONS

99. Graph of a function. Examples of simple functions.
Plotting values of the variable as abscissas, with corresponding values of the function as ordinates, and connecting the points gives a curve called the *graph* of the function. In studying functions it is often helpful to draw the graph.

Linear function, $ax + b$. The graph, that is, the locus of

(1) $$y = ax + b,$$

is a straight line. The change in y per unit change in x equals the slope a; that is, the *rate of change* of y is constant. In other words, if h and k are *corresponding* changes in the values of x and y respectively, the ratio of k to h equals a. *This property is characteristic for a linear function.*

Theorem 1. *If the differences of successive values of x in a linear function are equal (h), then the differences of the corresponding values of y will also be equal (ah).*

Quadratic function, $ax^2 + bx + c$. The graph, the locus of

(2) $$y = ax^2 + bx + c,$$

is a parabola with the axis of symmetry parallel to the y-axis (see Art. 59, equation (4)).

If $x + h$ and $y + k$ are corresponding values, then

(3) $$y + k = a(x + h)^2 + b(x + h) + c.$$

Expanding, and subtracting equation (2), we have

(4) $$k = 2\,ahx + (ah^2 + bh).$$

If h is constant, k is a linear function of x.

Theorem 2. *If the differences of successive values of x in a quadratic function are equal, then the difference of successive corresponding values of y is a linear function of x.*

If k_1, k_2, k_3, etc., are the differences in successive values of y, we see that $k_2 - k_1$, $k_3 - k_2$, etc. are equal, by the above property of a linear function. By (4), this difference is $2\,ah^2$. The numbers k_1, k_2, k_3, etc. are called the **first differences** of y, and $k_2 - k_1$, etc., the **second differences**. The latter are constant (not zero) in the case assumed in Theorem 2.

Notation. A first difference of y is denoted by Δy, a second difference by $\Delta^2 y$, and similarly for any variable.

EXAMPLE

Show that the values of x and y in the accompanying table satisfy

(2) $\qquad y = ax^2 + bx + c$

exactly, and find a, b, c.

Solution. Here $\Delta x = 1$ and is constant. The first and second differences of y are tabulated. Since the latter are constant (not zero), y is a quadratic function of x. To find a, b, c, we may proceed in either of two ways.

x	y	Δy	$\Delta^2 y$
1	25	16	-2
2	41	14	-2
3	55	12	-2
4	67	10	-2
5	77	8	-2
6	85	6	
7	91		

First method. By (4), since $k = \Delta y$, we must have

(5) $\qquad \Delta y = a'x + b'$, where $a' = 2\,ah$, $b' = ah^2 + bh$.

Also $\Delta^2 y = a'h$, by Theorem 1. Since $h = 1$, then $a' = -2$. Hence $-2 = 2\,ah$, and $a = -1$. Putting any pair of corresponding values of x and Δy in (5), say $x = 1$, $\Delta y = 16$, we find $b' = 18$. Hence $ah^2 + bh = 18$, and $b = 19$. Then (2) is $y = -x^2 + 19\,x + c$. To find c, substitute for x and y any pair of values given in the table. Then $c = 7$, and the relation sought is $y = 7 + 19\,x - x^2$. All given values of x and y satisfy this equation.

Second method. Substitute three pairs of values of x and y in (2), and solve for a, b, c; that is, determine a, b, c so that the parabola (2) shall pass through three of the given points.

PROBLEMS

1. In the tables below find Δx, Δy, and $\Delta^2 y$. Then show that the values of x and y satisfy exactly a linear relation $y = ax + b$, and find a and b.

(a)

x	1	2	3	4	5
y	-1	2	5	8	11

(b)

x	1	2	3	4
y	3	1	-1	-3

2. Construct a table of values of x and y satisfying an assumed linear relation. Find Δx, Δy, and $\Delta^2 y$. What is the rate of change of y?

3. In the tables below find Δx, Δy, and $\Delta^2 y$. Then show that the values of x and y satisfy exactly $y = ax^2 + bx + c$, and find a, b, c.

(a)

x	1	2	3	4	5
y	-3	2	13	30	53

(b)

x	-2	-1	0	1	2
y	13	8	5	4	5

4. Construct a table of values of x and y satisfying an assumed quadratic relation of the form (2). Find Δx, Δy, and $\Delta^2 y$. When is $\Delta^2 y$ constant?

5. Show that the rate of change of y is constant for the values given below. Express y as a function of x.

(a)

x	0	1.4	2	5
y	3.26	4.8	5.46	8.76

Ans. $y = 1.1\, x + 3.26$.

(b)

x	10	15	25	40
y	72.4	83.4	105.4	138.4

6. Find a, b, c in the parabolic law $y = ax^2 + bx + c$ which is satisfied exactly by

(a)

x	0	2	5	10	15
y	6	12	42	148	324

(b)

x	0	0.5	2	4	5
y	10.2	10.2	13.8	27	37.2

7. Given $f(x) = x^2 - 4\,x + 2$. Find the values of $f(3)$, $f(0)$, $f(-2)$.

For individual study or assignment

8. If $P_0(x_0, y_0)$ is a fixed point on the parabola $y = ax^2 + bx + c$, and $P(x, y)$ any other point, show that the slope of the chord PP_0 is a linear function of x.

9. Apply the theorem of Problem 8 to Problem 6.

10. Show that the real roots of $ax^2 + bx + c = 0$ are the intercepts on the x-axis of the graph of the left-hand member.

100. Setting up and graphing functions. When the functional relation is given in words, it is often easy to express it by a formula. We may then "graph the function."

EXAMPLES

1. Express the area of a rectangle inscribed in a circle of diameter 5 in. as a function of a side x.

Solution. The altitude is found to be $(25 - x^2)^{\frac{1}{2}}$. Hence if A denotes the area in square inches, we have

(1) $\quad A = f(x) = x(25 - x^2)^{\frac{1}{2}}$. *Ans.*

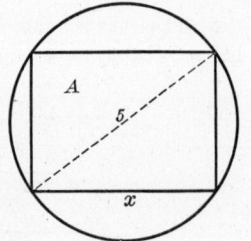

This equation gives the *functional* relation between the function A and the variable x. From it we are enabled to calculate the value of A corresponding to any value of x. For example, if $x = 3$ in.,

$$A = f(3) = 12 \text{ sq. in.}$$

The figure shows the graph of the function. The values of x range from 0 to 5, inclusive. Suitable scales must be chosen as in the figure.

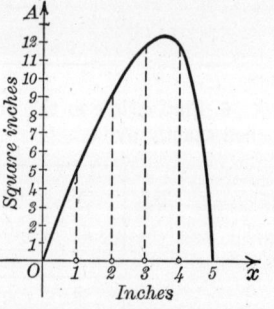

What do we learn from the graph?

1. If the graph is carefully drawn, we may measure from it the area of the inscribed rectangle with any side between $x = 0$ and $x = 5$.

2. Beginning with a small value, let x increase. Then the area *increases* until x attains a certain value between 3 and 4, then *decreases*. Hence the function defined by equation (1) has a **maximum value**. This value is the ordinate of the point of contact of the horizontal

FUNCTIONS, GRAPHS, EMPIRICAL EQUATIONS 209

tangent. Careful measurement will give for the base of the maximum rectangle, $x = 3.5$, and for the area, $A = 12.5$. These results, as may be shown by the methods of the differential calculus, are, in fact, correct to one place of decimals. The maximum rectangle is a square; that is, of all rectangles inscribed in a given circle, the square has the greatest area.

2. A wooden box, open at the top, is to be built to contain 108 cu. ft. The base must be square. Express the amount of material used as a function of a side x of the square base.

Solution. Let M = amount of lumber in square feet.

Then area of base = x^2 sq. ft.,

and area of sides = $4\,hx$ sq. ft.

Hence $M = x^2 + 4\,hx$.

But $hx^2 = 108$, and $h = \dfrac{108}{x^2}$.

Therefore

(2) $\qquad M = f(x) = x^2 + \dfrac{432}{x}.$ Ans.

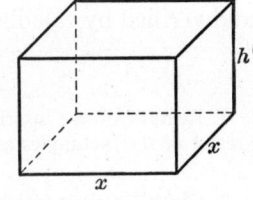

x	0	1	2	3	4	5	6	7	8	...	20 etc. feet
M	∞	433	220	153	124	111	108	111	118	...	422 etc. sq. ft.

Now graph equation (2), choosing scales as in the figure. Corresponding values of x and $M = f(x)$ are given in the table.

What do we learn from the graph?

1. If the graph is carefully drawn, we may measure from it the number of square feet of lumber in any box which contains 108 cu. ft. and has a square base.

2. Beginning with a small value, let x increase. Then the function *decreases* until x attains a certain value, then *increases*; that is, M has a minimum value. This value is the ordinate of the point of contact of

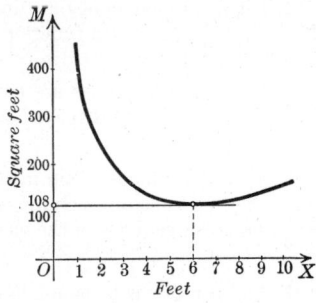

the horizontal tangent. This point on the graph can be determined exactly by Calculus, but careful measurement will in this case give the correct values, namely, $x = 6$, $M = 108$. That is, the construction will take the least lumber (108 sq. ft.) if the side of the base is 6 ft. and $h = 3$ ft.

210   NEW ANALYTIC GEOMETRY

In the following problems the student should work out the functional relation, draw the graph, and state any conclusions to be drawn from the figure. Care should be exercised in the selection of suitable scales on the axes, especially in the scale adopted for plotting values of the function. The graph should be neither very flat nor very steep. To avoid the latter we may select a large unit of length for the variable. The plot should be accurate, and the maximum or minimum value of the function should be measured and verified by calculation.

PROBLEMS

1. Rectangles are inscribed in a semicircle of radius 3 in. Plot the area A of the rectangles as a function of the width y.

Ans. $A = 2y\sqrt{9-y^2}$.

2. Given a right triangle with legs 15 and 20. Rectangles are drawn having one side x on the hypotenuse and the opposite vertices on the legs. Express the area A as a function of x and plot.

Ans. $A = \frac{12}{25}(25x - x^2)$.

3. Right circular cylinders are inscribed in a sphere of given radius r. Plot the area of the curved surface S as a function of the altitude x.

Ans. $S = \pi x (4r^2 - x^2)^{\frac{1}{2}}$.

4. Right circular cones are inscribed in a sphere of given radius r. Plot the volume V as a function of the altitude x.

Ans. $V = \frac{1}{3}\pi(2rx^2 - x^3)$.

5. Right circular cones are constructed with a given slant height L. Plot the area of the entire surface T as a function of the altitude x.

Ans. $T = \pi L(L^2 - x^2)^{\frac{1}{2}} + \pi(L^2 - x^2)$.

6. A funnel is made of tin in the shape of a right circular cone. If V represents its constant volume, express the amount of tin T used as a function of the radius x of the base, and plot.

Ans. $T = \dfrac{(\pi^2 x^6 + 9V^2)^{\frac{1}{2}}}{x}$.

7. An open box is to be made from a sheet of cardboard 16 by 12 in. by cutting equal squares from the four corners and bending up the sides. Plot the volume V as a function of the side x of the square cut out.

8. Plot the distance d from the point $(0, 5)$ to the point (x, y) on the ellipse $x^2 + 2y^2 = 98$.

Ans. $d = (123 - 10y - y^2)^{\frac{1}{2}}$.

FUNCTIONS, GRAPHS, EMPIRICAL EQUATIONS   211

9. A line is drawn through the fixed point $(3, 4)$. Plot the length of the line between the axes as a function of its x-intercept x.

10. A window consists of a rectangle surmounted by a semicircle. Given the area A, plot the perimeter P as a function of the radius x of the semicircle.
$$Ans. \ P = \frac{2\,A + 4\,x^2 + \pi x^2}{2\,x}..$$

11. Two poles 40 and 20 ft. high are 60 ft. apart on a level street. Stay wires are attached to the ground at the same point between them. Plot the length of the wires as a function of the distance x from one pole to the point where they are attached to the ground.

12. A carpenter has 96 sq. ft. of lumber with which to make a box with a square bottom and top. Express, plot, and discuss the volume of the box as a function of the side of the base.

13. Plot the length of the frame of a window of given area A as a function of its width if its shape is a rectangle surmounted by an equilateral triangle.

14. Given a piece of wire of length L. If it is cut into two pieces and one piece is bent into the shape of a square and the other into a circle, plot the combined areas of the two figures as a function of the radius of the circle.

15. The volume of a right prism having a regular hexagon as base is 16 cu. in. Plot the area of its total surface as a function of the edge of the base.

16. A wall 10 ft. high surrounds a square house which is 15 ft. from the wall. Express the length of a ladder placed without the wall, resting upon it and just reaching the house, as a function either of the distance of the foot of the ladder from the wall or of the inclination of the ladder to the horizontal. Plot and discuss.

17. A cylindrical boiler is to be constructed having a capacity of 1200 cu. ft. The material for the ends cost \$3.50 per square foot and that for the curved surface \$2.50 per square foot. Plot and discuss the cost as a function of the length of the boiler.

18. A person in a boat 3 mi. from the nearest point of a straight beach wishes to reach a house on the beach 5 mi. from that point. He can walk 4 mi. per hour and can row $3\frac{1}{2}$ mi. per hour. Plot the time required to reach the house as a function of the distance of his landing place from the house.

101. Function defined empirically. Information concerning the relation between variable and function may consist of a table of corresponding values which have been determined by experiment, that is, *empirically*. Usually the values of the variable are exact, while those of the function are inexact, being measured values and hence subject to errors of observation, errors due to defective instruments, etc. When the given values of the variable (x) and function (y) are plotted, and a relation between them is sought, it is observed at once that the graph of this relation is a curve which must "*fit*" the points but not necessarily *pass through* them, merely coming as near to them as the accuracy of the experiment demands. Heretofore we have always drawn the curve *through* the points plotted. This is no longer necessary (see the figure).

The problem is: *Given certain corresponding values of x and y, to find a formula* (or *law*) *which these values satisfy approximately, that is, within the degree of accuracy justified by the data.*

The general treatment of this important problem is beyond the scope of an elementary text, and the following articles are concerned with simple cases only.

102. Straight-line law. If the curve suggested by the plotted points is a straight line, assume the law

(1) $$y = mx + b,$$

and determine the values of m and b from the observed data. Note again that the straight line does not necessarily pass *through all* (or any) of the points plotted, for experimental work is subject to error. In general, it may be drawn through two of the plotted points, and m and b calculated from their coördinates.

FUNCTIONS, GRAPHS, EMPIRICAL EQUATIONS

EXAMPLE

In an experiment with a pulley, the effort, E pounds, required to raise a load of W pounds was found to be as follows:

W	10	20	30	40	50	60	70	80	90	100
E	$3\frac{1}{4}$	$4\frac{7}{8}$	$6\frac{1}{4}$	$7\frac{1}{2}$	9	$10\frac{1}{2}$	$12\frac{1}{4}$	$13\frac{3}{4}$	15	$16\frac{1}{2}$

Find a law to fit these data.

Solution. Plotting the points as in the figure, we see that the straight line drawn through (30, 6.25) and (100, 16.5) fits the observed data very well. To find its equation, substitute these values in the equation

(2) $\qquad E = mW + b.$

This gives $6.25 = 30\,m + b$, $16.5 = 100\,m + b$. Solving for m and b, and substituting in (2), we obtain

(3) $\quad E = 0.146\,W + 1.86,$

the required equation.

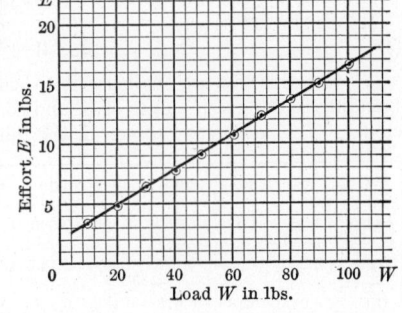

103. Method of averages. The preceding example illustrates the **method of selected points**; that is, two points were chosen to determine the straight line. A second method which takes into account all the points is the following:

First step. Substitute each pair of values x and y in the law

(1) $\qquad\qquad y = mx + b,$

thus obtaining as many equations as there are pairs of corresponding values. These are the **observation equations**.

Second step. Divide these equations into two groups as nearly equal in number as possible. Add the equations of each group, thus obtaining two equations in m and b.

Third step. Solve these equations for m and b and substitute their values in (1).

EXAMPLE

Apply the method of averages to the data of the example of Art. 102.

Solution. 1. Here $W = x$, $E = y$. Substituting in (1), we obtain ten equations, which we divide into two groups of five each, as follows:

(2)
$$3.250 = 10\,m + b, \qquad 10.500 = 60\,m + b,$$
$$4.875 = 20\,m + b, \qquad 12.250 = 70\,m + b,$$
$$6.250 = 30\,m + b, \qquad 13.750 = 80\,m + b,$$
$$7.500 = 40\,m + b, \qquad 15.000 = 90\,m + b,$$
$$9.000 = 50\,m + b. \qquad 16.500 = 100\,m + b.$$

2. Adding the equations in each group, we obtain

(3) $\qquad 30.875 = 150\,m + 5\,b. \qquad 68.000 = 400\,m + 5\,b.$

3. Solving these equations, $m = 0.1485$, $b = 1.720$.

Hence the law is

(4) $\qquad\qquad\qquad E = 0.1485\,W + 1.720.$

To test this law we shall use it to calculate the values of E corresponding to the given values of W and compare them with the observed values. The results are shown in the following table:

W	10	20	30	40	50	60	70	80	90	100
E obs.	3.250	4.875	6.250	7.500	9.000	10.500	12.250	13.750	15.000	16.500
E calc.	3.205	4.690	6.175	7.660	9.145	10.630	12.115	13.600	15.085	16.570
Diff.	+0.045	+0.185	+0.075	−0.160	−0.145	−0.130	+0.135	+0.150	−0.085	−0.070

The comparison shows that half of the differences are positive and half are negative. The sum of the positive differences is $+ 0.590$ and the sum of the negative differences is $- 0.590$; that is, the algebraic sum of the differences is zero. This indicates that the points are evenly distributed on the two sides of the line. No point plotted from the experimental values lies exactly on the line.

104. Comments on the preceding example. Denoting the difference (first difference, Art. 99) between any value of y and the preceding value by Δy, we obtain the table below, setting $W = x$, $E = y$, and observing that the first two values of y give $\Delta y = 4.875 - 3.25 = 1.625$, etc.

x	10	20	30	40	50	60	70	80	90	100
Δy	1.625	1.375	1.25	1.5	1.5	1.75	1.50	1.25	1.5	—

FUNCTIONS, GRAPHS, EMPIRICAL EQUATIONS

Here $\Delta x = 10$ and is constant. Hence if x and y satisfied $y = mx + b$ *exactly*, Δy would be constant (Art. 99). The values of Δy are, however, approximately equal, and do not on the whole increase or decrease. This test may be used for a straight-line law when the successive values of x have a constant difference Δx. In other cases the values of the ratio Δy to Δx (the rate of change of y) may be examined.

Residuals. The difference between an observed value of the function and the corresponding calculated value is called a *residual*. In the table at the end of Art. 103 the last line gives the residuals. When the values found for m and b are substituted in the right-hand members of equations (2) of that article, they become the calculated values of E. Then $3.25 - (10\,m + b)$ is the first residual. The sum of the first five residuals is therefore $30.875 - (150\,m + 5\,b)$. But this is zero by the first equation of (3). Hence the

Theorem. *When the constants in a straight-line law are found by the method of averages, the sum of the residuals for the values of y in each group of the equations in the second step will be zero.*

Practically, these sums will be zero only approximately. In the example both sums are exactly zero. The important theoretical point is that the residuals are positive and negative in such a way that their sum is zero.

Remark. In practical applications it is not always advisable to divide the observations into two equal groups, and this fact introduces an element of uncertainty depending upon judgment of the value of the different observations. Slightly different values of m and b may be obtained by dividing the observations into two groups in different ways. To avoid this uncertainty in the problems which follow, we agree to divide the data into two equal groups if the number of observations is even; if the number is odd, we shall take the extra observation with the second group.

NEW ANALYTIC GEOMETRY

The more elaborate method of least squares is adapted to the solution of the preceding problem, but it is beyond the scope of this book.

PROBLEMS

1. Find a straight-line law by the method of averages to fit the following data. Calculate the residuals. (See the theorem of Art. 104.)

(a)

x	0.5	1	1.5	2	2.5	3
y	0.31	0.82	1.29	1.85	2.51	3.02

Ans. $y = 1.10\,x - 0.29$.

(b)

x	0.5	1.0	1.5	2.0	2.5	3.0
y	2.1	6.8	12.0	17.2	21.8	27.1

(c)

x	0.9	3.0	5.2	7.0	8.8	10.7
y	5.6	4.4	3.3	2.6	1.6	0.7

(d)

x	0	2.2	4.0	5.8	7.9	10.0
y	3.8	8.2	12.1	15.7	19.8	24.0

Ans. $y = 2.02\,x + 3.90$.

(e)

x	10	20	30	40	50
y	0.75	1.15	1.74	2.18	2.67

2. Examine the values of the ratio Δy to Δx in Problem 1, and hence justify the use of the straight-line law.

3. Plot the points determined by the following values, and find a straight-line law $V = mt + b$ to fit them.

The volume (V cubic centimeters) of a certain quantity of gas under constant pressure and at different temperatures ($t°$ C.) was measured with results shown in the table below. (See Remark at the top of the next page.)

t	20	30	40	50	60	70
V	106.5	110.9	114	117.2	121.2	124.7

FUNCTIONS, GRAPHS, EMPIRICAL EQUATIONS 217

Remark. Values of t are plotted as abscissas, V as ordinates. It is convenient to consider the point of intersection of the axes as 20 on the t-scale and 105 on the V-scale, in order to have the points lie on the coördinate paper. This means simply that the axes have been translated to the new origin (20, 105).

4. Find straight-line laws for each of the following by the method of averages. Calculate the residuals. Plot the points and the straight line found.

(a) S is the weight of potassium bromide which will dissolve in 100 gm. of water at the temperature $t°$ C.

t	0	20	40	60	80
S	53.4	64.6	74.6	84.7	93.5

(b)

x	30	25	20	15	10	5
y	1	4	7.4	10.4	13.4	16.7

(c) Corresponding values of the speed and the induced volts in an arc-light dynamo were found to be

Revolutions per minute, R	200	320	495	621	744
Volts induced, V	165	270	410	525	625

(d) The resistance R ohms of a wire at $t°$ C. was measured as below.

t	0	5	10	15	20	25
R	25.00	25.49	25.98	26.48	26.99	27.51

105. Laws with two constants. When the straight-line law does not hold, the problem of finding a satisfactory formula for the given data falls under one of two heads: (1) the type of formula may be known from theoretical considerations; (2) nothing may be known about the formula in advance. The first of these cases only will b discussed. The formulas with two constants commonly used are

(1) $y = ax^n$ (power law);

(2) $y = be^{ax}$ (exponential law);

(3) $y = \dfrac{ax + b}{x}$ (first hyperbolic law);

(4) $y = \dfrac{x}{ax + b}$ (second hyperbolic law).

Each of these may be transformed into a straight-line law.

106. Power law. To find a and n in

(1) $$y = ax^n,$$

take logarithms of both members (3, p. 2); this gives

(2) $$\log y = \log a + n \log x.$$

Set $\log y = y'$, $\log a = a'$, $\log x = x'$, and (2) becomes

(3) $$y' = nx' + a'.$$

Equation (1) has thus been transformed into a straight-line law.

Theorem. *The power law holds when $\log x$ and $\log y$ satisfy a straight-line law.*

EXAMPLE

The following data satisfy approximately a law of the form $y = ax^n$. Find the values of a and n.

x	4	7	11	15	21
y	28.6	79.4	182	318	589

Solution. Tabulating the values of $\log x$ and $\log y$,

$\log x = x'$	0.6021	0.8451	1.0414	1.1761	1.3222
$\log y = y'$	1.4564	1.8998	2.2601	2.5024	2.7701

FUNCTIONS, GRAPHS, EMPIRICAL EQUATIONS 219

Plotting (x', y'), we find that a straight line will fit these points. Proceed with equation (3) as in Art. 103. The work is as follows:

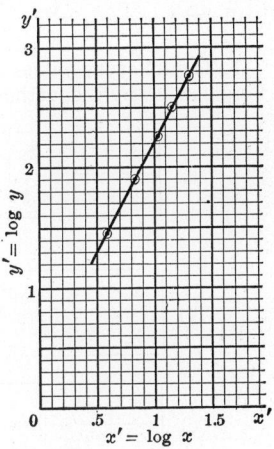

$$1.4564 = 0.6021\, n + a'$$
$$1.8998 = 0.8451\, n + a'$$
Adding, $\overline{3.3562 = 1.4472\, n + 2\, a'}$

$$2.2601 = 1.0414\, n + a'$$
$$2.5024 = 1.1761\, n + a'$$
$$2.7701 = 1.3222\, n + a'$$
Adding, $\overline{7.5326 = 3.5397\, n + 3\, a'}$

Solving, $n = 1.8251$, $a' = 0.3575$, and x', y' follow the law

(4) $\qquad y' = 1.8251\, x' + 0.3575.$

Calculating y' and comparing with the above values, we find

y' obs.	1.4564	1.8998	2.2601	2.5024	2.7701
y' cal.	1.4563	1.8998	2.2582	2.5039	2.7706
Diff.	+ 0.0001	0	+ 0.0019	− 0.0015	− 0.0005

These differences (residuals) conform to the theorem of Art. 104. Hence (4) is satisfactory. Since $\log a = a' = 0.3575$, we find $a = 2.278$, and the required power law is $y = 2.278\, x^{1.8251}$. *Ans.*

Finally, compare the observed and calculated values of y, using the calculated values of y'. This gives the table

y obs.	28.6	79.4	182	318	589
y cal.	28.6	79.4	181	319	590
Diff.	0	0	+ 1	− 1	− 1

The curve $\qquad y = 2.278\, x^{1.8251},$

which has been found to "fit" the given points x, y, passes through two of them.

In the example above, a graphical test of the correctness of the power law was afforded by plotting the points (x', y') and the straight line (3). This should be done in all cases.

PROBLEMS

1. The following values satisfy approximately a power law $y = ax^n$. Find a and n by the method of averages, and calculate the residuals.

(a)

x	1	2	3	4	5	6
y	9.2	6.1	4.7	3.9	3.5	3.2

Ans. $y = 9.18\, x^{-0.60}$.

(b)

x	5	10	15	20	25	30
y	2.56	3.23	3.70	4.07	4.39	4.66

(c)

x	4	4.5	5	5.5	6	7
y	110	97.1	86.8	78.4	71.5	60.7

2. The following table gives the diameter (D inches) of wrought-iron shafting required to transmit H horse power at 70 R.P.M. Find a law of the form $D = mH^n$.

H	10	20	30	40	50	60	70	80
D	2.11	2.67	3.04	3.36	3.61	3.82	4.02	4.22

Ans. $D = 0.991\, H^{0.330}$.

3. The following table gives the force (F dynes) between two magnetic poles at a distance of d centimeters. Find a law of the form $F = md^n$.

d	1.2	1.9	2.3	3.2	4.5
F	4.44	1.77	1.21	0.63	0.32

4. The following table gives the volume (u cubic feet) of 1 lb. of saturated steam at a pressure of p pounds per square inch. Find a law of the form $pu^n = $ constant.

u	26.43	22.40	19.08	16.32	14.04
p	14.70	17.53	20.80	24.54	28.83

5. The indicated horse power I required to drive a vessel with a displacement of D tons at a ten-knot speed is given by the following data. Find a law of the form $I = mD^n$.

D	1720	2300	3200	4100
I	655	789	1000	1164

107. Exponential and hyperbolic laws. To find a and b in
(1) $$y = be^{ax},$$
take logarithms of both members (3, p. 2), giving
(2) $$\log y = \log b + ax \log e,$$
and set $\log y = y'$, $\log b = b'$, $a \log e = a'$. Then we have
(3) $$y' = a'x + b'.$$
Equation (1) has now been transformed into the straight-line form.

Theorem 1. *The exponential law holds when x and $\log y$ satisfy a straight-line law.*

The law (1) is often called the *compound-interest law* (see Art. 85).

Writing (3), Art. 105, in the form $xy = ax + b$, and putting $u = xy$, we have
(4) $$u = ax + b.$$

Theorem 2. *The first hyperbolic law holds when x and xy satisfy a straight-line law.*

Again, the law (4), Art. 105, may be written
(5) $$\frac{x}{y} = ax + b, \quad \text{or} \quad u = \frac{x}{y} = ax + b.$$

Whence the result,

Theorem 3. *The second hyperbolic law holds if x and $\dfrac{x}{y}$ satisfy a straight-line law.*

For each of the laws of Art. 105 there is, therefore, a straight-line test. We find the values of a' and b', or a and b in this straight-line law by the method of averages, and from them the constants in the required formula.

EXAMPLE

Find a law of the form $y = be^{ax}$ for the values in the accompanying table.

Solution. Tabulate the values of $\log y = y'$, as indicated. Then, using equation (3) on p. 221, we have the observation equations

x	y	$\log y$	y cal.
0	20	1.3010	19.96
2.1	18.92	1.2769	18.94
5.6	17.34	1.2390	17.35
9.3	15.8	1.1987	15.8
11.5	14.96	1.1749	14.96

$$1.3010 = 0 + b'$$
$$1.2769 = 2.1\,a' + b'$$
Adding, $\overline{2.5779 = 2.1\,a' + 2\,b'}$

$$1.2390 = 5.6\,a' + b'$$
$$1.1987 = 9.3\,a' + b'$$
$$1.1749 = 11.5\,a' + b'$$
Adding, $\overline{3.6126 = 26.4\,a' + 3\,b'}$

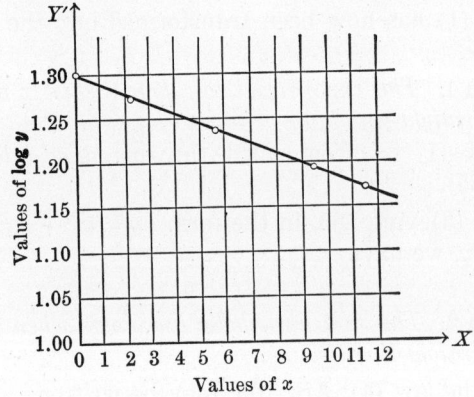

Solving, $a' = -0.01091$, $b' = 1.3003$. Hence the straight-line law is
$$y' = -0.01091\,x + 1.3003.$$

Calculating y' and comparing, the result is

y' obs.	1.3010	1.2769	1.2390	1.1987	1.1749
y' cal.	1.3003	1.2774	1.2392	1.1988	1.1748
Diff.	+0.0007	−0.0005	−0.0002	−0.0001	+0.0001

The differences (residuals) conform to the theorem of Art. 104.

FUNCTIONS, GRAPHS, EMPIRICAL EQUATIONS 223

Since $a' = a \log e$, we have $a = -0.01091 \times 2.3026 = -0.0251$, taking $\log e = 0.4343$. Also $\log b = b' = 1.3003$. Hence $b = 19.96$, and the required law is
$$y = 19.96 \, e^{-0.0251x}. \quad Ans.$$

The comparison of the observed and calculated values of y given in the table is left to the student. The figure on page 222 shows that x and $\log y \, (= y')$ satisfy nearly a straight-line law.

In the above example, the straight-line test (3) was applied, and the figure drawn. The straight-line test (3), (4), or (5) of page 221 should be carried through in each of the following problems.

PROBLEMS

1. Find a law of the form $y = be^{ax}$ for the following data. Calculate the residuals.

(a)

x	0	3.45	10.85	19.30	28.8	40.1	53.75
y	19.9	18.9	16.9	14.9	12.9	10.9	8.9

$Ans.\ y = 19.9 \, e^{-0.015x}.$

(b)

x	10	20	30	40	50	60
y	64.72	58.03	52	48.54	41.75	37.33

(c)

x	-2.4	-1.2	0	2	4	6
y	1.6	2.8	5.1	14	37.5	102

2. The following data follow the law $y = \dfrac{ax + b}{x}$. Find a and b by the method of averages, and calculate the residuals.

(a)

x	3	5	7	9	12
y	4.85	2.95	2.10	1.50	1.15

(b)

x	1.96	2.46	2.97	3.45	3.96	4.97
y	50.25	48.7	47.9	47.5	46.8	45.7

$Ans.\ y = \dfrac{43.2\,x + 13.8}{x}.$

(c)

x	1.5	2	2.5	3	3.5	4
y	3.08	3.12	3.14	3.15	3.162	3.174

3. Find a law of the form $y = \dfrac{x}{ax+b}$ for the following data. Calculate the residuals.

(a)

x	5	10	15	20	30
y	5.0	6.8	7.4	8.0	8.7

$$Ans.\ y = \dfrac{x}{0.1\,x + 0.5}.$$

(b)

x	10	20	30	40	50	60	70	80
y	12.8	17.1	20	22.2	23.1	23.8	23.8	24.2

(c)

x	8	15	30	60	80	100
y	13.0	15.4	17.2	18.5	18.9	19.2

4. Readings of the barometer in inches p for altitudes h in feet were as follows:

h	0	886	2753	4763	6942	10,593
p	30	29	27	25	23	20

Find a law of the form $p = be^{ah}$.

5. Find a law of the form $y = b + \dfrac{a}{x^2}$ for the data below, and find the residuals.

x	2	3	4	5
y	40	17	7	3

6. Find a law of the form $y = a\sqrt{x} + b$ for the given data and calculate the residuals.

x	3	6	9	12	16	20
y	6.2	8.8	11.1	13.2	15.3	17.0

FUNCTIONS, GRAPHS, EMPIRICAL EQUATIONS 225

108. Parabolic laws. The simple formula

(1) $\qquad y = a + bx^2 \quad (\textit{special parabolic law})$

has for its graph a parabola with the y-axis an **axis of symmetry**.

Letting $x^2 = t$, (1) becomes

(2) $\qquad y = a + bt.$

Hence x^2 *and* y *satisfy a straight-line law.*

EXAMPLE

An experiment to determine the coasting resistance R in pounds per ton of a motor wagon for the speed V miles per hour gave the following data:

V	0	$2\frac{1}{2}$	5	$7\frac{1}{2}$	10	$12\frac{1}{2}$	15
R	40	40	42	45	50	55	63

Solution. When these points are plotted the curve suggested (Fig. 1) appears to be a parabola with the equation

(3) $\qquad R = a + bV^2.$

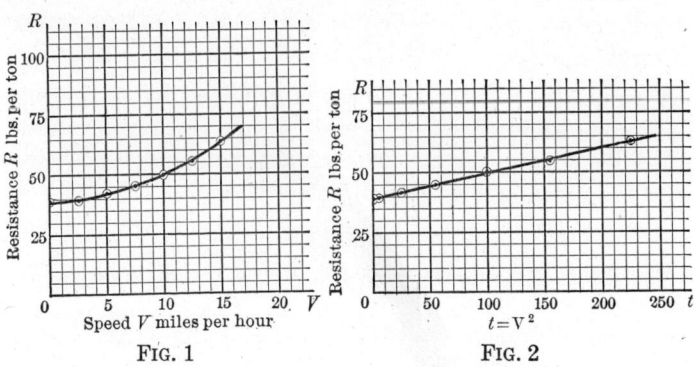

FIG. 1   FIG. 2

To check this, calculate the values of V^2, set $V^2 = t$, and retabulate the data thus:

$t\,(=V^2)$	0	$6\frac{1}{4}$	25	$56\frac{1}{4}$	100	$156\frac{1}{4}$	225
R	40	40	42	45	50	55	63

When these points are plotted (Fig. 2), it appears that they are fitted by a straight line. By the method of averages we find the equations determining a and b to be

$$122 = 31.25\, b + 3\, a, \quad 213 = 537.50\, b + 4\, a.$$

Solving, $a = 39.6$, $b = 0.102$, and the law is

$$R = 39.6 + 0.102\, V^2. \quad Ans.$$

The theorem of Art. 104 concerning the sums of the residuals applies also to the above law (1).

Turn now to the law with three constants,

(4) $\qquad y = ax^2 + bx + c \;\; \textit{(general parabolic law)},$

which often applies when none of the two-constant laws given above will hold. If $x + h$ and $y + \Delta y$ are corresponding values, then, by (4), Art. 99,

(5) $\qquad\qquad \Delta y = 2\,ahx + ah^2 + bh.$

If h is constant, put $a' = 2\,ah$, $b' = ah^2 + bh$; then

(6) $\qquad\qquad \Delta y = a'x + b'.$

Theorem. *If the successive values of x have a constant difference, the general parabolic law will hold if x and Δy follow a straight-line law.*

A numerical test for this case is provided by setting up the second differences of y and noting if they are substantially equal. We use $\Delta^2 y$ for a second difference (see Art. 99, following Theorem 2).

EXAMPLE

Find a law of the form $y = ax^2 + bx + c$ for the values in the accompanying table.

Solution. Since the values of x have a constant difference 5, we examine the values of $\Delta^2 y$ and find them substantially constant. Taking equation (6) above, and proceeding by the method of averages to find a' and b', we obtain the following observation equations:

x	y	Δy	$\Delta^2 y$	x^2
5	20	4.4	-0.4	25
10	24.4	4.0	-0.4	100
15	28.4	3.6	-0.4	225
20	32	3.2	-0.3	400
25	35.2	2.9		625
30	38.1	—	—	900
105	178.1			2275

FUNCTIONS, GRAPHS, EMPIRICAL EQUATIONS 227

$$4.4 = 5\,a' + b'$$
$$4.0 = 10\,a' + b'$$
Adding, $\overline{8.4 = 15\,a' + 2\,b'}$

$$3.6 = 15\,a' + b'$$
$$3.2 = 20\,a' + b'$$
$$2.9 = 25\,a' + b'$$
$$\overline{9.7 = 60\,a' + 3\,b'}$$

Solving, $a' = -0.0773$, $b' = 4.78$. But $a' = 2\,ah = 10\,a$. Hence

$$a = -0.00773.$$

Also $b' = ah^2 + bh = 25\,a + 5\,b$. Hence

$$b = -5\,a + \tfrac{1}{5}\,b' = 0.994.$$

To find c in (4), substitute the given values of x and y and add the resulting six equations. To help in this, x^2 has been tabulated, and the columns have been added in the table on page 226. Hence we have

$$178.1 = 2275\,a + 105\,b + 6\,c.$$

Substituting $a = -0.00773$, $b = 0.994$, we get $c = 15.21$. Hence the law is
$$y = 15.21 + 0.994\,x - 0.00773\,x^2. \quad \textit{Ans.}$$

The observed and calculated values of y are the same to one place of decimals.

109. Method of averages applied to the general parabolic law. A second method, which applies also when the values of x do not have a common difference, is the following. This is the method of averages applied to the formula

(4) $$y = ax^2 + bx + c.$$

Rule. *Substitute the given values of x and y in (4), divide the resulting equations into three groups, add the equations in each group, solve the three equations thus obtained for a, b, c, and substitute in (4).*

EXAMPLE

Solve the example worked out in Art. 108 by the above rule.

Solution. There will be six equations, namely,

$$20 = 25\,a + 5\,b + c,$$
$$24.4 = 100\,a + 10\,b + c;$$

$$28.4 = 225\,a + 15\,b + c,$$
$$32 = 400\,a + 20\,b + c;$$

$$35.2 = 625\,a + 25\,b + c,$$
$$38.1 = 900\,a + 30\,b + c.$$

Divide these into three groups as indicated, and add the two equations in each group. This gives

$$44.4 = 125\,a + 15\,b + 2\,c,$$
$$60.4 = 625\,a + 35\,b + 2\,c,$$
$$73.3 = 1525\,a + 55\,b + 2\,c.$$

Solving, $a = -0.00775$, $b = 0.994$, $c = 15.23$.

Hence the law is

$$y = -0.00775\,x^2 + 0.994\,x + 15.23. \quad Ans.$$

This result is substantially that found above.

The theorem on residuals in Art. 104 applies also to the parabolic law (4) with the single change from two groups to three.

PROBLEMS

1. Find a law $y = a + bx^2$ for the given data. Calculate the residuals. Plot the points and the parabola found.

(a)

x	1	1.5	2	2.5	3	3.5
y	1.0	4.1	8.5	14.1	21.0	29.1

Ans. $y = 2.5\,x^2 - 1.5.$

(b)

x	2	6	10	14	18	22
y	84	177	370	661	1040	1525

(c)

x	10	20	30	40	50
y	7	9.1	14.5	20	29

2. Find a parabolic law $y = ax^2 + bx + c$ satisfied approximately by the values below. Use the method of the second example of Art. 108. Calculate the residuals.

(a)

x	0	20	40	60	80	100
y	8290	8253	8215	8176	8136	8094

Ans. $y = -0.0014\,x^2 - 1.82\,x + 8290.$

FUNCTIONS, GRAPHS, EMPIRICAL EQUATIONS

(b)

x	0	0.5	1	1.5	2	2.5	3.0
y	5.4	6.3	6.6	6.1	5.0	3.2	0.6

(c)

x	0	20	40	60	80	100
y	290	253	215	176	136	94

3. Justify the use of the parabolic law in Problem 2 by examining the values of $\Delta^2 y$.

4. Work Problem 2 (b) by the method of averages (Art. 109).

5. $V =$ velocity of a train in miles per hour, $R =$ train resistance in pounds per ton.

V	20	40	60	80	100	120
R	5.5	9.1	14.9	22.8	33.3	46.0

Show that the values satisfy $R = aV^2 + bV + c$, approximately. Plot the points determined by the data, and the parabola represented by the law.

110. Solution of algebraic equations by graphs. The real roots of equations may be found approximately by drawing intersecting curves.

Quadratic equation. Solve the given equation for x^2. The result is of the form

$$x^2 = Ax + B,$$

where A and B are constants. Plot the parabola $y = x^2$ and the straight line $y = Ax + B$ on a large scale. The values of x at the points of intersection are the *real* roots of $x^2 = Ax + B$. (Why?) These values may be read from the diagram. Note the different cases:

If the line is a *secant*, the roots are real and unequal.

If the line is a *tangent*, the roots are real and equal.

If the line is *external to the parabola*, the roots are imaginary.

EXAMPLE

Solve $3x^2 + 4x - 5 = 0$ graphically.

Solution. Transposing and dividing by 3, we get

(1) $$x^2 = \tfrac{5}{3} - \tfrac{4}{3}x.$$

Plot the equations

(2) $$y = x^2 \quad \text{and} \quad y = \tfrac{5}{3} - \tfrac{4}{3}x$$

on the same axes. The abscissas of the points of intersection are 0.79, -2.12, the real roots of the given equation, approximately. By solving we find $x = 0.786, -2.120$.

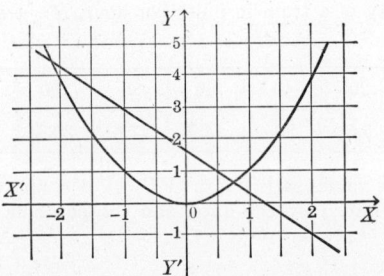

In the figure not all the lines parallel to OY at intervals of 0.1 have been drawn.

Cubic equation. To find approximately the real roots of the cubic,

(3) $$x^3 + px + q = 0,$$

where p and q are constants, by means of a graph, solve the equation for x^3, obtaining

$$x^3 = -px - q.$$

Draw the cubical parabola $y = x^3$ and the straight line $y = -px - q$, and read off the values of x at the points of intersection.

Equation (3) will have one or three real roots. Two of the three roots may be equal, namely, when the line used is tangent to the cubical parabola.

FUNCTIONS, GRAPHS, EMPIRICAL EQUATIONS

EXAMPLE

Find the real roots of

(1) $$x^3 - 4x - 8 = 0.$$

Solution. Draw the graphs of

$$y = x^3, \quad y = 4x + 8,$$

in the figure. There is one real root, $x = 2.65$. *Ans.*

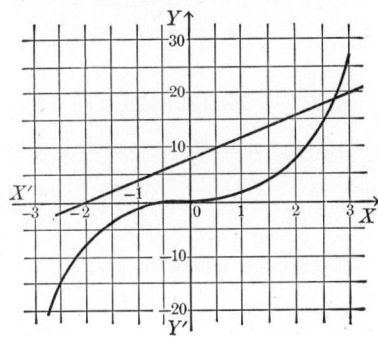

Checking by interpolation is shown in the appended calculation.

	x	x^3	$4x + 8$	$x^3 - (4x + 8)$
	2.7	19.683	18.8	$+ 0.883$
	$2.6 + z$		(root)	0
	2.6	17.576	18.4	$- 0.824$
Difference	0.1			$+ 1.707$

$$\frac{z}{0.1} = \frac{0.824}{1.707}. \quad z = 0.048. \quad x = 2.6 + z = 2.648.$$

Suppose all the terms of the equation to be solved are transposed to the left-hand member, as in (4) above, then, if we draw the graph of this function, *the intercepts on the x-axis will be the real roots.*

For example, the intercepts on OX of the graph of

(5) $$y = x^3 - 4x - 8$$

will be the real roots of equation (4). In the interpolation above, two points on this graph have been found, namely, $(2.6, -0.824)$ and $(2.7, + 0.883)$, since the last column gives values of y in (5). Obviously the graph will cross the x-axis between these points. Hence a root lies between $x = 2.6$ and $x = 2.7$. In interpolation, the portion of the graph joining these points is *replaced by a straight line*. This is justified by the fact that the two points on the graph are near together. The intercept of this line on the x-axis is calculated and taken as a close approximation to the correct root.

The graphical solution of general cubics of the form

(6) $$x^3 + ax^2 + bx + c = 0$$

is taken up below in Problem 3.

PROBLEMS

1. Solve the following quadratic equations graphically. Check by algebraic solution.

(a) $2x^2 - 4x - 5 = 0$.
(b) $2x^2 - 3x - 2 = 0$.
(c) $x^2 + 11x + 30 = 0$.
(d) $3x^2 + 4x + 6 = 0$.

2. Solve the following cubic equations graphically. Check by interpolation. Also note that, by higher algebra, the sum of all the roots is zero, since the term in x^2 is lacking.

(a) $x^3 - 9x - 5 = 0$.
    Ans. $-2.67, -0.58, 3.25$.
(b) $x^3 - 6x - 12 = 0$.
(c) $x^3 - 5x + 2 = 0$.
(d) $x^3 + 2x - 5 = 0$.
(e) $x^3 - 5x + 1 = 0$.
    Ans. $-2.33, 0.20, 2.13$.
(f) $x^3 + 8x - 7 = 0$.

For individual study or assignment

3. Prove the following statement: Equation (6) will reduce to the form (3), $x_1^3 + px_1 + q_1 = 0$, by the substitution $x = x_1 - \frac{1}{3}a$. Use this result to solve the following:

(a) $x^3 - 6x^2 + 3x + 5 = 0$.
(b) $x^3 - 3x^2 - 2x + 5 = 0$.

4. A cylindrical shell with a hemispherical end contains 700 cu. in. The length of the cylindrical part is 24 in. Find the diameter. *Ans.* 5.86 in.

5. The volume v of a spherical segment of one base and height h is $v = \pi(rh^2 - \frac{1}{3}h^3)$, where $r =$ radius of the sphere. Find h if $r = 2$ ft., $v = 20$ cu. ft.

111. Graphical solution of transcendental equations. Similar methods to those of the preceding section apply to equations not algebraic.

FUNCTIONS, GRAPHS, EMPIRICAL EQUATIONS

Consider the equation

(1) $\cot x = x$, or $\cot x - x = 0$.

To find values of x (in radians) for which this equation holds.

To aid in determining the roots, let us plot

(2) $y = \cot x$ and $y = x$.

Now *the abscissa of each point of intersection is a root of equation* (1), for, obviously, at each point of intersection of the curves (2) we must have $\cot x = x$; that is, equation (1) is satisfied.

$y = \cot x$		
Degrees	x radians	y
0	0	∞
10	0.174	5.67
20	0.349	2.75
30	0.524	1.73
40	0.698	1.19
45	0.785	1.000
50	0.873	0.839
60	1.047	0.577
70	1.222	0.364
80	1.396	0.176
90	1.571	0

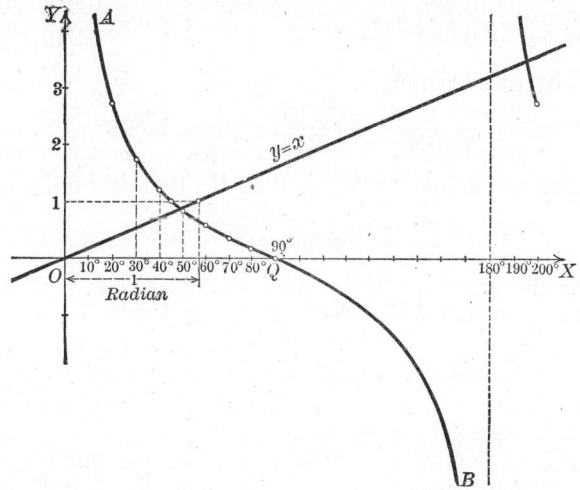

In plotting it is well to lay off carefully both scales (degrees* and radians) on OX.

* If a table is available in which natural values of the trigonometric functions are given for angles divided into decimal parts of a radian, it is not necessary to use degrees in the figure. See W. R. Longley's "Tables and Formulas" (Ginn and Company), p. 8.

234   NEW ANALYTIC GEOMETRY

Number of solutions. The curve $y = \cot x$ consists of an infinite number of branches congruent to AQB of the figure (Art. 89). The line $y = x$ will obviously cross each branch. Hence the equation (1) has an infinite number of solutions.

Smallest solution. From the figure this solution lies between 45° and 50°, or, in radians, between $x = 0.785$ and $x = 0.873$. Hence the first significant figure of the smallest root is 0.8. Interpolation is necessary to determine subsequent figures.

For this purpose arrange the work thus, using the preceding table.

x (radians)	$\cot x$	$\cot x - x$
0.873	0.839	− 0.034
0.785 + z	(root)	0
0.785	1.000	+ 0.215
Difference + 0.088		− 0.249

Then, by proportion,

$$\frac{z}{0.088} = \frac{-0.215}{-0.249}. \quad \therefore z = 0.076.$$

Hence $x = 0.785 + 0.076 = 0.86$ (to two decimal places).

PROBLEMS

Determine graphically the number of solutions in each of the following, and find the smallest root (different from zero).

1. $\cos x = x$.
   Ans. One solution; $x = 0.74$.
2. $\sin 2x = x$.
   Ans. Three solutions; $x = 0.95$.
3. $\tan x + x - 1 = 0$.
   Ans. Infinite number.
4. $3 \sin x - x = 0$.
5. $\cot x - 1 + x^2 = 0$.
6. $e^x + x - 2 = 0$.
   Ans. One solution; $x = 0.44$.
7. $\sin x - \log_{10} x = 0$.
   Ans. Three solutions.
8. $\cos x - \log_{10}(x+1) = 0$.
9. $\sin 2x - \cos 3x = 0$.
10. $e^{-x} - \tan \tfrac{1}{2} x = 0$.

For individual study or assignment

11. The area of a circular segment whose arc subtends a central angle of x radians is 5 sq. in. The radius is 2 in. Find x.   *Ans.* 2.82.

CHAPTER XIII

CARTESIAN COÖRDINATES IN SPACE

112. Cartesian coördinates. The study of solid analytic geometry is based on the determination of the position of a point in space by a set of *three* real numbers x, y, and z.

Let there be given three mutually perpendicular planes intersecting in the lines XX', YY', and ZZ'. These lines also are mutually perpendicular. The three planes are called the **coördinate planes** and may be distinguished as the XY-plane, the YZ-plane, and the ZX-plane. Their lines of intersection are the **axes of coördinates** and are called the x-axis, y-axis, and z-axis respectively. The positive directions on them are indicated by the arrowheads. The point of intersection of the coördinate planes is called the **origin**.

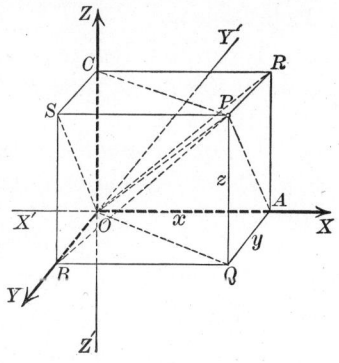

XX' and ZZ' are supposed to be in the plane of the paper, the positive direction on XX' being to the *right*, that on ZZ' being *upward*. YY' is supposed to be perpendicular to the plane of the paper, the positive direction being *in front* of the paper, that is, from the plane of the paper toward the reader.

Let P be any point in space and let three planes be drawn through P parallel to the coördinate planes and cutting the axes at A, B, and C. These three planes together with the coördinate planes bound a rectangular parallelepiped, of which P and the origin O are opposite vertices, as in the figure. The three edges $OA = x$, $OB = y$, and $OC = z$ are called the **rectangular coördinates** of P. Obviously $OA = SP$, $OB = RP$, $OC = QP$. That is, *the rectangular coördinates of P are equal numerically to its perpendicular distances from the coördinate planes.* The coördinates of P are written (x, y, z).

The coördinate planes divide all space into eight parts called **octants**, designated by O-XYZ, O-$X'YZ$, etc. The signs of the coördinates of a point in any octant may be determined by the

Rule *for signs.*

x is positive or negative according as P lies to the right or left of the YZ-plane.

y is positive or negative according as P lies in front or in back of the ZX-plane.

z is positive or negative according as P lies above or below the XY-plane.

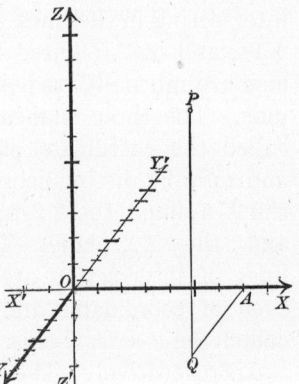

Points in space may be conveniently plotted by marking the same scale on XX' and ZZ' and a somewhat smaller scale on YY'. For example, draw OY making $\angle X'OY = 45°$ and lay off unit distance on OY equal to half unit distance on OX ("cabinet projection"). Then to plot any point, for example (7, 6, 10), we lay off $OA = 7$ on OX, and draw AQ parallel to OY and equal to 6 units on OY, and QP parallel to OZ and equal to 10 units on OZ. Note especially that Q in the XY-plane is plotted by the rule in Art. 7 for *oblique* coördinates. Points in the YZ-plane also are plotted by this **rule.**

CARTESIAN COÖRDINATES IN SPACE

113. Important relations. In the figure on page 235 we have
$$\overline{OP}^2 = \overline{OQ}^2 + \overline{QP}^2 = \overline{OA}^2 + \overline{OB}^2 + \overline{OC}^2.$$
Hence, if $OP = \rho$,

(1) $$\rho^2 = x^2 + y^2 + z^2.$$

Let the angles between OP and OX, OY and OZ be, respectively, α, β, and γ. The triangle OAP is a right triangle, for OA is perpendicular to AP. Also $\angle XOP = \alpha$. Hence $OA = OP \cos \alpha$, or $x = \rho \cos \alpha$. Similar values for y and z are found from the right triangles OBP and OCP. Hence

(2) $$x = \rho \cos \alpha, \quad y = \rho \cos \beta, \quad z = \rho \cos \gamma.$$

Squaring these equations, adding them, using (1), and dividing by ρ^2, we obtain the important relation

(3) $$\cos^2 \alpha + \cos^2 \beta + \cos^2 \gamma = 1.$$

Equations (2) may be written as a set of equal ratios, namely,

(4) $$\frac{\cos \alpha}{x} = \frac{\cos \beta}{y} = \frac{\cos \gamma}{z} = \frac{1}{\rho}.$$

Solving (2) for $\cos \alpha$, $\cos \beta$, $\cos \gamma$, and using the value of ρ from (1), we obtain

(5) $$\cos \alpha = \frac{x}{\sqrt{x^2 + y^2 + z^2}}, \quad \cos \beta = \frac{y}{\sqrt{x^2 + y^2 + z^2}},$$
$$\cos \gamma = \frac{z}{\sqrt{x^2 + y^2 + z^2}}.$$

The perpendicular distance of P from the x-axis in the figure on page 235 is AP. In the right triangle OAP, we have $\overline{AP}^2 = \overline{OP}^2 - \overline{OA}^2$. Substituting $OA = x$, and using (1), we obtain the result, *the perpendicular distance of $P(x, y, z)$ from the x-axis is $\sqrt{y^2 + z^2}$*. Similarly, the *perpendicular distances of $P(x, y, z)$ from the y-axis and the z-axis, respectively, are $\sqrt{z^2 + x^2}$ and $\sqrt{x^2 + y^2}$.*

PROBLEMS

1. Plot the following points and calculate the perpendicular distance of each from the axes and the distance from the origin:

(a) $(0, 0, 4)$, $(0, -2, 0)$, $(-4, 0, 0)$, $(3, 0, 5)$, $(7, 3, 0)$, $(0, -4, 3)$.

(b) $(1, 3, 5)$, $(1, 6, 1)$, $(-2, -1, 4)$, $(3, 4, -2)$, $(-3, -4, -6)$, $(-4, 5, 7)$.

(c) $(4, 5, 8)$, $(3, -4, 8)$, $(6, 4, -2)$, $(3, -2, 6)$, $(-2, 3, 1)$, $(-3, -6, -7)$.

2. Show that the following points lie on a circular cylinder whose axis is the z-axis:

$$(3, 4, 7), (5, 0, 4), (2\sqrt{5}, \sqrt{5}, -3), (2\sqrt{6}, -1, -4).$$

3. What is the locus of $P(x, y, z)$ if

(a) $x = 0$?
(b) $y = 0$?
(c) $z = 0$?
(d) $x = y = 0$?
(e) $x = z = 0$?
(f) $y = z = 0$?
(g) $x = y = z$?
(h) $x = y$, $z = 0$?
(i) $x = z$?

4. Draw a rectangular parallelepiped with its edges lying in or parallel to the coördinate planes if $(0, 0, 0)$ and $(3, 6, 7)$ are the extremities of a diagonal.

5. What are the distance from the origin and the perpendicular distances from the axes to each of the points (a, b, c), $(a, b, -c)$, $(a, -b, c)$, $(-a, -b, c)$, $(-a, b, -c)$, $(a, -b, -c)$, $(-a, b, c)$, $(-a, -b, -c)$? What pairs of these points are symmetric with respect to a coördinate plane? a coördinate axis? the origin?

6. Find the angle between each axis and the line drawn from the origin to

(a) $(1, -1, -1)$;   *Ans.* $\alpha = 54° 44'$, $\beta = \gamma = 125° 16'$.
(b) $(1, -2, -2)$;
(c) $(4, 3, 12)$;   *Ans.* $\alpha = 72° 5'$, $\beta = 76° 40'$, $\gamma = 22° 37'$.
(d) $(4, -4, 7)$;
(e) $(-6, 2, 3)$;   *Ans.* $\alpha = 149°$, $\beta = 73° 24'$, $\gamma = 64° 37'$.
(f) $(4, -2, -3)$.

7. A line is drawn through the point $(-6, 5, 2)$ parallel to the y-axis. Find the coördinates of the points on this line that are at a distance of 9 units from the origin.

8. Solve Problem 7 if the line is drawn parallel to the x-axis; the z-axis.

9. Describe the locus of a point if it moves so that

(a) its perpendicular distance from the y-axis is 3;
(b) its distance from the origin is 6;

CARTESIAN COÖRDINATES IN SPACE

(c) its perpendicular distances from the coördinate planes XY and YZ are equal;

(d) its perpendicular distance from the plane ZX is -5.

114. Direction cosines of a line. The angles α, β, and γ between a directed line OP and the axes of coördinates are called the **direction angles** of the line. If the line does not pass through O, then its direction angles α, β, and γ are the angles between the axes and a line drawn through the origin parallel to the given line and agreeing with it in direction.

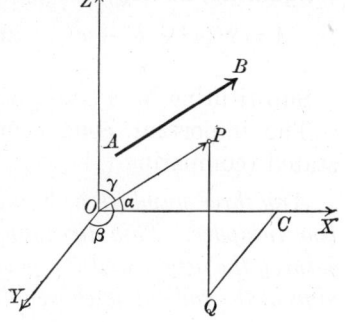

The cosines of the direction angles of a line are called its *direction cosines*.

Reversing the direction of a line changes the signs of its direction cosines; for reversing the direction of a line changes α, β, and γ into $\pi - \alpha$, $\pi - \beta$, and $\pi - \gamma$ respectively, and $\cos(\pi - x) = -\cos x$ (**8**, p. 3).

From (3) in Art. 113, we have the

Theorem. *The sum of the squares of the direction cosines of a line is unity; that is,*

(I) $$\cos^2 \alpha + \cos^2 \beta + \cos^2 \gamma = 1.$$

115. Direction numbers of a line. Instead of using the direction cosines, we employ more often three numbers to which they are proportional, called *direction numbers* of the line.

Theorem. *If a, b, c are direction numbers of a line, its direction cosines are given by the formulas*

(II) $$\cos \alpha = \frac{a}{\pm \sqrt{a^2 + b^2 + c^2}}, \quad \cos \beta = \frac{b}{\pm \sqrt{a^2 + b^2 + c^2}},$$
$$\cos \gamma = \frac{c}{\pm \sqrt{a^2 + b^2 + c^2}}.$$

Proof. By definition,
$$\frac{\cos\alpha}{a} = \frac{\cos\beta}{b} = \frac{\cos\gamma}{c}.$$

Let r denote the common value of the ratios. Then
(1) $\qquad \cos\alpha = ar, \quad \cos\beta = br, \quad \cos\gamma = cr.$

Squaring, adding, and applying (I), Art. 114,
$$1 = r^2(a^2 + b^2 + c^2), \quad \text{and} \quad r = \frac{1}{\pm\sqrt{a^2 + b^2 + c^2}}.$$

Substituting in (1), we get the formulas. Q.E.D.

The important conclusion just derived may be thus stated (comparing (II) with (5), Art. 113):

Any three numbers a, b, and c determine the direction of a line in space. This direction is the same as that of the line joining the origin and the point (a, b, c) when the positive sign of the radical is chosen in (II); *otherwise this direction reversed.*

If one direction number is zero, the line is perpendicular to the corresponding axis of coördinates. If two are zero, it is parallel to the remaining axis.

If a line cuts the XY-plane, it will be *directed upward* or *downward* according as $\cos\gamma$ is *positive* or *negative*.

If a line is parallel to the XY-plane, $\cos\gamma = 0$, and it will be *directed in front* or *in back of the ZX-plane* according as $\cos\beta$ is *positive* or *negative*.

If a line is parallel to the x-axis, $\cos\beta = \cos\gamma = 0$, and its positive direction will *agree or disagree with that of the x-axis* according as $\cos\alpha = 1$ or -1.

These considerations enable us to choose the sign of the radical in the theorem so that the positive direction on the line shall be that given in advance.

PROBLEMS

1. The numbers given in each case are direction numbers for a line. Write down other sets of direction numbers for the same line, and calculate the direction cosines.

(a) $2, -3, 4$.   (b) $3, 0, -1$.   (c) $\frac{1}{5}, \frac{3}{2}, \frac{2}{3}$.   (d) $0, -\frac{1}{2}, \frac{4}{5}$.

Construct a line with the given direction numbers in each case.

CARTESIAN COÖRDINATES IN SPACE

2. Find the direction cosines and angles of a line directed upward if its direction numbers are

(a) $-6, 2, 3$;   *Ans.* $\alpha = 149°$, $\beta = 73° 24'$, $\gamma = 64° 37'$.
(b) $1, 2, 3$;
(c) $4, 1, 0$;
(d) $-2, -3, 1$;
(e) $1, -1, -1$;   *Ans.* $\alpha = 125° 16'$, $\beta = \gamma = 54° 44'$.
(f) $5, -4, 7$;
(g) $5, 0, -6$.

In each case draw a line with the given direction numbers.

3. Describe the direction of a line if

(a) $\cos \alpha = 0$;
(b) $\cos \gamma = 0$;
(c) $\cos \beta = 0$;
(d) $\cos \alpha = \cos \beta = 0$;
(e) $\cos \alpha = \cos \gamma = 0$;
(f) $\cos \beta = \cos \gamma = 0$.

4. A line makes equal angles with the axes of coördinates. Find the angle.

5. A line makes an angle of $45°$ with the x-axis and an angle of $60°$ with the y-axis. What angle does it make with the z-axis?

6. Find the direction cosines of a line which makes an angle of $30°$ with the z-axis and equal angles with the x- and y-axes.

Ans. $\pm \frac{1}{4}\sqrt{2}, \pm \frac{1}{4}\sqrt{2}, \frac{1}{2}\sqrt{3}$.

7. Can any of the following sets of numbers be the direction cosines of a line:

(a) $(\frac{1}{15}, 1, -\frac{2}{15})$? (b) $(\frac{1}{2}, \frac{1}{3}, \frac{2}{3})$? (c) $(0, \frac{1}{2}\sqrt{2}, -\frac{1}{2}\sqrt{2})$? (d) $(\frac{1}{4}, \frac{1}{5}, \frac{3}{7})$?

8. If two of the direction angles of a line are $60°$ and $30°$, what is the third?

9. Two direction cosines of a line are $\frac{1}{3}$ and $-\frac{2}{3}$. What is the third?

10. In what octant ($O\text{-}XYZ$, $O\text{-}X'YZ$, etc.) will the positive part of a line through O lie if

(a) $\cos \alpha > 0$, $\cos \beta > 0$, $\cos \gamma > 0$?
(b) $\cos \alpha > 0$, $\cos \beta > 0$, $\cos \gamma < 0$?
(c) $\cos \alpha > 0$, $\cos \beta < 0$, $\cos \gamma < 0$?
(d) $\cos \alpha > 0$, $\cos \beta < 0$, $\cos \gamma > 0$?
(e) $\cos \alpha < 0$, $\cos \beta > 0$, $\cos \gamma > 0$?
(f) $\cos \alpha < 0$, $\cos \beta < 0$, $\cos \gamma > 0$?
(g) $\cos \alpha < 0$, $\cos \beta < 0$, $\cos \gamma < 0$?
(h) $\cos \alpha < 0$, $\cos \beta > 0$, $\cos \gamma < 0$?

116. Lengths.

Theorem. *The length l of the line joining two points $P_1(x_1, y_1, z_1)$ and $P_2(x_2, y_2, z_2)$ is given by*

(III) $\quad l = \sqrt{(x_1 - x_2)^2 + (y_1 - y_2)^2 + (z_1 - z_2)^2}.$

Proof. Construct a rectangular parallelepiped by passing planes through P_1 and P_2 parallel to the coördinate planes. Its edges will be parallel to the axes and equal respectively to $x_2 - x_1$, $y_2 - y_1$, $z_2 - z_1$. P_1P_2 will be a diagonal of this parallelepiped, and hence l^2 will equal the sum of the squares of its three edges. Q.E.D.

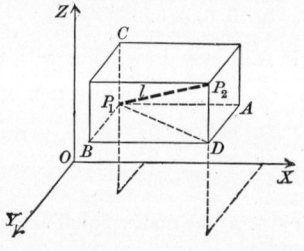

Let α, β, γ be the direction angles of P_1P_2. Then, from the figure, $\angle AP_1P_2 = \alpha$, and $P_1A = l \cos \alpha$. Similarly $P_1B = l \cos \beta$, $P_1C = l \cos \gamma$.

Hence we have the equations

(1) $\quad x_2 - x_1 = l \cos \alpha, \quad y_2 - y_1 = l \cos \beta, \quad z_2 - z_1 = l \cos \gamma.$

Then $x_2 - x_1$, $y_2 - y_1$, $z_2 - z_1$, or *numbers proportional to them, may be taken as direction numbers of P_1P_2.*

117. Angle between two directed lines.

Theorem. *If α, β, γ and α', β', γ' are the direction angles of two directed lines, then the angle θ between them is given by*

(IV) $\quad \cos \theta = \cos \alpha \cos \alpha' + \cos \beta \cos \beta' + \cos \gamma \cos \gamma'.$

Proof. Draw OP and OP' parallel to the given lines. Then we define the angle between the given lines by

$$\angle POP' = \theta.$$

Let $OP = \rho$, $OP' = \rho'$, $PP' = d$ (Fig. p. 243). Then, by the law of cosines (**11**, p. 4),

(1) $\quad\quad\quad \cos \theta = \dfrac{\rho^2 + \rho'^2 - d^2}{2\,\rho\rho'}.$

If (x, y, z) and (x', y', z')
are the coördinates of P and
P' respectively, we have

$$\rho^2 = x^2 + y^2 + z^2,$$
$$\rho'^2 = x'^2 + y'^2 + z'^2,$$
$$d^2 = (x' - x)^2 + (y' - y)^2 + (z' - z)^2.$$

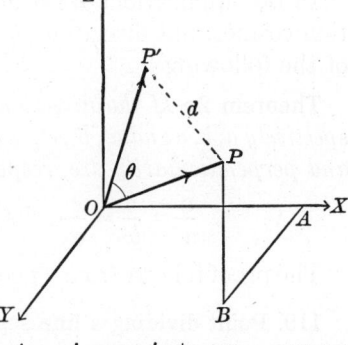

Hence
$$\rho^2 + \rho'^2 - d^2 = 2(x'x + y'y + z'z).$$

By (2), Art. 113, we have $x' = \rho' \cos \alpha'$ etc., $x = \rho \cos \alpha$ etc. Substituting these values in (1), we obtain (IV). Q.E.D.

118. Test for parallel lines or perpendicular lines.

Theorem 1. *Two lines are parallel and in the same direction when and only when their direction angles are equal, and perpendicular when and only when the sum of the products of their direction cosines is zero.*

Proof. The condition for parallelism follows from the fact that both lines will be parallel to and agree in direction with the same line through the origin when and only when their direction angles are equal.

The condition for perpendicularity follows from (IV), for if $\theta = 90°$ then $\cos \theta = 0$, and conversely. Q.E.D.

Two lines will be parallel and have opposite directions when and only when the direction angles are supplementary. Two lines in space are said to be perpendicular when the angle between them is 90°, but the lines do not necessarily intersect.

When two parallel lines are constructed by using Cartesian coördinates in space, they are parallel in the drawing. Two perpendicular lines so constructed do not necessarily appear perpendicular, however. (See the figure at the beginning of Art. 112.)

In the applications we usually have given not the direction cosines, but direction numbers. Hence the importance of the following

Theorem 2. *If the direction numbers of two lines are respectively a, b, c and a', b', c', then the conditions for parallelism and perpendicularity are, respectively,*

$$\frac{a}{a'} = \frac{b}{b'} = \frac{c}{c'}, \quad aa' + bb' + cc' = 0.$$

The proof follows from Theorem 1 above and (II), Art. 115.

119. Point dividing a line segment in a given ratio.

Theorem. *The coördinates (x, y, z) of the point P dividing the line joining $P_1(x_1, y_1, z_1)$ and $P_2(x_2, y_2, z_2)$ so that*

$$\frac{P_1P}{PP_2} = r$$

are given by the formulas

(V) $\quad x = \dfrac{x_1 + rx_2}{1 + r}, \quad y = \dfrac{y_1 + ry_2}{1 + r}, \quad z = \dfrac{z_1 + rz_2}{1 + r}.$

This is proved as in Art. 10.

Corollary. *The coördinates (x, y, z) of the mid-point of $P_1(x_1, y_1, z_1)$ and $P_2(x_2, y_2, z_2)$ are*

$$x = \tfrac{1}{2}(x_1 + x_2), \quad y = \tfrac{1}{2}(y_1 + y_2), \quad z = \tfrac{1}{2}(z_1 + z_2).$$

EXAMPLES

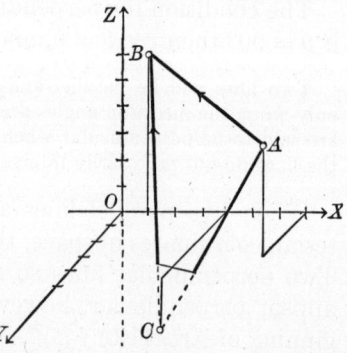

1. Show that the triangle with vertices $A(7, 3, 4)$, $B(1, 0, 6)$, $C(4, 5, -2)$ is a right triangle.

Solution. By Art. 116, the direction numbers are:

of AB, $6, 3, -2$; of BC, $-3, -5, 8$; of CA, $-3, 2, -6$.

The condition $a'a + b'b + c'c = 0$ applies to the direction numbers of AB and CA. Hence $\angle A$ is $90°$. *Ans.*

CARTESIAN COÖRDINATES IN SPACE

2. Find $\angle B$ in the triangle of Example 1.

Solution. Take positive directions of AB and CB (Art. 115) as in the figure. Let α, β, γ, and α', β', γ' be their direction angles. Then γ and γ' are acute. By (II), Art. 115,

$$\cos \alpha = -\frac{6}{7}, \cos \beta = -\frac{3}{7}, \cos \gamma = \frac{2}{7};$$

$$\cos \alpha' = -\frac{3\sqrt{2}}{14}, \cos \beta' = -\frac{5\sqrt{2}}{14}, \cos \gamma' = \frac{8\sqrt{2}}{14}.$$

Hence, by (IV), $\cos B = \dfrac{(18 + 15 + 16)\sqrt{2}}{98} = \dfrac{1}{2}\sqrt{2}.$ $B = 45°$. *Ans.*

PROBLEMS

1. Show by the length formula that the triangle with vertices $(7, 3, 4)$, $(1, 0, 6)$, and $(4, 5, -2)$ is an isosceles right triangle (see example above).

2. Find the angle at the first vertex given in each of the following triangles. The triangle should be drawn in each case. Also the student must determine if the angle desired is that between the sides directed upward (Art. 115) or its supplement.

(a) $(2, 1, 4)$, $(3, -1, 2)$, $(5, 0, 6)$. *Ans.* 84° 53'
(b) $(2, -4, 7)$, $(3, -2, 0)$, $(4, -5, 4)$.
(c) $(4, 3, -4)$, $(-2, 9, -4)$, $(-2, 3, 2)$.
(d) $(4, 3, -2)$, $(7, -1, 4)$, $(-2, 1, -4)$.
(e) $(3, 2, 2)$, $(1, 2, 1)$, $(2, 4, -1)$.

3. Determine the nature of each triangle in Problem 2 by the length formula.

4. What kind of quadrilateral has the vertices $(5, 5, 2)$, $(7, 5, -3)$, $(3, 2, -1)$, $(1, 2, 4)$? Draw it.

5. Find the mid-point of and the points which trisect the lines joining

(a) $(3, 2, -1)$ and $(4, -2, 6)$;
    Ans. $(3\tfrac{1}{2}, 0, 2\tfrac{1}{2})$, $(3\tfrac{1}{3}, \tfrac{2}{3}, 1\tfrac{1}{3})$, $(3\tfrac{2}{3}, -\tfrac{2}{3}, 3\tfrac{2}{3})$.
(b) $(4, -7, 3)$ and $(-6, 3, -5)$;
(c) $(4, 3, -2)$ and $(-2, 1, -5)$;
(d) $(4, 7, -2)$ and $(3, 5, -4)$;
(e) $(3, -8, 6)$ and $(6, -4, 6)$.

6. By comparing directions and lengths determine the type of figure with the following vertices (given in order around the perimeter):

(a) $(7, 3, -4)$, $(1, 0, -6)$, $(4, 5, 2)$.
(b) $(2, -1, 5)$, $(3, 4, -2)$, $(6, 2, 2)$, $(5, -3, 9)$.
(c) $(6, 7, 3)$, $(3, 11, 1)$, $(-3, 7, 2)$, $(0, 3, 4)$.
(d) $(-6, 3, 2)$, $(3, -2, 4)$, $(5, 7, 3)$, $(-13, 17, -1)$.
(e) $(2, 3, 0)$, $(4, 5, -1)$, $(3, 7, 1)$, $(1, 5, 2)$.

(f) $(6, -6, 0)$, $(3, -4, 4)$, $(2, -9, 2)$, $(-1, -7, 6)$.
(g) $(3, 2, 2)$, $(1, 2, 1)$, $(2, 4, -1)$, $(4, 4, 0)$.
(h) $(2, 1, 4)$, $(0, 0, 0)$, $(3, -1, 2)$, $(5, 0, 6)$.

7. Examine each group of points given to determine if they lie on a straight line. Draw the figure.

(a) $(3, 2, 7)$, $(1, 4, 6)$, $(7, -2, 9)$.
(b) $(13, 4, 9)$, $(1, 7, 13)$, $(7, 5.5, 11)$, $(5, 6, 11\frac{2}{3})$.
(c) $(3, 6, -2)$, $(7, -4, 3)$, $(-1, 16, -7)$, $(-5, 25, -12)$.
(d) $(2, -15, -4)$, $(-3, -5, -9)$, $(3, -17, -3)$, $(4, -19, -2)$.

8. Find the area of each of the following triangles with the vertices given:

(a) $(1, 3, 3)$, $(0, 1, 0)$, $(4, -1, 0)$. *Ans.* $\sqrt{70}$.
(b) $(3, 1, 2)$, $(2, -1, 5)$, $(1, 0, -1)$. *Ans.* $\frac{3}{2}\sqrt{19}$.
(c) $(4, -4, 2)$, $(9, -1, 10)$, $(6, -7, 8)$.
(d) $(3, -4, 4)$, $(2, -9, 2)$, $(-1, -7, 6)$.

9. If the lines L_1 and L_2 have direction numbers $(0, -1, 1)$ and $(-1, -1, 0)$ respectively, find the direction cosines of the line L_3 if it is perpendicular to L_1 and makes an angle of $30°$ with L_2.

10. If one end of a line is $(2, -3, 5)$ and its mid-point is $(4, 2, 3)$, find the coördinates of the other end.

11. Show that $(0, 0, 0)$, $(0, -1, -1)$, $(-1, 0, -1)$, and $(-1, -1, 0)$ are the vertices of a regular tetraedron.

12. If one end of a line is $(6, -1, -7)$ and a point three fifths of the way along it from this end is $(3, 2, -1)$, find the other end.

13. If the direction numbers of three lines are $(12, -3, -4)$, $(4, 12, 3)$, and $(3, -4, 12)$ respectively, show that the lines are mutually perpendicular.

14. The x-coördinate of a point on the line joining $(2, -3, 4)$ and $(8, 0, 10)$ is 4. Find the other coördinates of the point.

PROBLEMS FOR INDIVIDUAL STUDY OR ASSIGNMENT

1. If the direction numbers of two lines L_1 and L_2 are, respectively, $(2, -3, 4)$ and $(-1, 2, -3)$, find direction numbers for a line perpendicular to L_1 and L_2.

2. Find the area of $\triangle ABC$ with vertices $A(2, 1, 4)$, $B(3, -1, 2)$, $C(5, 0, 6)$, using the formula, area $= \frac{1}{2} AB \cdot AC \sin A$.

3. Show that the line joining $(2, 3, 4)$ and $(-1, 2, 6)$ intersects the line joining $(1, 2, -5)$ and $(6, 3, -18)$, and find the point of intersection.

4. Find the coördinates of the centroid of any triangle.
Ans. $\frac{1}{3}(x_1 + x_2 + x_3)$, $\frac{1}{3}(y_1 + y_2 + y_3)$, $\frac{1}{3}(z_1 + z_2 + z_3)$.

5. Show that the lines joining the mid-points of the opposite sides of any quadrilateral (not necessarily plane) bisect each other.

6. The three lines joining the mid-points of opposite edges of a tetraedron bisect each other.

7. In any tetraedron the lines from the vertices to the centroids of the opposite faces meet in a point which divides each line in the ratio $r = 3$. (Centroid of the tetraedron.)

8. The sum of the squares of the diagonals of any quadrilateral is twice the sum of the squares of the lines which join the mid-points of the opposite sides.

9. The sum of the squares of two pairs of opposite edges of a tetraedron is equal to the sum of the squares of the third pair of opposite edges increased by four times the square of the line joining the mid-points of the third pair.

120. Loci in space. In solid geometry it is necessary to consider two kinds of loci:

1. The locus of a point in space which satisfies *one* given condition is, in general, a *surface*.

Thus the locus of a point at a given distance from a fixed point is a sphere. The locus of a point equidistant from two fixed points is the plane which is perpendicular to the line joining the given points at its mid-point.

2. The locus of a point in space which satisfies *two* conditions is, in general, a *curve*. For the locus of a point which satisfies either condition is a surface, and hence the points which satisfy both conditions lie on two surfaces, that is, on their curve of intersection.

Thus the locus of a point which is (1) at a given distance r from a fixed point P_1 and (2) equally distant from two fixed points P_2 and P_3 is a circle, namely, the intersection of the sphere with center P_1 and radius r with the plane perpendicular to P_2P_3 at its mid-point.

The number of conditions must be counted carefully. Thus, if a point is to be equidistant from three fixed points P_1, P_2, and P_3, it satisfies *two* conditions, namely, that of being equidistant from P_1 and P_2 and that of being equidistant from P_2 and P_3.

These two kinds of loci must be carefully distinguished.

121. Equation of a surface. If any point P which lies on a surface is given the coördinates (x, y, z), then the condition which defines the surface as a locus will lead to an equation involving the variables x, y, and z. This equation is called the *equation of the surface*, and may be found in many cases by a rule analogous to that in Art. 16, as we shall see below.

The *equation of a surface* is the equation in x, y, and z which is satisfied by the coördinates of every point on the surface and by those of no other point.

The plane is the simplest surface, and this we take up in the next chapter. At this point the truth of the following statement should be obvious:

Theorem. *The equation of a plane which is*
parallel to the XY-plane has the form $z = $ constant;
parallel to the YZ-plane has the form $x = $ constant;
parallel to the ZX-plane has the form $y = $ constant.

122. Equations of a curve. If any point P on a curve is given the coördinates (x, y, z), then the two conditions which define the curve as a locus will lead to two equations involving the variables x, y, and z. The equation of the surface defined by each condition separately may be found in many cases by a rule analogous to that of Art. 16. The two equations considered as *simultaneous* will be the equations of the curve, which is the *curve of intersection of the surfaces*.

The *equations of a curve* are two simultaneous equations in x, y, and z which are satisfied by the coördinates of every point on the curve and by those of no other point.

It will appear later that the equations of the same curve may have an endless variety of forms.

The straight line, as the intersection of two planes, affords the simplest example of a "curve" in space (see the next chapter). A simple example is provided by the obvious

CARTESIAN COÖRDINATES IN SPACE

Theorem. *The equations of a line which is
parallel to the x-axis have the form $y = $ constant, $z = $ constant;
parallel to the y-axis have the form $z = $ constant, $x = $ constant;
parallel to the z-axis have the form $x = $ constant, $y = $ constant.*

123. Locus of an equation. The locus of an equation in three variables (one or two may be lacking) representing coördinates in space is the *surface* passing through all points whose coördinates satisfy that equation, and no other points.

Discussion of the equation and construction of the surface are taken up in a later chapter.

The **locus of two simultaneous equations** is the *curve of intersection* of the surfaces defined by the equations taken separately.

PROBLEMS

1. What are the equations of the coördinate planes? of the coördinate axes?

2. Find the equation of the locus of a point

(a) 4 units below the XY-plane;
(b) 5 units to the left of the YZ-plane;
(c) 3 units in front of the XZ-plane;
(d) 4 units to the right of the YZ-plane;
(e) 10 units above the XY-plane;
(f) 6 units back of the XZ-plane.

3. Find the equation of the locus of a point

(a) at a distance of 6 units from $(1, -1, 3)$;
(b) at a distance of 5 units from $(3, 0, 4)$;
      Ans. Sphere $x^2 + y^2 + z^2 - 6x - 8z = 0$.
(c) equidistant from $(2, -2, 1)$ and $(4, 5, 6)$;
(d) equidistant from $(4, -6, -8)$ and $(-2, 7, 9)$.
      Ans. Plane $6x - 13y - 17z + 9 = 0$.

4. Find the equation of the plane which bisects the line joining the given pair of points and is perpendicular to this line.

(a) $(6, 3, 2)$ and $(4, 2, 0)$.   *Ans.* $4x + 2y + 4z - 29 = 0$.
(b) $(7, -6, 0)$ and $(-5, -2, 3)$.
(c) $(4, -3, 6)$ and $(2, -4, 2)$.   *Ans.* $4x + 2y + 8z - 37 = 0$.
(d) $(4, -5, -12)$ and $(-2, 4, 6)$.

5. Find the equation of the sphere

(a) of radius 4 and center $(3, -4, -5)$;

(b) having the line joining $(-3, 4, 2)$ and $(7, -2, 6)$ as a diameter;
Ans. $x^2 + y^2 + z^2 - 4x - 2y - 8z - 17 = 0$.

(c) with center $(2, 1, 4)$ and tangent to the YZ-plane;

(d) with center $(3, 2, 7)$ and passing through $(5, -3, 8)$;
Ans. $x^2 + y^2 + z^2 - 6x - 4y - 14z + 32 = 0$.

(e) of radius 3 and tangent to all three coördinate planes (eight cases);

(f) passing through $(2, 0, 0)$, $(0, -4, 0)$, $(0, 0, 4)$, $(8, 0, 0)$.

6. Find the equation of the locus of a point

(a) twice as far from $(5, 4, 0)$ as from $(-4, 3, 4)$;

(b) the sum of whose distances from $(5, 0, 0)$ and $(-5, 0, 0)$ is 20;
Ans. $3x^2 + 4y^2 + 4z^2 = 300$.

(c) the sum of the squares of whose distances from $(7, -5, 9)$ and $(5, -3, 8)$ is 6;

(d) whose distance from $(-4, 3, 4)$ equals its distance from the XY-plane;

(e) whose distance from the x-axis is 4 times its distance from $(4, -2, 4)$;

(f) the sum of whose distances from the coördinate planes equals its distance from the origin. *Ans.* $xy + yz + zx = 0$.

7. Find the equations of the six planes each of which bisects perpendicularly an edge of the tetraedron $(4, 8, 0)$, $(2, 5, -2)$, $(3, 2, 2)$, $(5, 1, 2)$. Do the planes meet in a common point?

8. Write the equation of the circular cylinder

(a) of radius 5 with the z-axis for its axis;

(b) of radius 4 with the y-axis for its axis;

(c) of radius 3 with the x-axis for its axis.

9. Find the equations of the locus of a point equidistant from $(1, 3, 8)$, $(-6, -4, 2)$, and $(3, 2, 1)$.

10. Find the equations of the locus of a point if it is

(a) equidistant from $(1, 3, 2)$ and $(0, 0, 1)$ and also from $(3, 0, 3)$ and $(0, -2, 0)$;

(b) 3 units from $(1, 2, 1)$ and 2 units from $(2, 0, 1)$;

(c) 2 units from the x-axis and from the y-axis;

(d) equidistant from the y-axis, the XZ-plane, and the point $(3, 3, 2)$;

(e) the vertex of an isosceles triangle whose base joins $(4, 5, 6)$ and $(-2, -1, 2)$.

CHAPTER XIV

THE PLANE AND THE STRAIGHT LINE IN SPACE

124. The normal form of the equation of the plane. Let ABC be any plane, and let ON be drawn from the origin perpendicular to ABC at D. *Let the positive direction on ON be from O toward N, that is, from the origin toward the plane,* and denote the directed length OD by p and the direction angles of ON by $\alpha, \beta,$ and γ. Then *the position of any plane is determined by given positive values of $p, \alpha, \beta,$ and γ.*

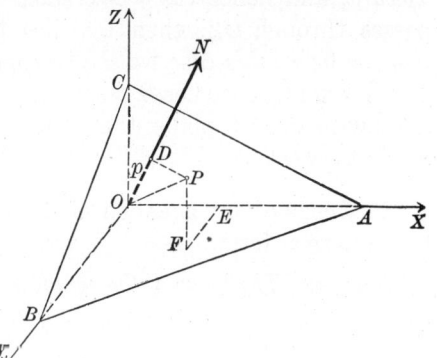

The plane surface ABC may be defined as the locus of a point P which lies on a line perpendicular to ON at D.

We now prove the

Theorem. *Normal form. The equation of a plane is*

(I) $\quad\quad x \cos \alpha + y \cos \beta + z \cos \gamma - p = 0,$

where p is the perpendicular distance from the origin to the plane, and α, β, and γ are the direction cosines of that perpendicular.

Proof. Let $P(x, y, z)$ be any point on the given plane ABC. Let α', β', γ' be the direction angles of OP, and let $\theta = \angle PON$. Then, by (IV), Art. 117,

(1) $\quad \cos \theta = \cos \alpha \cos \alpha' + \cos \beta \cos \beta' + \cos \gamma \cos \gamma'.$

251

In the right triangle DOP, $OD = p = OP \cos \theta$. Also, by (2), Art. 113, $x = OP \cos \alpha'$, $y = OP \cos \beta'$, $z = OP \cos \gamma'$. Substituting in (1) the values of $\cos \theta$, $\cos \alpha'$, etc., we obtain, after simplifying, the result (I). Q.E.D.

Corollary. *The equation of any plane is of the first degree in x, y, and z.*

The change necessary in the proof when $p = 0$ offers no difficulty, for then $\theta = 90°$, and $\cos \theta$ in (1) equals zero.

Special cases. If $p = 0$, we shall suppose that ON is directed upward, and hence $\cos \gamma > 0$ since $\gamma < \frac{1}{2}\pi$. If the plane passes through OZ, then ON lies in the XY-plane and $\cos \gamma = 0$; *in this case we shall suppose ON so directed that $\beta < \frac{1}{2}\pi$* and hence $\cos \beta > 0$. Finally, if the plane coincides with the YZ-plane, the positive direction on ON shall be that on OX.

125. Locus of any equation of the first degree. Reduction to the normal form.

Theorem. *The locus of the equation*

(II) $$Ax + By + Cz + D = 0,$$

is a plane.

Proof. We shall prove the theorem by showing that (II) may be reduced to the normal form (I) by multiplying by a proper constant. (Compare Art. 30.) To determine this constant, multiply (II) by k, which gives

(1) $$kAx + kBy + kCz + kD = 0.$$

Equating corresponding coefficients of (1) and (I),

(2) $\quad kA = \cos \alpha, \quad kB = \cos \beta, \quad kC = \cos \gamma, \quad kD = -p.$

Squaring the first three of equations (2) and adding,

$$k^2(A^2 + B^2 + C^2) = \cos^2 \alpha + \cos^2 \beta + \cos^2 \gamma = 1.$$

(3) $$\therefore k = \frac{1}{\pm\sqrt{A^2 + B^2 + C^2}}.$$

PLANE AND STRAIGHT LINE IN SPACE 253

From the last of equations (2) we see that the sign of the radical must be *opposite to that of D* in order that p shall be positive.

Substituting from (3) in (2), we get

$$(4) \begin{cases} \cos\alpha = \dfrac{A}{\pm\sqrt{A^2+B^2+C^2}}, & \cos\beta = \dfrac{B}{\pm\sqrt{A^2+B^2+C^2}}, \\ \cos\gamma = \dfrac{C}{\pm\sqrt{A^2+B^2+C^2}}, & p = \dfrac{-D}{\pm\sqrt{A^2+B^2+C^2}}. \end{cases}$$

We have thus determined values of α, β, γ, and p such that (I) and (II) have the same locus. Hence the locus of (II) is a plane. Q.E.D.

Equation (II) is called the **general equation of the first degree** in x, y, and z. The discussion gives the

Rule *to reduce the equation of a plane to the normal form.*
Divide the equation by $\pm\sqrt{A^2+B^2+C^2}$, *choosing the sign of the radical opposite to that of D.*

When $D = 0$, then $p = 0$, and the sign of the radical must be the same as that of C, the same as that of B if $C = D = 0$, and the same as that of A if $B = C = D = 0$ (see Art. 124).

From (4) we have the important

Theorem. *The coefficients of x, y, and z in the equation of a plane are proportional to the direction cosines (or are direction numbers) of a line perpendicular to the plane.*

From this theorem and Art. 118 we easily prove the following

Corollary 1. *Two planes whose equations are*

$$Ax + By + Cz + D = 0, \quad A'x + B'y + C'z + D' = 0$$

are parallel when and only when the coefficients of x, y, and z are proportional, that is,

$$\frac{A}{A'} = \frac{B}{B'} = \frac{C}{C'}.$$

Corollary 2. *Two planes are perpendicular when and only when the sum of the products of the coefficients of x, y, and z is zero, that is,*
$$AA' + BB' + CC' = 0.$$

126. Special planes.

Theorem. *A plane whose equation has the form*

$Ax + By + D = 0$ *is perpendicular to the XY-plane;*
$By + Cz + D = 0$ *is perpendicular to the YZ-plane;*
$Ax + Cz + D = 0$ *is perpendicular to the ZX-plane.*

That is, if one variable is lacking, the plane is perpendicular to the coördinate plane corresponding to the two remaining variables.

Proof. The direction numbers of a line perpendicular to $Ax + By + D = 0$ are A, B, 0; of a line perpendicular to $z = 0$ they are 0, 0, 1. The sum of their products is zero. The proof is similar in the other cases. Q.E.D.

Corollary. *A plane whose equation has the form*

$Ax + D = 0$ *is perpendicular to the axis of x;*
$By + D = 0$ *is perpendicular to the axis of y;*
$Cz + D = 0$ *is perpendicular to the axis of z.*

That is, if two variables are lacking, the plane is perpendicular to the axis corresponding to the remaining variable.

For example, the plane $Ax + D = 0$ is perpendicular to both the XY-plane and the ZX-plane, and hence is also perpendicular to their line of intersection.

127. Intercepts and traces of a plane. In a manner analogous to the rule in Art. 18, we may state for a plane (or any surface) the

Rule *to find the intercepts on the axes of coördinates.*

Set each pair of the variables x, y, z in turn equal to zero, and solve for real values of the remaining variable.

PLANE AND STRAIGHT LINE IN SPACE

The straight lines in which a plane intersects the coördinate planes are called its *traces*. The equation of the trace on the XY-plane referred to OX and OY as axes is found by substituting $z=0$ in the equation of the plane. Proceed similarly for the other traces.

To construct a plane from its equation, find the intercepts, lay them off on the axes, and connect the points thus determined. These lines are the traces. If the intercepts are zero, plot one or more traces, and proceed as in the following

EXAMPLES

1. Find the intercepts and traces of the plane
(1) $\qquad 2x + 2y - z - 6 = 0,$
and draw the plane.

Solution. Following the rule and referring to the figure, we find the intercepts to be

$\qquad OA = 3, \ OB = 3, \ OC = -6.$ *Ans.*

The traces are

$\qquad AB: x + y - 3 = 0; \ BC: 2y - z - 6 = 0;$
$\qquad CA: 2x - z - 6 = 0.$ *Ans.*

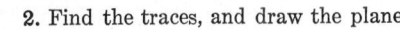

The line DE is drawn parallel to BA to set off part of the plane in the first octant.

2. Find the traces, and draw the plane

(2) $\qquad x - y - 2z = 0.$

Solution. The traces are.

$\qquad OA: x - y = 0; \ OB: y + 2z = 0;$
$\qquad OC: x - 2z = 0.$ *Ans.*

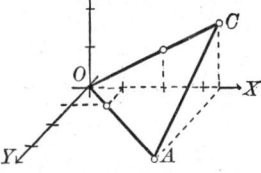

Draw OA and OC and the line CA to display part of the plane in the first octant.

PROBLEMS

1. Find the intercepts on the axes and the traces on the coördinate planes of each of the following planes. Construct the figures.

(a) $6x - 2y + 3z - 20 = 0.$
(b) $x + 2y + 3z + 12 = 0.$
(c) $6x - 4y + z - 12 = 0.$
(d) $2x + y - z = 0.$
(e) $3x + 2y - 6z - 10 = 0.$
(f) $3x - y + z - 14 = 0.$
(g) $4y + 3z + 36 = 0.$
(h) $5x + 3z + 45 = 0.$

2. Find the equations of the following planes and construct them:

(a) $p = 5$, $\alpha = 120°$, $\beta = 45°$, $\gamma = 120°$.

Ans. $x - \sqrt{2}\,y + z + 10 = 0$.

(b) $p = 7$, $\alpha = 45°$, $\beta = 60°$, $\gamma = 60°$.

(c) $p = 4$, $\alpha = 90°$, $\beta = 135°$, $\gamma = 45°$. *Ans.* $y - z + 4\sqrt{2} = 0$.

(d) $p = 2$, $\alpha = 60°$, $\beta = 45°$, $\gamma = 120°$.

(e) $p = 4$, $\dfrac{\cos \alpha}{6} = \dfrac{\cos \beta}{-2} = \dfrac{\cos \gamma}{3}$. *Ans.* $6x - 2y + 3z \pm 28 = 0$.

(f) $p = 6$, $\dfrac{\cos \alpha}{-2} = \dfrac{\cos \beta}{-1} = \dfrac{\cos \gamma}{-2}$.

(g) $p = 3$, $\dfrac{\cos \alpha}{6} = \dfrac{\cos \beta}{-3} = \dfrac{\cos \gamma}{2}$.

(h) $p = 0$, $\dfrac{\cos \alpha}{-3} = \dfrac{\cos \beta}{4} = \dfrac{\cos \gamma}{12}$. *Ans.* $3x - 4y - 12z = 0$.

3. Find the equation of the plane such that the foot of the perpendicular from the origin to the plane is

(a) $(-2, -2, 1)$;
Ans. $2x + 2y - z + 9 = 0$.
(b) $(1, 4, 2)$;
Ans. $x + 4y + 2z - 21 = 0$.
(c) $(-4, 3, -12)$;
(d) $(2, -1, 3)$;
(e) $(-1, 6, 3)$;
(f) $(1, 0, 2)$.

4. Reduce the equations of the planes of Problem 1 to normal form. Determine in each case the direction cosines of the perpendicular drawn from the origin and the perpendicular distance from the origin.

Ans. (a) $\cos \alpha = \tfrac{6}{7}$, $\cos \beta = -\tfrac{2}{7}$, $\cos \gamma = \tfrac{3}{7}$, $p = 2\tfrac{6}{7}$.

5. Write the equation of the plane which is perpendicular to the line drawn from the origin

(a) to $(4, 5, 3)$ and passing through $(1, 3, 2)$;
(b) to $(2, -4, 3)$ and passing through $(3, -4, -5)$.

6. Write the equation of the plane passing through $(1, -3, 2)$ and perpendicular to the line joining $(0, 0, 3)$ and $(1, -3, -4)$.

7. If the vertex of the right angle of a right triangle is $(4, -2, -2)$ and another vertex is $(3, 1, 1)$, find the equation of the locus of the third vertex.

8. In each of the following show that the planes are parallel and find the perpendicular distance between them:

(a) $x - y - z + 5 = 0$, $2x - 2y - 2z - 7 = 0$.
(b) $3x - y + 2z + 10 = 0$, $3x - y + 2z - 7 = 0$.
(c) $6x + 2y - 3z - 63 = 0$, $6x + 2y - 3z + 49 = 0$.   *Ans.* **16.**
(d) $x + 2y + 2z - 7 = 0$, $3x + 6y + 6z - 1 = 0$.

PLANE AND STRAIGHT LINE IN SPACE

9. Examine each pair of planes in each case below for parallel planes or perpendicular planes.

(a) $2x + 3y - z = 0$, $3x - y + 3z + 2 = 0$, $4x + 6y - 2z + 8 = 0$.
(b) $2x - 5y + 4 = 0$, $5x + 2y - 8 = 0$, $x - 2y = 0$.

10. Derive the equation of the plane which

(a) is perpendicular to the XY-plane and passes through the points $(2, -1, 0)$ and $(3, 0, 5)$; *Ans.* $x - y - 3 = 0$.

(b) is perpendicular to the YZ-plane with intercepts 5 and -2, respectively, on the y-axis and the z-axis;

(c) is parallel to the plane $x - 2y - 2z - 15 = 0$ and 2 units nearer the origin.

11. Find the point of intersection of the planes

(a) $x + 2y + z = 0$, $x - 2y - 8 = 0$, $x + y + z - 3 = 0$;
Ans. $(2, -3, 4)$.
(b) $3x - 5y - 4z + 7 = 0$, $6x + 2y + 2z - 7 = 0$, $x + y = 5$.

12. Show that the four planes $4x + y + z + 4 = 0$, $y - 5z + 14 = 0$, $x + 2y - z + 3 = 0$, $x + y + z - 2 = 0$ have a common point.

13. Find the area of the triangle which the coördinate planes cut from each of the following planes:

(a) $2x + 2y + z - 12 = 0$. *Ans.* 54.

Hint. Use intercepts and express the volume of the tetraedron bounded by the given plane and the coördinate planes in two ways.

(b) $7x - 7y + 2z - 6 = 0$.
(c) $2x - y - 3z + 12 = 0$.
(d) $x + 5y + 7z - 3 = 0$.
Ans. $\frac{9}{14}\sqrt{3}$.

128. The angle between two planes. The plane angle of one pair of diedral angles formed by two intersecting planes is evidently equal to the angle between the positive directions of the lines drawn perpendicular to the planes from the origin. That angle is called *the angle between the planes*.

Theorem. *The angle θ between the two planes*
$$A_1x + B_1y + C_1z + D_1 = 0 \text{ and } A_2x + B_2y + C_2z + D_2 = 0$$
is given by

(III) $\quad \cos\theta = \dfrac{A_1A_2 + B_1B_2 + C_1C_2}{\pm\sqrt{A_1^2 + B_1^2 + C_1^2} \times \pm\sqrt{A_2^2 + B_2^2 + C_2^2}},$

the signs of the radicals being chosen as in Art. 125.

Proof. The direction cosines of the lines drawn perpendicular to the planes from the origin are

$$\cos \alpha_1 = \frac{A_1}{\pm \sqrt{A_1^2 + B_1^2 + C_1^2}}, \quad \cos \alpha_2 = \frac{A_2}{\pm \sqrt{A_2^2 + B_2^2 + C_2^2}},$$

$$\cos \beta_1 = \frac{B_1}{\pm \sqrt{A_1^2 + B_1^2 + C_1^2}}, \quad \cos \beta_2 = \frac{B_2}{\pm \sqrt{A_2^2 + B_2^2 + C_2^2}},$$

$$\cos \gamma_1 = \frac{C_1}{\pm \sqrt{A_1^2 + B_1^2 + C_1^2}}, \quad \cos \gamma_2 = \frac{C_2}{\pm \sqrt{A_2^2 + B_2^2 + C_2^2}}.$$

The angle θ equals the angle between these lines. Hence, by (IV), Art. 117, we have

$$\cos \theta = \cos \alpha_1 \cos \alpha_2 + \cos \beta_1 \cos \beta_2 + \cos \gamma_1 \cos \gamma_2.$$

Substituting the values of the direction cosines, we obtain (III). Q.E.D.

129. Planes determined by three conditions. The equation

(1) $$Ax + By + Cz + D = 0$$

represents, as we know, all planes. The statement of a problem to find the equation of a certain plane may be such that we are able to write down three homogeneous equations in the coefficients A, B, C, D, which we can then solve for three coefficients in terms of the fourth. When these values are substituted in (1), the fourth coefficient will divide out, giving the required equation.

EXAMPLES

1. Find the equation of the plane which passes through the point $P_1(2, -7, \frac{3}{2})$ and is parallel to the plane $21x - 12y + 28z - 84 = 0$.

Solution. Let the equation of the required plane be

(2) $$Ax + By + Cz + D = 0.$$

Since P_1 lies on (2), we may substitute $x = 2$, $y = -7$, $z = \frac{3}{2}$, giving

(3) $$2A - 7B + \tfrac{3}{2}C + D = 0.$$

PLANE AND STRAIGHT LINE IN SPACE

Since (2) is parallel to the given plane (Corollary 1, p. 253),

(4) $\quad \dfrac{A}{21} = \dfrac{B}{-12} = \dfrac{C}{28}.$

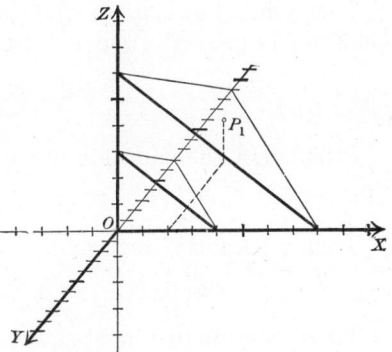

Equations (3) and (4) are three homogeneous equations in A, B, C, D.

Solving (3) and (4) for A, B, and D in terms of C,

$$A = \tfrac{3}{4} C, \quad B = -\tfrac{3}{7} C,$$
$$D = -6\, C.$$

Substituting in (2),

$$\tfrac{3}{4} Cx - \tfrac{3}{7} Cy + Cz - 6\, C = 0.$$

Clearing of fractions and dividing by C,

$$21\, x - 12\, y + 28\, z - 168 = 0. \quad \textit{Ans.}$$

2. To find the equation of a plane passing through three points, substitute for x, y, and z in (1) the coördinates of each of the three points. Then *three* equations involving A, B, C, and D will be obtained, which may be solved for three of these coefficients in terms of the fourth.

It is convenient to write down the equation of a plane passing through three given points (x_1, y_1, z_1), (x_2, y_2, z_2), (x_3, y_3, z_3) in the form of a determinant. This is

(5) $\quad \begin{vmatrix} x & y & z & 1 \\ x_1 & y_1 & z_1 & 1 \\ x_2 & y_2 & z_2 & 1 \\ x_3 & y_3 & z_3 & 1 \end{vmatrix} = 0.$

In fact, when (5) is expanded in terms of the elements of the first row, an equation of the first degree in x, y, and z results. Hence (5) is the equation of a plane. Further, (5) is satisfied when the coördinates of any one of the three given points are substituted for x, y, and z, since then two rows become identical. Hence the plane (5) passes through the given points.

The equation (5) may be used also to determine whether four given points lie in a plane.

If we write (5), when expanded, in the form

$$Ax + By + Cz + D = 0,$$

then the coefficients are the determinants of the third order,

$$A = \begin{vmatrix} y_1 & z_1 & 1 \\ y_2 & z_2 & 1 \\ y_3 & z_3 & 1 \end{vmatrix}, \; B = -\begin{vmatrix} x_1 & z_1 & 1 \\ x_2 & z_2 & 1 \\ x_3 & z_3 & 1 \end{vmatrix}, \; C = \begin{vmatrix} x_1 & y_1 & 1 \\ x_2 & y_2 & 1 \\ x_3 & y_3 & 1 \end{vmatrix}, \; D = -\begin{vmatrix} x_1 & y_1 & z_1 \\ x_2 & y_2 & z_2 \\ x_3 & y_3 & z_3 \end{vmatrix}.$$

130. The equation of a plane in terms of its intercepts.

Theorem. *If a, b, and c are, respectively, the intercepts of a plane on the axes of x, y, and z, then the equation of the plane is*

(IV) $$\frac{x}{a} + \frac{y}{b} + \frac{z}{c} = 1.$$

Proof. Let the equation of the required plane be

(1) $$Ax + By + Cz + D = 0.$$

Then we know three points in the plane, namely

$$(a, 0, 0), \quad (0, b, 0), \quad (0, 0, c).$$

These coördinates must satisfy (1). Hence

$$Aa + D = 0, \quad Bb + D = 0, \quad Cc + D = 0.$$

Whence $A = -\dfrac{D}{a}, \quad B = -\dfrac{D}{b}, \quad C = -\dfrac{D}{c}.$

Substituting in (1), dividing by $-D$, and transposing, we obtain (IV). Q.E.D.

PROBLEMS

1. Find the equation of the plane which passes through the points given. Check the answer.

(a) $(0, 0, 3), (4, 0, 0), (8, 0, 0)$.
(b) $(2, 3, 0), (-2, -3, 4), (0, 6, 0)$.   *Ans.* $3x + 2y + 6z - 12 = 0$.
(c) $(-4, 0, 6), (8, 2, -1), (2, 4, 6)$.
(d) $(4, 2, 1), (-1, -2, 2), (0, 4, -5)$.   *Ans.* $11x - 17y - 13z + 3 = 0$.
(e) $(1, 2, 3), (2, 3, 4), (5, 4, 3)$.
(f) $(1, 1, -1), (-2, -2, 2), (1, -1, 2)$.   *Ans.* $x - 3y - 2z = 0$.

2. Find the equation of the plane which passes

(a) through $(2, 1, -1)$ and is parallel to the plane $7x + 4y - 4z = 0$;
(b) through $(3, -4, 5)$ and is parallel to the plane $3x - y + z + 6 = 0$.
   Ans. (b) $3x - y + z = 18$.

3. Write the equation of the plane whose intercepts are as given, and draw the plane.

(a) 3, 4, 5.   (c) 2, 4, −7.   (e) $a, -b, -c$.
(b) −1, −3, 5.   (d) 7, 0, −4.   (f) $2a, -a, 3a$.

PLANE AND STRAIGHT LINE IN SPACE

4. Write the equation of the plane which passes

(a) through $(2, 1, -1)$ and $(1, 1, 2)$ and is perpendicular to the plane $7x + 4y - 4z + 30 = 0$;   *Ans.* $12x - 17y + 4z - 3 = 0$.

(b) through $(6, 4, -1)$ and $(2, 4, 1)$ and is perpendicular to the plane $4x + 6y - 3z - 7 = 0$.

5. Write the equation of the plane passing

(a) through $(7, 0, 3)$ and perpendicular to each of the planes $2x - 4y + 3z = 0$ and $7x + 2y + z = 14$;

Ans. $10x - 19y - 32z + 26 = 0$.

(b) through $(3, 4, 5)$ and perpendicular to each of the planes $2x + 3y - 7 = 0$ and $4x - 3z = 7$.

6. Show that the four points given lie in a plane in each case.

(a) $(-1, 0, 0)$, $(0, 2, -3)$, $(2, 10, -5)$, $(1, 0, -10)$.
(b) $(1, 0, -1)$, $(3, 4, -3)$, $(8, -2, 6)$, $(2, 2, -2)$.

7. Find the angle between each pair of planes given below.

(a) $4x - 3y + 5z = 8$, $2x + 3y - z = 4$.
(b) $2x - y + z = 7$, $x + y + 2z = 11$.   *Ans.* $60°$.
(c) $4x - 3y + z = 6$, $2x + 3y - 5z = 4$.
(d) $x + 2y - z = 12$, $x - 2y - 2z = 7$.   *Ans.* $97° 49'$.
(e) $3x - z + 12 = 0$, $x + 3y + 17 = 0$.
(f) $x + 5y - 3z = 10$, $2x - 3y + z = 10$.

8. Show that the angle given by (III), Art. 128, is equal to the plane angle of the diedral angle which does not contain the origin.

9. Find the vertex and the diedral angles of the triedral angle formed by the planes $x + y + z = 2$, $x - y - 2z - 4 = 0$, $2x + y - z = 2$.
Ans. Vertex $(4, -4, 2)$, one diedral angle $120°$.

10. Find the equation of each of the following planes:

(a) Passes through $(0, -1, 0)$ and $(0, 0, 1)$ and makes an angle of $60°$ with the XY-plane.   *Ans.* $\sqrt{2}\,x - y + z - 1 = 0$.

(b) Passes through $(0, -1, 0)$ and $(0, 0, 1)$ and makes an angle of $120°$ with the plane $y - z - 2 = 0$.

For individual study or assignment

11. The equations of three faces of a parallelepiped are $x - 4y = 3$, $2x - y + z = 3$, and $3x + y - 2z = 0$, and one vertex is the point $(3, 7, -2)$. What are the equations of the other three faces? What are the coördinates of the other vertices?

12. Find the equation of the plane which passes through the point $P_1(x_1, y_1, z_1)$ and is parallel to the plane $A_1x + B_1y + C_1z + D_1 = 0$.
Ans. $A_1(x - x_1) + B_1(y - y_1) + C_1(z - z_1) = 0$.

13. Find the equation of the plane which passes through the origin and $P_1(x_1, y_1, z_1)$ and is perpendicular to the plane $A_1x + B_1y + C_1z + D_1 = 0$.

Ans. $(B_1z_1 - C_1y_1)x + (C_1x_1 - A_1z_1)y + (A_1y_1 - B_1x_1)z = 0$.

14. Find the equation of the plane passing through $P_1(x_1, y_1, z_1)$ and $P_2(x_2, y_2, z_2)$, and perpendicular to the plane $Ax + By + Cz + D = 0$.

131. The perpendicular distance from a plane to a point. The positive direction on any line perpendicular to a plane is assumed to agree with that on the line drawn through the origin perpendicular to the plane (Art. 124). Hence the perpendicular distance *from* a plane *to* the point P_1 is *positive* or *negative* according as P_1 and the origin are on opposite sides of the plane or not.

If the plane passes through the origin, the sign of the distance from the plane to P_1 must be determined by the conventions for the special cases in Art. 124.

We now solve the problem: Given the equation of a plane and the coördinates of a point, to find the perpendicular distance from the plane to the point. (Compare Art. 31.)

Solution. Let the point be $P_1(x_1, y_1, z_1)$ and assume that the equation of the given plane is in the normal form

(1) $x \cos \alpha + y \cos \beta + z \cos \gamma - p = 0$.

Let d equal the required distance.

Through P_1 pass a plane $A'B'C'$ parallel to the given plane ABC. The equation of this plane is

$x \cos \alpha + y \cos \beta + z \cos \gamma - (p + d) = 0$.

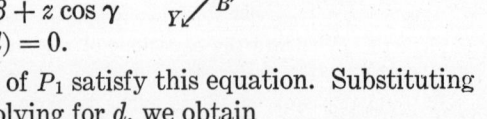

The coördinates of P_1 satisfy this equation. Substituting $x = x_1$, etc., and solving for d, we obtain

$d = x_1 \cos \alpha + y_1 \cos \beta + z_1 \cos \gamma - p$. *Ans.*

PLANE AND STRAIGHT LINE IN SPACE

Hence the perpendicular distance d is the result obtained by substituting the coördinates of the given point for x, y, and z in the left-hand member of (1). Whence the

Rule *to find the perpendicular distance d from a given plane to a given point.*

Reduce the equation of the plane to the normal form. Place d equal to the left-hand member of this equation.

Substitute the coördinates of the given point for x, y, and z. The result is the required distance.

EXAMPLE

To find the perpendicular distance from the plane $2x + y - 2z + 8 = 0$ to the point $(-1, 2, 3)$.

Solution. Dividing the equation by -3 and following the rule, we have
$$d = \frac{2x + y - 2z + 8}{-3} = \frac{2(-1) + 2 - 2(3) + 8}{-3} = -\tfrac{2}{3}. \text{ Ans.}$$

Hence the required distance is $\tfrac{2}{3}$ and the given point is on the same side of the plane as the origin. *Ans.*

The rule gives for the perpendicular distance d from the plane
$$Ax + By + Cz + D = 0$$
to the point (x_1, y_1, z_1) the result

(2) $$d = \frac{Ax_1 + By_1 + Cz_1 + D}{\pm \sqrt{A^2 + B^2 + C^2}},$$

the sign of the radical being determined as above (Art. 125).

PROBLEMS

1. Find the perpendicular distance from the plane
   (a) $6x - 3y + 2z - 10 = 0$ to the point $(4, 2, 10)$; *Ans.* 4.
   (b) $x + 2y - 2z - 12 = 0$ to the point $(1, -2, 3)$; *Ans.* -7.
   (c) $4x + 3y + 12z + 6 = 0$ to the point $(9, -1, 0)$;
   (d) $2x - 5y + 3z + 4 = 0$ to the point $(-2, 1, 7)$;
   (e) $3x - 4y + 12z + 26 = 0$ to the point $(1, 5, 9)$;
   (f) $3x + 4y - 12z + 10 = 0$ to the point $(1, 6, 5)$;
   In each case state the meaning of the algebraic sign of the result.

2. Find the lengths of the altitudes of the tetraedron whose vertices are $(0, 3, 1)$, $(2, -7, 1)$, $(0, 5, -4)$, and $(2, 0, 1)$. *Ans.* $\frac{10}{29}\sqrt{29}$, etc.

3. Find the volume of the tetraedron whose vertices are the point $(1, 2, 1)$ and the points where the plane $3x + 4y + 2z + 12 = 0$ intersects the coördinate axes.

4. Find the volumes of the tetraedrons having the following vertices:

(a) $(3, 4, 0)$, $(4, -1, 0)$, $(1, 2, 0)$, $(6, -1, 4)$. *Ans.* 8.
(b) $(0, 0, 4)$, $(3, 0, 0)$, $(0, 2, 0)$, $(7, 7, 3)$.
(c) $(4, 0, 0)$, $(0, 4, 0)$, $(0, 0, 4)$, $(7, 3, 2)$.
(d) $(3, 0, 0)$, $(0, -2, 0)$, $(0, 0, -1)$, $(3, -1, -1)$. *Ans.* $\frac{3}{2}$.
(e) $(1, 0, 0)$, $(0, 1, 0)$, $(0, 0, -2)$, $(4, -1, 3)$.
(f) $(3, 0, 0)$, $(0, 5, 0)$, $(0, 0, -1)$, $(3, -4, 0)$.

5. Find the equation of the locus of a point whose perpendicular distances from the planes $2x - y - 2z - 3 = 0$ and $6x + 3y + 2z + 4 = 0$ are equal numerically.

Ans. Two planes; one is $32x + 2y - 8z - 9 = 0$.

6. Find the equation of the locus of a point which is three times as far from the plane $3x - 6y - 2z = 0$ as from the plane $2x + y + 2z = 9$.

7. Find the equation of the locus of a point whose distance from the plane $x + y + z + 12 = 0$ is equal to its distance from the origin.

8. Find the equation of the locus of a point whose distance from the plane $x + y = 1$ equals its distance from the z-axis.

Ans. $(x - y)^2 + 2(x + y) - 1 = 0$.

9. Find the equation of the locus of a point the sum of the squares of whose distances from the planes $x + y - z - 1 = 0$ and $x + y + z + 1 = 0$ is equal to unity.   *Ans.* $2(x + y)^2 + 2z(z + 2) - 1 = 0$.

10. Write the equation of the plane equally inclined to the coördinate planes and at the perpendicular distance p from the origin.

11. Find the relation between the perpendicular distance p from the origin and the intercepts a, b, c of a plane.

132. Systems of planes. The equation of a plane which satisfies *two* conditions will, in general, contain an arbitrary constant, for it takes three conditions to determine a plane. Such an equation therefore represents a *system* of planes.

Systems of planes are used to find the equation of a plane satisfying three conditions in the same manner that systems of lines are used to find the equation of a line (Art. 32).

PLANE AND STRAIGHT LINE IN SPACE

Three important systems of planes are the following:

The system of planes parallel to a given plane
$$Ax + By + Cz + D = 0$$
is represented by
(V) $\qquad Ax + By + Cz + k = 0,$
where k is an arbitrary constant.

The plane (V) is obviously parallel to the given plane (Corollary 1, Art. 125).

The system of planes passing through the line of intersection of two given planes
$$A_1x + B_1y + C_1z + D_1 = 0, \quad A_2x + B_2y + C_2z + D_2 = 0$$
is represented by

(VI) $A_1x + B_1y + C_1z + D_1 + k(A_2x + B_2y + C_2z + D_2) = 0,$
where k is an arbitrary constant.

Clearly, the coördinates of any point on the line of intersection will satisfy the equations of both of the given planes, and hence will satisfy (VI) also.

The equation of a system of planes which satisfy a single condition must contain two arbitrary constants. One of the most important systems of this sort is the following:

The system of planes passing through a given point $P_1(x_1, y_1, z_1)$ is represented by
(VII) $\qquad A(x - x_1) + B(y - y_1) + C(z - z_1) = 0.$

Equation (VII) is the equation of a plane which passes through P_1, for the coördinates of P_1 obviously satisfy Again, if any plane whose equation is
$$Ax + By + Cz + D = 0$$
passes through P_1, then
$$Ax_1 + By_1 + Cz_1 + D = 0.$$

Subtracting, we get (VII). Hence (VII) represents all planes passing through P_1.

Equation (VII) contains two essential arbitrary constants, namely, the ratios of any two coefficients to the third.

In the following problems write down the equation of the appropriate system of planes and then determine the unknown parameters from the remaining data.

PROBLEMS

1. Determine the value of k such that the plane $x + ky - 2z - 9 = 0$ shall

(a) pass through the point $(5, -4, -6)$; *Ans.* 2.
(b) be parallel to the plane $6x + 2y - 12z = 7$;
(c) be perpendicular to the plane $2x + 4y + 3z = 3$; *Ans.* 1.
(d) be 5 units from the origin;
(e) make an angle of $45°$ with the plane $2x - 3y + z = 0$.
Ans. $-\frac{1}{2}\sqrt{70}$.

2. Find the equation of the plane which passes through the point $(3, -2, -1)$ and is parallel to the plane $7x - y - z = 14$.

3. Find the equation of the plane which passes through the line of intersection of the planes $2x + y - 4 = 0$ and $y + 2z = 0$ and

(a) passes through the point $(2, -1, -1)$; *Ans.* $3x + y - z = 6$.
(b) is perpendicular to the plane $3x + 2y + 3z = 6$.

4. Find the equations of the planes passing through the line of intersection of the planes $2x + y - z = 4$ and $x - y + 2z = 0$ which are perpendicular to the coördinate planes.

Ans. $5x + y = 8$, $3x + z = 4$, $3y - 5z = 4$.

5. Find the equation of a plane parallel to $6x + 3y + 2z + 21 = 0$ and tangent to a sphere of unit radius whose center is the origin.

6. Find the equation of a plane parallel to $6x - 2y + 3z + 15 = 0$ and such that the point $(0, -2, -1)$ lies midway between the two planes.

7. Find the equation of a plane through the point $(2, -3, 0)$ and having the same trace on the XZ-plane as $x - 3y + 7z + 12 = 0$.

8. Find the equation of a plane parallel to $2x + y + 2z + 5 = 0$ and forming a tetraedron of unit volume with the three coördinate planes.

9. Find the equation of a plane parallel to $5x + 3y + 2z + 7 = 0$ if the sum of its intercepts is 23.

PLANE AND STRAIGHT LINE IN SPACE

For individual study or assignment

10. Find the equation of a plane parallel to $2x + 6y + 3z - 8 = 0$, upon which the area intercepted by the coördinate planes in the first octant is $\frac{7}{8}$. *Ans.* $2x + 6y + 3z - 3 = 0$.

11. Find the equation of a plane parallel to $12x + y + 2z + 5 = 0$ and such that the entire surface of the tetraedron which it forms with the coördinate planes is unity.

12. Find the equation of a plane having the trace $x + 3y - 2 = 0$ and forming a tetraedron of volume $\frac{8}{3}$ with the coördinate planes.

13. Find the equation of a plane passing through the line of intersection of the two planes $6x + 2y + 3z - 6 = 0$ and $-x + y + z + 1 = 0$ and forming a tetraedron of volume $\frac{1}{6}$ with the coördinate planes.

14. Show that $x + 2y - 3z + 1 = 0$, $3x + 4y - 19z + 5 = 0$, and $y + 5z = 1$ have a common line of intersection.

15. Find the equation of the plane passing through the line of intersection of $3x + y - z + 5 = 0$ and $x - y + z - 2 = 0$ and making an angle of $45°$ with the plane $y - z = 0$.

16. Find the equation of the plane which passes through the line of intersection of the planes
$$A_1x + B_1y + C_1z + D_1 = 0 \text{ and } A_2x + B_2y + C_2z + D_2 = 0$$
and through the origin.
Ans. $(A_1D_2 - A_2D_1)x + (B_1D_2 - B_2D_1)y + (C_1D_2 - C_2D_1)z = 0$.

17. Find the equations of the planes which pass through the line of intersection of the planes
$$A_1x + B_1y + C_1z + D_1 = 0 \text{ and } A_2x + B_2y + C_2z + D_2 = 0$$
and are perpendicular to a coördinate plane.
Ans. $(A_1B_2 - A_2B_1)y - (C_1A_2 - C_2A_1)z + A_1D_2 - A_2D_1 = 0$, etc.

18. Find the equation of the plane which passes through the origin and $P_1(x_1, y_1, z_1)$ and is perpendicular to $A_1x + B_1y + C_1z + D_1 = 0$.
Ans. $(B_1z_1 - C_1y_1)x + (C_1x_1 - A_1z_1)y + (A_1y_1 - B_1x_1)z = 0$.

133. General equations of the straight line. A straight line may be regarded as the intersection of any two planes which pass through it. The equations of the planes considered as simultaneous are the equations of the line of intersection.

The locus of two simultaneous equations of the first degree is a straight line unless the planes which are the

NEW ANALYTIC GEOMETRY

loci of the separate equations are parallel. Hence we have the

Theorem. *The locus of two simultaneous equations of the first degree,*

(VIII) $\quad \begin{cases} A_1x + B_1y + C_1z + D_1 = 0, \\ A_2x + B_2y + C_2z + D_2 = 0, \end{cases}$

is a straight line, unless the coefficients of x, y, and z are proportional.

The direction of a line is known when its direction numbers are known. The method of obtaining them will now be illustrated.

EXAMPLES

1. Find direction numbers for the line whose equations are

(1) $\quad 3x + 2y - z - 1 = 0, \quad 2x - y + 2z - 3 = 0.$

Solution. Let a, b, c be the required direction numbers.

The coefficients 3, 2, and -1 in the first plane of (1) are proportional to the direction cosines of a perpendicular to that plane. The given line lies in this plane. Hence, by Theorem 2, Art. 118,

(2) $\quad 3a + 2b - c = 0.$

For the same reason, using the second plane in (1),

(3) $\quad 2a - b + 2c = 0.$

Solving (2) and (3) for a, b, in terms of c, the result is

$$7b = 8c, \quad 7a = -3c,$$

(4) $\quad \therefore \dfrac{a}{3} = \dfrac{b}{-8} = \dfrac{c}{-7}.$

That is, 3, -8, -7 are direction numbers. *Ans.*

2. Find direction numbers a, b, c, for the line

(5) $\quad 2x + y + 3z + 2 = 0, \quad 3x + y + 3z - 5 = 0.$

Solution. Following Example 1, we have to solve the equations

(6) $\quad 2a + b + 3c = 0, \quad 3a + b + 3c = 0.$

Solving, we get $a = 0$, $b = -3c$.
Hence 0, -3, 1 are the required direction numbers. *Ans.*
The line is parallel to the *YZ*-plane.

PLANE AND STRAIGHT LINE IN SPACE

To plot a straight line, we need to know one point on it and direction numbers. It is easy to find the point in which the line intersects a coördinate plane, called the trace of the line on that plane. For example, the values of x and y for the trace on the XY-plane are found by setting $z = 0$ in the equations of the line and solving for x and y.

3. Show how to draw the line (1) of Example 1.

Solution. Set $z = 0$ in (1), giving $3x + 2y - 1 = 0$, $2x - y - 3 = 0$, from which $x = 1$, $y = -1$. The trace on the XY-plane is $A(1, -1, 0)$. The direction numbers are $3, -8, -7$. Hence draw a line through A parallel to the line joining the origin and the point $(3, -8, -7)$, or through A and $B(4, -9, -7)$, since the direction numbers of AB are $3, -8, -7$ (Art. 116).

4. Find the direction cosines of the line (VIII).

Solution. The direction cosines $\cos \alpha$, $\cos \beta$, $\cos \gamma$ must satisfy
$A_1 \cos \alpha + B_1 \cos \beta + C_1 \cos \gamma = 0$, $A_2 \cos \alpha + B_2 \cos \beta + C_2 \cos \gamma = 0$,
by the reasoning of Example 1.

Solving these equations for the ratios, we have the

Theorem. *If α, β, and γ are the direction angles of the line* (VIII), *then*

$$\frac{\cos \alpha}{B_1 C_2 - B_2 C_1} = \frac{\cos \beta}{C_1 A_2 - C_2 A_1} = \frac{\cos \gamma}{A_1 B_2 - A_2 B_1}.$$

The denominators are readily remembered as the three determinants of the second order

$$\begin{vmatrix} B_1 & C_1 \\ B_2 & C_2 \end{vmatrix}, \quad \begin{vmatrix} C_1 & A_1 \\ C_2 & A_2 \end{vmatrix}, \quad \begin{vmatrix} A_1 & B_1 \\ A_2 & B_2 \end{vmatrix},$$

formed from the coefficients of x, y, and z in (VIII).

PROBLEMS

1. Find one of the traces for each of the following lines and direction numbers for the line. Construct the line.

(a) $x + 5y + 7z - 3 = 0$, $x - 2y + 3z - 6 = 0$.

$$Ans.\ \frac{\cos \alpha}{29} = \frac{\cos \beta}{4} = \frac{\cos \gamma}{-7}.$$

(b) $3x - 5y - 4z + 12 = 0$, $6x + 2y + 2z - 12 = 0$.
(c) $6x - 3y + 6z - 7 = 0$, $3x + 2y + 3z + 28 = 0$.
(d) $5x - 7y + 3z - 10 = 0$, $3x + 5y - 8z + 4 = 0$.
(e) $x + 2y = 8$, $2x - 4y = 7$. *Ans.* Direction numbers, $0, 0, 1$.
(f) $y + z = 4$, $x + y - 2z = 12$.

2. Find the angles between the following lines, assuming that they are directed upward (or in front of the ZX-plane if $\cos \gamma = 0$ (Art. 115), or to the right if $\cos \beta = \cos \gamma = 0$):

(a) $x + y - z = 0$, $y + z = 0$, and $x - y = 1$, $x - 3y + z = 0$.
Ans. $60°$.

(b) $2x + y - z = 2$, $x - y + 2z = 4$, and $4x + 3y - 6z = 0$, $4x - 3y = 2$.

(c) $x + y + z = 5$, $x - y + z = 3$, and $y + 3z = 4$, $3y - 5z = 1$.
Ans. $45°$.

(d) $2x - y + 2z = 5$, $x + 2y - 2z = 4$, and $3x - 2y - 6z + 49 = 0$, $2x + 2y - z = 9$.

(e) $x - 2y + z = 2$, $2y - z = 1$,
and $x - 2y + z = 2$, $x - 2y + 2z = 4$. *Ans.* $78° 28'$.

(f) $x + y - 3z = 6$, $2x - y + 3z = 3$, and $x + y = 6$, $2x - 3z = 5$.

(g) $3x + 2y - z = 4$, $x - 2y - 2z = 5$,
and $5x - 14z = 7$, $2x + 7z = 19$. *Ans.* $63° 19'$.

(h) $6x - 3y + 2z - 7 = 0$, $2x - 2y - z + 12 = 0$,
and $2x + 2y - z = 9$, $6x + 4y - z + 12 = 0$.

3. Show that the lines defined by the following pairs of equations are parallel, and construct the lines:

(a) $2y + z = 0$, $3y - 4z = 7$, and $5y - 2z = 8$, $4y + z = 44$.

(b) $x + 2y - z = 7$, $y + z - 2x = 6$, and $3x + 6y - 3z = 8$, $2x - y - z = 0$.

(c) $3x + z = 4$, $y + 2z = 9$, and $6x - y = 7$, $3y + 6z = 1$.

4. Show that the lines of intersection of each of the following pairs of planes meet in a point and are perpendicular:

(a) $x + 2y = 1$, $2y - z = 1$, and $x - y = 1$, $x - 2z = 3$.
(b) $4x + y - 3z + 24 = 0$, $z = 5$, and $x + y + 3 = 0$, $x + 2 = 0$.
(c) $3x + y - z = 1$, $2x - z = 2$, and $2x - y + 2z = 4$, $x - y + 2z = 3$.

5. Show that the lines of intersection of $x + 2y + 3z = 3$ and $3x + 6y + 9z = 20$ with $4x - y + z = 0$ are parallel lines.

6. Find the point of intersection of the lines $3x - y - 3z - 8 = 0$, $x - y + z + 2 = 0$, and $x + y - z = 0$, $6x - 6y - 3z - 15 = 0$.
Ans. $(-1, -2, -3)$.

7. Show analytically that the lines of intersection of two parallel planes with any third plane are parallel.

8. Show analytically that the plane $y - z = 0$ intersects the planes $3x + y - z + 5 = 0$ and $x - y + z - 2 = 0$ in parallel lines.

PLANE AND STRAIGHT LINE IN SPACE

134. Various forms of the equations of a straight line.

Theorem 1. *Parametric form.* *The coördinates of any point* $P(x, y, z)$ *on the line through a given point* $P_1(x_1, y_1, z_1)$ *with direction angles* α, β, *and* γ *are given by*

(IX) $\quad x = x_1 + t \cos \alpha, \quad y = y_1 + t \cos \beta, \quad z = z_1 + t \cos \gamma,$

where t, the parameter, denotes the variable directed length P_1P.

The proof follows immediately from (1), Art. 116, setting $l = t$.

Theorem 2. *Symmetric form.* *The equations of the line passing through* $P_1(x_1, y_1, z_1)$ *with direction angles* α, β, *and* γ *have the form*

(X) $\quad\dfrac{x - x_1}{\cos \alpha} = \dfrac{y - y_1}{\cos \beta} = \dfrac{z - z_1}{\cos \gamma}.$

To obtain (X), solve each of the equations of (IX) for t and equate results.

Corollary. *If* a, b, *and* c *are direction numbers, then the symmetric equations of the line may be written in the form*

(XI) $\quad\dfrac{x - x_1}{a} = \dfrac{y - y_1}{b} = \dfrac{z - z_1}{c}.$

Theorem 3. *Two-point form.* *The equations of the straight line passing through* $P_1(x_1, y_1, z_1)$ *and* $P_2(x_2, y_2, z_2)$ *are*

(XII) $\quad\dfrac{x - x_1}{x_2 - x_1} = \dfrac{y - y_1}{y_2 - y_1} = \dfrac{z - z_1}{z_2 - z_1}.$

Proof. By Art. 116, the denominators in (XII) are direction numbers for the line. Hence (XII) follows from (XI).
Q.E.D.

The three equal ratios in (X)–(XII) are equivalent to *two* independent equations, each of which represents a plane through the line (see the following article). The proof of (X) fails when a direction angle is 90°, and also that of (XI) and (XII) in these cases (see Problems 2, 3, pp. 274–275).

135. The projecting planes of a line.

A plane passing through a given line and perpendicular to one of the coördinate planes is called a *projecting plane*.

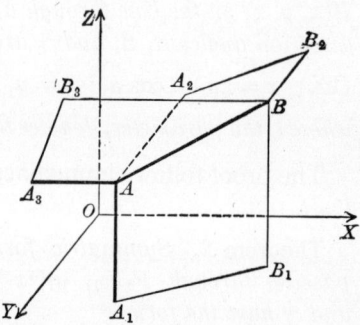

If the line is perpendicular to one of the coördinate planes, any plane containing the line is perpendicular to that plane. In this case we speak of but two projecting planes, namely, those drawn through the line perpendicular to the other coördinate planes.

If the line is parallel to one of the coördinate planes, two of the projecting planes coincide.

By (VI), Art. 132, the equation of any plane through the line

(1) $\quad 3x + 2y - z - 1 = 0, \quad 2x - y + 2z - 3 = 0$

has the form

$$3x + 2y - z - 1 + k(2x - y + 2z - 3) = 0.$$

Multiplying out and collecting terms,

(2) $\quad (3 + 2k)x + (2 - k)y + (-1 + 2k)z - 1 - 3k = 0.$

This plane will be perpendicular to the XY-plane when the coefficient of z equals zero, that is, if $k = \frac{1}{2}$ (Art. 126). Writing this value of k in (2) and reducing,

(3) $\quad 4x + \frac{3}{2}y - \frac{5}{2} = 0, \quad \text{or} \quad 8x + 3y - 5 = 0.$

This is therefore the equation of the projecting plane of the line (1) on XY, that is, of the plane ABB_1A_1 of the figure.

Now equation (3) is simply the result obtained by *eliminating z from the equations* (1); namely, we multiply the first of equations (1) by 2 and add it to the second. Hence the result:

To find the equations of the projecting planes of a line, eliminate x, y, and z in turn from the given equations.

Thus, to finish the example begun, eliminating y from (1), we find $7x + 3z - 7 = 0$ for the projecting plane on XZ. Eliminating x, we get $7y - 8z + 7 = 0$ for the equation of the projecting plane on YZ.

The forms (X)–(XII) of Art. 134 give at once the projecting planes. For example, in (XI),

(4) $$\frac{x - x_1}{a} = \frac{y - y_1}{b},$$

or $b(x - x_1) - a(y - y_1) = 0$, is the projecting plane on XY.

The projections form. The simultaneous equations
(XIII) $\qquad x = mz + p, \quad y = nz + q$

define a line as the intersection of its projecting planes on XZ and YZ. Solving each equation for z, and equating results, we obtain the symmetric equations,

(5) $$\frac{x - p}{m} = \frac{y - q}{n} = \frac{z}{1}.$$

Comparing with (XI), Art. 134, we have the

Theorem. *In the projections form* (XIII), *the line passes through $(p, q, 0)$, and m, n, 1 are direction numbers.*

The form (XIII) is often useful. It may be used for any line not parallel to the XY-plane. Obviously, two other projecting planes also might be employed.

EXAMPLE

Reduce the following equations of a line to the symmetric form (XI):
$$x - 2y + z = 8, \quad 2x - 3y = 13.$$

Solution. Find the equations of two projecting planes. The second plane is already the projecting plane on XY. Eliminating x, we get $y - 2z = -3$. From the two projecting planes thus found,
(6) $\qquad 2x - 3y = 13 \quad \text{and} \quad y - 2z = -3,$

by solving the first for x and the second for z, we obtain the projections form
(7) $\qquad x = \frac{3}{2}y + \frac{13}{2}, \quad z = \frac{1}{2}y + \frac{3}{2}.$

Solving each for y and equating results, we get

(8) $$\frac{x - 1\tfrac{3}{2}}{\tfrac{3}{2}} = \frac{y}{1} = \frac{z - \tfrac{3}{2}}{\tfrac{1}{2}}.$$

Multiplying all denominators by 2, the result is

$$\frac{x - 1\tfrac{3}{2}}{3} = \frac{y}{2} = \frac{z - \tfrac{3}{2}}{1}. \quad Ans.$$

Comparison with (XI) gives $x_1 = 1\tfrac{3}{2}$, $y_1 = 0$, $z_1 = \tfrac{3}{2}$, $a = 3$, $b = 2$, $c = 1$. Hence the line passes through $(1\tfrac{3}{2}, 0, \tfrac{3}{2})$, and its direction cosines are proportional to 3, 2, 1. Thus we have a second method of finding direction numbers for a line. (See examples, p. 268.)

A remark here is important. In (XI), x_1, y_1, and z_1 are the coördinates of any known point on the line. Hence for a given line the numerators in (XI) may be quite different. For example, putting $z = 0$ in (6), we find $x = 2$, $y = -3$. Hence the equations $\dfrac{x - 2}{3} = \dfrac{y + 3}{2} = \dfrac{z}{1}$ represent the given line also. Notice that in equations (XI) the coefficients of x, y, and z *must be unity*. This explains the form of (8).

PROBLEMS

1. Find the equations of the projecting planes of each of the following lines. Write equations for the line in the projections form.

(a) $2x + y - z = 0$, $x - y + 2z = 3$.
  Ans. $5x + y = 3$, $3x + z = 3$, $3y - 5z + 6 = 0$;
  $y = -5x + 3$ and $z = -3x + 3$.
(b) $2x + y + z = 6$, $x + 3y - 2z = 2$.
(c) $2x + y - z = 1$, $x - y + z = 2$.
  Ans. Line is parallel to YZ. $x = 1$, $y = z - 1$.
(d) $3x + y - 4z = 10$, $2x + 2y + 3z = 10$.
(e) $2y + 3z = 6$, $2y - 3z = 18$.
  Ans. Line is parallel to OX. $y = 6$, $z = -2$.
(f) $12x + y + z = 0$, $4x + 3y + 2z = 16$.
(g) $x + z = 1$, $x - z = 3$.

2. Prove the following formulas, which replace (X)–(XII) in the special cases given. Derive them from (IX).

(a) When $\gamma = 90°$, $\dfrac{x - x_1}{\cos \alpha} = \dfrac{y - y_1}{\cos \beta}$, $z = z_1$.
(b) When $c = 0$, $\dfrac{x - x_1}{a} = \dfrac{y - y_1}{b}$, $z = z_1$.
(c) When $z_1 = z_2$, $\dfrac{x - x_1}{x_2 - x_1} = \dfrac{y - y_1}{y_2 - y_1}$, $z = z_1$.

PLANE AND STRAIGHT LINE IN SPACE

3. Prove the following formulas, to replace (X)–(XII) (see Problem 2).

(a) When $\beta = \gamma = 90°$, $y = y_1$, $z = z_1$.
(b) When $b = c = 0$, $y = y_1$, $z = z_1$.
(c) When $y_1 = y_2$, $z_1 = z_2$, $y = y_1$, $z = z_1$.

4. Derive equations for each of the following lines. In special cases use the results of Problems 2 and 3.

(a) Passes through $(3, 4, -4)$, with direction angles $60°, 45°, 120°$.
(b) Passes through $(1, -2, 3)$, with direction angles $45°, 90°, 135°$.
$\qquad$ Ans. $y = -2$, $x + z - 4 = 0$.
(c) Passes through $(3, -2, 1)$, $(2, 3, 4)$.
$\qquad$ Ans. $5x + y - 13 = 0$, $3x + z - 10 = 0$.
(d) Passes through $(3, -2, 1)$, $(3, -4, 5)$.
(e) Passes through $(3, 2, -1)$, with direction numbers $0, 1, 0$.
(f) Passes through $(1, 4, 6)$ and $(-1, 4, 6)$.
(g) Passes through $(0, -3, 2)$ and is parallel to the line joining $(3, 4, -7)$ and $(2, 7, -6)$. $\qquad$ Ans. $x = -z + 2$, $y = 3z - 9$.

5. Show that the conditions that the three points $P_1(x_1, y_1, z_1)$, $P_2(x_2, y_2, z_2)$, and $P_3(x_3, y_3, z_3)$ should lie on a straight line are
$$\frac{x_3 - x_1}{x_2 - x_1} = \frac{y_3 - y_1}{y_2 - y_1} = \frac{z_3 - z_1}{z_2 - z_1}.$$

6. Reduce the equations of the following lines to the symmetric form (XI) (see Problems 2, 3, above), and interpret the results.

(a) $4x + 5y + 3z = 3$, $4x - 5y + z + 9 = 0$.
(b) $2x + y + 5 = 0$, $x + 3z - 5 = 0$.
(c) $x + 2y + 6z = 5$, $3x - 2y - 10z = 7$. Ans. $\dfrac{x-3}{2} = \dfrac{y-1}{-7} = \dfrac{z}{2}$.
(d) $3x + y - 2z = 0$, $6x - 3y + 4z + 9 = 0$.
(e) $2x + y + 2z = 7$, $x + 3y + 6z = 11$. Ans. $\dfrac{y-3}{2} = \dfrac{z}{-1}$, $x = 2$.
(f) $3x - 3y + z = 4$, $4x - 6y - z = 5$.

7. Find equations of the line through the point $(-2, 4, 0)$ which is parallel to the line $\dfrac{x}{4} = \dfrac{y+2}{-3} = \dfrac{z-4}{-1}$. Ans. $x = -4z - 2$, $y = 3z + 4$.

8. Show that the lines $\dfrac{x+2}{-6} = \dfrac{y+3}{-3} = \dfrac{z-11}{2}$ and $\dfrac{x+3}{-2} = \dfrac{y}{6} = \dfrac{z+3}{3}$ are perpendicular.

9. Find the angle between the lines $\dfrac{x-3}{2} = \dfrac{y+1}{1} = \dfrac{z-3}{-1}$ and $\dfrac{x+2}{1} = \dfrac{y-7}{2} = \dfrac{z}{1}$, if both are directed upward. $\qquad$ Ans. $120°$.

10. Find equations for each of the following lines:

(a) Passing through $(-1, 2, 6)$ and parallel to the line $x = 2z - 3$, $y = -3z - 5$.

(b) Passing through $(-1, 2, 6)$ and perpendicular to and intersecting the x-axis.

(c) Passing through the origin and perpendicular to each of the lines $x = 2z - 4$, $y = -z + 2$, and $y = x + 5$, $z = 2x - 8$.

(d) Passing through $(0, 2, 0)$ and at right angles to the line $x = z$, $y = 2z$, and the y-axis.

(e) Perpendicular to each of the lines $y = -x + 6$, $z = 2x - 11$, and $x = 2z + 10$, $y = 2z + 8$, at their point of intersection.

11. Find the parametric equations of the line passing through the point $(2, 3, 4)$ whose direction cosines are proportional to $1, -4,$ and 2.

12. Construct the lines whose parametric equations are

(a) $x = 2 + \frac{2}{3}t,\ y = 4 + \frac{1}{3}t,\ z = 6 + \frac{2}{3}t$;

(b) $x = -3 + \frac{2}{7}t,\ y = 6 - \frac{6}{7}t,\ z = 4 + \frac{3}{7}t$.

13. Find the distance, measured along the line whose equations are $x = 2 - \frac{3}{13}t,\ y = 4 + \frac{12}{13}t,\ z = -3 + \frac{4}{13}t$, from the point $(2, 4, -3)$ to the intersection of the line with the plane $4x + y - 2z = 16$. *Ans.* $3\frac{1}{4}$.

136. Relative positions of a line and a plane. If the equations of the line L have the projections form (XIII), Art. 135, we may determine if L **lies in a given plane** as follows: Substitute the values of x and y in the equation of the plane. Then if the result is true for *all* values of z, the line lies in the plane.

We next easily prove the

Theorem. *A line L whose direction numbers are a, b, and c and the plane $Ax + By + Cz + D = 0$ are*

(a) *parallel when and only when*

(1) $$Aa + Bb + Cc = 0;$$

(b) *perpendicular when and only when*

(2) $$\frac{A}{a} = \frac{B}{b} = \frac{C}{c}.$$

Proof. The direction numbers of a perpendicular L_2 to the plane are A, B, and C.

The line L and the plane are parallel when and only when L and L_2 are perpendicular, that is, when and only when (1) holds.

PLANE AND STRAIGHT LINE IN SPACE

The line L and the plane are perpendicular when and only when L and L_2 are parallel, that is, when and only when (2) holds.   Q.E.D.

Equation (1) holds, of course, when L lies in the plane.

PROBLEMS

1. Show that the line $\frac{x+3}{-2} = \frac{y+4}{-7} = \frac{z}{3}$ is parallel to the plane $4x - 2y - 2z = 9$.

2. Show that the line $\frac{x}{3} = \frac{y}{-2} = \frac{z}{7}$ is perpendicular to the plane $3x - 2y + 7z = 8$.

3. Show that

(a) the line $x = z + 4$, $y = 2z + 3$ lies in the plane $2x + 3y - 8z - 17 = 0$;

(b) the line $\frac{x-2}{3} = \frac{y+2}{1} = \frac{z-3}{-4}$ lies in the plane $2x + 2y + 2z - 6 = 0$.

4. Find equations for each of the following lines:

(a) Passing through $(2, -3, 4)$ and perpendicular to the plane $3x - y + 2z = 4$.   *Ans.* $x = -3y - 7$, $z = -2y - 2$.

(b) Passing through $(-1, 3, 2)$ and perpendicular to the plane $x - 3z = 4$.

(c) Passing through $(0, 2, 4)$ and parallel to each of the planes $x + 2z = 1$, $y - 3z = 2$.

(d) Passing through $(1, -2, 3)$ and parallel to each of the planes $2x - y = 4$, $x + y - z = 4$.

5. Find the equation of each of the following planes:

(a) Passing through $(1, 2, -3)$ and perpendicular to the line $3x - y = 4$, $y + 2z = 5$.   *Ans.* $2x + 6y - 3z - 23 = 0$.

(b) Passing through $(-4, 0, 1)$ and perpendicular to the line whose equations are $x + y - 4z = 0$, $y - z = 2$.

(c) Passing through $(3, 6, -12)$ and parallel to each of the lines $x + 3y - 1 = 0$, $3y + z - 2 = 0$, and $z = 2x + 1$, $y = 3$.
    Ans. $2x + 3y - z - 36 = 0$.

(d) Determined by the intersecting lines $x = 2z + 1$, $y = 3z + 2$, and $2x = 2 - z$, $3y = z + 6$.

(e) Passing through the line $x + 2z - 4 = 0$, $3y - z + 8 = 0$ and parallel to the line $x = y + 4$, $z = y - 6$.
    Ans. $2x - 9y + 7z - 32 = 0$.

(f) Determined by the point $(2, 3, -4)$ and the line
$$\frac{x+2}{-2} = \frac{y+3}{-2} = \frac{z-1}{1}.$$

(g) Determined by the parallel lines

$$\frac{x+1}{3} = \frac{y+2}{-2} = \frac{z}{1}, \text{ and } \frac{x+3}{3} = \frac{y+4}{-2} = \frac{z+1}{1}.$$

6. Find equations for the lines determined as follows:

(a) Lying in the plane $x + 3y - z + 4 = 0$ and perpendicular to the line $x = 2z + 3$, $y = 2z$ at the point where this line meets the plane.
  Ans. $3x + 5y + 7 = 0$, $4x + 5z + 1 = 0$.

(b) Passing through $(4, 2, -3)$, parallel to the plane $x + y + z - 10 = 0$, and perpendicular to the line $x + 2y - z = 5$, $z = 10$.

(c) Perpendicular to the line $3x + 2y - z = 8$, $x - 3y + 1 = 0$ at the point where it meets the plane $2x - y + z - 3 = 0$.

(d) Passing through $(2, 5, -3)$, perpendicular to the line from the origin to this point, and parallel to the plane $2x - 3y + 16 = 0$.

PROBLEMS FOR INDIVIDUAL STUDY OR ASSIGNMENT

1. Find the perpendicular distance from $(3, 4, -6)$ to the line $3x - 2y + 7 = 0$, $2y + z - 3 = 0$.

2. The line from $A(3, -7, 5)$ with direction numbers 4, 1, 8, meets the plane $2x + 3y - z + 7 = 0$ at B. Find the length AB.

3. Derive equations for the following lines, each of which passes through $P_1(x_1, y_1, z_1)$:

(a) Parallel to the line $x = mz + a$, $y = nz + b$.

(b) Perpendicular to each of the lines $x = m_1z + a_1$, $y = n_1z + b_1$, and $x = m_2z + a_2$, $y = n_2z + b_2$.

(c) Perpendicular to the plane $Ax + By + Cz + D = 0$.

(d) Parallel to each of the planes $A_1x + B_1y + C_1z + D_1 = 0$ and $A_2x + B_2y + C_2z + D_2 = 0$.

4. Find the equation of the plane passing through $P_1(x_1, y_1, z_1)$ and perpendicular to the line $x = mz + p$, $y = nz + q$.

5. Prove that when the lines of Problem 3 (b) lie in a plane,

$$(a_1 - a_2)(n_1 - n_2) = (b_1 - b_2)(m_1 - m_2).$$

6. Find the angle θ between the line $\dfrac{x - x_1}{a} = \dfrac{y - y_1}{b} = \dfrac{z - z_1}{c}$ and the plane $Ax + By + Cz + D = 0$.

Ans. $\sin \theta = \dfrac{Aa + Bb + Cc}{\sqrt{A^2 + B^2 + C^2} \sqrt{a^2 + b^2 + c^2}}.$

Hint. The angle between a line and a plane is the acute angle between the line and its orthogonal projection on the plane. This angle equals $\frac{1}{2}\pi$ increased or decreased by the angle between the line and the normal to the plane.

PLANE AND STRAIGHT LINE IN SPACE

7. Find the equation of the plane passing through $P_3(x_3, y_3, z_3)$ and parallel to each of the lines

$$\frac{x-x_1}{a_1}=\frac{y-y_1}{b_1}=\frac{z-z_1}{c_1} \text{ and } \frac{x-x_2}{a_2}=\frac{y-y_2}{b_2}=\frac{z-z_2}{c_2}.$$

Ans. $(b_1c_2 - b_2c_1)(x - x_3) + (c_1a_2 - a_2c_1)(y - y_3)$
$\qquad\qquad + (a_1b_2 - a_2b_1)(z - z_3) = 0.$

8. Find the condition that the plane $A_1x + B_1y + C_1z + D_1 = 0$ should be parallel to the line whose equations are $A_2x + B_2y + C_2x + D_2 = 0$, $A_3x + B_3y + C_3z + D_3 = 0$.

Ans. $A_1(B_2C_3 - B_3C_2) + B_1(C_2A_3 - C_3A_2) + C_1(A_2B_3 - A_3B_2) = 0.$

9. Find the equation of the plane determined by the point $P_1(x_1, y_1, z_1)$ and the line $A_1x + B_1y + C_1z + D_1 = 0$, $A_2x + B_2y + C_2z + D_2 = 0$.

Ans. $(A_2x_1 + B_2y_1 + C_2z_1 + D_2)(A_1x + B_1y + C_1z + D_1)$
$\qquad = (A_1x_1 + B_1y_1 + C_1z_1 + D_1)(A_2x + B_2y + C_2z + D_2).$

10. Find the equation of the plane determined by the intersecting lines $\dfrac{x-x_1}{a_1}=\dfrac{y-y_1}{b_1}=\dfrac{z-z_1}{c_1}$ and $\dfrac{x-x_1}{a_2}=\dfrac{y-y_1}{b_2}=\dfrac{z-z_1}{c_2}$.

Ans. $(b_1c_2 - b_2c_1)(x - x_1) + (c_1a_2 - c_2a_1)(y - y_1)$
$\qquad\qquad + (a_1b_2 - a_2b_1)(z - z_1) = 0.$

11. Find the equation of the plane determined by the parallel lines $\dfrac{x-x_1}{a}=\dfrac{y-y_1}{b}=\dfrac{z-z_1}{c}$ and $\dfrac{x-x_2}{a}=\dfrac{y-y_2}{b}=\dfrac{z-z_2}{c}$.

Ans. $[(y_1 - y_2)c - (z_1 - z_2)b]x + [(z_1 - z_2)a - (x_1 - x_2)c]y$
$\quad + [(x_1 - x_2)b - (y_1 - y_2)a]z + (y_1z_2 - y_2z_1)a$
$\quad + (z_1x_2 - z_2x_1)b + (x_1y_2 - x_2y_1)c = 0.$

12. Find the conditions that the line $x = mz + a$, $y = nz + b$ should lie in the plane $Ax + By + Cz + D = 0$.

Ans. $Aa + Bb + D = 0$, $Am + Bn + C = 0$.

13. Find the equation of the plane passing through the line $\dfrac{x-x_1}{a_1} = \dfrac{y-y_1}{b_1} = \dfrac{z-z_1}{c_1}$ and parallel to the line $\dfrac{x-x_2}{a_2} = \dfrac{y-y_2}{b_2} = \dfrac{z-z_2}{c_2}$.

Ans. $(b_1c_2 - b_2c_1)(x - x_1) + (c_1a_2 - c_2a_1)(y - y_1)$
$\qquad\qquad + (a_1b_2 - a_2b_1)(z - z_1) = 0.$

14. Find the equation of the plane determined by $P_1(x_1, y_1, z_1)$ and the line through $P_2(x_2, y_2, z_2)$ with direction numbers a, b, c.

CHAPTER XV

SPECIAL SURFACES

137. The sphere. In this chapter we shall consider spheres, cylinders, and cones (surfaces considered in elementary geometry), and also quadric surfaces.

In analytic geometry the terms "sphere," "cylinder," and "cone" are usually used to denote the spherical surface, cylindrical surface, and conical surface of elementary geometry, and not the solids bounded wholly or in part by such surfaces.

Theorem. *The equation of the sphere with center (h, k, l) and radius r is*

(I) $$(x - h)^2 + (y - k)^2 + (z - l)^2 = r^2.$$

Proof. Let $P(x, y, z)$ be any point on the sphere, and denote the center of the sphere by C. Then, by definition, $PC = r$. Substituting the value of PC given by the length formula, and squaring, we obtain (I). Q.E.D.

When (I) is multiplied out, it is

$$x^2 + y^2 + z^2 - 2hx - 2ky - 2lz + h^2 + k^2 + l^2 - r^2 = 0;$$

that is, it is in the form

(1) $$x^2 + y^2 + z^2 + Gx + Hy + Iz + K = 0.$$

The question now is, What is the locus of an equation of this form? (Compare Art. 35.)

To answer this, collect the terms thus:

$$(x^2 + Gx) + (y^2 + Hy) + (z^2 + Iz) = -K.$$

Completing the squares within the parentheses, we obtain

$$(x + \tfrac{1}{2}G)^2 + (y + \tfrac{1}{2}H)^2 + (z + \tfrac{1}{2}I)^2$$
$$= \tfrac{1}{4}(G^2 + H^2 + I^2 - 4K).$$

SPECIAL SURFACES

The right-hand member may be positive, zero, or negative. Hence, comparing with (I), we see that the locus is a sphere, or a **point sphere** ($r = 0$), or there is no locus.

The presence of the four constants, G, H, I, K, in (1) indicates that a sphere is *determined by four conditions* (compare Art. 36). To find the equation of a sphere satisfying given conditions, we use (I) or (1), as may be more convenient.

If (I) is used, we have to find h, k, l, and r. If (1) is used, we need four equations in G, H, I, K, and we find the values of these constants by solving the equations.

EXAMPLE

What is the locus of the equation $x^2 + y^2 + z^2 - 2x + 3y + 1 = 0$?

Solution. Collecting terms,
$$(x^2 - 2x) + (y^2 + 3y) + z^2 = -1.$$

Completing the squares,
$$(x^2 - 2x + 1) + (y^2 + 3y + \tfrac{9}{4}) + z^2 = -1 + 1 + \tfrac{9}{4},$$
or
$$(x - 1)^2 + (y + \tfrac{3}{2})^2 + z^2 = \tfrac{9}{4}.$$

The locus is a sphere of radius $\tfrac{3}{2}$ and center $(1, -\tfrac{3}{2}, 0)$. *Ans.*

PROBLEMS

1. Determine the nature of the loci of the following equations and find the center and radius if the locus is a sphere, or the coördinates of the center if the locus is a point sphere.

(a) $x^2 + y^2 + z^2 + 4x - 6z = 0$.
(b) $x^2 + y^2 + z^2 - 4x + 2y - 5 = 0$.
(c) $x^2 + y^2 + z^2 - x + 4y + 10 = 0$.
(d) $x^2 + y^2 + z^2 - 12y + 6z = 5$.
(e) $x^2 + y^2 + z^2 - 4x + 6y + 8z + 29 = 0$.
(f) $x^2 + y^2 + z^2 + 2x + 2y + 4z = 0$.

2. Find the equation of the locus of a point

(a) whose distance from $(0, \tfrac{1}{2}, -2)$ is $\tfrac{1}{2}$;
(b) whose distance from $(-2, \tfrac{1}{3}, 0)$ is $\sqrt{5}$;
(c) whose distance from $(-3, 2, 1)$ is 4;

Ans. $x^2 + y^2 + z^2 + 6x - 4y - 2z - 2 = 0.$

(d) whose distance from $(-1, 3, \tfrac{2}{3})$ is $\sqrt{3}$.

3. Find the equation of the sphere

(a) having the line joining $(3, 0, 4)$ and $(4, 6, 0)$ as a radius and the first point as center;

(b) having the line joining $(3, 0, 7)$ and $(-2, 1, 1)$ as a diameter;
$$\text{Ans. } x^2 + y^2 + z^2 - x - y - 8z + 1 = 0.$$

(c) whose center is $(2, -2, 1)$ and which is tangent to the XZ-plane;
$$\text{Ans. } x^2 + y^2 + z^2 - 4x + 4y - 2z + 5 = 0.$$

(d) passing through the four points $(2, 0, 0)$, $(0, 4, 0)$, $(0, 0, -4)$, and $(-8, 0, 0)$.

4. Prove that the locus of a point satisfying the condition given below is in every case a sphere, and find the radius and center.

(a) Its distance from $(7, 1, 3)$ is twice its distance from $(-\frac{5}{4}, -2, \frac{3}{2})$.
$$\text{Ans. } h = -4, \ k = -3, \ l = 1, \ r = \tfrac{1}{2}\sqrt{141}.$$

(b) Its distance from $(-3, 4, 5)$ is four times its distance from the origin.

(c) The sum of the squares of its distances from $(4, -5, 1)$ and $(0, 2, -4)$ is 64.

(d) The sum of the squares of its perpendicular distances from three planes $x + y + z = 5$, $2x - 3y - 2z - 1 = 0$, $3x - 2y + 3z = 6$ is 5.

5. Find the equation of a sphere which

(a) is concentric with $x^2 + y^2 + z^2 - 6x + 4z - 36 = 0$ and passes through $(2, 5, -7)$; $\quad$ Ans. $x^2 + y^2 + z^2 - 6x + 4z = 38.$

(b) has the center $(4, -4, 3)$ and is tangent to the plane whose equation is $3x + 2y - z = 7$;

(c) has its center in the XZ-plane and passes through the three points $(1, 0, 2)$, $(1, 3, 1)$, $(-3, 0, 0)$; $\quad$ Ans. $x^2 + y^2 + z^2 - 2x + 6z = 15.$

(d) has its center on the z-axis and passes through $(3, 4, 0)$ and $(-2, 3, 5)$; $\quad$ Ans. $5x^2 + 5y^2 + 5z^2 - 13z = 125.$

(e) passes through $(1, 5, -3)$ and $(-3, 0, 0)$ with center on the line $3x + y + z = 0, x + 2y + 1 = 0$;
$$\text{Ans. } 9x^2 + 9y^2 + 9z^2 - 34x + 26y + 76z - 183 = 0.$$

(f) passes through $(2, 2, 0)$, $(0, 2, 2)$, and $(2, 0, 2)$ and has the radius 5.

6. Find the equation of the tangent plane to each of the following spheres at the given point:

(a) $x^2 + y^2 + z^2 - 14 = 0$, at $(3, -2, 1)$.

(b) $x^2 + y^2 + z^2 - 6x + 4z - 36 = 0$, at $(1, 6, -5)$.
$$\text{Ans. } 2x - 6y + 3z + 49 = 0.$$

(c) $x^2 + y^2 + z^2 - 4x - 2y + 6z = 0$, at $(0, 0, -6)$.

(d) $x^2 + y^2 + z^2 - 2x + 6z = 15$, at $(1, 5, -3)$.

7. Given two spheres, $A: x^2 + y^2 + z^2 - 6x + 8y - 10z + 41 = 0$, and $B: x^2 + y^2 + z^2 + 6x + 2y - 6z + 10 = 0$. Find the equation of a third sphere if

(a) the line joining the centers of A and B is a diameter;
(b) it has the same center as A and is tangent to B (two cases);
Its center lies on the line passing through the centers of A and B, and
(c) it is tangent to both A and B (four cases);
(d) its center is on B and it is tangent to A (four cases).

8. Find the equations of the planes which are tangent to the sphere $x^2 + y^2 + z^2 - 10x + 5y - 2z - 24 = 0$ at the points where it intersects the coördinate axes.

9. Find the equation of a sphere inscribed in the tetraedron formed by any four of the following planes:

$14x + 5y - 2z - 168 = 0$, $\quad 10x + 11y + 2z + 88 = 0$,
$14x - 5y + 2z + 28 = 0$, $\quad 2x - y - 2z + 12 = 0$,
$10x - 11y + 2z + 33 = 0$, $\quad 2x - y + 2z + 8 = 0$.

10. Find the equation of the smallest sphere tangent to the two spheres
$$x^2 + y^2 + z^2 - 2x - 6y + 1 = 0,$$
$$x^2 + y^2 + z^2 + 6x + 2y - 4z + 5 = 0.$$
$$\text{Ans. } x^2 + y^2 + z^2 + 2x - 2y - 2z + 3 = 0.$$

138. Cylinders. A surface generated by a straight line which moves parallel to itself and intersects a given curve is called a *cylinder*. The curve is called the **directrix**. We now consider equations whose loci are cylinders.

EXAMPLES

1. Find the equation of a circular cylinder, with radius r, whose axis is the z-axis.

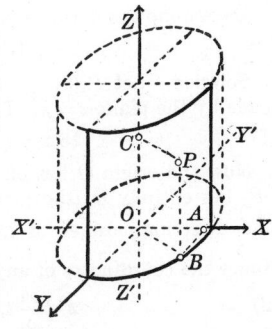

Solution. Let $P(x, y, z)$ be any point on the cylinder. Then, in the figure, $OA = x$, $AB = y$, $BP = z$. If CP is perpendicular to OZ, then the condition that P lies on the cylinder is

(1) $\qquad CP = OB = r$.

But $OB = \sqrt{x^2 + y^2}$. Hence the equation desired is

(2) $\qquad x^2 + y^2 = r^2$. *Ans.*

Note that the circle $x^2 + y^2 = r^2$ *in the XY-plane* is the directrix of the cylinder.

2. Determine the nature of the surface whose equation is $y^2 - 4x = 0$

Solution. If $M(a, b)$ is any point on the parabola $y^2 - 4x = 0$ in the XY-plane, then *every* point on the line drawn through M parallel to OZ will lie on the given surface. For $b^2 - 4a = 0$, since M is on the parabola. Hence the coördinates (a, b, z), where z has any value, satisfy the equation of the surface. *The locus is therefore a cylinder with directrix the parabola* $y^2 - 4x = 0$ *in the XY-plane and with elements parallel to OZ.* Ans.

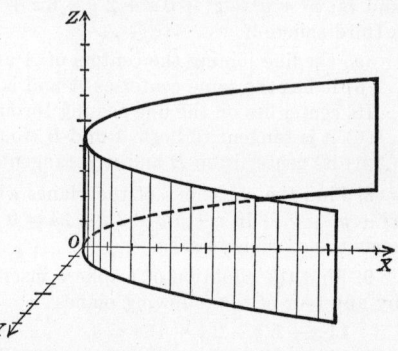

These examples lead at once to the

Theorem. *The locus of an equation in which one variable is lacking is a cylinder whose elements are parallel to the axis along which that variable is measured. The given equation considered as a **plane locus** in the corresponding coördinate plane represents the directrix.*

139. Cones. The surface generated by a straight line turning around one of its points and intersecting a given curve is called a *cone*.

EXAMPLE

Determine the nature of the surface whose equation is
$$16x^2 + y^2 - z^2 = 0.$$

Solution. Let $P_1(x_1, y_1, z_1)$ be a point on a section of the surface made by the plane $z = k$. Then

(1) $\qquad 16x_1^2 + y_1^2 - z_1^2 = 0, \quad z_1 = k.$

Now the origin O lies on the surface. We shall show that the line OP_1 lies entirely on the surface and hence that the surface is a cone. The direction cosines of OP_1 are $\dfrac{x_1}{\rho_1}$, $\dfrac{y_1}{\rho_1}$, and $\dfrac{z_1}{\rho_1}$, where $\rho_1 = OP_1$. Hence the coördinates of any point on OP_1 are, by (IX), Art. 134,

(2) $\qquad x = \dfrac{x_1}{\rho_1} t, \quad y = \dfrac{y_1}{\rho_1} t, \quad z = \dfrac{z_1}{\rho_1} t.$

SPECIAL SURFACES

Substituting these values of x, y, and z in the left-hand member of the given equation, we obtain

(3) $\quad \dfrac{t^2}{\rho_1{}^2}(16\,x_1{}^2 + y_1{}^2 - z_1{}^2).$

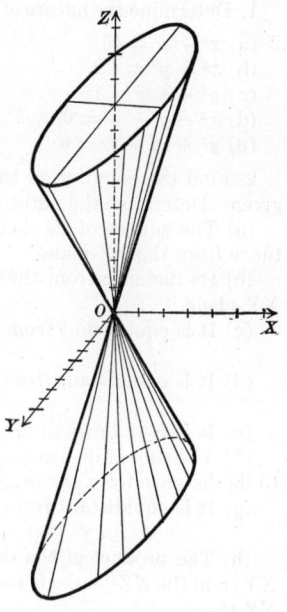

But from the first of equations (1) the expression in the parenthesis in (3) equals zero. Hence the product in (3) also vanishes for *any value of t*. This means that every point (x, y, z) on the line (2) lies on the surface, that is, the entire line lies on the surface. Hence the surface is a cone whose vertex is the origin. *Ans.*

The same proof will apply to any equation in x, y, z in which all the terms are of the same degree. Such an equation is said to be **homogeneous in x, y, and z**. Hence the

Theorem. *The locus of an equation which is homogeneous in the variables x, y, and z is a cone whose vertex is the origin.*

In the figure for the above example, the cone is cut by the plane $z = 8$. The equations of the curve of intersection of the cone $16\,x^2 + y^2 - z^2 = 0$ with this plane are obviously

$$z = 8, \quad 16\,x^2 + y^2 - 64 = 0.$$

The curve is an ellipse and is plotted in the plane $z = 8$, using oblique coördinates.

To construct the locus of the equation of a cone, find the equations of the curve of intersection of the cone with a suitably chosen plane parallel to one of the coördinate planes, construct this plane curve, and then draw the elements from the points on this curve to the vertex of the cone.

PROBLEMS

1. Determine the nature of the following surfaces and construct them:

(a) $x^2 + z^2 = 16$.
(b) $x^2 + y^2 = 4x$.
(c) $y^2 + 4x^2 = 16$.
(d) $x^2 - y^2 - z^2 = 0$.
(e) $y^2 + xz + yz = 0$.
(f) $xz - 6 = 0$.
(g) $y^2 + z^2 - 2xz = 0$.
(h) $y^2 - 2z^3 = 0$.
(i) $x^2 - 4y^2 + 6z^2 = 0$.
(j) $x^2 - z^2 = 25$.

2. Find the equation of the locus of a point satisfying the condition given. Determine the nature of the locus and draw the figure.

(a) The square of its distance from the z-axis equals twice its distance from the YZ-plane. *Ans.* $x^2 + y^2 - 2x = 0$.

(b) Its distance from the z-axis is three times its distance from the XY-plane.

(c) It is equidistant from the point $(4, 0, 0)$ and the XY-plane.
Ans. $x^2 + y^2 - 8x + 16 = 0$.

(d) It is equidistant from the XY-plane and the z-axis.
Ans. $x^2 + y^2 - z^2 = 0$.

(e) It is four times as far from the y-axis as from the z-axis.

(f) The sum of its distances from the three coördinate planes is equal to its distance from the origin.

(g) It is equidistant from the point $(0, 0, 5)$ and the x-axis.
Ans. $x^2 - 10z + 25 = 0$.

(h) The product of the sum and difference of its distances from the XY- and the XZ-planes is four times the square of its distance from the YZ-plane.

3. Find the equation of the cone whose vertex is the origin and whose elements cut the circle $y^2 + z^2 = 4$, $x = 1$.

4. Find the equation of the cone with the origin as a vertex whose elements cut the ellipse $2x^2 + 3z^2 = 6$, $y = 1$.
Ans. $2x^2 + 3z^2 - 6y^2 = 0$.

For individual study or assignment

5. A point moves so that the difference between the squares of its distances from two intersecting perpendicular lines is constant. What is the locus?

6. What is the locus of a point equidistant from a plane and a line perpendicular to the plane?

7. What is the locus of a point which moves so that the ratio of its distances from two perpendicular intersecting lines is constant?

8. A point moves so that its distance from a fixed point is always equal to its distance from a fixed line. What is the locus?

9. The sum of the distances of a point from three mutually perpendicular planes is equal to half its distance from their common point of intersection. What is the locus?

140. Discussion of the equation of a surface. Some properties of a surface can be determined by methods analogous to those in Art. 18.

1. *Intercepts on the axes of coördinates.*

Rule *to find the intercepts of a surface.*
Set each pair of variables in turn equal to zero and solve for real values of the third.

2. *Traces on the coördinate planes.*

The curves in which a surface intersects the coördinate planes are called its **traces**.

Rule *to find the traces.*
The equations of the traces of a surface are obtained by successively setting $x = 0$, $y = 0$, and $z = 0$ in the equation of the surface.

3. *Symmetry.*

Theorem. *If an equation is unaffected by changing the sign of one variable, the locus is symmetric with respect to the coördinate plane from which that variable is measured.*

If an equation is unaffected by changing the signs of two variables, the locus is symmetric with respect to the axis along which the third variable is measured.

If an equation is unaffected by changing the signs of all three variables, the locus is symmetric with respect to the origin.

The definition of symmetry and the proof are analogous to those of Art. 18.

4. *Sections by planes parallel to the coördinate planes.*

The *general appearance of a surface* is determined by considering the curves in which it is cut by systems of planes parallel to a coördinate plane. This also enables us *to determine whether the surface is closed or recedes to infinity.*

The examples below illustrate the method.

To *discuss the equation of a surface,* find (1) the intercepts and (2) the traces, examine (3) the question of symmetry and (4) the nature of plane sections lying in planes parallel to a coördinate plane.

EXAMPLE

Determine the nature of the curve in which the plane $z = 4$ intersects the surface whose equation is $y^2 + z^2 = 4x$.

Solution. The equations of the curve are, by definition (Art. 122),

(1) $\qquad y^2 + z^2 = 4x, \quad z = 4.$

Eliminate z by substituting from the second equation in the first. This gives

(2) $\qquad y^2 - 4x + 16 = 0, \quad z = 4.$

Equations (2) are also equations of the curve and define it as the curve of intersection of the parabolic cylinder $y^2 - 4x + 16 = 0$ and the plane $z = 4$.

For every set of values of (x, y, z) which satisfy both of equations (1) will evidently satisfy both of equations (2), and conversely.

If we take as axes in the plane $z = 4$ the lines $O'X'$ and $O'Y'$ in which the plane cuts the ZX-plane and the YZ-plane respectively, then the equation of the curve when *referred to these axes* is the first of equations (2), namely,

(3) $\qquad y^2 - 4x + 16 = 0.$

The locus of (3) is a parabola. The vertex, in the plane $z = 4$, is the point $(4, 0)$; also $p = 2$. *Ans.*

In plotting the locus of (3) in the plane $X'O'Y'$ the values of x and y must be laid off *parallel* to $O'X'$ and $O'Y'$ respectively, as in plotting oblique coördinates (Art. 7).

From the preceding example we may state the

Rule to *determine the nature of the curve in which a plane parallel to one of the coördinate planes cuts a given surface.*

Eliminate the variable occurring in the equation of the plane from the equations of the plane and surface. The result is the equation of the curve referred to the lines in which the given plane cuts the other two coördinate planes as axes. Discuss this curve by the methods of plane analytic geometry.

EXAMPLE

Discuss the locus of the equation

(4) $$y^2 + z^2 = 4x.$$

Solution. 1. The intercept on each axis is zero.

2. The traces are, respectively, the point circle $y^2 + z^2 = 0$ and the parabolas $z^2 = 4x$ and $y^2 = 4x$.

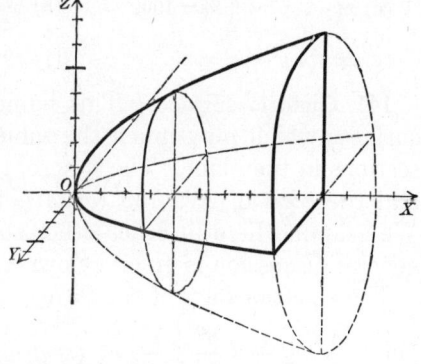

3. The surface is symmetric with respect to the XY-plane, the ZX-plane, and the x-axis.

4. Putting $x = k$ in the equation (4), we obtain the equation of the section in that plane, namely,

$$y^2 + z^2 = 4k.$$

This curve is a circle whose center is on the x-axis and whose radius is $2\sqrt{k}$ if $k > 0$, but there is no locus if $k < 0$. Hence the surface lies entirely to the right of the YZ-plane. If k increases from zero to infinity, the radius of the circle increases from zero to infinity while the plane $x = k$ recedes from the YZ-plane. In the figure the circles are plotted in the planes $x = 4$ and $x = 10$.

The intersection with a plane $z = k$ or $y = k'$, parallel to the XY- or the ZX-plane, is seen to be a parabola whose equation is

$$y^2 = 4x - k^2 \quad \text{or} \quad z^2 = 4x - k'^2.$$

These parabolas have the same value of p, namely, $p = 2$, and their vertices recede from the YZ- or the ZX-plane as k or k' increases numerically.

PROBLEMS

1. Plot carefully the curve of intersection of the given surface and given plane.

(a) $4x^2 + y^2 - 8z = 0$, $z = 2$.
(b) $x^2 + 3y^2 + 4z^2 = 45$, $z = 3$.
(c) $x^2 + 3y^2 + 4z^2 = 45$, $x = 3$.
(d) $x^2 + 3y^2 - 4z^2 = 9$, $z = 3$.
(e) $x^2 + 3y^2 - 4z^2 = 16$, $x = 2$.

2. Discuss the equation of each of the following surfaces. Plot the traces.

(a) $x^2 + 4y^2 + 9z^2 = 36$.
(b) $x^2 + 4y^2 = 8z$.
(c) $x^2 + y^2 + z^2 = 25$.
(d) $z^2 + 7xy = 0$.
(e) $x^2 - y^2 + z^2 = 25$.
(f) $x^2 - y^2 - 4z^2 = 8$.
(g) $x^2 + 9y^2 - 9z^2 = 0$.
(h) $xy - 4 = 0$.

3. Discuss and draw the locus of each of the following equations:

(a) $x^2 + 4y^2 = 8z$.
(b) $x^2 + 4z^2 = 8y$.
(c) $x^2 + 4y^2 + 9z^2 = 100$.
(d) $x^2 - 9y^2 = 10z$.
(e) $x^2 + 4y^2 - z^2 = 25$.
(f) $y^2 + z^2 - 4z + 8 = 0$.
(g) $x^2 + 4y^2 - 16x = 0$.
(h) $x^2 - y^2 - z^2 - 1 = 0$.
(i) $x^2 + y^2 - 2zx = 0$.
(j) $y^2 + z^2 - x - 4 = 0$.

141. Quadric surfaces. This name is given to a class of surfaces which play much the same rôle in space as conic sections in the plane. The sphere, the cylinder of Art. 138, and the cone of Art. 139 (*quadric cone*) are special cases. We examine here in order other surfaces in this class. A general discussion is given below.

The equations are of the form

(1) $$\pm \frac{x^2}{a^2} \pm \frac{y^2}{b^2} \pm \frac{z^2}{c^2} = 1 \ (central \ quadrics);$$

(2) $$\frac{x^2}{a^2} \pm \frac{y^2}{b^2} = 2cz \ (noncentral \ quadrics).$$

142. The ellipsoid $\dfrac{x^2}{a^2} + \dfrac{y^2}{b^2} + \dfrac{z^2}{c^2} = 1$. If all the signs in (1), Art. 141, are positive, the locus is called an *ellipsoid*. A discussion of its equation gives us the following properties:

1. The intercepts on the axes are, respectively,

$$x = \pm a, \quad y = \pm b, \quad z = \pm c.$$

SPECIAL SURFACES

The lines $AA' = 2\,a$, $BB' = 2\,b$, $CC' = 2\,c$ are called the **principal axes** of the ellipsoid (see figure below).

2. The traces on the principal planes are the ellipses $ABA'B'$, $BCB'C'$, and $ACA'C'$, whose equations are

$$\frac{x^2}{a^2} + \frac{y^2}{b^2} = 1, \quad \frac{y^2}{b^2} + \frac{z^2}{c^2} = 1, \quad \frac{x^2}{a^2} + \frac{z^2}{c^2} = 1.$$

3. The surface is symmetric with respect to each coördinate plane, each axis, and the origin. These planes of symmetry are called the **principal planes** of the ellipsoid.

4. The equation of the section in a plane parallel to the XY-plane, $z = k$, is

(1) $\quad \dfrac{x^2}{a^2} + \dfrac{y^2}{b^2} = 1 - \dfrac{k^2}{c^2}, \quad$ or $\quad \dfrac{x^2}{\dfrac{a^2}{c^2}(c^2 - k^2)} + \dfrac{y^2}{\dfrac{b^2}{c^2}(c^2 - k^2)} = 1.$

The locus of this equation is an ellipse. If k increases from 0 to c, or decreases from 0 to $-c$, the plane recedes from the XY-plane, and the axes of the ellipse decrease from $2\,a$ and $2\,b$, respectively, to 0, when the ellipse degenerates into a point. If $k > c$ or $k < -c$, there is no locus. Hence the ellipsoid lies entirely between the planes $z = \pm c$.

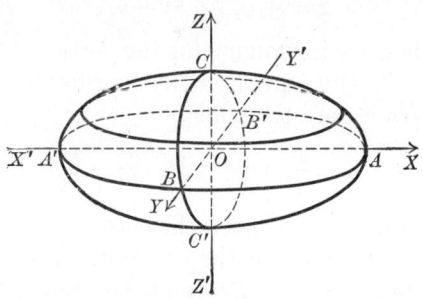

In like manner the sections parallel to the YZ-plane and the ZX-plane are ellipses whose axes decrease as the planes recede. Hence the ellipsoid lies entirely between the planes $x = \pm a$ and $y = \pm b$. The ellipsoid is therefore a closed surface. (See Plate I.)

If $a = b$, the section (1) is a circle for values of k such that $-c < k < c$, and hence the ellipsoid is now an "ellipsoid of revolution" whose axis is the z-axis. The surface is generated by revolving the trace on XZ about OZ. If $b = c$ or $c = a$, the surface is an ellipsoid of revolution whose axis is the x-axis or the y-axis.

If $a = b = c$, the ellipsoid is a sphere, for its equation may be written in the form $x^2 + y^2 + z^2 = a^2$.

143. The hyperboloid of one sheet $\dfrac{x^2}{a^2} + \dfrac{y^2}{b^2} - \dfrac{z^2}{c^2} = 1$. If two of the signs in (1), Art. 141, are positive and one is negative, the locus is called a *hyperboloid of one sheet*. Consider first the equation

(1) $\qquad \dfrac{x^2}{a^2} + \dfrac{y^2}{b^2} - \dfrac{z^2}{c^2} = 1.$

A discussion of this equation gives us the following properties:

1. The intercepts on the x-axis and the y-axis are, respectively,

$$x = \pm a, \quad y = \pm b,$$

but are imaginary for the z-axis.

2. The traces on the coördinate planes are the conics

$$\dfrac{x^2}{a^2} + \dfrac{y^2}{b^2} = 1, \quad \dfrac{y^2}{b^2} - \dfrac{z^2}{c^2} = 1, \quad \dfrac{x^2}{a^2} - \dfrac{z^2}{c^2} = 1,$$

of which the first is the ellipse whose axes are $AA' = 2a$ and $BB' = 2b$, and the others are the hyperbolas whose transverse axes are BB' and AA' respectively.

3. The surface is symmetric with respect to each coördinate plane, each axis, and the origin.

4. The equation of the section in a plane parallel to the XY-plane, $z = k$, is

(2) $\dfrac{x^2}{a^2} + \dfrac{y^2}{b^2} = 1 + \dfrac{k^2}{c^2},$ or $\dfrac{x^2}{\dfrac{a^2}{c^2}(c^2 + k^2)} + \dfrac{y^2}{\dfrac{b^2}{c^2}(c^2 + k^2)} = 1.$

PLATE I

Ellipsoid

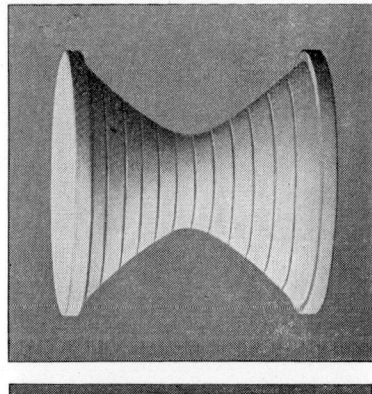
Hyperboloid of one sheet

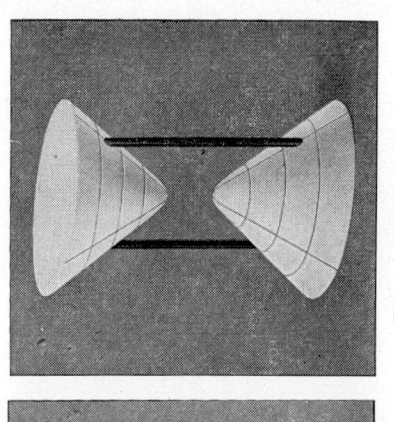
Hyperboloid of two sheets

CENTRAL QUADRICS

SPECIAL SURFACES

The locus of this equation is an ellipse. If k increases from 0 to ∞, or decreases from 0 to $-\infty$, the plane recedes from the XY-plane, and the axes of the ellipse increase indefinitely from $2a$ and $2b$ respectively. Hence the surface recedes indefinitely from the XY-plane and from the z-axis.

In like manner the sections formed by the planes $x = k'$ and $y = k''$ are seen to be hyperbolas. As k' and k'' increase numerically, the axes of the hyperbolas decrease, and when $k' = \pm a$ or $k'' = \pm b$, the hyperbolas degenerate into intersecting lines. As k' and k'' increase beyond this point, the directions of the transverse and conjugate axes are interchanged, and the lengths of these axes increase indefinitely. (See Plate I opposite page 292.)

The hyperboloid (1), which does not intersect OZ, is said to "lie along the z-axis."

The equations

(3) $$\frac{x^2}{a^2} - \frac{y^2}{b^2} + \frac{z^2}{c^2} = 1, \quad -\frac{x^2}{a^2} + \frac{y^2}{b^2} + \frac{z^2}{c^2} = 1,$$

are the equations of hyperboloids of one sheet which lie along the y-axis and the x-axis respectively.

If $a = b$, the hyperboloid (1) is a surface of revolution whose axis is the z-axis, because the section (2) becomes a circle. The hyperboloids (3) will be hyperboloids of revolution if $a = c$ and $b = c$ respectively.

144. The hyperboloid of two sheets $\dfrac{x_2}{a^2} - \dfrac{y^2}{b^2} - \dfrac{z^2}{c^2} = 1$. If only one of the signs in (1), Art. 141, is positive, the locus is called a *hyperboloid of two sheets*. Consider first the equation

(1) $$\frac{x^2}{a^2} - \frac{y^2}{b^2} - \frac{z^2}{c^2} = 1.$$

1. The intercepts on the x-axis are $x = \pm a$, but there are none on the y-axis and the z-axis.

2. The traces on the XY-plane and the XZ-plane are, respectively, the hyperbolas

$$\frac{x^2}{a^2} - \frac{y^2}{b^2} = 1, \quad \frac{x^2}{a^2} - \frac{z^2}{c^2} = 1,$$

which have the same transverse axis $AA' = 2a$, but there is no trace on the YZ-plane.

3. The surface is symmetric with respect to each coördinate plane, each axis, and the origin.

4. The equation of the section in a plane parallel to the YZ-plane, $x = k$, is

$$\frac{y^2}{b^2} + \frac{z^2}{c^2} = \frac{k^2}{a^2} - 1, \quad \text{or} \quad \frac{y^2}{\frac{b^2}{a^2}(k^2 - a^2)} + \frac{z^2}{\frac{c^2}{a^2}(k^2 - a^2)} = 1.$$

This equation has no locus if $-a < k < a$. If $k = \pm a$, the locus is a point ellipse, and as k increases from a to ∞, or decreases from $-a$ to $-\infty$, the locus is an ellipse whose axes increase indefinitely. Hence the surface consists of two sheets which recede indefinitely from the YZ-plane and from the x-axis.

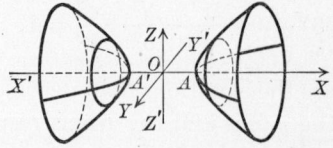

In like manner the sections formed by *all* planes parallel to the XY-plane and the ZX-plane are hyperbolas whose axes increase indefinitely as their planes recede from the coördinate planes. (See Plate I opposite page 292.)

The hyperboloid (1) is said to "lie along the x-axis."

The equations

(2) $\quad -\dfrac{x^2}{a^2} + \dfrac{y^2}{b^2} - \dfrac{z^2}{c^2} = 1, \quad -\dfrac{x^2}{a^2} - \dfrac{y^2}{b^2} + \dfrac{z^2}{c^2} = 1,$

are the equations of hyperboloids of two sheets which lie along the y-axis and the z-axis respectively.

If $b = c$, or $c = a$, or $a = b$, the hyperboloids (1) and (2) are hyperboloids of revolution.

SPECIAL SURFACES

PROBLEMS

1. Discuss, construct, and name the locus of each of the following equations:

(a) $x^2 + 4y^2 + 9z^2 = 36$.
(b) $x^2 + 4y^2 - 9z^2 = 36$.
(c) $x^2 - 4y^2 - 9z^2 = 36$.
(d) $4x^2 + 9y^2 - 9z^2 = 36$.
(e) $x^2 - y^2 - z^2 = 1$.
(f) $9x^2 - 4y^2 - z^2 = 36$.
(g) $9x^2 + y^2 - z^2 = 36$.
(h) $9x^2 - 16y^2 + 4z^2 = 64$.
(i) $x^2 - 4y^2 + 9z^2 + 36 = 0$.
(j) $4x^2 + 4y^2 + z^2 = 16$.
(k) $x^2 + y^2 - 9z^2 = 1$.
(l) $x^2 + 4y^2 - z^2 = 16$.
(m) $4x^2 + 16y^2 - z^2 = 64$.
(n) $x^2 - 8y^2 + 2z^2 = 16$.

2. Assuming that the equation of a central quadric surface is

$$Ax^2 + By^2 + Cz^2 + D = 0,$$

find its equation if it passes through the given points. Name the surface.

(a) $(2, -1, 1)$, $(-3, 0, 0)$, $(1, -1, -2)$. *Ans.* $x^2 + 4y^2 + z^2 = 9$.
(b) $(-1, 5, 4)$, $(-7, 1, -8)$, $(8, -2, 10)$.
(c) $(4, -2, -1)$, $(0, 1, -3)$, $(3, 5, 2)$.
(d) $(-1, -1, \sqrt{5})$, $(2\sqrt{5}, -2, 4)$, $(0, 0, -2)$.

Ans. $x^2 + y^2 - 2z^2 + 8 = 0$.

3. Find the equation of the locus of a point whose distance from the point $(1, 0, 0)$ is half its perpendicular distance from the plane $x = 4$. Discuss, name, and draw the locus.

Ans. $3x^2 + 4y^2 + 4z^2 - 12 = 0$.

4. Find the equation of the locus of a point if its distance from $(0, -4, 0)$ is twice its perpendicular distance from the plane $y + 1 = 0$. Discuss, construct, and name the surface.

5. Assuming the equation of Problem 2, find the equation of the quadric surface passing through $(2, 1, 3)$ and the curve whose equations are

(a) $z = 4, 3x^2 + y^2 - 9 = 0$; *Ans.* $21x^2 + 7y^2 + 4z^2 - 127 = 0$.
(b) $z = 4, x^2 + y^2 - 25 = 0$.

6. A point moves so that the sum of the squares of its distances from two intersecting perpendicular lines in space is constant. Prove that the locus is an ellipsoid of revolution.

145. The elliptic paraboloid $\dfrac{x^2}{a^2} + \dfrac{y^2}{b^2} = 2cz$. If the coefficient of y^2 in (2), Art. 141, is positive, the locus is called an *elliptic* *paraboloid*. A discussion of its equation gives us the following properties:

1. The intercepts are all zero.
2. The traces on the coördinate planes are, respectively, the conics

$$\frac{x^2}{a^2}+\frac{y^2}{b^2}=0, \quad \frac{x^2}{a^2}=2\,cz, \quad \frac{y^2}{b^2}=2\,cz,$$

of which the first is a point ellipse and the other two parabolas.

3. The surface is symmetric with respect to the YZ-plane, the ZX-plane, and the z-axis.

4. The equation of the section in a plane parallel to the XY-plane, $z = k$, is

$$\frac{x^2}{a^2}+\frac{y^2}{b^2}=2\,ck,$$

or $\quad\dfrac{x^2}{2\,a^2ck}+\dfrac{y^2}{2\,b^2ck}=1.$

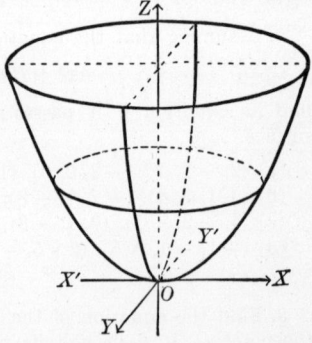

The curve is an ellipse if c and k have the same sign, but there is no locus if c and k have opposite signs. Hence, if c is positive, the surface lies entirely above the XY-plane. If k increases from 0 to ∞, the plane recedes from the XY-plane and the axes of the ellipse increase indefinitely. Hence the surface recedes indefinitely from the XY-plane and from the z-axis.

In like manner the sections parallel to the YZ-plane and the ZX-plane are parabolas whose vertices recede from the XY-plane as their planes recede from the coördinate planes. (See Plate II opposite page 298.)

The paraboloid is said to "lie along the z-axis."

The loci of the equations

(1) $\qquad \dfrac{y^2}{b^2}+\dfrac{z^2}{c^2}=2\,ax, \quad \dfrac{x^2}{a^2}+\dfrac{z^2}{c^2}=2\,by,$

SPECIAL SURFACES

are elliptic paraboloids which lie along the x-axis and the y-axis respectively.

If $a = b$, the first surface considered is a paraboloid of revolution whose axis is the z-axis; and if $b = c$ and $a = c$, the paraboloids (1) are surfaces of revolution whose axes are, respectively, the x-axis and the y-axis.

An elliptic paraboloid lies along the axis corresponding to the term of the first degree in its equation, and in the positive or negative direction of the axis according as that term is positive or negative.

146. The hyperbolic paraboloid $\dfrac{x^2}{a^2} - \dfrac{y^2}{b^2} = 2\,cz$. If the coefficient of y^2 in (2), Art. 141, is negative, the locus is called a *hyperbolic paraboloid*.

1. The intercepts are all zero.

2. The traces on the coördinate planes are, respectively, the conics
$$\frac{x^2}{a^2} - \frac{y^2}{b^2} = 0, \quad \frac{x^2}{a^2} = 2\,cz, \quad -\frac{y^2}{b^2} = 2\,cz,$$
of which the first is a pair of intersecting lines and the other two are parabolas.

3. The surface is symmetric with respect to the YZ-plane, the ZX-plane, and the z-axis.

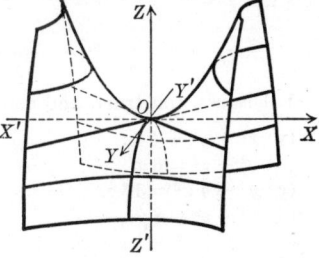

4. The equation of the section in a plane parallel to the XY-plane, $z = k$, is
$$\frac{x^2}{a^2} - \frac{y^2}{b^2} = 2\,ck,$$
or $\quad \dfrac{x^2}{2\,a^2 ck} - \dfrac{y^2}{2\,b^2 ck} = 1.$

The locus is a hyperbola. If c is positive, the transverse axis of the hyperbola is parallel to the x-axis or y-axis according as k is positive or negative. If k increases from 0 to ∞, or decreases from 0 to $-\infty$, the plane recedes from the XY-plane, and the axes of the hyperbolas increase indefinitely. Hence the surface recedes indefinitely from the XY-plane and the z-axis. The surface has approximately the shape of a saddle.

In like manner the sections parallel to the other coördinate planes are parabolas whose vertices recede from the XY-plane as their planes recede from the coördinate planes. (See Plate II on the opposite page.)

The surface is said to "lie along the z-axis."

The loci of the equations

$$\frac{x^2}{a^2} - \frac{z^2}{c^2} = 2\,by, \quad \frac{y^2}{b^2} - \frac{z^2}{c^2} = 2\,ax,$$

are hyperbolic paraboloids lying along the y-axis and the x-axis respectively. A hyperbolic paraboloid lies along the axis which corresponds to the first-degree term in its equation.

A plane of symmetry of a quadric is called a **principal plane**. Each paraboloid has two principal planes; each central quadric, three. Axes of symmetry are called **principal axes**. A paraboloid possesses one such axis; a central quadric, three. The existence of a center of symmetry for a *central* quadric explains the designation "central quadric."

PROBLEMS

1. Discuss, construct, and name the following surfaces:

(a) $x^2 + y^2 = 4\,z$.
(b) $y^2 - z^2 = 6\,x$.
(c) $y^2 - 4\,x^2 = 16\,z$.
(d) $x^2 + z^2 = 8\,x$.
(e) $3\,x^2 + z^2 - 4\,y = 0$.
(f) $y^2 - 2\,x^2 - 4\,z = 0$.
(g) $9\,y^2 - 4\,z^2 = 288\,x$.
(h) $x^2 - y^2 - z = 0$.
(i) $2\,y^2 + 3\,z^2 + 2\,x = 0$.
(j) $y^2 - 2\,z^2 - 4\,x = 0$.
(k) $\dfrac{x^2}{9} + \dfrac{y^2}{4} = 6\,z$.
(l) $\dfrac{x^2}{9} - \dfrac{z^2}{4} = 2\,y$.

2. Taking the equation of a noncentral quadric surface in the form $Ax^2 + By^2 + Cz = 0$, find its equation if the surface passes through the points given. Name the surface.

PLATE II

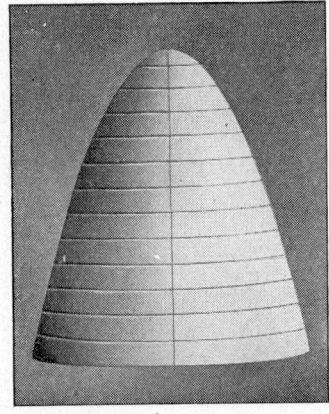

Elliptic Paraboloid   Hyperbolic Paraboloid

NONCENTRAL QUADRICS

Hyperboloid of one sheet   Hyperbolic Paraboloid

RULED QUADRICS

SPECIAL SURFACES

(a) $(1, 0, 1)$, $(0, 2, 1)$.   Ans. $4x^2 + y^2 - 4z = 0$.
(b) $(1, 0, 1)$, $(0, 2, -1)$.
(c) $(1, 2, 1)$, $(2, 1, 1)$.

3. Using the formula of Problem 2, find the equation of the paraboloid passing through the curve whose equations are $z = 4$, $2x^2 + y^2 = 4$.

PROBLEMS FOR INDIVIDUAL STUDY OR ASSIGNMENT

1. Prove that the parabolas obtained by cutting (1) an elliptic paraboloid or (2) a hyperbolic paraboloid by planes parallel to one of the principal planes are congruent.

2. The equation $\dfrac{x^2}{a^2 - k} + \dfrac{y^2}{b^2 - k} + \dfrac{z^2}{c^2 - k} = 1$, $a > b > c$, in which k is a parameter, represents a *system* of central quadrics. What values of k are excluded? For what values of k is the quadric an ellipsoid? a hyperboloid of one sheet? a hyperboloid of two sheets?

3. Show that the traces of the quadrics in Problem 2 on each coordinate plane are confocal conics (see example, Art. 55).

4. The equation $\dfrac{x^2}{a^2 - k} + \dfrac{y^2}{b^2 - k} = 2cz$, in which k is a parameter, represents a *system* of noncentral quadrics. For what values of k is the quadric an elliptic paraboloid? a hyperbolic paraboloid?

5. How may a paraboloid be generated by moving a parabola? (See Problem 1.)

6. In Problem 2, show that the surface, an ellipsoid, becomes more and more flat as k increases and approaches c^2. Clear the equation of fractions and show that the limiting surface when $k = c^2$ is the interior of an ellipse in the XY-plane. What is the equation of this ellipse?

CHAPTER XVI

SUPPLEMENTARY TOPICS IN THE GEOMETRY OF SPACE

In this chapter are assembled important topics, some or all of which may well be included if time permits.

147. Surfaces of revolution. The surface generated by revolving a curve about a line lying in its plane is called a *surface of revolution*.

Familiar examples are afforded by the sphere, the right circular cylinder, and the right circular cone.

EXAMPLE

Find the equation of the surface of revolution generated by revolving the ellipse $x^2 + 4y^2 - 12x = 0$, $z = 0$, about the x-axis.

Solution. Let $P(x, y, z)$ be any point on the surface. Pass a plane through P and OX which cuts the surface along the ellipse in one position. In this plane draw OY' perpendicular to OX. Referred to OX and OY' as axes, the equation of the ellipse is evidently

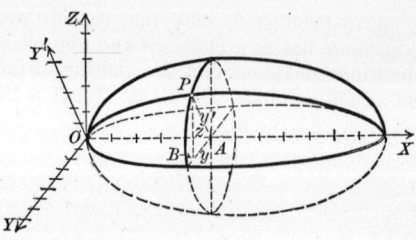

(1) $$x^2 + 4y'^2 - 12x = 0.$$

But from the right $\triangle PAB$ we get
$$y'^2 = y^2 + z^2.$$

Substituting in (1),

(2) $$x^2 + 4y^2 + 4z^2 - 12x = 0. \ Ans.$$

This equation expresses the relation which any point on the surface must satisfy, and it is therefore the equation of the surface.

SUPPLEMENTARY TOPICS

The method of the solution enables us to state the

Rule *to find the equation of the surface generated by revolving a curve in one of the coördinate planes about one of the axes in that plane.*

Substitute in the equation of the curve the square root of the sum of the squares of the two variables not measured along the axis of revolution for that one of these two variables which occurs in the equation of the curve.

The line about which the given curve is revolved is called the **axis** of the surface. Sections of the surface by planes perpendicular to its axis are obviously circles whose centers lie on the axis.

If the sections of a surface by all planes perpendicular to one of the coördinate axes are circles whose centers lie on that axis, then the surface is evidently a surface of revolution whose axis is this coördinate axis. This enables us to determine whether or not a given surface is a surface of revolution whose axis is one of the coördinate axes.

PROBLEMS

1. Find the equation of the surface of revolution generated by revolving the given curve lying in a coördinate plane about the given axis, and name and construct the surface.

(a) $4x - y = 2$, x-axis.
(b) $x^2 + 4z^2 = 16$, z-axis. *Ans.* $x^2 + y^2 + 4z^2 = 16$.
(c) $9x^2 + 4y^2 = 36$, y-axis.
(d) $9x^2 - 4y^2 = 36$, x-axis; y-axis.
(e) $y^2 = 8x$, x-axis. *Ans.* $y^2 + z^2 = 8x$.
(f) $2x^2 - 4z^2 = 1$, its transverse axis; its conjugate axis.
(g) $x^2 = y^3$, y-axis.
(h) $2x^2 = 4 - y$, y-axis.
(i) $xz = 8$, z-axis.
(j) $y = \sin x$, x-axis.
(k) $x^2 + 4y^2 - 4x = 0$, x-axis; y-axis; $x = 2$.
(l) $xy = a$ about its asymptotes.
  Ans. $y^2(x^2 + z^2) = a^2$; $x^2(y^2 + z^2) = a^2$.

2. Find the equation of the surface of revolution generated by revolving the given curve about the axis indicated. Name and construct the surface.

(a) $y^2 = 2\,pz$, z-axis. *Ans.* A paraboloid of revolution, $x^2 + y^2 = 2\,pz$.

(b) $\dfrac{x^2}{a^2} + \dfrac{y^2}{b^2} = 1$, x-axis. \hspace{1em} *Ans.* $\dfrac{x^2}{a^2} + \dfrac{y^2}{b^2} + \dfrac{z^2}{b^2} = 1$.

(c) $\dfrac{x^2}{a^2} - \dfrac{y^2}{b^2} = 1$, y-axis.

(d) $\dfrac{x^2}{a^2} - \dfrac{y^2}{b^2} = 1$, x-axis.

3. Find the equation of and construct the surface formed by revolving the curve $z = e^x$ about (1) the x-axis; (2) the z-axis.

4. Verify analytically that a sphere is generated by revolving a circle about a diameter.

5. Find the equation of the surface of revolution generated by revolving the circle $x^2 + y^2 - 2\,hx + h^2 - r^2 = 0$ about the y-axis. Discuss the surface when $h > r$, $h = r$, and $h < r$.

Ans. $(x^2 + y^2 + z^2 + h^2 - r^2)^2 = 4\,h^2(x^2 + z^2)$.

When $h > r$ the surface is called an **anchor ring** or **torus**.

6. Find the equations of the cylinders of revolution whose axes are the coördinate axes and whose radii equal r.

7. Find the equations of the cones of revolution whose axes are the coördinate axes and whose elements make an angle of ϕ with the axis of revolution.

Ans. $y^2 + z^2 = x^2 \tan^2\phi$; $z^2 + x^2 = y^2 \tan^2\phi$; $x^2 + y^2 = z^2 \tan^2\phi$.

8. Show that the following loci are surfaces of revolution:

(a) $y^2 + z^2 = 4\,x$.
(b) $x^2 - 4\,y^2 + z^2 = 0$.
(c) $4\,x^2 + 4\,y^2 - z^2 = 16$.
(d) $x^2 - 4\,y^2 + z^2 - 3\,y = 0$.
(e) $xz^2 + xy^2 = 3$.
(f) $(x^2 + z^2)y = 4\,a^2(2\,a - y)$.
(g) $x^2 + y^2 + zx^2 + zy^2 - z + 3 = 0$.
(h) $x^2 + y^2 + z^3 - 2\,y + 1 = 0$.
(i) $y^2 + z^2 + xy^2 + xz^2 - 8 = 0$.

9. A point moves so that its perpendicular distance from a fixed plane is in a constant ratio to its distance from a fixed point. Show that the locus is a surface of revolution.

10. A point moves so that its perpendicular distance from a fixed line is in a constant ratio to its distance from a fixed point on that line. Prove analytically that the locus is a cone of revolution. What values of the ratio are excluded?

SUPPLEMENTARY TOPICS

148. Ruled surfaces. A surface generated by a moving straight line is called a *ruled surface*. If the equations of a straight line involve an arbitrary constant, then they represent a system of lines which form a ruled surface. If we eliminate the parameter from the equations of the line, the result will be the equation of the ruled surface.

For if (x_1, y_1, z_1) satisfy the given equations for some value of the parameter, they will satisfy the equation obtained by eliminating the parameter; that is, the coördinates of every point on every line of the system satisfy that equation.

Cylinders and cones are the simplest ruled surfaces.

EXAMPLES

1. Find the equation of the surface generated by the system of lines whose equations are
$$x + y = kz, \quad x - y = \frac{1}{k}z.$$

Solution. We may eliminate k from these equations of the line by multiplying them. This gives

(1) $$x^2 - y^2 = z^2.$$

This is the equation of a cone (Art. 139) whose vertex is the origin. As the sections made by the planes $x = k$ are circles, it is a cone of revolution whose axis is the x-axis.

We may verify that the given lines lie on the surface (1) for all values of k as follows:

Solving the equations of the lines for x and y in terms of z, we get
$$x = \frac{1}{2}\left(k + \frac{1}{k}\right)z, \quad y = \frac{1}{2}\left(k - \frac{1}{k}\right)z.$$

Substituting in (1),
$$\frac{1}{4}\left(k + \frac{1}{k}\right)^2 z^2 - \frac{1}{4}\left(k - \frac{1}{k}\right)^2 z^2 = z^2,$$

This equation is true for all values of k and z, as is seen by removing the parentheses. Hence every point on any line of the system lies on (1), since its coördinates satisfy (1).

2. Determine the nature of the surface $z^3 - 3zx + 8y = 0$.

Solution. The intersection of the surface with the plane $z = k$ is the straight line
$$k^3 - 3kx + 8y = 0, \quad z = k.$$

Hence the surface is the ruled surface generated by this line as k varies. To construct the surface consider the intersections with the planes $x = 0$ and $x = 8$. Their equations are, respectively,

$$x = 0,$$
$$8y + z^3 = 0,$$
and
$$x = 8,$$
$$8y - 24z + z^3 = 0.$$

Joining the points on these curves which have the same value of z gives the lines generating the surface.

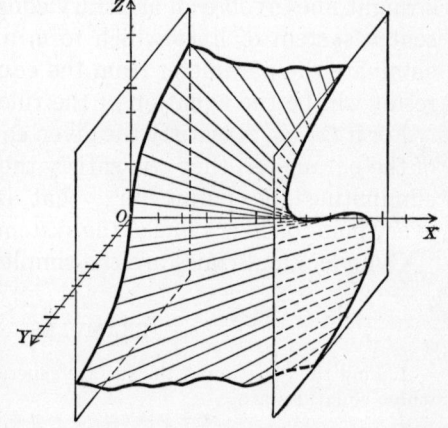

The method used in Example 2 is adapted to the determination and construction of ruled surfaces. An examination of the equation of such a surface will suggest a system of planes whose intersections with the surface are a system of lines, as illustrated in Problem 1 on page 305.

149. Ruled quadrics. Rectilinear generators. The equation of the hyperboloid of one sheet (Art. 143) may be written in the form

(1) $$\frac{x^2}{a^2} - \frac{z^2}{c^2} = 1 - \frac{y^2}{b^2}.$$

As this equation is the result of eliminating k from the equations of the system of lines

$$\frac{x}{a} + \frac{z}{c} = k\left(1 + \frac{y}{b}\right), \quad \frac{x}{a} - \frac{z}{c} = \frac{1}{k}\left(1 - \frac{y}{b}\right),$$

the hyperboloid is a ruled surface. Equation (1) is also the result of eliminating k from the equations of the system of lines

$$\frac{x}{a} + \frac{z}{c} = k\left(1 - \frac{y}{b}\right), \quad \frac{x}{a} - \frac{z}{c} = \frac{1}{k}\left(1 + \frac{y}{b}\right),$$

SUPPLEMENTARY TOPICS

and the hyperboloid may therefore be regarded in two ways as a ruled surface. (See Plate II, opposite page 298.)

In like manner the hyperbolic paraboloid (Art. 146) contains the two systems of lines

$$\frac{x}{a} + \frac{y}{b} = 2\,ck, \quad \frac{x}{a} - \frac{y}{b} = \frac{z}{k},$$

and
$$\frac{x}{a} + \frac{y}{b} = kz, \quad \frac{x}{a} - \frac{y}{b} = \frac{2\,c}{k}.$$

These lines are called the *rectilinear generators* of these surfaces. Hence the

Theorem. *The hyperboloid of one sheet and the hyperbolic paraboloid have two systems of rectilinear generators; that is, they may be regarded in two ways as ruled surfaces.*

The two systems of generators are shown in Plate II.

PROBLEMS

1. Show that the following are ruled surfaces with rectilinear generators parallel to one of the coördinate planes. Find equations for the rectilinear generators, and construct the surfaces by means of these equations.

   (a) $xy = z$.
   (b) $yz = x + z^2$.
   (c) $y^2 = x + yz$.
   (d) $x^2y + xz = y$.
   (e) $xy = y^2 - 3\,z$.
   (f) $x^2y - x^2 + z = 0$.
   (g) $xz - z^2 + y = 0$.
   (h) $x^2 = y^2(z + 1)$.

2. Find two systems of rectilinear generators for each of the following quadric surfaces. Draw the surfaces, using the equations of one system of generators.

   (a) $x^2 - z^2 - y^2 + 1 = 0$.
   (b) $x^2 + yz - 1 = 0$.
   (c) $9\,x^2 + 4\,y^2 - 36\,z^2 = 36$.
   (d) $y^2 - 4\,z^2 + 2\,x = 0$.
   (e) $x^2 - 4\,y^2 = 4\,z$.
   (f) $x^2 + y^2 - yz - 1 = 0$.

3. Find the equations of the ruled surfaces whose generators are the following. Construct the surfaces.

   (a) $x + 2\,z + k(1 - y) = 0$, $k(x - 2\,z) + 1 + y = 0$.
                                                   Ans. $x^2 + y^2 - 4\,z^2 = 1$.
   (b) $2\,x + y - 3\,k = 0$, $k(2\,x - y) - z = 0$.
   (c) $x + 2\,ky + 4\,z = 4\,k$, $kx - 2\,y - 4\,kz = 4$.
   (d) $5 - x - ky = 0$, $k(5 + x) - y = 0$.
   (e) $y - 4\,k = 0$, $ky - x = 0$.
   (f) $3\,x - 4\,y = kz$, $k(3\,x + 4\,y) = z$.

For individual study or assignment

4. Show that every rectilinear generator of the hyperbolic paraboloid $\frac{x^2}{a^2} - \frac{y^2}{b^2} = 2\,cz$ is parallel to one of the planes $\frac{x}{a} \pm \frac{y}{b} = 0$.

5. Prove that the projections of the rectilinear generators of (1) the hyperboloid of one sheet, (2) the hyperbolic paraboloid, on a principal plane are tangent to the traces of the surface on that plane.

6. A plane passed through the center and a generator of a hyperboloid of one sheet intersects the surface in a second generator which is parallel to the first.

7. Show that two rectilinear generators of (1) a hyperbolic paraboloid and (2) a hyperboloid of one sheet pass through each point of the surface.

8. If a plane passes through a rectilinear generator of a quadric, show that it will also pass through a second generator, and that these generators do not belong to the same system.

9. The equation of the hyperboloid of one sheet may be written in the form $\frac{y^2}{b^2} - \frac{z^2}{c^2} = 1 - \frac{x^2}{a^2}$. By treating this equation as in Art. 149, we obtain the equations of two systems of lines on the surface. Show that these systems of lines are identical with those already obtained.

150. Cylinders with elements oblique to the axes. The student should not infer from the statement of Art. 138 that the equations of all cylinders lack one variable. In case the elements are not parallel to an axis of coördinates, all three variables will appear in the equation. This is illustrated by the following

EXAMPLE

Determine the nature of the locus of
$$x^2 + 2\,xz + z^2 = 1 - y^2.$$

Solution. The surface is obviously a ruled surface with rectilinear generators
$$y = k, \quad x + z = \pm\sqrt{1 - k^2}.$$

These equations define a system of parallel lines, for the direction numbers are $-1, 0, 1$, and are independent of k. That is, the lines are parallel to the line joining the point $(-1, 0, 1)$ to the origin. We conclude, then, that the surface is **a cylinder**. *Ans.*

To construct the surface, draw one of its traces and pass lines through points on it having the above direction. The trace in the YZ-plane is the circle $y^2 + z^2 = 1$; in the XY-plane, the circle $x^2 + y^2 = 1$.

Either of these circles may be used as directrix.

It is evident that in order to prove that a surface is cylindrical it is only necessary to show that it is a ruled surface whose generators are parallel lines.

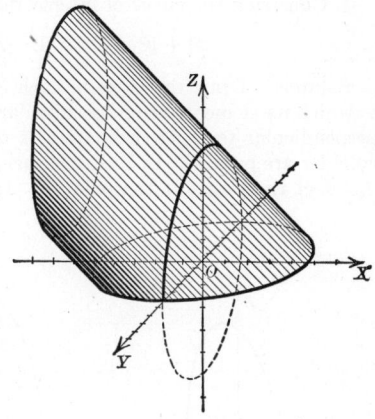

151. The projecting cylinders of a curve. The cylinders whose elements intersect a given curve and are parallel to one of the coördinate axes are called *projecting cylinders* of the curve. The equations may be found by eliminating in turn each of the variables x, y, and z from the equations of the curve. For if we eliminate z, for example, the result, by Art. 138, is the equation of a cylinder with elements parallel to the z-axis. Also, this cylinder passes through the curve, since values of x, y, and z which satisfy the two equations of the curve satisfy an equation obtained from them by eliminating one variable.

In general, the equations of a curve may be replaced by any two independent equations to which they are equivalent, that is, by two independent equations which are derived by combining the given equations. This amounts to stating that a curve is defined by the simultaneous equations of any two surfaces passing through it.

The equations of two of the projecting cylinders may conveniently be used as the equations of the curve. Hence the problem of constructing the original curve reduces to that of constructing the curve of intersection of two cylinders whose elements are parallel to the coördinate axes. The method is illustrated in the following examples.

EXAMPLES

1. Construct the curve of intersection of the two cylinders

$$x^2 + y^2 - 2y = 0, \quad y^2 + z^2 - 4 = 0.$$

Solution. Draw the trace of each cylinder on the coördinate plane to which its elements are perpendicular (Fig. 1). Then consider a plane perpendicular to the coördinate axis to which the elements of neither cylinder are parallel. In this case such a plane is $y = k$. Let this plane intersect the y-axis at the point K. It will intersect the traces at the

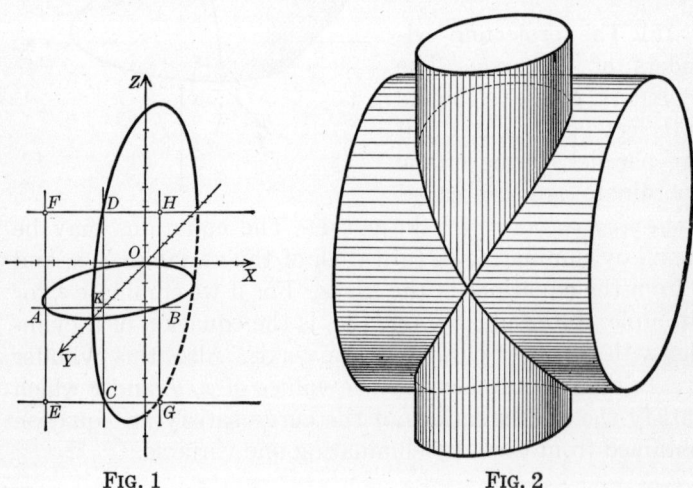

FIG. 1   FIG. 2

points A, B, C, and D. Through each of these points will pass an element of the corresponding cylinder, all four elements lying in this plane. The points of intersection E, F, G, and H of these elements are points on the curve of intersection of the two cylinders. By taking several positions of the plane $y = k$, we obtain a sufficient number of points to construct the entire curve as shown in Fig. 2.

2. Find the equations of the projecting cylinders of the curve whose equations are

$$2y^2 + z^2 + 4x = 4z, \quad y^2 + 3z^2 - 8x = 12z,$$

and construct the curve. (See also the example on page 312 for a second solution).

Solution. Eliminating x, y, and z in turn, we obtain the equations of the projecting cylinders

$$y^2 + z^2 = 4z, \quad z^2 - 4x = 4z, \quad y^2 + 4x = 0.$$

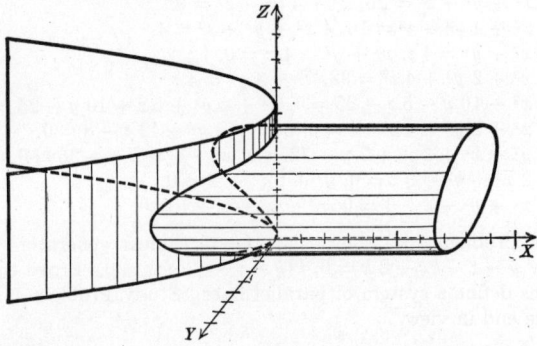

The figure shows the first and third of these cylinders, intersecting in the original curve, constructed by the method explained in the previous example.

It is usually wise to deduce the equations of all three of the projecting cylinders, for it may be that two of them are distinguished for simplicity and hence are most convenient to construct.

For a straight line the "projecting cylinders" are the projecting planes.

PROBLEMS

1. Prove that the following surfaces are cylinders. Discuss the equations and construct the surfaces.

(a) $x - y^2 + z = 0$.
(b) $xz + yz - 1 = 0$.
(c) $y^2 - 2x - 3z = 0$.
(d) $y^2 - 4(x + z) + 8 = 0$.
(e) $x^2 + 2xy + y^2 = 4z$.
(f) $y^2 - 2yz + z^2 = 4 - x^2$.
(g) $x^2 - 4xy + 4y^2 = z - 1$.
(h) $x^2 + 9y^2 + 4z^2 - 12yz = 4$.

2. Show that the following surfaces are cylinders. Construct the surfaces.

(a) $(x + z)(y + z) = 4$.
(b) $(x + z)^2 = y + z$.
(c) $(x + y)^2 + (x - z)^2 = a^2$.
(d) $(y + z - a)^2 + (x - z)^2 = a^2$.

3. Construct the curve of intersection of each of the following pairs of surfaces:

(a) $x^2 + y^2 = 36$, $y - z = 0$.
(b) $x^2 + y^2 - 4x = 0$, $x^2 + z^2 - 4 = 0$.
(c) $x^2 + 4z^2 - 8z = 0$, $x + y - 1 = 0$.
(d) $y^2 - 4z = 0$, $x^2 - z - 4 = 0$.

4. Find the equations of the projecting cylinders of the following curves and construct the curve as the intersection of two of these cylinders:

(a) $x^2 + y^2 + z^2 = 25$, $x^2 + 4\,y^2 - z^2 = 0$.
(b) $x^2 + 4\,y^2 - z^2 = 16$, $4\,x^2 + y^2 + z^2 = 4$.
(c) $x^2 + y^2 = 4\,z$, $x^2 + y^2 - 4\,x = 0$.
(d) $x^2 + 2\,y^2 + 4\,z^2 = 32$, $x^2 + 4\,y^2 = 4\,z$.
(e) $x^2 - 10\,y - 5\,z - 25 = 0$, $x^2 + 2\,y^2 + 5\,z + 10\,y - 25 = 0$.
(f) $x^2 + 2\,y^2 + 4\,z - 4 = 0$, $2\,x^2 + 5\,y^2 + 12\,z - 8 = 0$.
(g) $y^2 - x^2 + 2\,z^2 + 7\,y - 72 = 0$, $x^2 - z^2 - 7\,y + 36 = 0$.
(h) $2\,x^2 + y^2 - 9\,z = 0$, $y^2 + 9\,z - 72 = 0$.
(i) $x^2 + y^2 - z - 1 = 0$, $x^2 - y^2 - z + 1 = 0$.

5. In Problem 1 (f) show that the rectilinear generators are also given by $y - z - kx - 2\,k = 0$, $k(y - z) - 2 + x = 0$. Prove that these equations define a system of parallel lines. Study Problem 1 (h) with the same end in view.

For individual study or assignment

6. Show that the planes of the two systems $4\,x \pm 12\,z = k$ intersect the ellipsoid $9\,x^2 + 25\,y^2 + 169\,z^2 = 100$ in circles.

7. Show that the plane $3\,x + y = 10$ is tangent to the cylinder $x^2 + y^2 - 10 = 0$. Write the equations of the element along which the plane touches the cylinder.

8. Construct the following surfaces and shade that part of the first intercepted by the second:

(a) $x^2 + 4\,y^2 + 9\,z^2 = 36$, $x^2 + y^2 + z^2 = 16$.
(b) $x^2 + y^2 + z^2 = 64$, $x^2 + y^2 - 8\,x = 0$.
(c) $4\,x^2 + y^2 - 4\,z = 0$, $x^2 + 4\,y^2 - z^2 = 0$.

9. Construct and describe the solids bounded by the surfaces

(a) $x^2 + y^2 = a^2$, $z = mx$, $z = 0$;
(b) $x^2 + y^2 = az$, $x^2 + y^2 = 2\,ax$, $z = 0$.

10. A point moves so that its distance from a fixed point is always equal to its distance from a fixed line. Prove that the locus is a parabolic cylinder.

11. A point moves so that the difference between the squares of its distances from two intersecting perpendicular lines is constant. Prove that the locus is a hyperbolic cylinder.

12. A point moves so that the sum of its distances from two planes is equal to the square of its distance from a third plane. The three planes are mutually perpendicular. Prove that the locus is a cylinder.

Solution. Choose the axes of coördinates so that the equation of the cylinder is
(5) $$x^2 + y^2 = a^2,$$
as in the figure.

Let P_0 on OX be one position of the moving point, and P any other position. Then, by definition, the distance NP ($=z$) varies as the angle XON ($=\theta$); that is, $z = b\theta$, where b is a constant. Furthermore, from the figure,

$$x = OM = ON \cos \theta = a \cos \theta,$$
$$y = MN = ON \sin \theta = a \sin \theta.$$

Hence the equations of the helix are
(6) $x = a \cos \theta, \quad y = a \sin \theta, \quad z = b\theta,$
where θ is a parameter. *Ans.*

Eliminating θ from the first two of equations (6), we obtain (5), as we should.

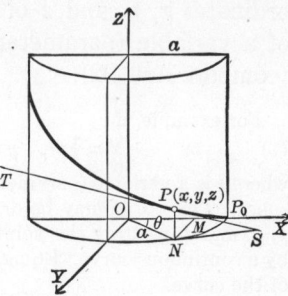

Given the equations of the projecting cylinders, to find parametric equations for the curve. It was shown in Art. 94 that an indefinite number of parametric equations could be obtained for the same plane curve. The same statement holds for space curves, as illustrated in the following

EXAMPLE

Find parametric equations for the curve
$$2y^2 + z^2 + 4x = 4z, \quad y^2 + 3z^2 - 8x = 12z.$$

Solution. The projecting cylinders are (see Example 2, Art. 151),
(7) $\quad y^2 + z^2 = 4z, \quad z^2 - 4x = 4z, \quad y^2 + 4x = 0.$

If we assume $y = 2t$, then the last equation will give $x = -t^2$. From either of the other two cylinders we find
$$z = 2 \pm 2\sqrt{1 - t^2}.$$

Hence the given curve is the locus of
(8) $\qquad x = -t^2, \quad y = 2t, \quad z = 2 \pm 2\sqrt{1 - t^2}.$ *Ans.*

The curve may now be drawn from these equations.

Other parametric equations result when we set one of the coördinates in (7) equal to some other function of a parameter. The aim is, of course, to find *simple* parametric equations. The method adopted must depend upon the given problem.

SUPPLEMENTARY TOPICS

13. A point moves so that the sum of its distances from two planes [is] equal to the square root of its distance from a third plane. Prove t[hat] the locus is a parabolic cylinder when the three planes are mutua[lly] perpendicular.

152. Parametric equations of curves in space. If the c[o-]ordinates x, y, and z of a point P in space are function[s] of a variable (parameter), then the locus of P is a curv[e] (compare Art. 92).

For example, if
$$(1) \qquad x = \tfrac{1}{4} t^2, \quad y = 1 - 2t, \quad z = 3 t^3 + 2,$$
where t is a variable (parameter), then the locus of (x, y, z) is a curve in space. This curve may be drawn by assuming values for t, computing x, y, and z, plotting the points, and then joining these points in order by a continuous curve. Equations (1) are called the *parametric equations* of the curve.

The equations of the projecting cylinders of the curve, the locus of (1), result when the parameter t is eliminated from each pair of the equations. Thus, taking the first two,
$$(2) \qquad x = \tfrac{1}{4} t^2, \quad y = 1 - 2t,$$
we find, from the second, $t = \tfrac{1}{2}(1 - y)$ and, substituting in the first,
$$(3) \qquad 4x = \tfrac{1}{4}(1-y)^2, \quad \text{or} \quad (y-1)^2 - 16x = 0,$$
and the locus lies on this parabolic cylinder.

Similarly, eliminating t from the first and third equations of (1),
$$x = \tfrac{1}{4} t^2, \quad z = 3 t^3 + 2,$$
we obtain the cubic cylinder
$$(4) \qquad (z-2)^2 = 576 x^3.$$

Hence the curve (1) is the curve of intersection of the cylinders (3) and (4).

In some cases it is convenient to find the equations of a curve in space by using a parameter.

EXAMPLE

Equations of the *helix*. A point moves on a right circular cylinder in such a manner that the distance it moves parallel to the axis varies directly as the angle it turns through around the axis. Find the equations of the locus.

SUPPLEMENTARY TOPICS

PROBLEMS

1. Find simple parametric equations for the curve of intersection of each pair of the surfaces given. Plot the curve from the parametric equations.

(a) $y^2 - 4z = 0$, $4x + z^2 = 0$. Ans. $x = -\frac{1}{4} t^4$, $y = 2t$, $z = t^2$.
(b) $x^2 - 9z + 36 = 0$, $x^2 + y^2 - 36 = 0$.
(c) $x^2 + y^2 - 25 = 0$, $3x - z^2 = 0$.
(d) $x^2 + y^2 - 2y = 0$, $y^2 + z^2 - 4 = 0$.
(e) $x^2 + y^2 - 25 = 0$, $x^2 + z^2 - 25 = 0$.
(f) $2y^2 + z^2 + 4x - 4z = 0$, $y^2 + 3z^2 - 8x - 12z = 0$.

2. Check each curve constructed in Problems 3 and 4 of Art. 151 by finding parametric equations and plotting the locus from them.

CHAPTER XVII

TRANSFORMATION OF COÖRDINATES. DIFFERENT SYSTEMS OF COÖRDINATES

153. Translation of the axes. Formulas applicable to space, entirely analogous to those established in Chapter VII for the plane, are derived as explained below.

Theorem. *The equations for translating the axes to a new origin $O'(h, k, l)$ are*

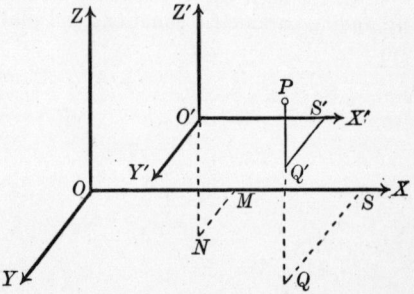

(I) $\begin{cases} x = x' + h, \\ y = y' + k, \\ z = z' + l. \end{cases}$

Proof. Let the coördinates of any point before and after the translation of the axes be (x, y, z) and (x', y', z') respectively. In the figure, $OM = h$, $OS = x$, $O'S' = x'$. But $OS = OM + MS = OM + O'S'$. Hence $x = x' + h$. The proof is similar for the other formulas. Q.E.D.

154. Rotation of the axes. Simple formulas for rotation arise if two of the axes are rotated about the third. For example, when the axes OX and OY are turned through an angle θ about the z-axis, the z-coördinate of any point P does not change, and the new x- and y-coördinates are given by formulas (II), Art. 61. Hence the

Theorem. *The equations for rotating the axes about the z-axis through an angle θ are*

(II) $x = x' \cos\theta - y' \sin\theta, \quad y = x' \sin\theta + y' \cos\theta, \quad z = z'.$

TRANSFORMATION OF COÖRDINATES

Similar formulas result when the axes are rotated about the x-axis or the y-axis.

If the axes are rotated about the origin into a new position $O\text{-}X'Y'Z'$, and if the coördinates of any point P before and after the rotation are, respectively, (x, y, z) and (x', y', z'), we have the

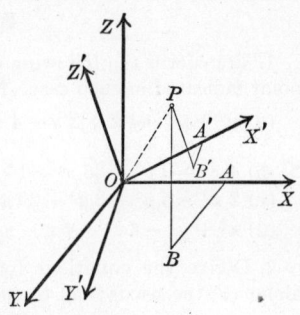

Theorem. *If $\alpha_1, \beta_1, \gamma_1, \alpha_2, \beta_2, \gamma_2,$ and $\alpha_3, \beta_3, \gamma_3,$ are, respectively, the direction angles of the three mutually perpendicular lines OX', OY', and OZ', then the equations for rotating the axes into the position $O\text{-}X'Y'Z'$ are*

(III) $\quad\begin{cases} x = x' \cos \alpha_1 + y' \cos \alpha_2 + z' \cos \alpha_3, \\ y = x' \cos \beta_1 + y' \cos \beta_2 + z' \cos \beta_3, \\ z = x' \cos \gamma_1 + y' \cos \gamma_2 + z' \cos \gamma_3. \end{cases}$

Proof. Let $\angle XOP = \theta$. Refer OX and OP to the new axes OX', OY', OZ'. The direction angles of OX are α_1, α_2, α_3. Let those of OP be α', β', γ'. Then, by (IV), Art. 117,

$$\cos \theta = \cos \alpha' \cos \alpha_1 + \cos \beta' \cos \alpha_2 + \cos \gamma' \cos \alpha_3.$$

Multiplying both members by $\rho = OP$, and remembering that $\rho \cos \theta = x$, $\rho \cos \alpha' = x'$, $\rho \cos \beta' = y'$, $\rho \cos \gamma' = z'$, we have the first formula in (III). The others are proved in the same way. Q.E.D.

The direction cosines of OX', OY', and OZ' obviously satisfy the six equations
$$\cos^2 \alpha_1 + \cos^2 \beta_1 + \cos^2 \gamma_1 = 1,$$
$$\cos \alpha_1 \cos \alpha_2 + \cos \beta_1 \cos \beta_2 + \cos \gamma_1 \cos \gamma_2 = 0,$$
$$\cos^2 \alpha_2 + \cos^2 \beta_2 + \cos^2 \gamma_2 = 1,$$
$$\cos \alpha_2 \cos \alpha_3 + \cos \beta_2 \cos \beta_3 + \cos \gamma_2 \cos \gamma_3 = 0,$$
$$\cos^2 \alpha_3 + \cos^2 \beta_3 + \cos^2 \gamma_3 = 1,$$
$$\cos \alpha_3 \cos \alpha_1 + \cos \beta_3 \cos \beta_1 + \cos \gamma_3 \cos \gamma_1 = 0.$$

Hence only *three* of the nine constants in (III) are independent.

Theorem. *The degree of an equation is unchanged by a transformation of coördinates.*

This may be shown by reasoning as in Art. 68.

PROBLEMS

1. Transform the following equations by translating the axes to the point indicated in each case. Name the surface.

(a) $x^2 + y^2 - 4x + 2y - 4z + 1 = 0$; $(2, -1, -1)$.
$$Ans. \; x^2 + y^2 - 4z = 0.$$
(b) $4x^2 + 9y^2 - 36z^2 - 16x - 18y + 216z - 385 = 0$; $(2, 1, 3)$.
(c) $2x^2 - 5y^2 - 3z^2 + 20x - 4z - 46 = 0$; $(-5, 0, \frac{2}{3})$.
(d) $x^2 + y^2 - 4z^2 - 4x - y - 4z - 3 = 0$; $(2, \frac{1}{2}, -\frac{1}{2})$.

2. Derive the equations for rotating the axes through an angle θ about (1) the x-axis; (2) the y-axis.

3. Show that the following equations may be transformed into the given answers by translating the axes or by rotating them about one of the coördinate axes (see Arts. 58, 64). Name the surface and describe its relation to the original axes.

(a) $x^2 + y^2 - z^2 - 6x - 8y + 10z = 0$.   *Ans.* $x^2 + y^2 - z^2 = 0$.
(b) $3x^2 - 8xy + 3y^2 - 5z^2 + 5 = 0$.   *Ans.* $x^2 - 7y^2 + 5z^2 = 5$.
(c) $y^2 + 4z^2 - 16x - 6y + 16z + 9 = 0$.   *Ans.* $y^2 + 4z^2 = 16x$.
(d) $2x^2 - 5y^2 - 5z^2 - 6yz = 0$.   *Ans.* $x^2 - 4y^2 - z^2 = 0$.
(e) $9x^2 - 25y^2 + 16z^2 - 24zx - 80x - 60z = 0$.
$$Ans. \; x^2 - y^2 = 4z.$$

4. Reduce each of the following by transformation to one of the standard forms (1) or (2) of Art. 141 for a quadric.

(a) $x^2 + 4y^2 + 6z^2 - 8x + 8y = 0$.   (d) $x^2 + 3xy + y^2 + z^2 - 6z = 0$.
(b) $x^2 + xy + y^2 + z^2 - 3 = 0$.   (e) $x^2 + y^2 + 6y - 6z - 18 = 0$.
(c) $3y^2 - 5yz + 3z^2 - 8x = 0$.   (f) $x^2 + xy + y^2 - 2z^2 + 5x = 0$.

5. Transform the equation
$$5x^2 + 8y^2 + 5z^2 - 4yz + 8zx + 4xy - 4x + 2y + 4z = 0$$
by rotating the axes to a position in which their direction cosines are, respectively, $\frac{2}{3}, \frac{2}{3}, \frac{1}{3}$; $\frac{1}{3}, -\frac{2}{3}, \frac{2}{3}$; $\frac{2}{3}, -\frac{1}{3}, -\frac{2}{3}$.   *Ans.* $3x^2 + 3y^2 = 2z$.

6. Transform the equation
$$5x^2 - 2y^2 + 11z^2 + 12xy + 12yz - 16 = 0$$
by rotation about the x-axis so that the y'-axis has direction cosines $(0, \frac{1}{2}\sqrt{3}, \frac{1}{2})$.

TRANSFORMATION OF COÖRDINATES

7. Transform
$$5x^2 + 5y^2 + 2z^2 + 2xy - 4yz + 4xz + 6x - 6y - 12z = 0$$
by rotating the axes so that the new direction cosines are $-\frac{1}{3}, \frac{2}{3}, \frac{2}{3}$; $\frac{2}{3}, -\frac{2}{3}, \frac{1}{3}$; $-\frac{2}{3}, \frac{1}{3}, -\frac{2}{3}$.

8. Transform $x^2 + 2y^2 + 6z^2 - 2x - 2y + 18z + 9 = 0$ by rotating the axes to the position in which their direction numbers are $2, -1, -1$; $0, 1, -1$; $1, 1, 1$.

9. Show that the xy-term may always be removed from the equation $Ax^2 + By^2 + Cz^2 + Fxy + K = 0$ by a rotation about the z-axis.

10. If (x, y, z) and (x', y', z') are, respectively, the coördinates of a point before and after a rotation of the axes, show that
$$x^2 + y^2 + z^2 = x'^2 + y'^2 + z'^2.$$

11. Reduce by transformation of coördinates each of the following to a standard form (Art. 141) and determine the type of paraboloid it represents:

(a) $z = xy$.   (c) $x^2 + 2y^2 - 6x + 4y + 3z + 11 = 0$.
(b) $z = x^2 + xy + y^2$.   (d) $z^2 - 3y^2 - 4x + 2z - 6y + 1 = 0$.

12. A point is equidistant from a fixed plane and a fixed point. Show that the locus is an elliptic paraboloid of revolution.

13. A point is equidistant from two nonintersecting perpendicular lines. Show that the locus is a hyperbolic paraboloid.

155. The locus of an equation of the second degree in x, y, and z, of which the most general form is

(1) $Ax^2 + By^2 + Cz^2 + Dyz + Ezx + Fxy + Gx + Hy + Iz + K = 0$,

is called a **quadric surface** or **conicoid**. We may learn something of the nature of such a surface by taking cross sections. We first obtain

Theorem 1. *The intersection of a quadric with any plane is a conic or a degenerate conic.*

Proof. By a transformation of coördinates any plane may be made the XY-plane, $z = 0$. Referred to any axes, the equation of a quadric has the form (1) (by last theorem, Art. 154). Hence the equation of the curve of intersection referred to axes in its own plane, $z = 0$, is of the form

$$Ax^2 + Fxy + By^2 + Gx + Hy + K = 0,$$

and the locus is therefore a conic or a degenerate conic, by Art. 63. Q.E.D.

As already pointed out in Art. 54, the parabola, ellipse, and hyperbola were originally studied as conic sections, — plane sections of a conical surface of revolution. Such a surface is generated by a straight line revolving about an intersecting axis, and consists of two sheets (or nappes). From the preceding theorem and by intuition the truth of the following statement is manifest:

Corollary. *The section of a cone of revolution by a plane is an ellipse when the plane cuts all the elements of one sheet; a parabola when the plane cuts all the elements of one sheet except one element to which it is parallel; a hyperbola when the plane cuts the elements of both sheets.*

For sections of a quadric by a set of parallel planes the following result is important:

Theorem 2. *The sections of a quadric with a system of parallel planes are conics of the same species.*

Proof. Reasoning as in Theorem 1, we need only consider sections in a system of planes $z = k$. Putting $z = k$ in (1), the equation of the section in this plane is

(2) $$Ax^2 + Fxy + By^2 + D'x + E'y + G' = 0,$$

in which D', E', G', only are functions of k. Hence the discriminant, $F^2 - 4AB$, is independent of k. Then the theorem follows by Art. 63. Q.E.D.

The meaning of the theorem is this: A set of parallel sections will all be ellipses, or all hyperbolas, or all parabolas, the exceptional cases (Art. 63) under each species being included.

156. Simplification of the general equation of the second degree in three variables. It is shown in more advanced treatises that if equation (1) is transformed by rotating

TRANSFORMATION OF COÖRDINATES

the axes, the new axes may be so chosen that the terms in yz, zx, and xy drop out. Hence (1) reduces to the form
$$A'x^2 + B'y^2 + C'z^2 + G'x + H'y + I'z + K' = 0.$$

If we transform this equation by translating the axes, it is easy to show that the new axes may be so chosen that the transformed equation will have one of the two forms

(1) $\qquad A''x^2 + B''y^2 + C''z^2 + K'' = 0,$

(2) $\qquad A''x^2 + B''y^2 + I''z = 0.$

Note the difference in (1) and (2). In (1) all the squares and no first powers are represented, in (2) only two squares and the first power of the other variable.

If all the coefficients in (1) and (2) are different from zero, they may, with a change in notation, be written, respectively, in the forms

(3) $\qquad \pm \dfrac{x^2}{a^2} \pm \dfrac{y^2}{b^2} \pm \dfrac{z^2}{c^2} = 1,$

(4) $\qquad \dfrac{x^2}{a^2} \pm \dfrac{y^2}{b^2} = 2\,cz.$

Equations (3) and (4) have been discussed in Arts. 142–146. The loci are the general quadric surfaces.

If one or more of the coefficients in (1) or (2) are zero, the locus is called a **degenerate quadric**.

Special cases are readily disposed of by means of former results.

If $K'' = 0$, the locus of (1) is a *cone* (theorem, Art. 139) unless the signs of A'', B'', and C'' are the same, in which case the locus is a *point*, namely, the origin.

If *one* of the coefficients A'', B'', or C'' is zero, the locus of (1) is a *cylinder* whose elements are parallel to one of the axes and whose directrix is a conic of the elliptic or hyperbolic type. If also $K'' = 0$, the locus will be a *pair of intersecting planes*, or the equation will be satisfied only by all points on one of the axes of coördinates.

If *two* of the coefficients A'', B'', and C'' are zero, the locus of (1) is a *pair of parallel planes* (coincident if $K'' = 0$) or there is *no locus*.

If *one* of the coefficients in (2) is zero, the locus is a *cylinder* whose directrix is a parabola, or a *pair of intersecting planes*, or the *z-axis*. If *two* of the coefficients are zero, the locus is a *pair of coincident planes*. (A'' and B'' cannot be zero simultaneously, as the equation would cease to be of the second degree.)

PROBLEMS

1. Name each of the following degenerate quadrics:

(a) $9x^2 - 36y^2 + 4z^2 = 0$.
(b) $16x^2 - 4y^2 - z^2 = 0$.
(c) $4x^2 + z^2 - 16 = 0$.
(d) $y^2 - 9z^2 + 36 = 0$.
(e) $4y^2 - 25 = 0$.
(f) $3y^2 + 7z^2 = 0$.
(g) $8y^2 + 25z = 0$.
(h) $z^2 + 16 = 0$.

2. Show by transformation of coördinates that the following quadrics are degenerate:

(a) $x^2 - y^2 + z^2 - 6z + 9 = 0$.
(b) $x^2 + 4y^2 - z^2 - 2x + 8y + 5 = 0$.
(c) $x^2 + y^2 + z^2 + 2x - 2y + 4z + 6 = 0$.
(d) $x^2 + y^2 - 2z^2 + 2y + 4z - 1 = 0$.
(e) $x^2 + yz = 0$.
(f) $4x^2 - y^2 + 9z^2 + 16x + 6y + 18z + 16 = 0$.
(g) $3x^2 - 6xy + xz - 2yz + 12x - 6y + 3z + 6 = 0$.

157. Polar coördinates. The line OP drawn from the origin to any point P is called the **radius vector** of P. The radius vector ρ, and the direction angles of OP, namely, α, β, and γ, are called the *polar coördinates* of P.

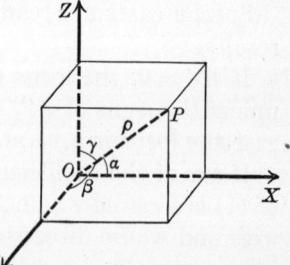

These numbers are not all independent, since α, β, and γ satisfy (I), Art. 114. If two are known, the third may then be found, but all three are retained for the sake of symmetry.

TRANSFORMATION OF COÖRDINATES

Theorem. *The relations between rectangular and polar coördinates are*

(IV) $\quad x = \rho \cos \alpha, \quad y = \rho \cos \beta, \quad z = \rho \cos \gamma.$

Obviously

(1) $\quad\quad\quad\quad \rho^2 = x^2 + y^2 + z^2,$

which expresses the radius vector in terms of x, y, and z.

158. Spherical coördinates. The radius vector ρ of a point P, the angle θ between OP and the z-axis, and the angle ϕ between the projection of OP on the XY-plane and the x-axis are called the *spherical coördinates* of P. θ is called the **colatitude** and ϕ the **longitude**. The spherical coördinates of P are written (ρ, θ, ϕ).

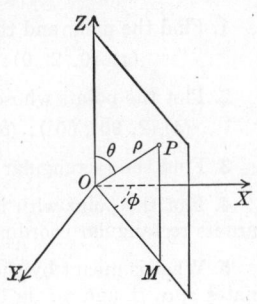

From the figure,
$$z = MP = \rho \cos \theta,$$
$$OM = \rho \sin \theta;$$
also
$$x = OM \cos \phi,$$
$$y = OM \sin \phi.$$

Hence we have the

Theorem. *The relations between rectangular and spherical coördinates are*

(V) $\quad x = \rho \sin \theta \cos \phi, \quad y = \rho \sin \theta \sin \phi, \quad z = \rho \cos \theta.$

Other relations may be obtained by solving (V) for ρ, θ, and ϕ.

159. Cylindrical coördinates. The distance z of a point $P(x, y, z)$ from the XY-plane and the polar coördinates (r, ϕ) of its projection $(x, y, 0)$ on the XY-plane are called the *cylindrical coördinates* of P. The cylindrical coördinates of P are written (r, ϕ, z).

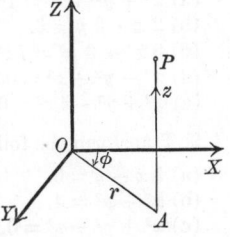

NEW ANALYTIC GEOMETRY

Theorem. *The relations between rectangular and cylindrical coördinates are*

(VI) $\qquad x = r \cos\phi, \quad y = r \sin\phi, \quad z = z.$

Other relations may be obtained by solving (VI) for r and ϕ.

PROBLEMS

1. Find the polar and the spherical coördinates of

(a) (0, 2, 0); (b) (3, 4, 12); (c) (− 2, 2, − 1).

2. Plot the points whose spherical coördinates are

(a) (2, 90°, 60°); (b) (5, 120°, 90°); (c) (9, − 135°, 120°).

3. Find the rectangular coördinates of the points in Problem 2.

4. Plot the point with the cylindrical coördinates (4, 45°, 6). What are its rectangular coördinates?

5. What is meant by the "locus of an equation" in the polar coördinates ρ, α, β, and γ? in the spherical coördinates ρ, θ, and ϕ? in the cylindrical coördinates r, ϕ, and z?

6. How may the intercepts of a surface on the rectangular axes be found if its equation in polar coördinates is given? if its equation in spherical coördinates is given? if its equation in cylindrical coördinates is given?

7. Transform the following equations into polar coördinates:

(a) $x^2 + y^2 + z^2 = 25.$ *Ans.* $\rho = 5.$
(b) $x^2 + y^2 - z^2 = 0.$ *Ans.* $\gamma = \frac{1}{4}\pi.$
(c) $2x^2 - y^2 - z^2 = 0.$ *Ans.* $\alpha = \arccos \frac{1}{3}\sqrt{3}.$
(d) $x^2 - y^2 + z^2 = 0.$

8. Transform the following equations into spherical coördinates:

(a) $x^2 + y^2 + z^2 = 16.$ *Ans.* $\rho = 4.$
(b) $2x + 3y = 0.$ *Ans.* $\phi = \arctan(-\frac{2}{3}).$
(c) $3x^2 + 3y^2 = 7z^2.$ *Ans.* $\theta = \arctan \frac{1}{3}\sqrt{21}.$
(d) $x^2 - y^2 + z^2 = 0.$
(e) $x^2 + y^2 - 4z^2 = 0.$

9. Transform the following equations into cylindrical coördinates:

(a) $5x - y = 0.$ *Ans.* $\phi = \arctan 5.$
(b) $x^2 + y^2 = 4.$ *Ans.* $r = 2.$
(c) $x^2 + y^2 - z^2 = 0.$

10. Describe the locus of each of the following equations:

Polar coördinates. (a) $\rho =$ constant. (b) $\alpha =$ constant.
Spherical coördinates. (a) $\rho =$ constant. (b) $\theta =$ constant.
(c) $\phi =$ constant.
Cylindrical coördinates. (a) $r =$ constant. (b) $\phi =$ constant.

11. The point $P(a, b, c)$ is the point of intersection of the three mutually perpendicular planes $x = a$, $y = b$, $z = c$. By the aid of the preceding problem describe three surfaces which intersect at P when P has

(a) the spherical coördinates $(\rho_1, \theta_1, \phi_1)$;
(b) the cylindrical coördinates (r_1, ϕ_1, z_1).

12. Show that the square of the distance r between two points whose polar coördinates are $(\rho_1, \alpha_1, \beta_1, \gamma_1)$ and $(\rho_2, \alpha_2, \beta_2, \gamma_2)$ is
$r^2 = \rho_1^2 + \rho_2^2 - 2\,\rho_1\rho_2(\cos\alpha_1\cos\alpha_2 + \cos\beta_1\cos\beta_2 + \cos\gamma_1\cos\gamma_2).$

13. Find the general equation of a sphere in polar coördinates.
Ans. $\rho^2 + \rho(G\cos\alpha + H\cos\beta + I\cos\gamma) + K = 0.$

Principal axes, 291, 298
Principal planes, 291, 298
Probability curve, 170
Prolate cycloid, 195

Radian, 2
Radius vector, 148, 320
Reciprocal spiral, 165
Rose, three-leaved, 154, 155; four-leaved, 155; eight-leaved, 155

Semicubical parabola, 184
Spiral, parabolic, 164; hyperbolic or reciprocal, 165; logarithmic or equiangular, 165

Spiral of Archimedes, 164
Strophoid, 43, 199
Symmetry, 33
System of logarithms, common, 166; natural, 166

Torus, 302
Traces of a surface, 287
Triangle problems, 69

Vertex of a conic, 85

Whispering gallery, 144
Witch of Agnesi, 194

INDEX

Abscissa, 6
Algebraic curve, 33
Amplitude, 174
Anchor ring, 302
Angle, eccentric, 94, 193; vectorial, 148
Arch, parabolic, 88
Asymptotes, 39, 102
Auxiliary circle, 94
Axis, major, 92; minor, 92; transverse, 98; conjugate, 98
Axis of parabola, 85

Cardioid, 153, 161, 162
Catenary, 170
Center, instantaneous, 196
Center of conic, 92, 98
Central quadric, 290, 298
Circle, point, 72
Cissoid of Diocles, 43, 190, 195, 198
Cocked hat, 43
Colatitude, 321
Compound-interest curve, 169
Compound-interest law, 221
Conchoid of Nicomedes, 153, 162
Confocal conics, 106
Conicoid, 317
Conjugate diameters, 202
Coördinates, oblique, 7
Cubical parabola, 35
Curtate cycloid, 195
Cycloid, 187, 191

Degenerate ellipse, 122
Degenerate hyperbola, 122
Degenerate parabola, 122
Degenerate quadric, 319
Director circle, 198
Directrix, 85, 159, 283

Eccentricity, 93, 99
Ellipse, point, 95
Epicycloid, 194
Exponential curves, 167

Focal radii of conics, 143, 145
Focus, 85, 92, 159
Folium of Descartes, 189
Four-leaved rose, 155

Helix, 311
Hyperbolic spiral, 165
Hypocycloid, 192; of three cusps, 185; of four cusps, 190, 193

Intercepts, 32
Involute of a circle, 195

Latus rectum, 86, 93
Lemniscate of Bernoulli, 43, 153, 198
Limaçon of Pascal, 43, 153, 163, 199
Lituus, 165
Logarithmic curves, 167
Longitude, 321

Maximum value of a function, 208
Minimum value of a function, 209

Octant, 236
Ordinate, 6

Parabola, cubical, 35; semicubical, 184
Parabolic spiral, 164
Parameter, 64, 184
Period of sine curves, 172, 173
Point circle, 72
Point of contact, 133
Polar axis, 148
Pole, 148